To ra do ra s☆

VOL. ❷

Based on the novels by Yuyuko Takemiya
Manga artwork by Zekkyou
Original character design by Yasu

CONTENTS

To ra do ra ♪

VOLUME 2

STORY BY
YUYUKO TAKEMIYA

ART BY
ZEKKYOU

CHARACTER DESIGN BY YASU

STAFF CREDITS

translation   Adrienne Beck

adaptation   Bambi Eloriaga-Amago

retouch & lettering   Roland Amago

cover design   Nicky Lim

layout   Bambi Eloriaga-Amago

copy editor   Shanti Whitesides

editor   Adam Arnold

publisher   Jason DeAngelis
Seven Seas Entertainment

TORADORA! VOL. 2
Copyright © 2009 Yuyuko Takemiya / Zekkyou
First published in 2009 by Media Works Inc., Tokyo, Japan.
English translation rights arranged with ASCII MEDIA WORKS.

Visit us online at www.gomanga.com.

ISBN: 978-1-934876-60-2

Printed in Canada

First Printing: July 2011

10 9 8 7 6 5 4 3 2

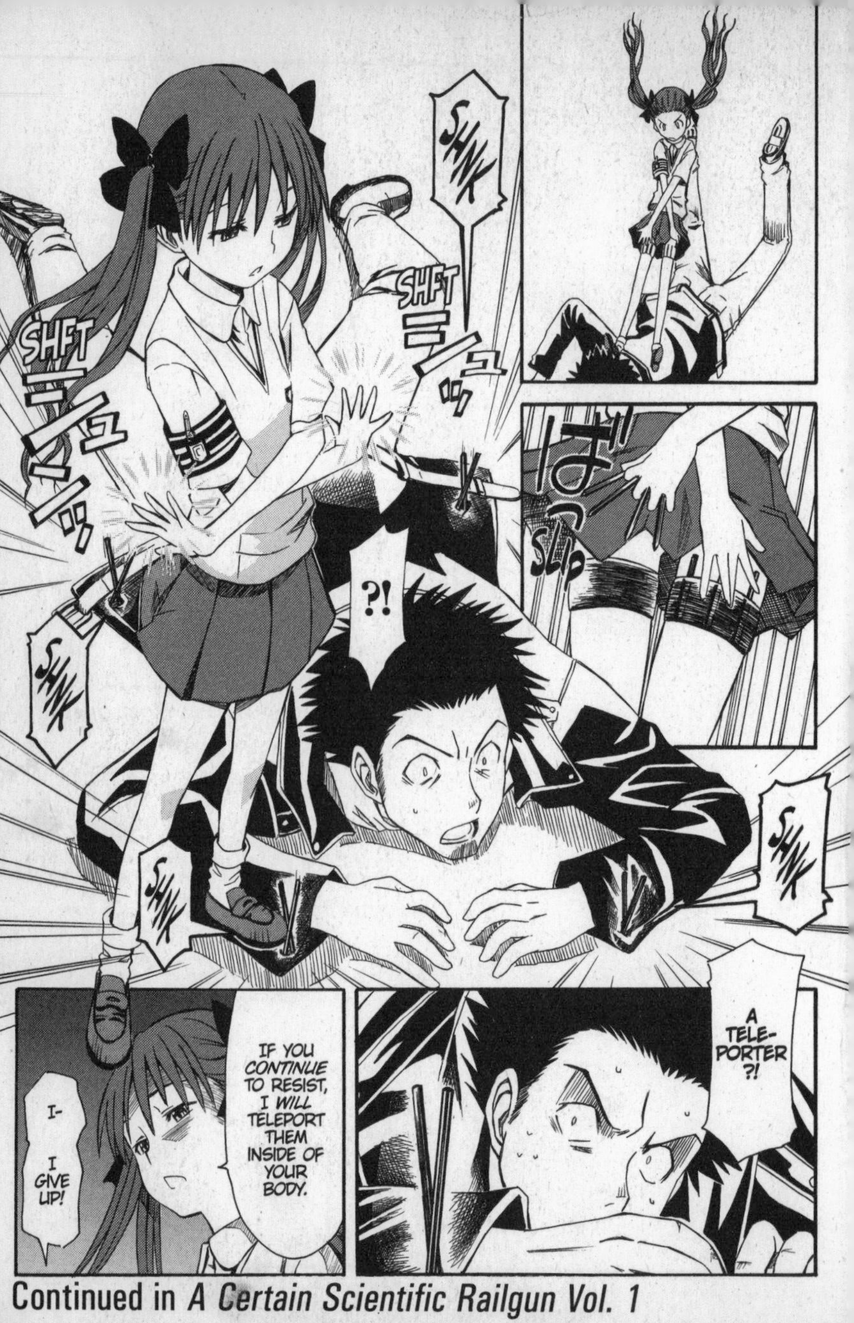
ぱっ
SLIP
SHNK
SHFT
ニュッ
SHFT
ニュッ
?!
SHNK
SHNK
SHNK
A TELE-PORTER?!
IF YOU CONTINUE TO RESIST, I *WILL* TELEPORT THEM INSIDE OF YOUR BODY.
I-
I GIVE UP!

Continued in *A Certain Scientific Railgun Vol. 1*

Chapter 7
A BEAUTIFUL COUPLE

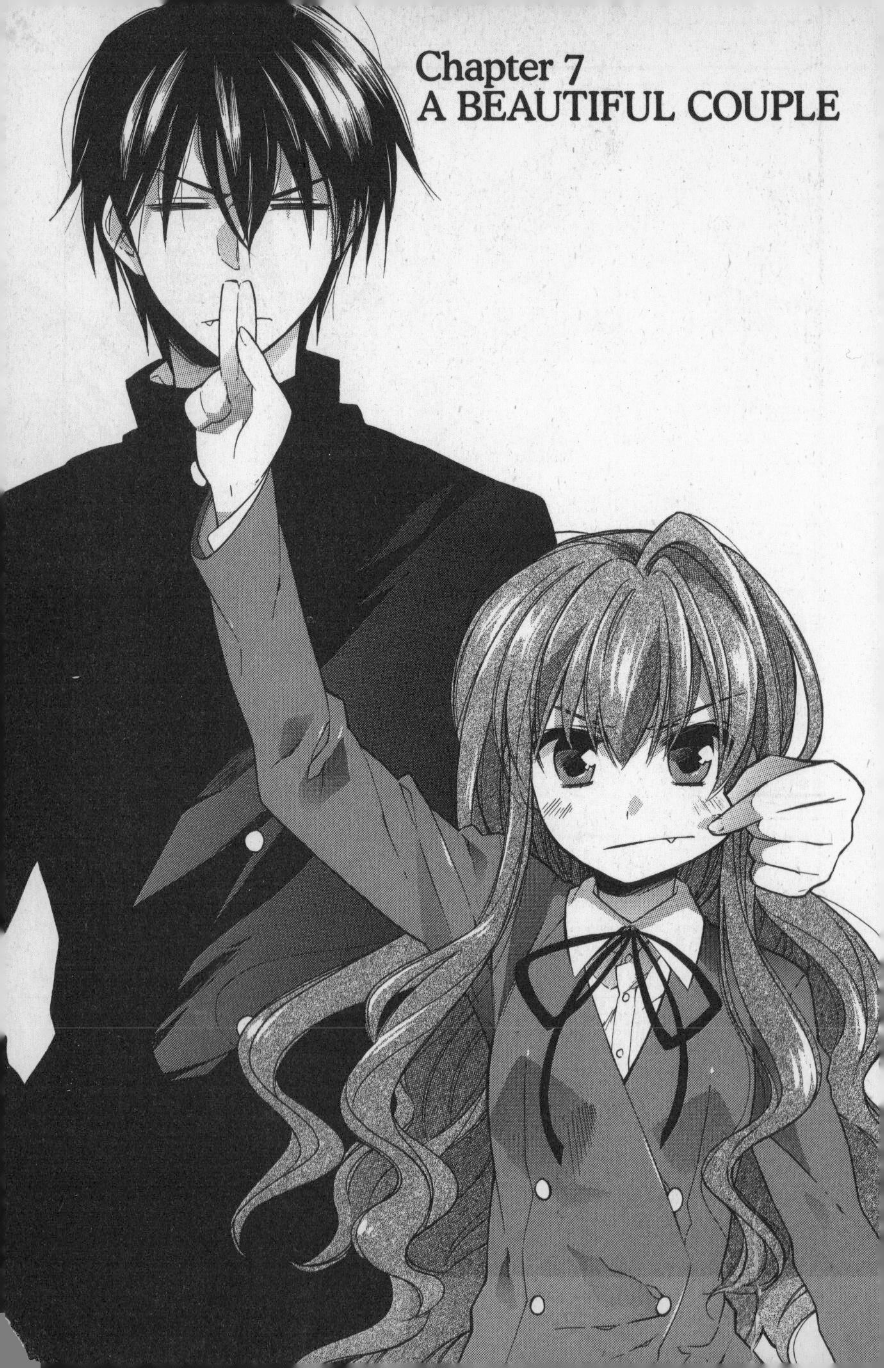

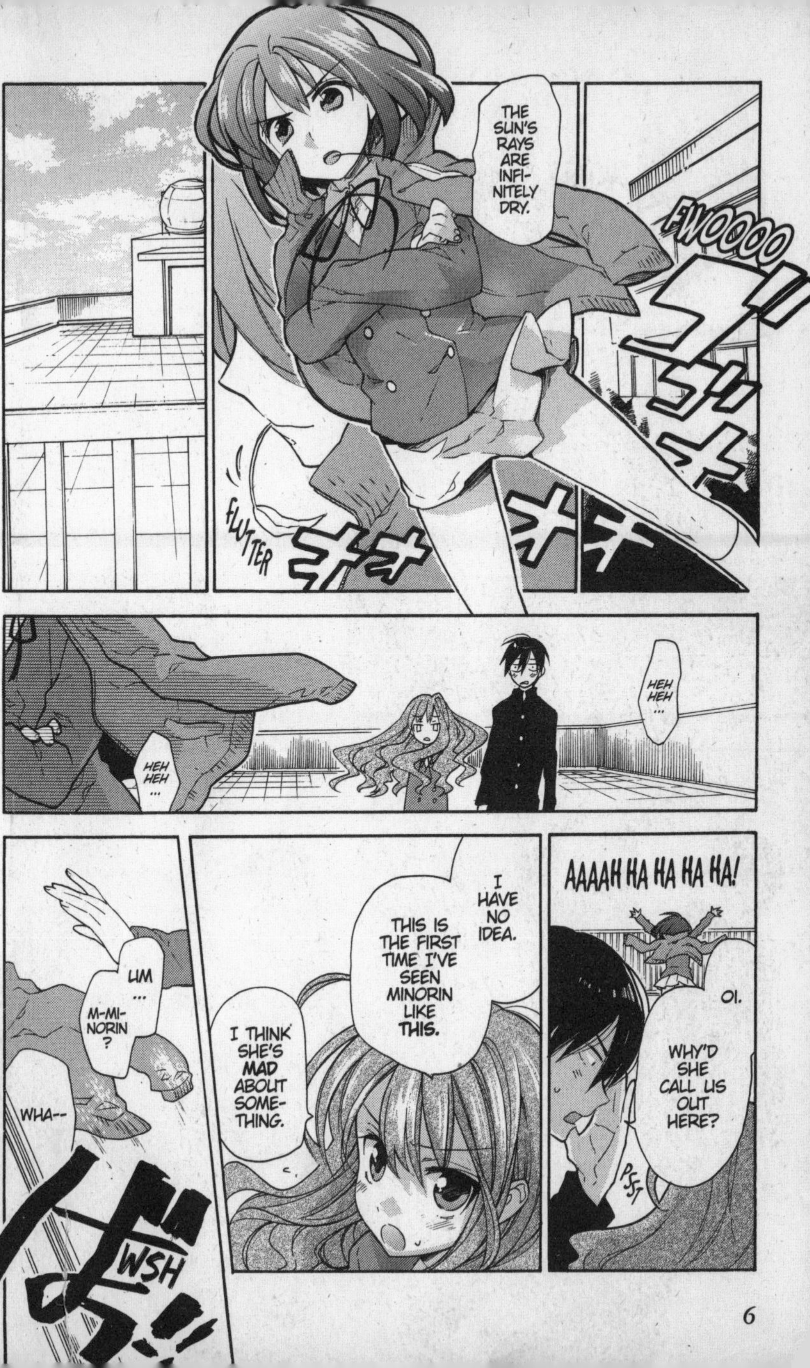
THE SUN'S RAYS ARE INFINITELY DRY.
FWOOOO
FLUTTER
HEH HEH ...
HEH HEH ...
AAAAH HA HA HA HA!
OI.
WHY'D SHE CALL US OUT HERE?
PSST
I HAVE NO IDEA.
THIS IS THE FIRST TIME I'VE SEEN MINORIN LIKE **THIS.**
I THINK SHE'S **MAD** ABOUT SOMETHING.
UM ...
M-MINORIN?
WHA--
WSH

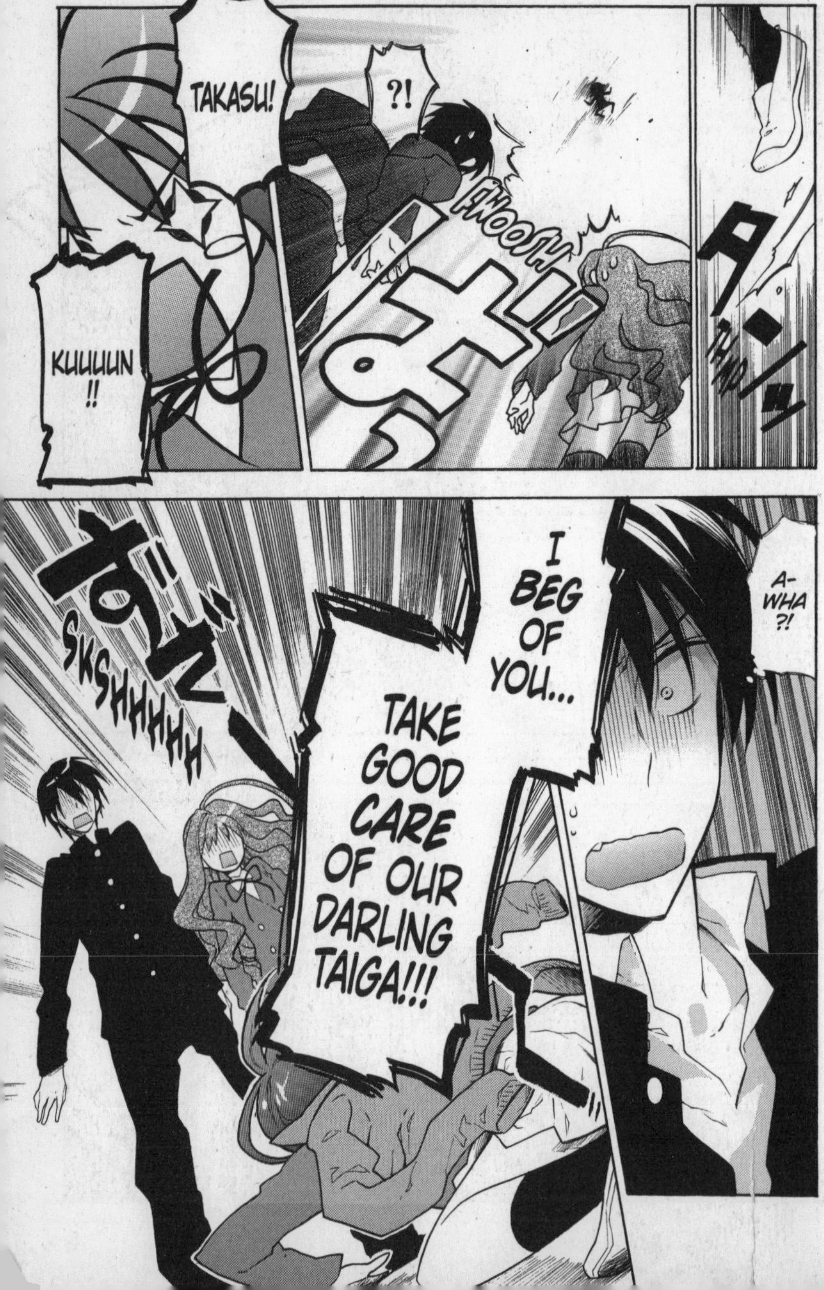
TAP
?!
WHOOSH
TAKASU!
KUUUUN!!
A-WHA?!
I BEG OF YOU...
TAKE GOOD CARE OF OUR DARLING TAIGA!!!
SKSHHHHHH

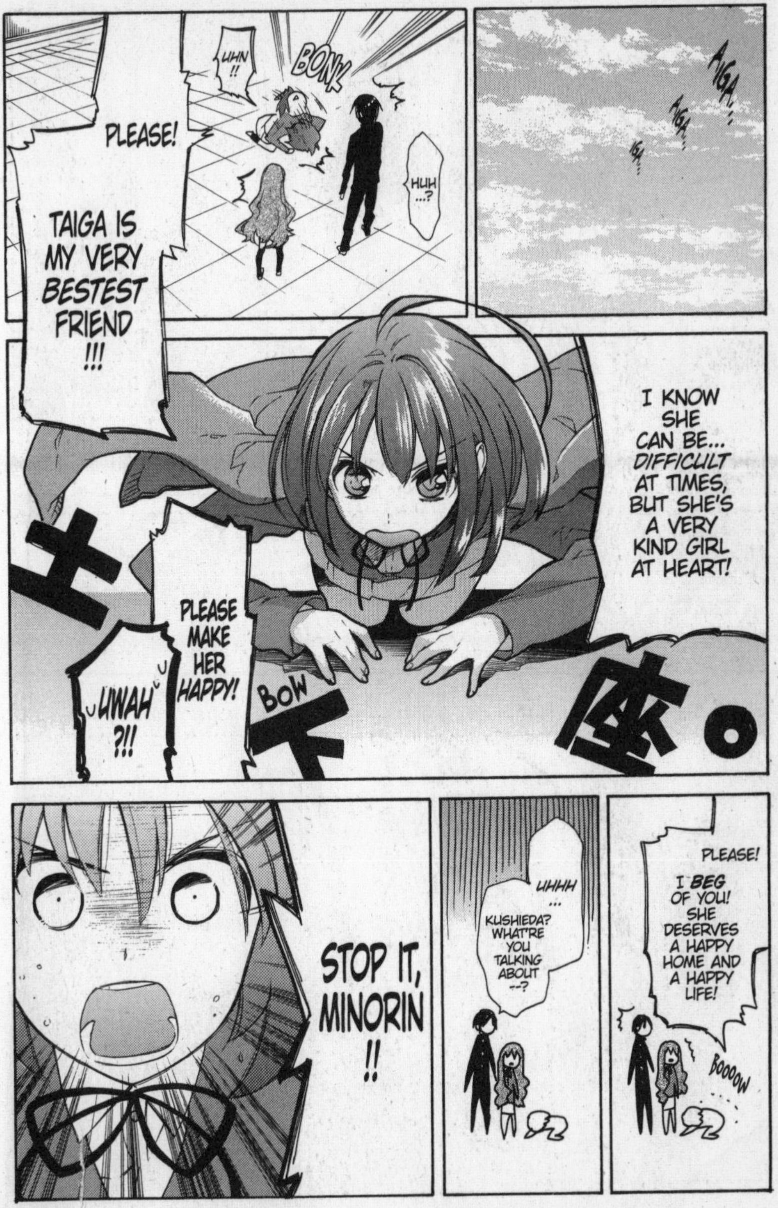
AIGA...
AIGA...
IGA...
BONK!
UHN !!
HUH ...?
PLEASE!
TAIGA IS MY VERY BESTEST FRIEND !!!
I KNOW SHE CAN BE... DIFFICULT AT TIMES, BUT SHE'S A VERY KIND GIRL AT HEART!
PLEASE MAKE HER HAPPY!
UWAH ?!!
BOW
土下座。
PLEASE!
I BEG OF YOU! SHE DESERVES A HAPPY HOME AND A HAPPY LIFE!
BOOOOW
UHHH ...
KUSHIEDA? WHAT'RE YOU TALKING ABOUT --?
STOP IT, MINORIN !!

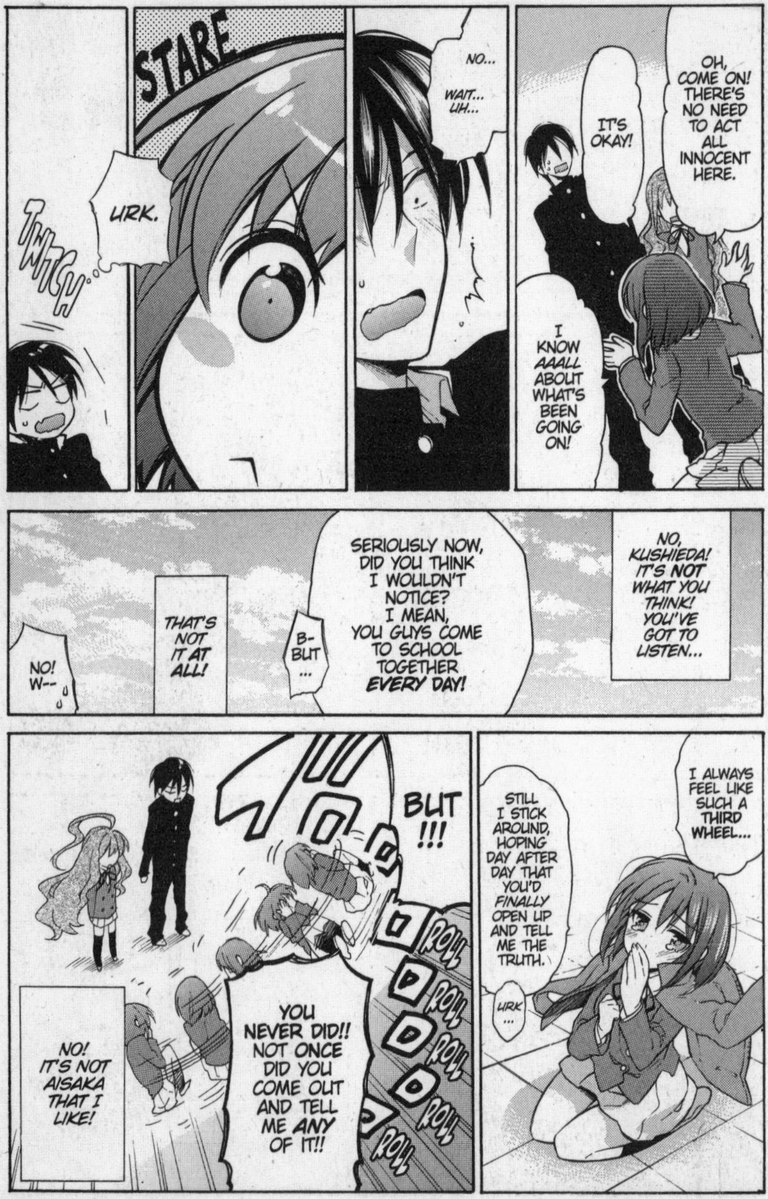
OH, COME ON! THERE'S NO NEED TO ACT ALL INNOCENT HERE.
IT'S OKAY!
I KNOW AAALL ABOUT WHAT'S BEEN GOING ON!
NO...
WAIT... UH...
STARE
URK.
TWITCH
NO, KUSHIEDA! IT'S NOT WHAT YOU THINK! YOU'VE GOT TO LISTEN...
SERIOUSLY NOW, DID YOU THINK I WOULDN'T NOTICE? I MEAN, YOU GUYS COME TO SCHOOL TOGETHER EVERY DAY!
B-BUT...
THAT'S NOT IT AT ALL!
NO! W--
I ALWAYS FEEL LIKE SUCH A THIRD WHEEL...
STILL I STICK AROUND, HOPING DAY AFTER DAY THAT YOU'D FINALLY OPEN UP AND TELL ME THE TRUTH.
URK...
BUT!!!
ROLL
ROLL
ROLL
ROLL
ROLL
YOU NEVER DID!! NOT ONCE DID YOU COME OUT AND TELL ME ANY OF IT!!
NO! IT'S NOT AISAKA THAT I LIKE!

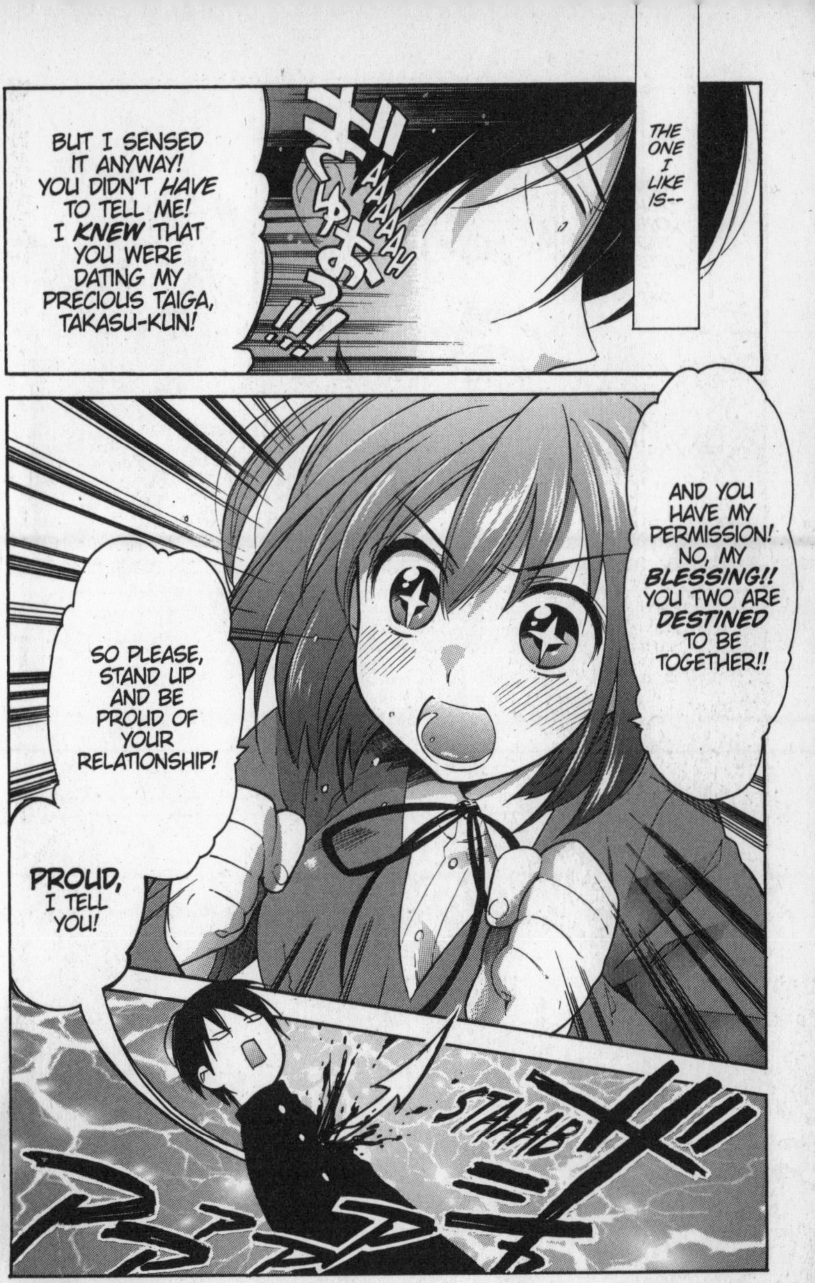
THE ONE I LIKE IS--
BUT I SENSED IT ANYWAY! YOU DIDN'T *HAVE* TO TELL ME! I ***KNEW*** THAT YOU WERE DATING MY PRECIOUS TAIGA, TAKASU-KUN!
AAAAAAH
AND YOU HAVE MY PERMISSION! NO, MY ***BLESSING!!*** YOU TWO ARE ***DESTINED*** TO BE TOGETHER!!
SO PLEASE, STAND UP AND BE PROUD OF YOUR RELATIONSHIP!
PROUD, I TELL YOU!
STAAAB!!

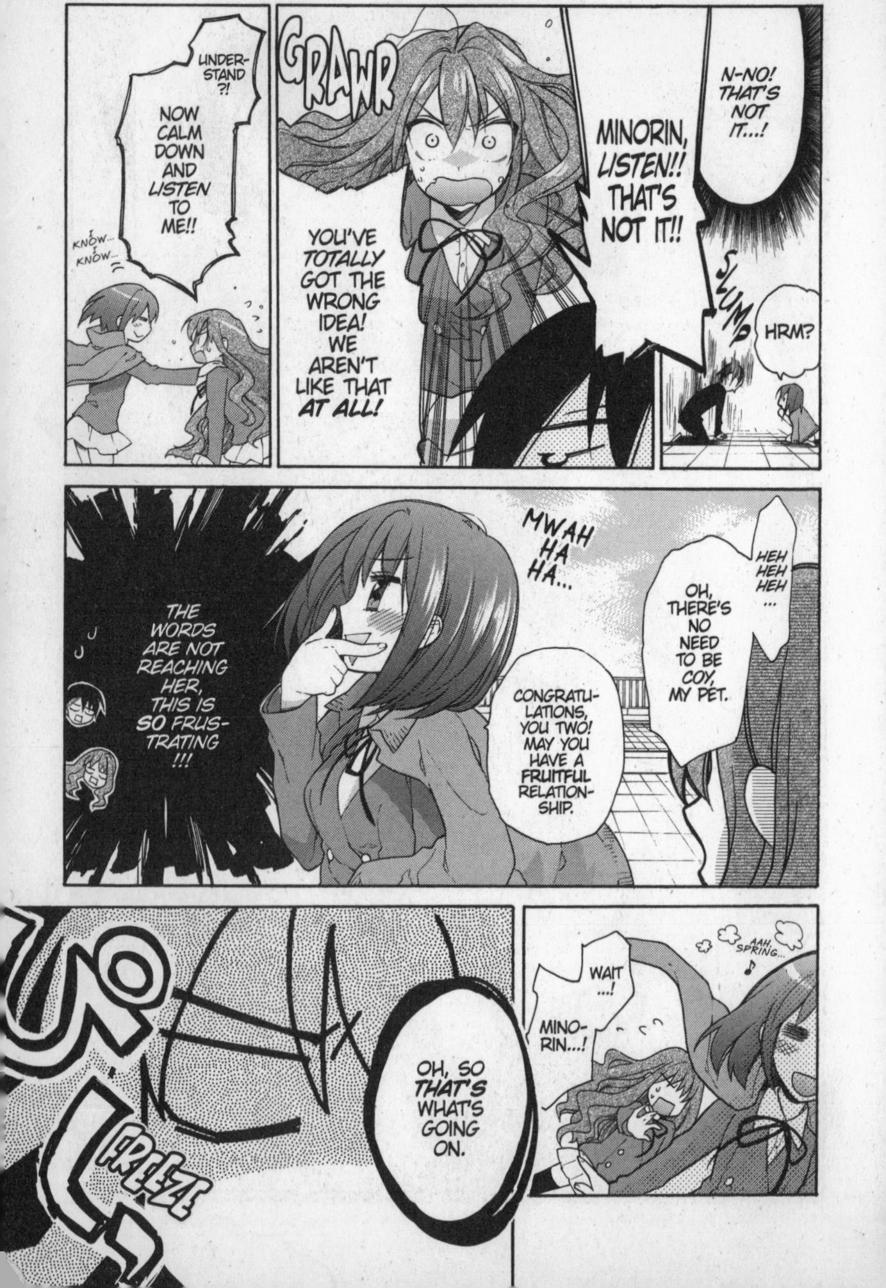
N-NO! THAT'S NOT IT...!
SLUMP
HRM?
GRAWR
MINORIN, LISTEN!! THAT'S NOT IT!!
YOU'VE TOTALLY GOT THE WRONG IDEA! WE AREN'T LIKE THAT AT ALL!
UNDER-STAND ?!
NOW CALM DOWN AND LISTEN TO ME!!
I KNOW... I KNOW...
HEH HEH HEH ...
OH, THERE'S NO NEED TO BE COY, MY PET.
MWAH HA HA...
CONGRATULATIONS, YOU TWO! MAY YOU HAVE A FRUITFUL RELATIONSHIP.
THE WORDS ARE NOT REACHING HER, THIS IS SO FRUS-TRATING !!!
AAH, SPRING...
WAIT ...!
MINO-RIN...!
OH, SO THAT'S WHAT'S GOING ON.
FREEZE

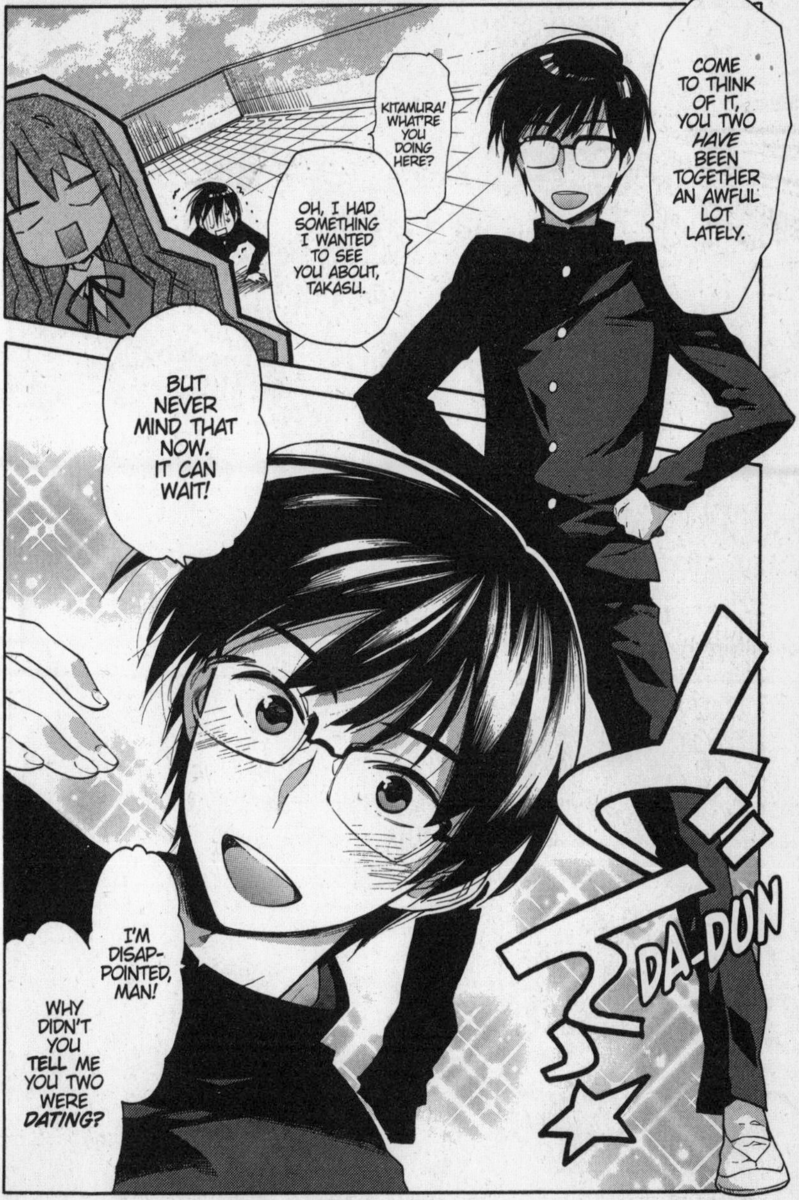
COME TO THINK OF IT, YOU TWO *HAVE* BEEN TOGETHER AN AWFUL LOT LATELY.
KITAMURA! WHAT'RE YOU DOING HERE?
OH, I HAD SOMETHING I WANTED TO SEE YOU ABOUT, TAKASU.
BUT NEVER MIND THAT NOW. IT CAN WAIT!
DA-DUN
I'M DISAP-POINTED, MAN!
WHY DIDN'T YOU TELL ME YOU TWO WERE *DATING*?

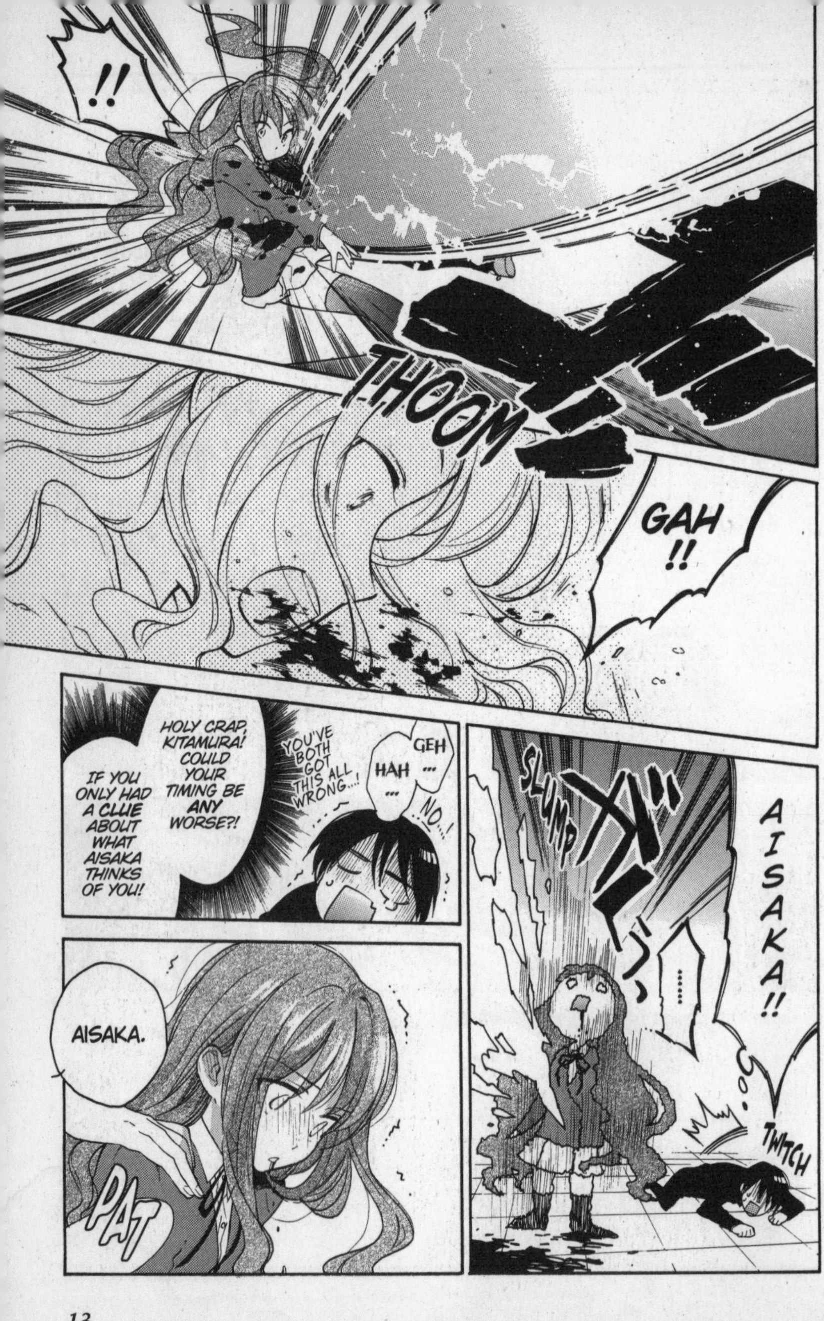
!!
THOOM
GAH !!
AISAKA!!
SLUMP
......
TWITCH
GEH ...
HAH ...
NO...!
YOU'VE BOTH GOT THIS ALL WRONG...!
HOLY CRAP, KITAMURA! COULD YOUR TIMING BE ANY WORSE?!
IF YOU ONLY HAD A CLUE ABOUT WHAT AISAKA THINKS OF YOU!
AISAKA.
PAT

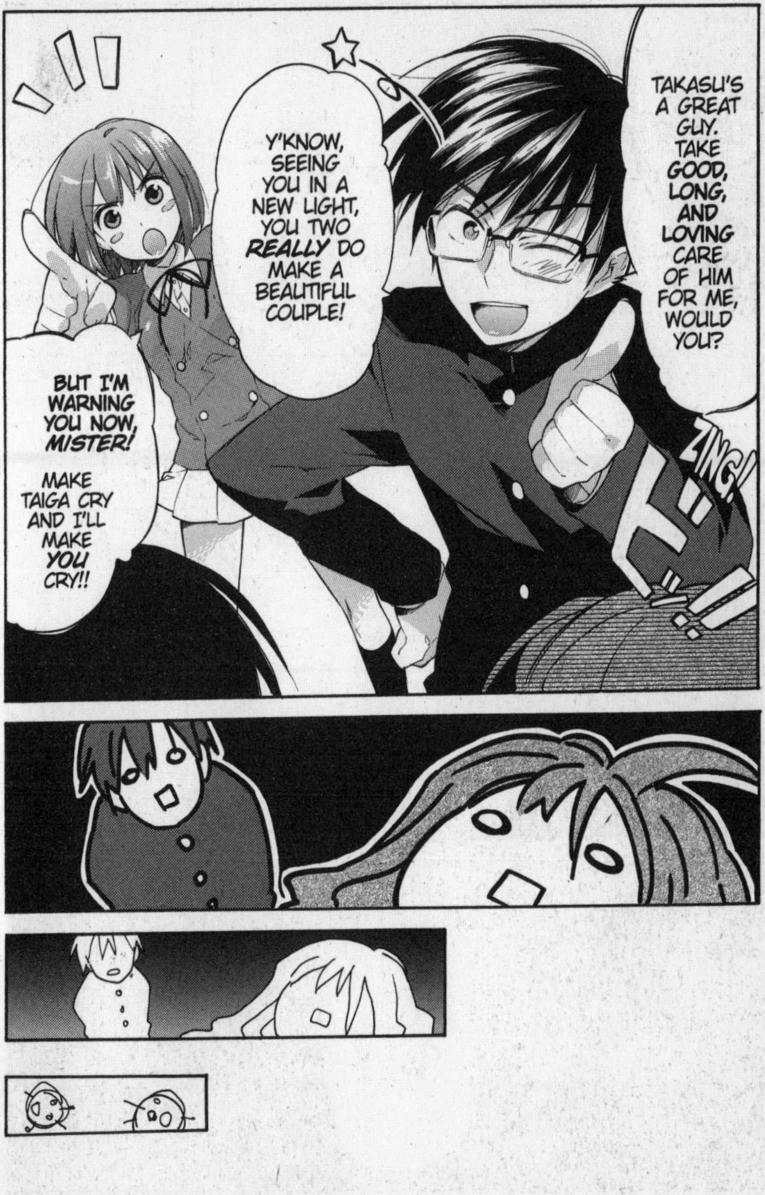
TAKASU'S A GREAT GUY. TAKE GOOD, LONG, AND LOVING CARE OF HIM FOR ME, WOULD YOU?
Y'KNOW, SEEING YOU IN A NEW LIGHT, YOU TWO *REALLY* DO MAKE A BEAUTIFUL COUPLE!
ZING!
BUT I'M WARNING YOU NOW, *MISTER*!
MAKE TAIGA CRY AND I'LL MAKE *YOU* CRY!!

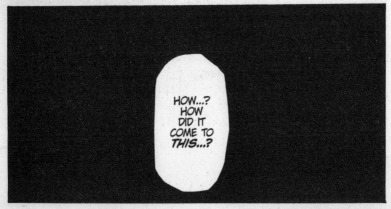

HOW...?
HOW
DID IT
COME TO
THIS...?

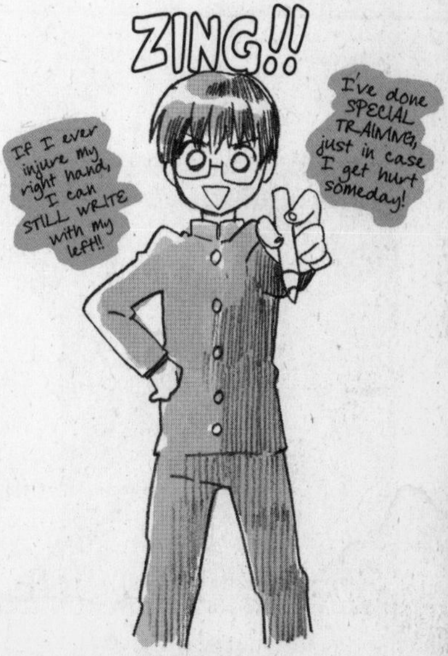
ZING!!
I've done SPECIAL TRAINING, just in case I get hurt someday!
If I ever injure my right hand, I can STILL WRITE with my left!!

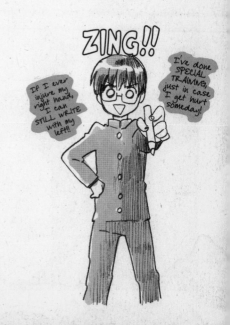

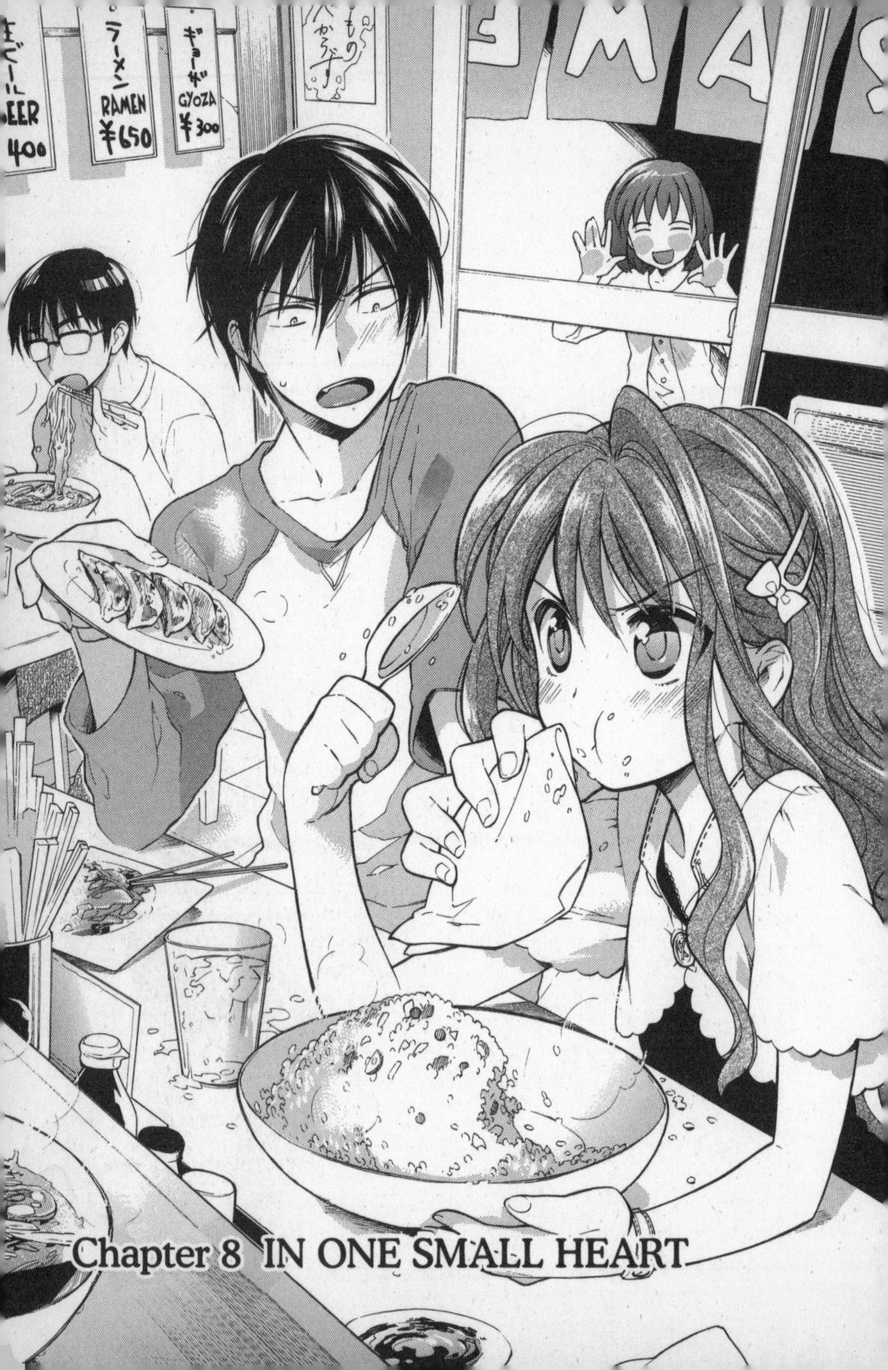
ラーメン
RAMEN
¥650
ギョーザ
GYOZA
¥300

Chapter 8 IN ONE SMALL HEART

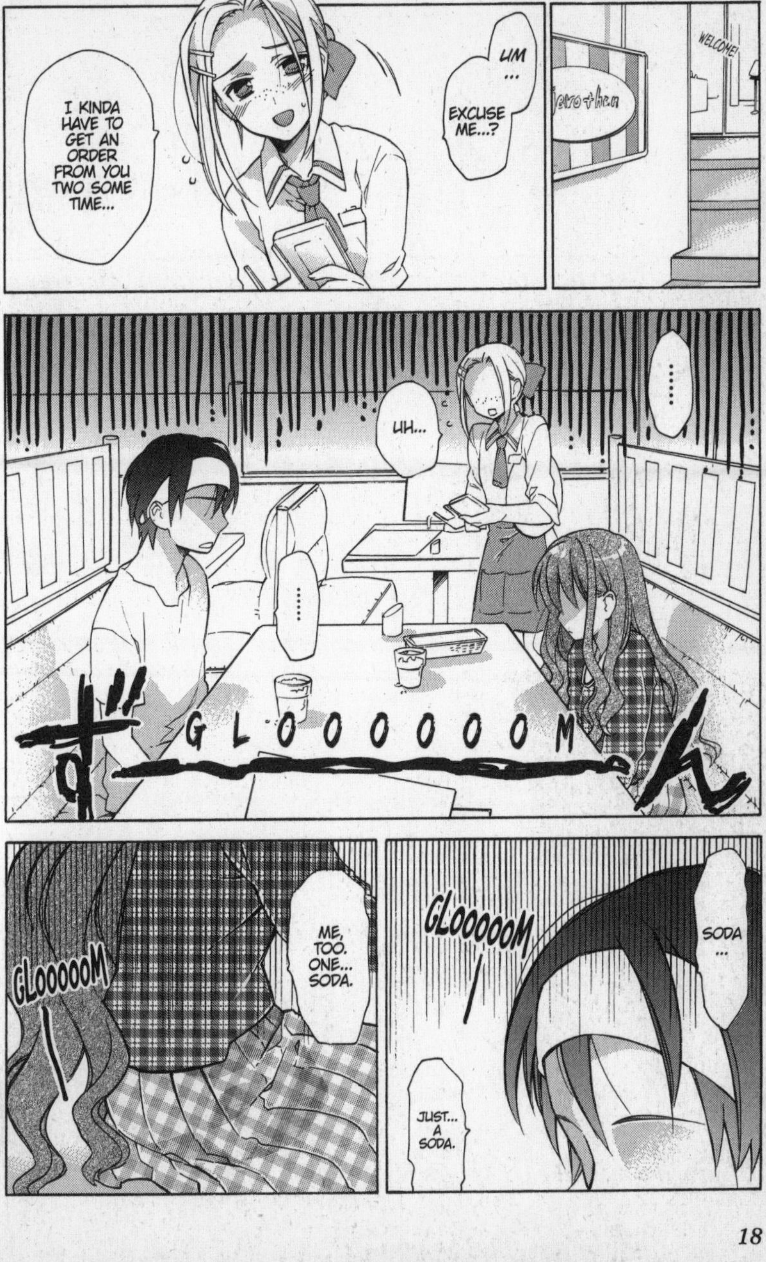
WELCOME!
UM ... EXCUSE ME...?
I KINDA HAVE TO GET AN ORDER FROM YOU TWO SOME TIME...
......
UH...
......
GLOOOOOOOM
GLOOOOOM
SODA ...
JUST... A SODA.
ME, TOO. ONE... SODA.
GLOOOOOM

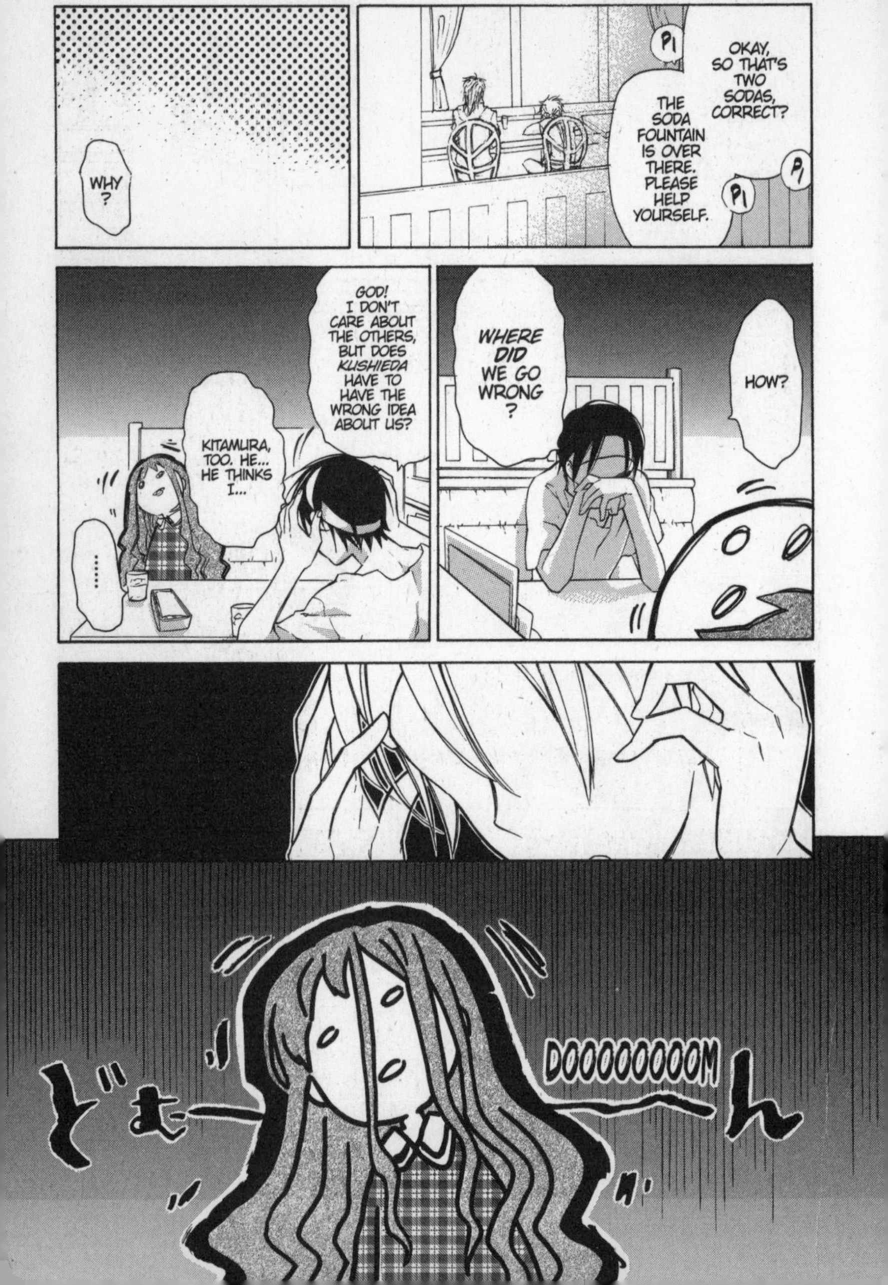
PI
OKAY, SO THAT'S TWO SODAS, CORRECT?
THE SODA FOUNTAIN IS OVER THERE. PLEASE HELP YOURSELF.
PI
PI
WHY?
HOW?
WHERE DID WE GO WRONG?
GOD! I DON'T CARE ABOUT THE OTHERS, BUT DOES KUSHIEDA HAVE TO HAVE THE WRONG IDEA ABOUT US?
KITAMURA, TOO. HE... HE THINKS I...
......
DOOOOOOOOM
どむ—ん

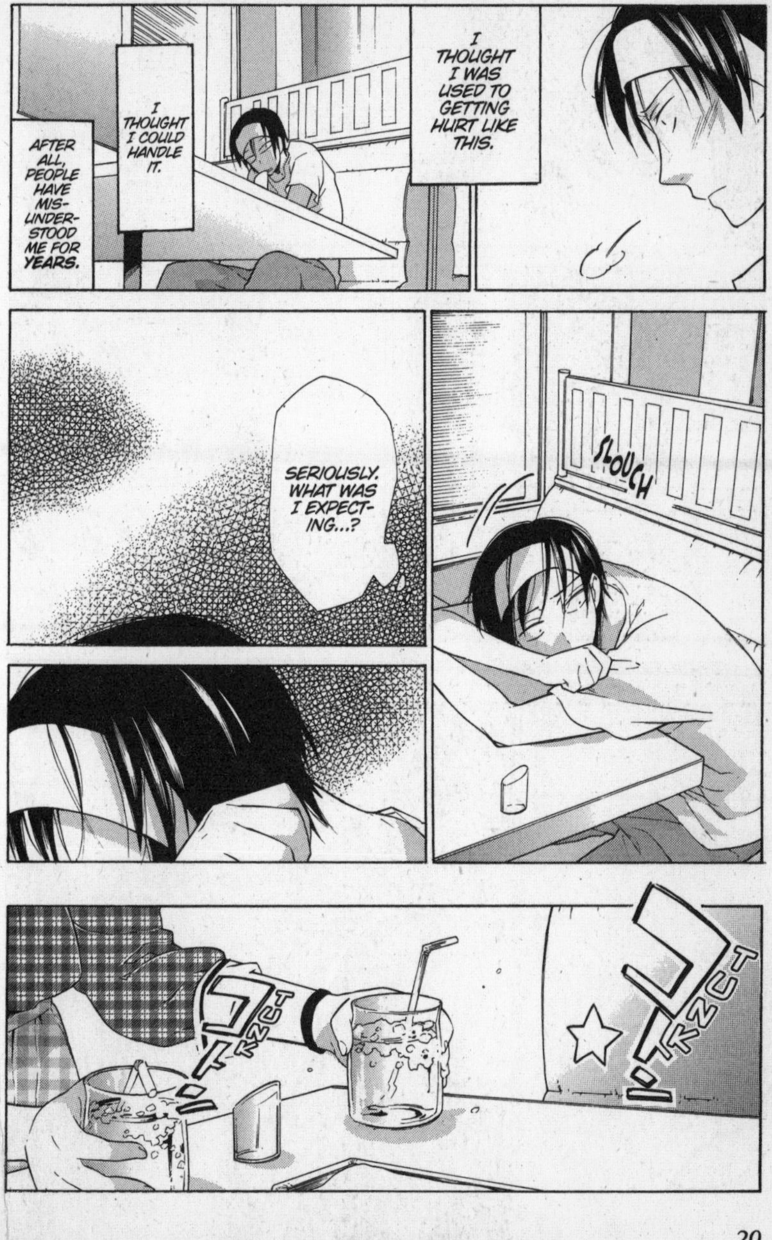
I THOUGHT I WAS USED TO GETTING HURT LIKE THIS.
I THOUGHT I COULD HANDLE IT.
AFTER ALL, PEOPLE HAVE MISUNDERSTOOD ME FOR YEARS.
SLOUCH
SERIOUSLY. WHAT WAS I EXPECTING...?
TUNK
TUNK

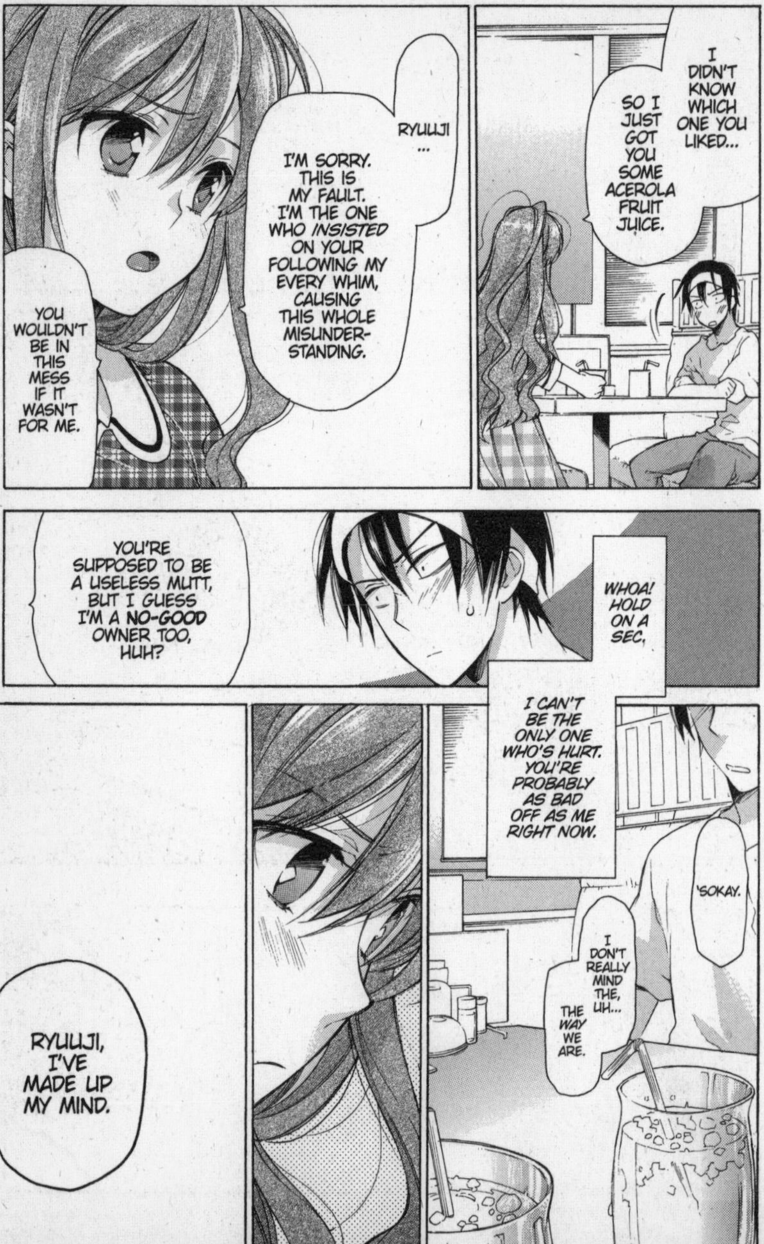
I DIDN'T KNOW WHICH ONE YOU LIKED...
SO I JUST GOT YOU SOME ACEROLA FRUIT JUICE.
RYUUJI ...
I'M SORRY. THIS IS MY FAULT. I'M THE ONE WHO *INSISTED* ON YOUR FOLLOWING MY EVERY WHIM, CAUSING THIS WHOLE MISUNDER-STANDING.
YOU WOULDN'T BE IN THIS MESS IF IT WASN'T FOR ME.
WHOA! HOLD ON A SEC.
YOU'RE SUPPOSED TO BE A USELESS MUTT, BUT I GUESS I'M A **NO-GOOD** OWNER TOO, HUH?
I CAN'T BE THE ONLY ONE WHO'S HURT. YOU'RE PROBABLY AS BAD OFF AS ME RIGHT NOW.
'SOKAY.
I DON'T REALLY MIND THE, UH... *THE WAY WE ARE.*
RYUUJI, I'VE MADE UP MY MIND.

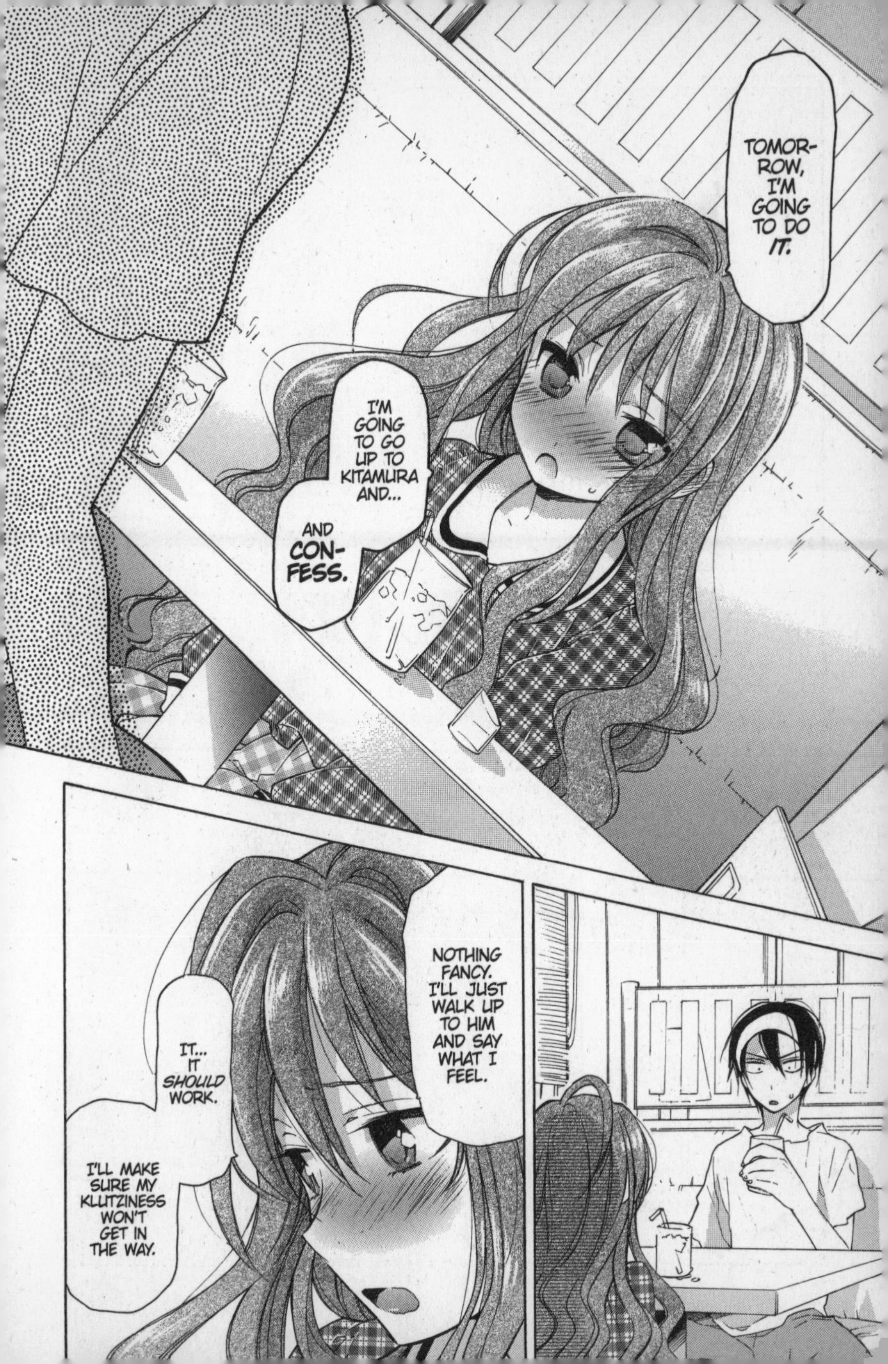
TOMOR-ROW, I'M GOING TO DO IT.
I'M GOING TO GO UP TO KITAMURA AND...
AND CON-FESS.
NOTHING FANCY. I'LL JUST WALK UP TO HIM AND SAY WHAT I FEEL.
IT... IT SHOULD WORK.
I'LL MAKE SURE MY KLUTZINESS WON'T GET IN THE WAY.

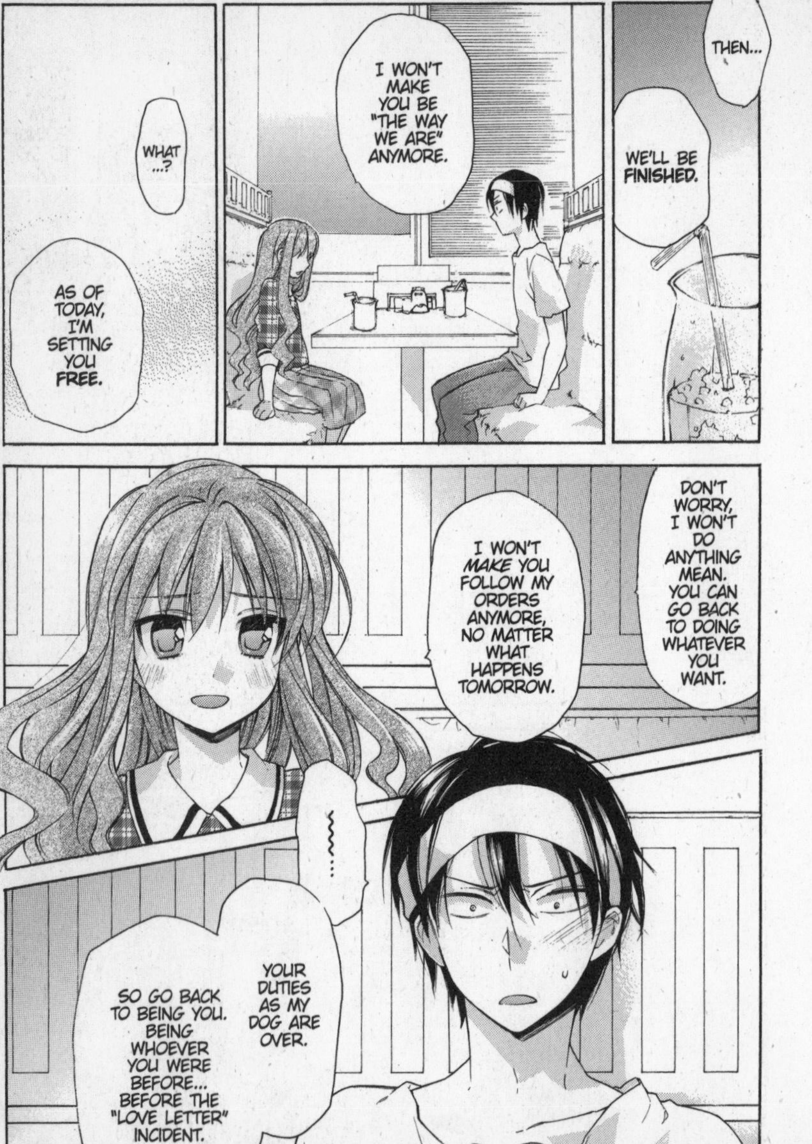
THEN...
WE'LL BE FINISHED.
I WON'T MAKE YOU BE "THE WAY WE ARE" ANYMORE.
WHAT ...?
AS OF TODAY, I'M SETTING YOU FREE.
DON'T WORRY, I WON'T DO ANYTHING MEAN. YOU CAN GO BACK TO DOING WHATEVER YOU WANT.
I WON'T *MAKE* YOU FOLLOW MY ORDERS ANYMORE, NO MATTER WHAT HAPPENS TOMORROW.
......
YOUR DUTIES AS MY DOG ARE OVER.
SO GO BACK TO BEING YOU. BEING WHOEVER YOU WERE BEFORE... BEFORE THE "LOVE LETTER" INCIDENT.

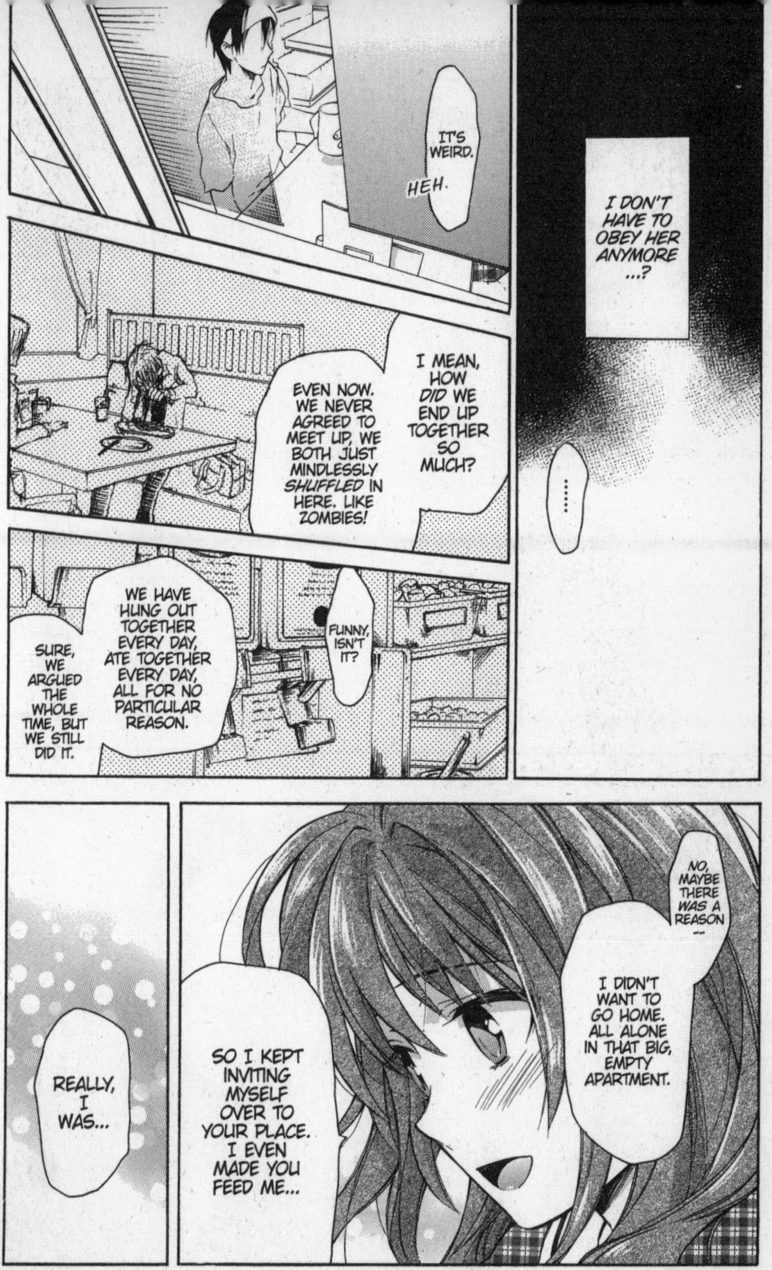
I DON'T HAVE TO OBEY HER ANYMORE ...?
......
IT'S WEIRD.
HEH.
I MEAN, HOW *DID* WE END UP TOGETHER SO MUCH?
EVEN NOW. WE NEVER AGREED TO MEET UP, WE BOTH JUST MINDLESSLY *SHUFFLED* IN HERE. LIKE ZOMBIES!
FUNNY, ISN'T IT?
WE HAVE HUNG OUT TOGETHER EVERY DAY, ATE TOGETHER EVERY DAY, ALL FOR NO PARTICULAR REASON.
SURE, WE ARGUED THE WHOLE TIME, BUT WE STILL DID IT.
NO, MAYBE THERE WAS A REASON --
I DIDN'T WANT TO GO HOME. ALL ALONE IN THAT BIG, EMPTY APARTMENT.
SO I KEPT INVITING MYSELF OVER TO YOUR PLACE. I EVEN MADE YOU FEED ME...
REALLY, I WAS...

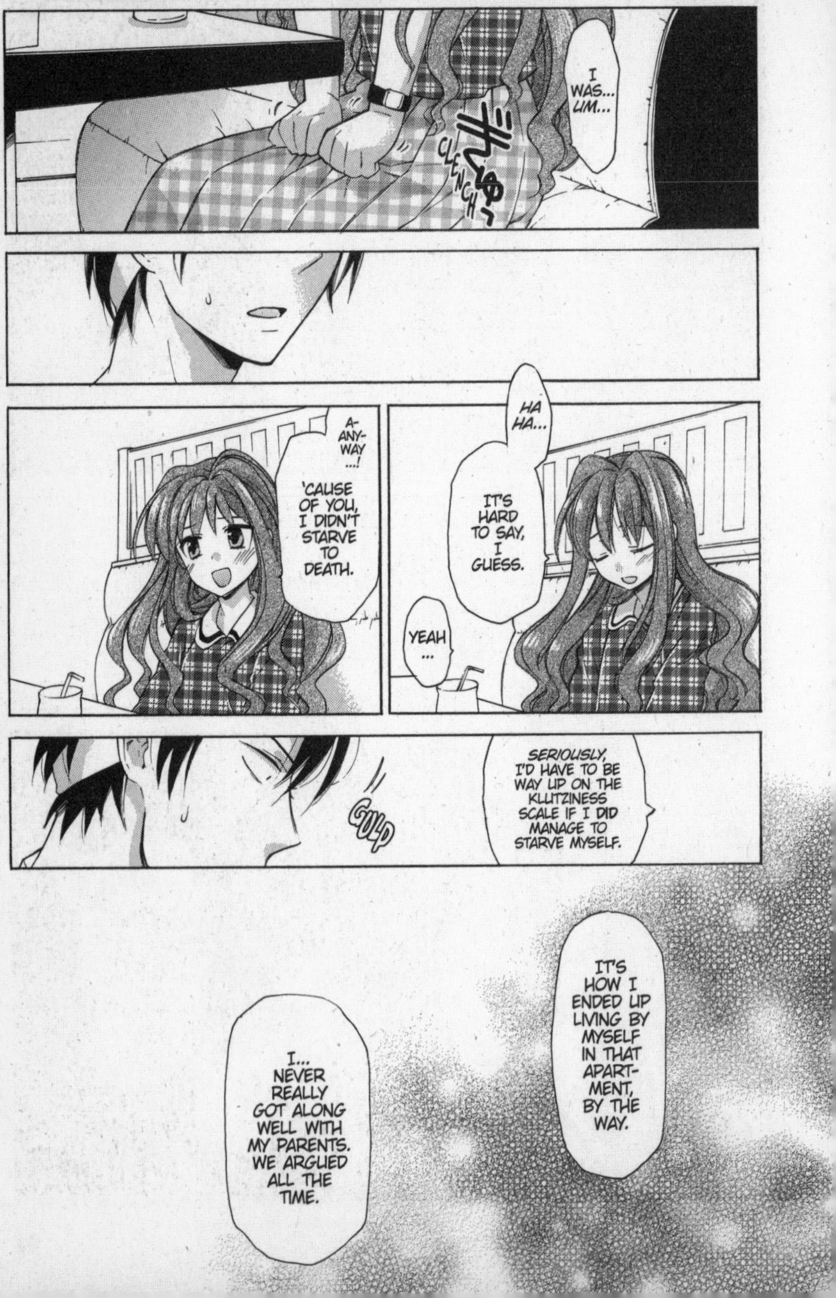
I WAS... UM...
CLENCH
HA HA...
IT'S HARD TO SAY, I GUESS.
YEAH ...
A-ANYWAY ...!
'CAUSE OF YOU, I DIDN'T STARVE TO DEATH.
SERIOUSLY, I'D HAVE TO BE WAY UP ON THE KLUTZINESS SCALE IF I DID MANAGE TO STARVE MYSELF.
GULP
IT'S HOW I ENDED UP LIVING BY MYSELF IN THAT APARTMENT, BY THE WAY.
I... NEVER REALLY GOT ALONG WELL WITH MY PARENTS. WE ARGUED ALL THE TIME.

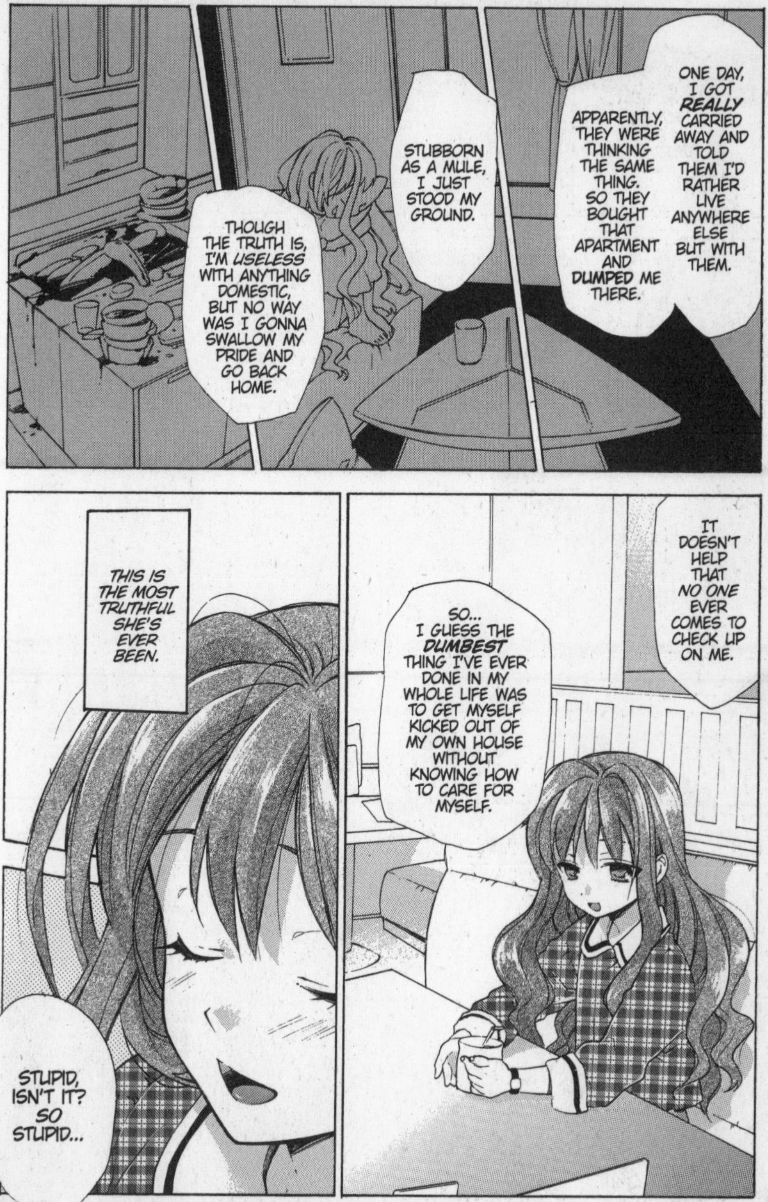
ONE DAY, I GOT *REALLY* CARRIED AWAY AND TOLD THEM I'D RATHER LIVE ANYWHERE ELSE BUT WITH THEM.
APPARENTLY, THEY WERE THINKING THE SAME THING. SO THEY BOUGHT THAT APARTMENT AND DUMPED ME THERE.
STUBBORN AS A MULE, I JUST STOOD MY GROUND.
THOUGH THE TRUTH IS, I'M *USELESS* WITH ANYTHING DOMESTIC, BUT NO WAY WAS I GONNA SWALLOW MY PRIDE AND GO BACK HOME.
IT DOESN'T HELP THAT *NO ONE* EVER COMES TO CHECK UP ON ME.
SO... I GUESS THE ***DUMBEST*** THING I'VE EVER DONE IN MY WHOLE LIFE WAS TO GET MYSELF KICKED OUT OF MY OWN HOUSE WITHOUT KNOWING HOW TO CARE FOR MYSELF.
THIS IS THE MOST TRUTHFUL SHE'S EVER BEEN.
STUPID, ISN'T IT? *SO* STUPID...

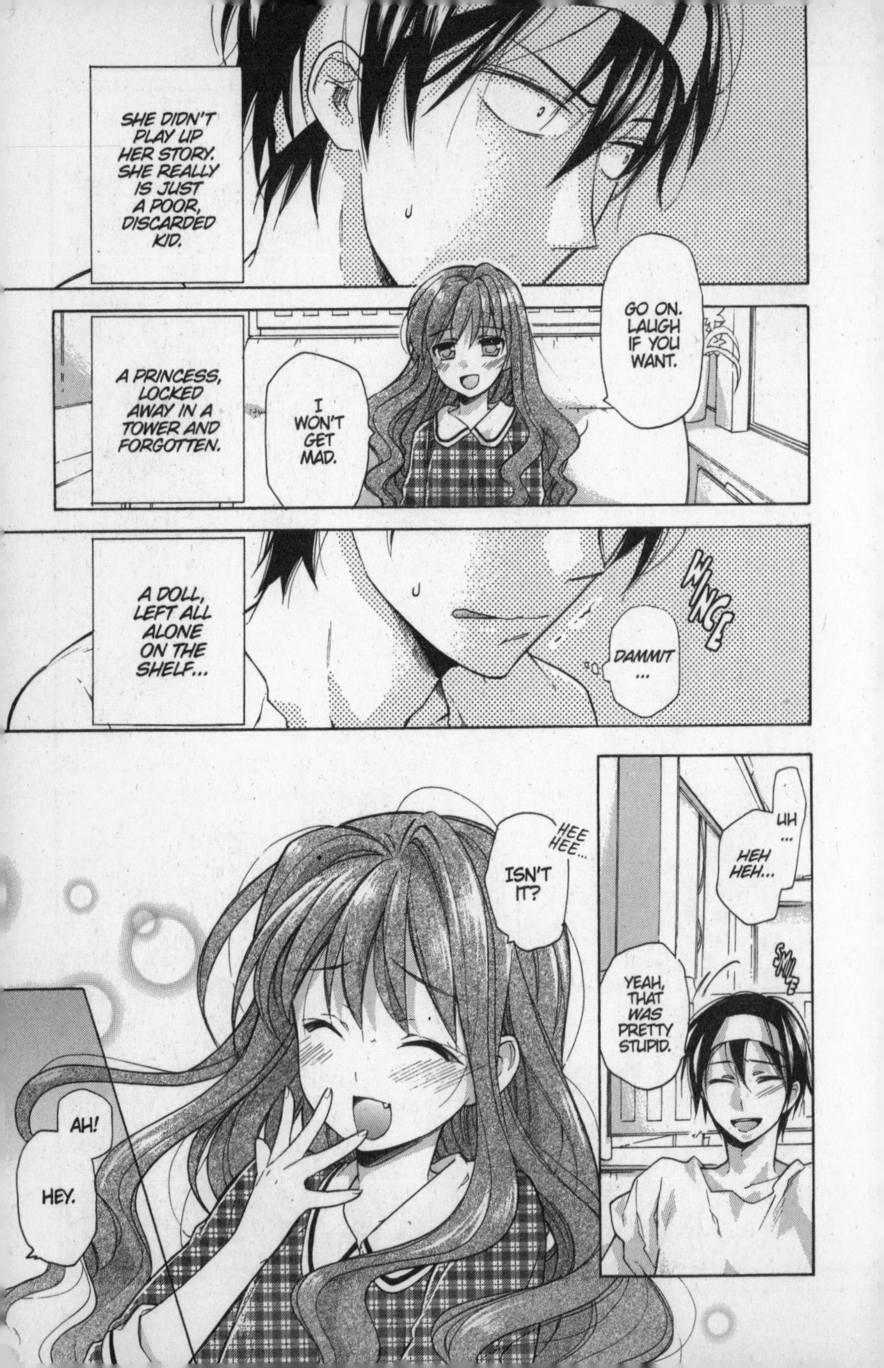
SHE DIDN'T PLAY UP HER STORY. SHE REALLY IS JUST A POOR, DISCARDED KID.
GO ON. LAUGH IF YOU WANT.
I WON'T GET MAD.
A PRINCESS, LOCKED AWAY IN A TOWER AND FORGOTTEN.
WINCE
DAMMIT ...
A DOLL, LEFT ALL ALONE ON THE SHELF...
UH ... HEH HEH...
SMILE
YEAH, THAT WAS PRETTY STUPID.
HEE HEE... ISN'T IT?
AH! HEY.

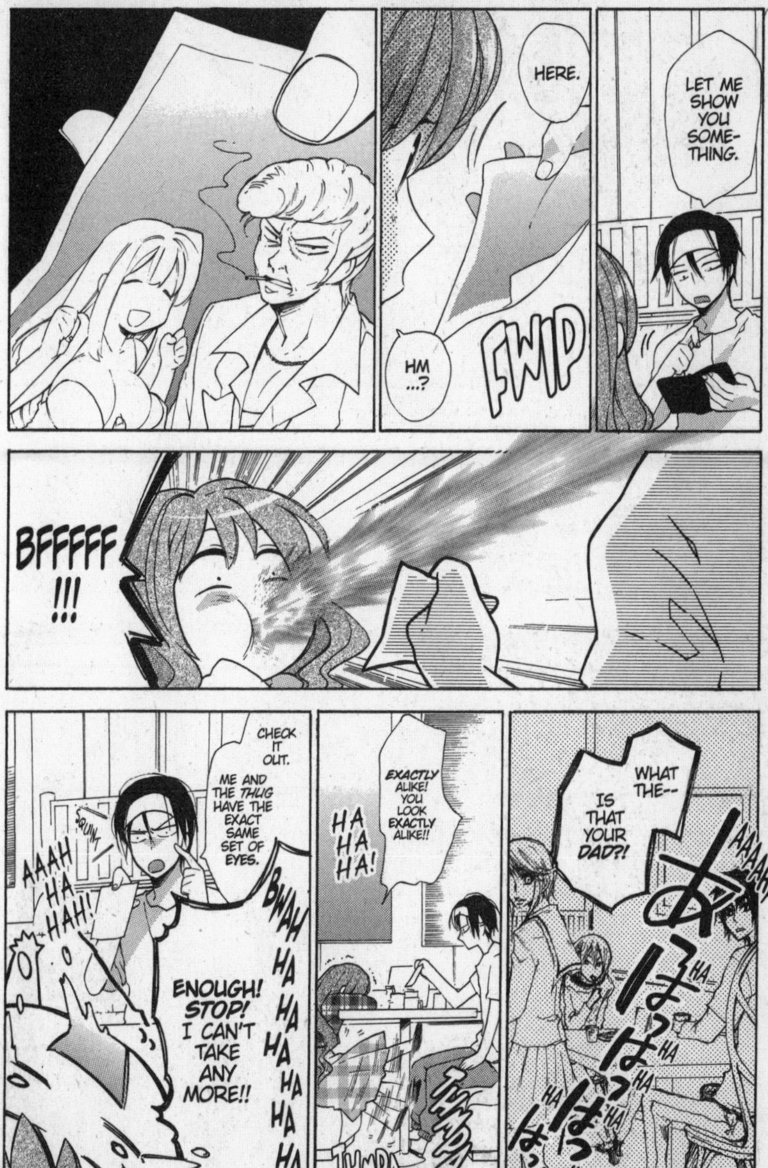

LET ME SHOW YOU SOME-THING.
HERE.
FWIP
HM ...?
BFFFFF !!!
WHAT THE--
IS THAT YOUR DAD?!
AAAAAHA
HA HA HA HA HA HA
EXACTLY ALIKE! YOU LOOK EXACTLY ALIKE!!
HA HA HA HA!
THMPA
THMPA
CHECK IT OUT.
ME AND THE THUG HAVE THE EXACT SAME SET OF EYES.
SQUINT
AAAH HA HAH!
BWAH HA HA HA HA HA HA HA HA
ENOUGH! STOP! I CAN'T TAKE ANY MORE!!

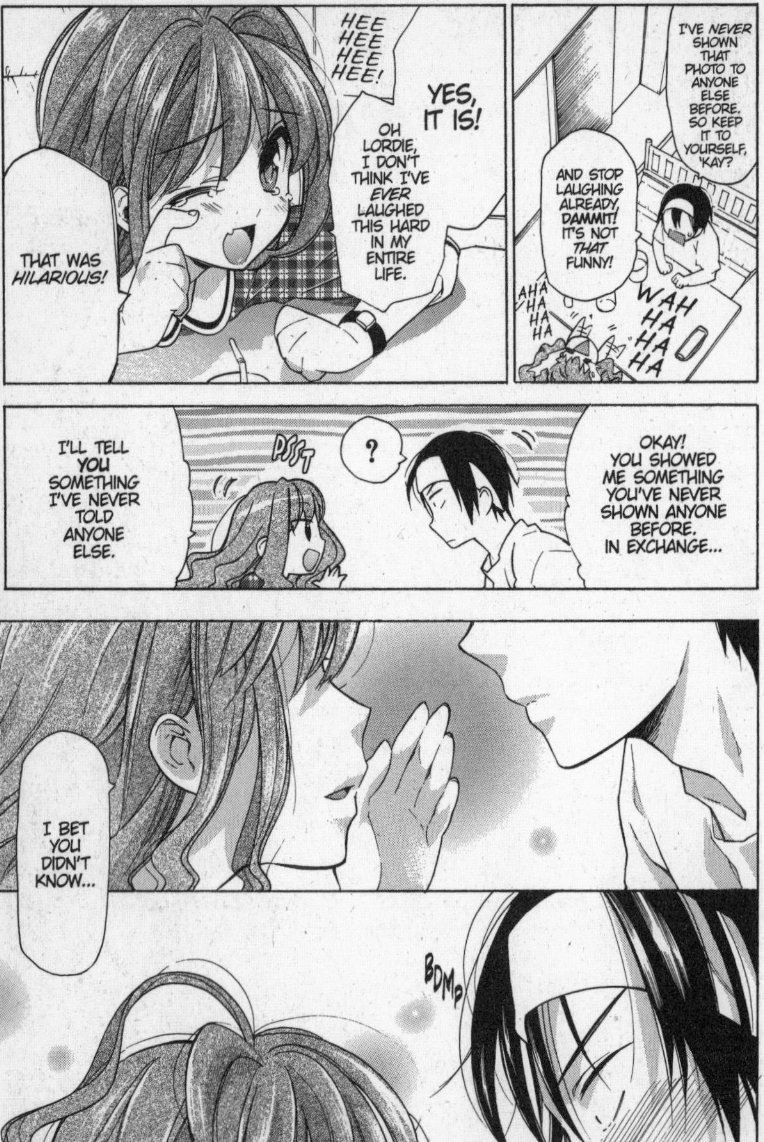
I'VE NEVER SHOWN THAT PHOTO TO ANYONE ELSE BEFORE. SO KEEP IT TO YOURSELF, 'KAY?
AND STOP LAUGHING ALREADY, DAMMIT! IT'S NOT THAT FUNNY!
WAH HA HA HA HA
AHA HA HA HA
YES, IT IS!
HEE HEE HEE HEE!
OH LORDIE, I DON'T THINK I'VE EVER LAUGHED THIS HARD IN MY ENTIRE LIFE.
THAT WAS HILARIOUS!
OKAY! YOU SHOWED ME SOMETHING YOU'VE NEVER SHOWN ANYONE BEFORE. IN EXCHANGE...
?
PSST
I'LL TELL YOU SOMETHING I'VE NEVER TOLD ANYONE ELSE.
I BET YOU DIDN'T KNOW...
BDMP

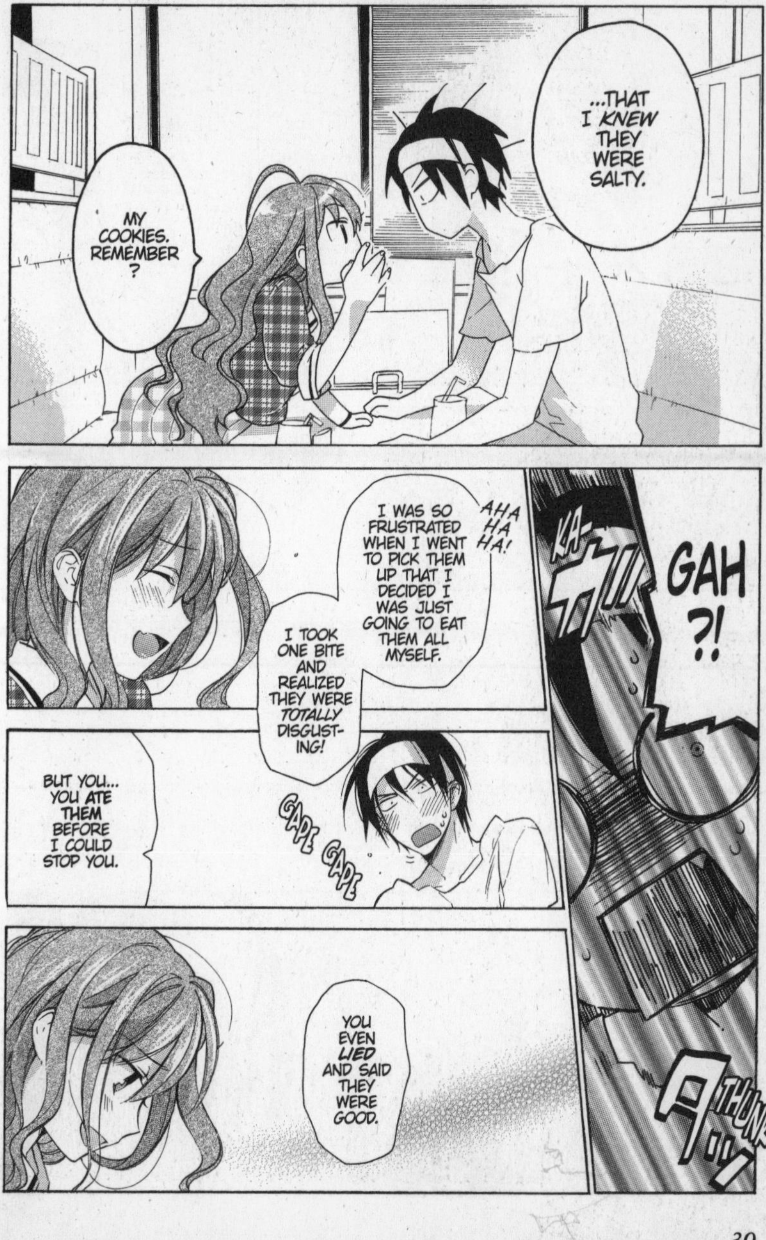
...THAT I *KNEW* THEY WERE SALTY.
MY COOKIES. REMEMBER?
KA-
GAH?!
THUNK
AHA HA HA!
I WAS SO FRUSTRATED WHEN I WENT TO PICK THEM UP THAT I DECIDED I WAS JUST GOING TO EAT THEM ALL MYSELF.
I TOOK ONE BITE AND REALIZED THEY WERE *TOTALLY* DISGUST-ING!
GAPE GAPE
BUT YOU... YOU ATE THEM BEFORE I COULD STOP YOU.
YOU EVEN ***LIED*** AND SAID THEY WERE GOOD.

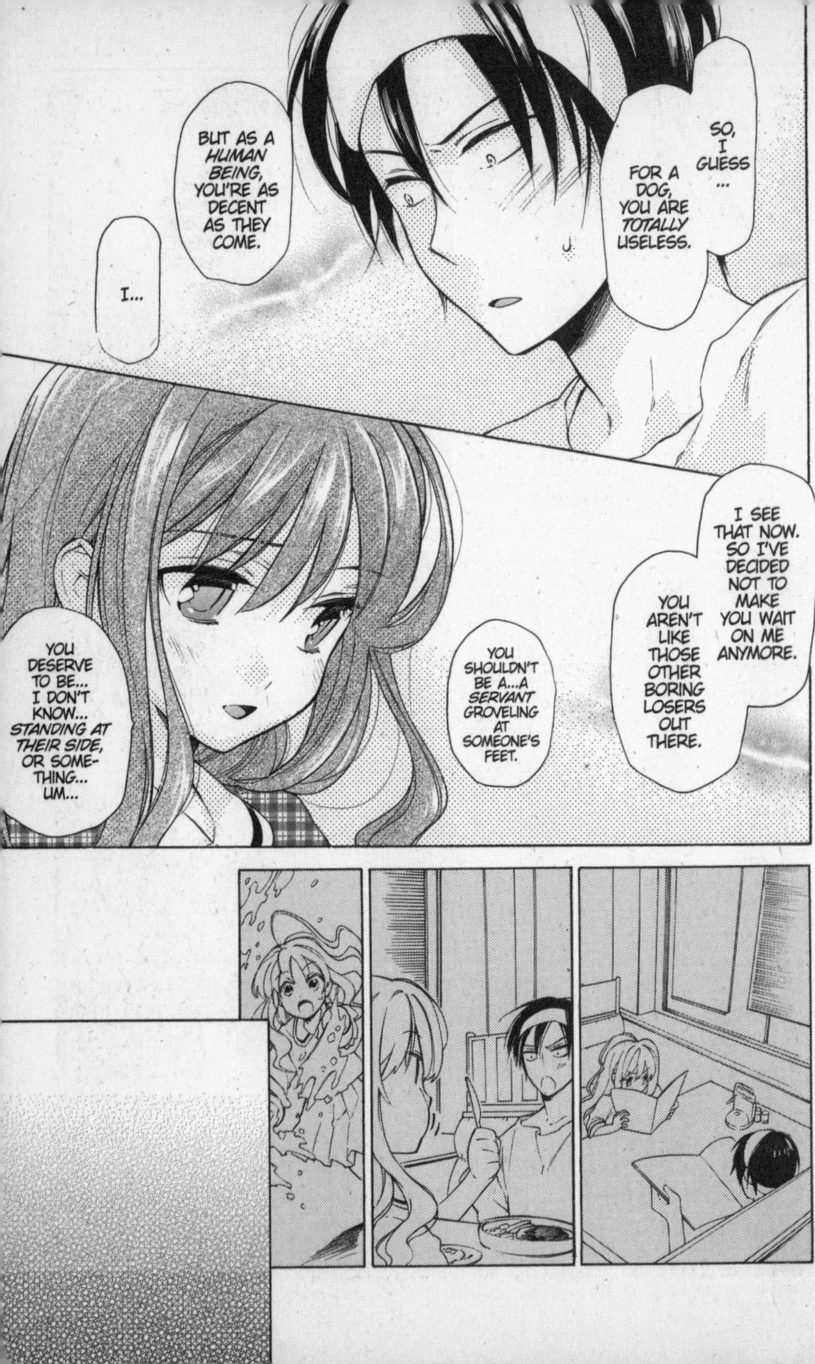
SO, I GUESS...
FOR A DOG, YOU ARE TOTALLY USELESS.
BUT AS A HUMAN BEING, YOU'RE AS DECENT AS THEY COME.
I...
I SEE THAT NOW. SO I'VE DECIDED NOT TO MAKE YOU WAIT ON ME ANYMORE.
YOU AREN'T LIKE THOSE OTHER BORING LOSERS OUT THERE.
YOU SHOULDN'T BE A...A SERVANT GROVELING AT SOMEONE'S FEET.
YOU DESERVE TO BE... I DON'T KNOW... STANDING AT THEIR SIDE, OR SOME-THING... UM...

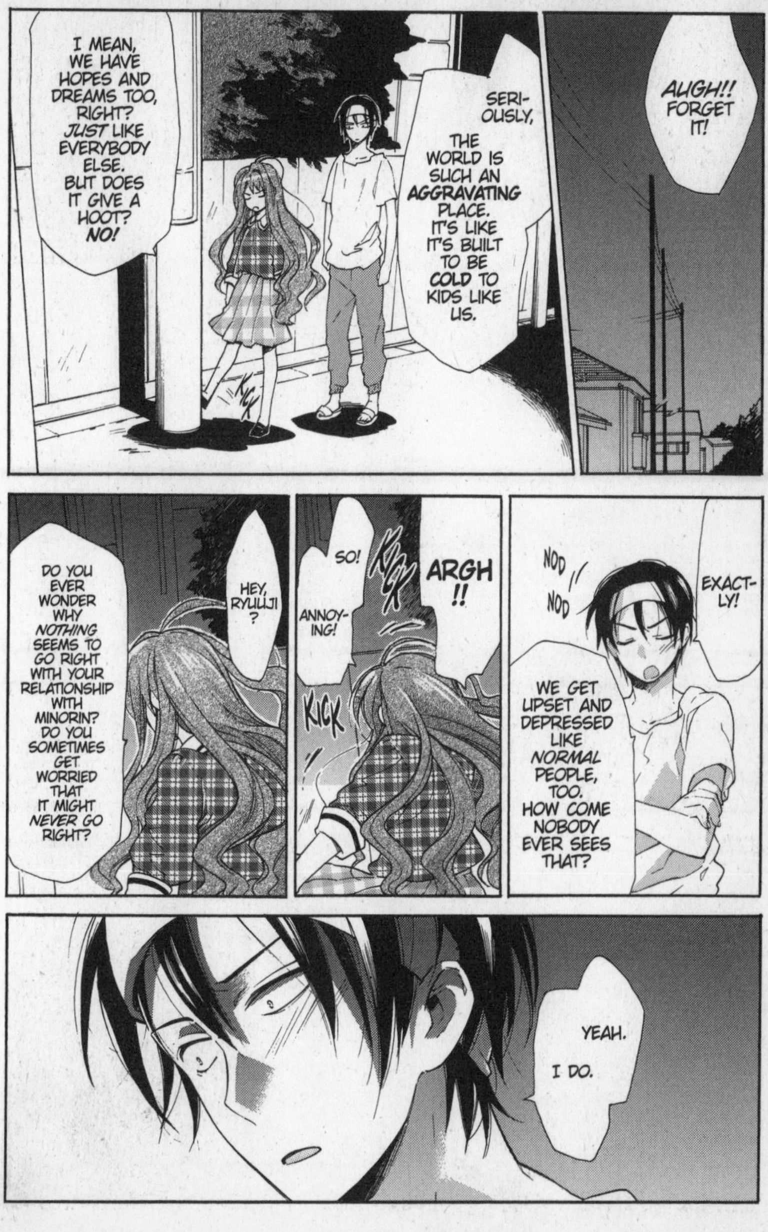
AUGH!! FORGET IT!
SERI-OUSLY, THE WORLD IS SUCH AN AGGRAVATING PLACE. IT'S LIKE IT'S BUILT TO BE COLD TO KIDS LIKE US.
I MEAN, WE HAVE HOPES AND DREAMS TOO, RIGHT? JUST LIKE EVERYBODY ELSE. BUT DOES IT GIVE A HOOT? NO!
KICK
EXACT-LY!
NOD NOD
WE GET UPSET AND DEPRESSED LIKE NORMAL PEOPLE, TOO. HOW COME NOBODY EVER SEES THAT?
ARGH!!
KICK
SO!
ANNOY-ING!
KICK
HEY, RYUUJI?
DO YOU EVER WONDER WHY NOTHING SEEMS TO GO RIGHT WITH YOUR RELATIONSHIP WITH MINORIN? DO YOU SOMETIMES GET WORRIED THAT IT MIGHT NEVER GO RIGHT?
YEAH.
I DO.

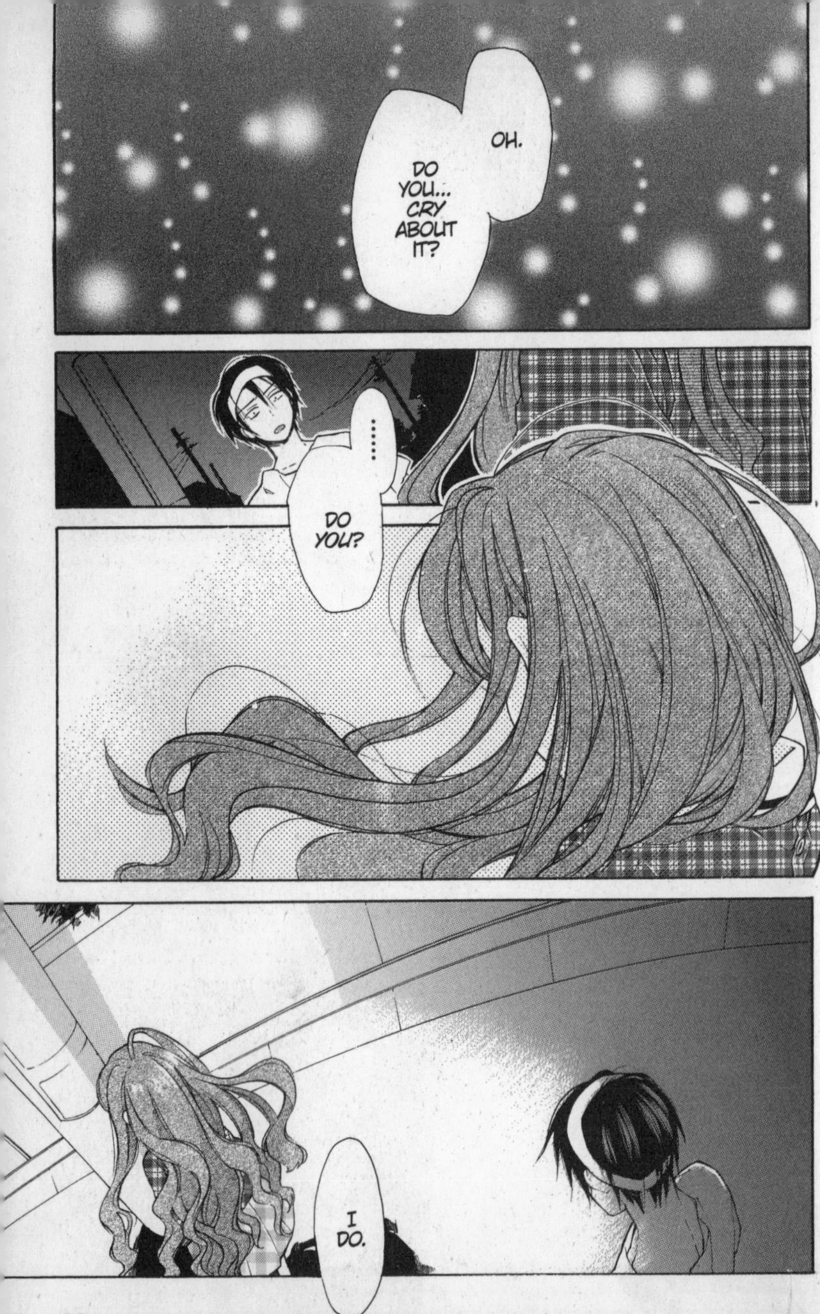
OH.
DO YOU... CRY ABOUT IT?
......
DO YOU?
I DO.

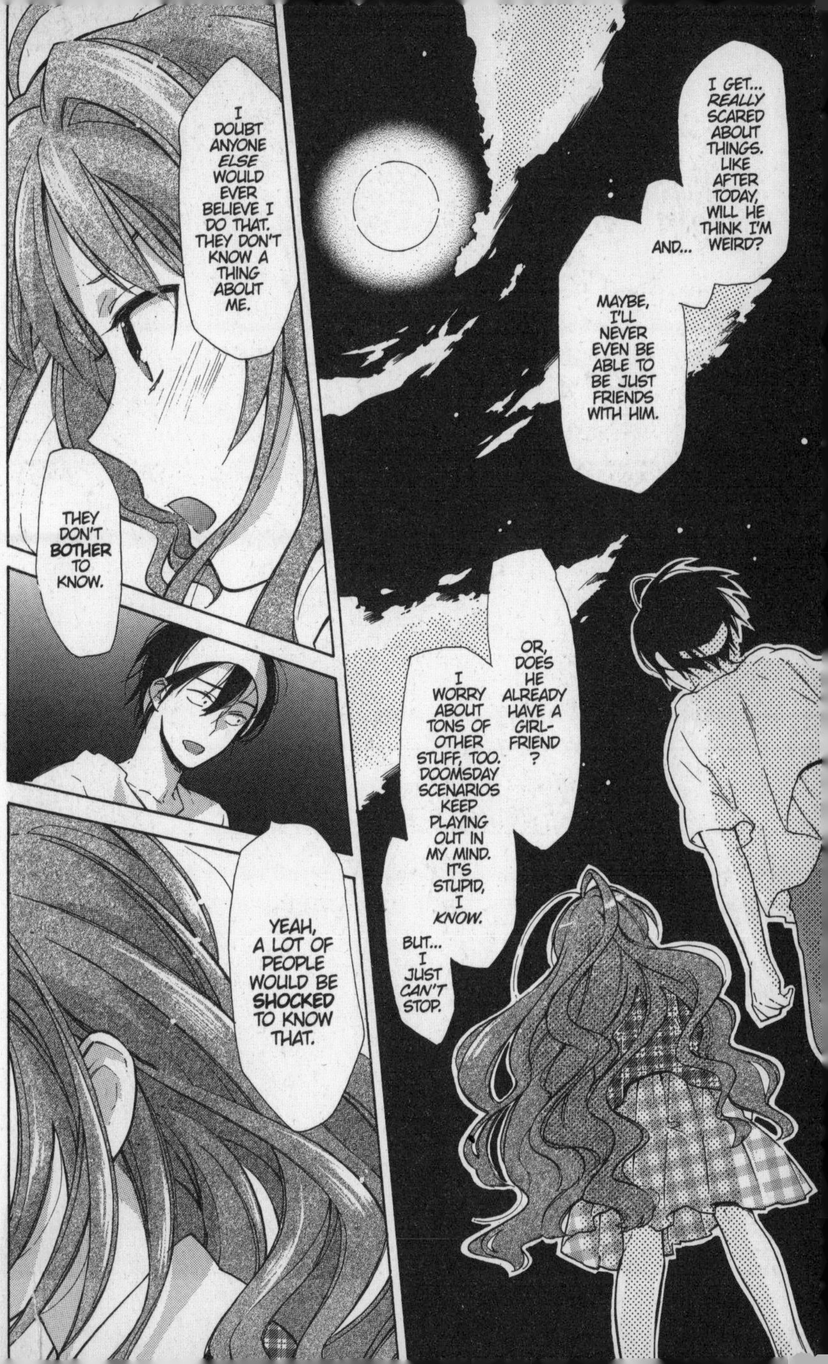
I GET... REALLY SCARED ABOUT THINGS. LIKE AFTER TODAY, WILL HE THINK I'M WEIRD?
AND...
MAYBE, I'LL NEVER EVEN BE ABLE TO BE JUST FRIENDS WITH HIM.
OR, DOES HE ALREADY HAVE A GIRL-FRIEND?
I WORRY ABOUT TONS OF OTHER STUFF, TOO. DOOMSDAY SCENARIOS KEEP PLAYING OUT IN MY MIND. IT'S STUPID, I KNOW.
BUT... I JUST CAN'T STOP.
I DOUBT ANYONE ELSE WOULD EVER BELIEVE I DO THAT. THEY DON'T KNOW A THING ABOUT ME.
THEY DON'T BOTHER TO KNOW.
YEAH, A LOT OF PEOPLE WOULD BE SHOCKED TO KNOW THAT.

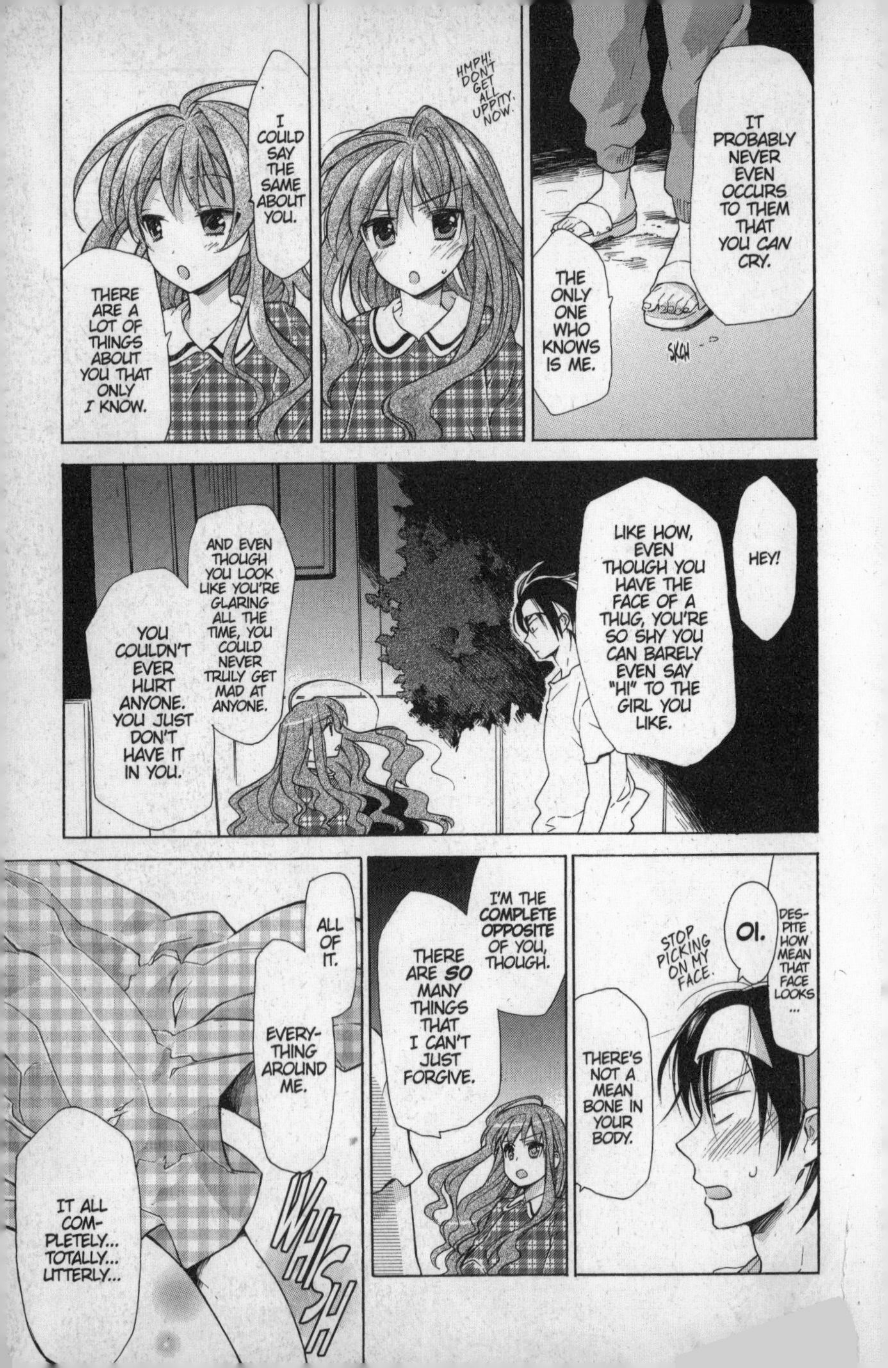
IT PROBABLY NEVER EVEN OCCURS TO THEM THAT YOU CAN CRY.
THE ONLY ONE WHO KNOWS IS ME.
SKCH
HMPH! DON'T GET ALL UPPITY, NOW.
I COULD SAY THE SAME ABOUT YOU.
THERE ARE A LOT OF THINGS ABOUT YOU THAT ONLY I KNOW.
HEY!
LIKE HOW, EVEN THOUGH YOU HAVE THE FACE OF A THUG, YOU'RE SO SHY YOU CAN BARELY EVEN SAY "HI" TO THE GIRL YOU LIKE.
AND EVEN THOUGH YOU LOOK LIKE YOU'RE GLARING ALL THE TIME, YOU COULD NEVER TRULY GET MAD AT ANYONE.
YOU COULDN'T EVER HURT ANYONE. YOU JUST DON'T HAVE IT IN YOU.
DESPITE HOW MEAN THAT FACE LOOKS...
OI.
STOP PICKING ON MY FACE.
THERE'S NOT A MEAN BONE IN YOUR BODY.
I'M THE COMPLETE OPPOSITE OF YOU, THOUGH.
THERE ARE SO MANY THINGS THAT I CAN'T JUST FORGIVE.
ALL OF IT.
EVERYTHING AROUND ME.
IT ALL COMPLETELY... TOTALLY... UTTERLY...
WHSH

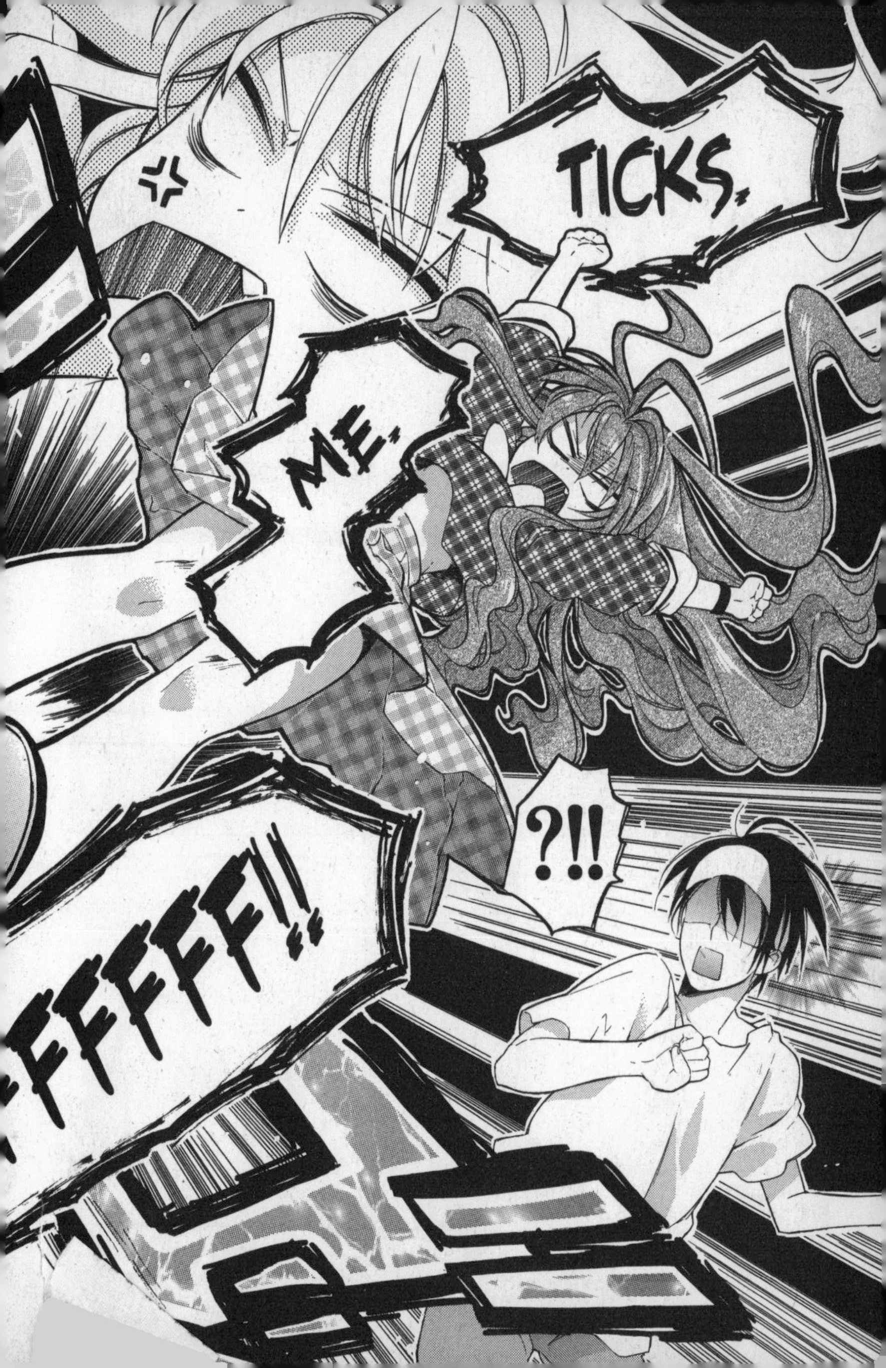
TICKS.
ME,
?!!
FFFFF!!

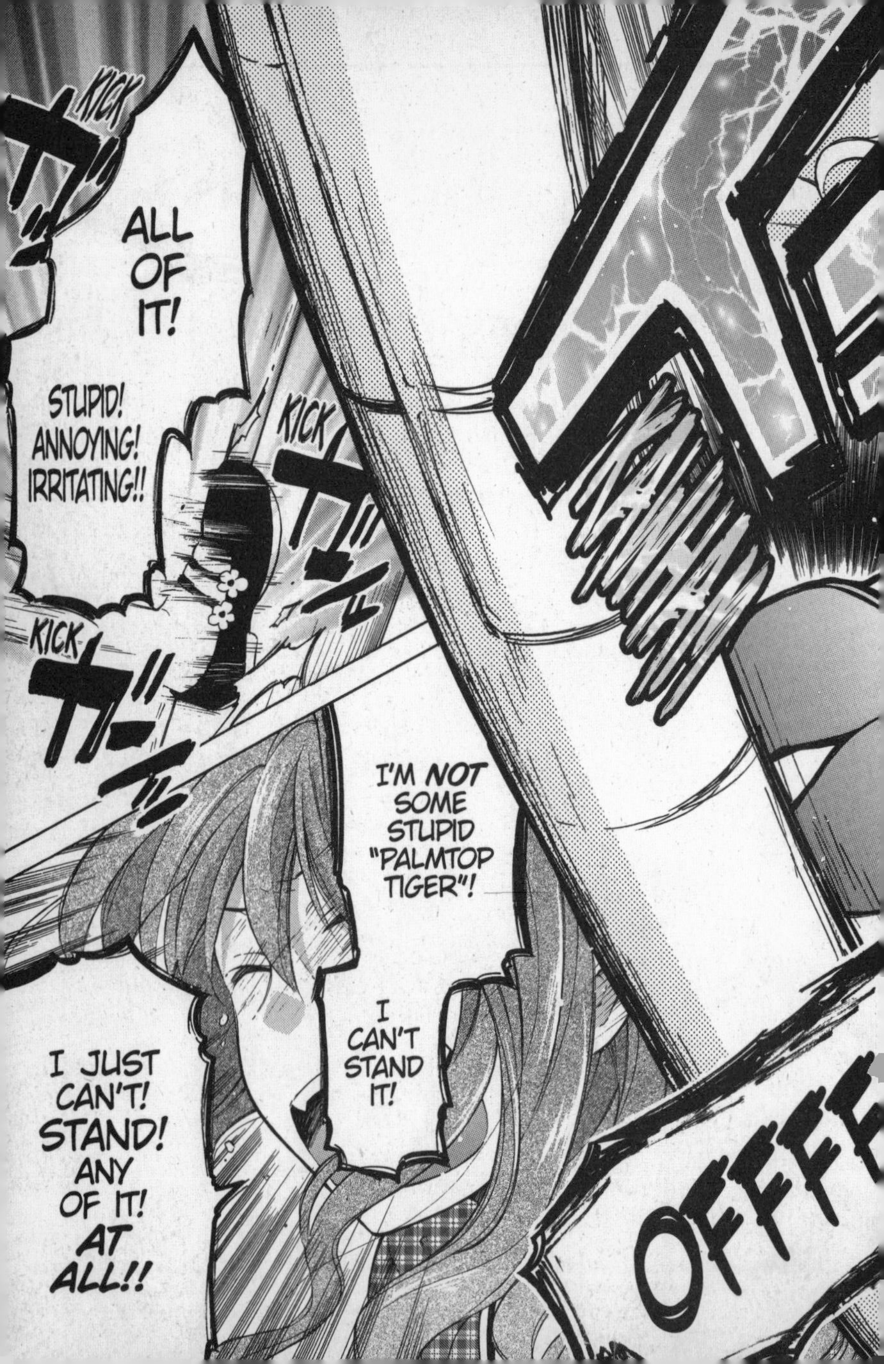
KICK
ALL OF IT!
KICK
STUPID! ANNOYING! IRRITATING!!
KICK
I'M *NOT* SOME STUPID "PALMTOP TIGER"!
I CAN'T STAND IT!
I JUST CAN'T! STAND! ANY OF IT! *AT ALL!!*
OFFFF

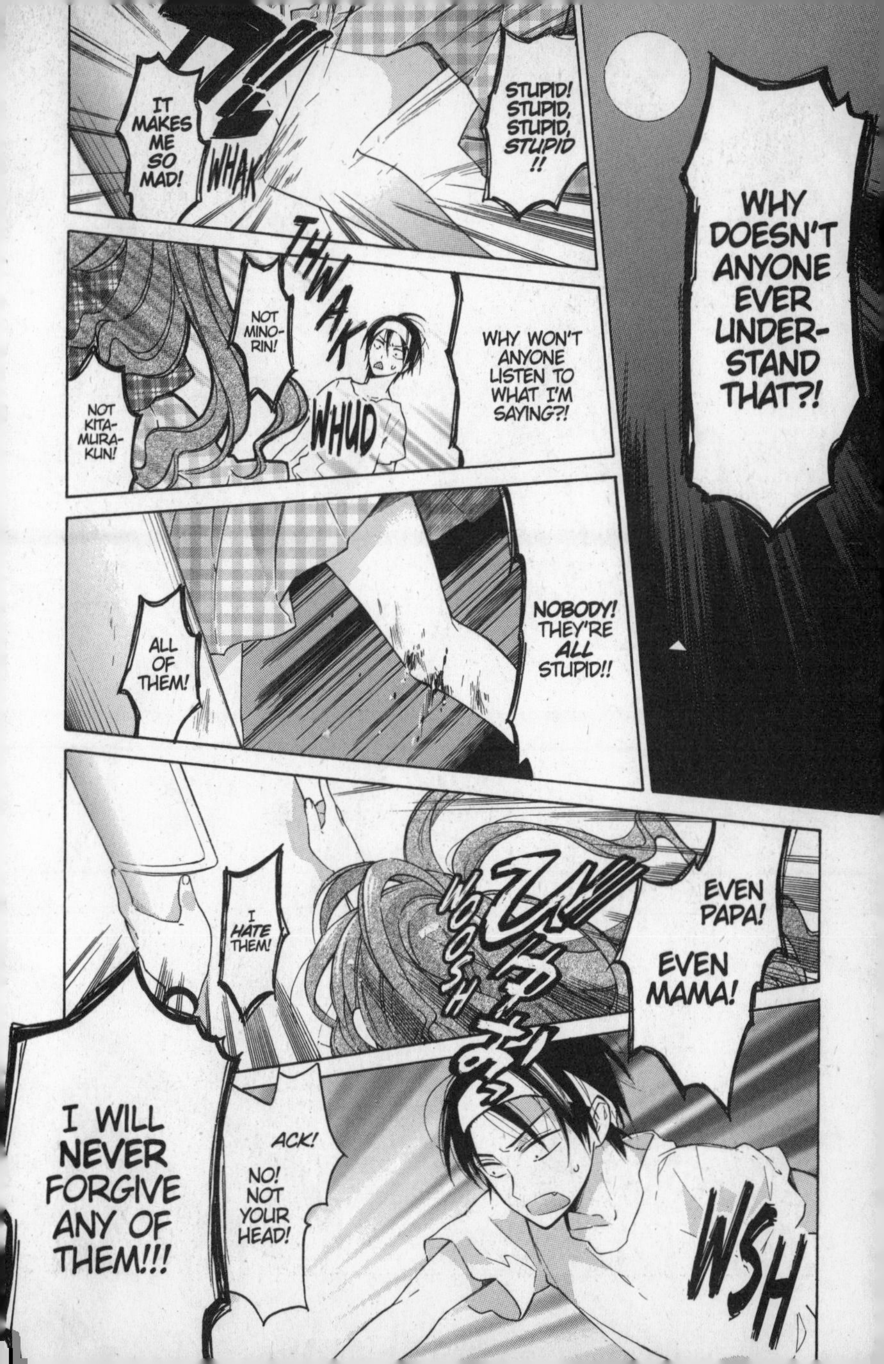
WHY DOESN'T ANYONE EVER UNDER-STAND THAT?!
STUPID! STUPID, STUPID, STUPID!!
WHAK
IT MAKES ME SO MAD!
THWAK
WHY WON'T ANYONE LISTEN TO WHAT I'M SAYING?!
WHUD
NOT MINO-RIN!
NOT KITA-MURA-KUN!
NOBODY! THEY'RE ALL STUPID!!
ALL OF THEM!
EVEN PAPA!
EVEN MAMA!
WHOOSH
I HATE THEM!
WSH
NO! NOT YOUR HEAD!
ACK!
I WILL NEVER FORGIVE ANY OF THEM!!!

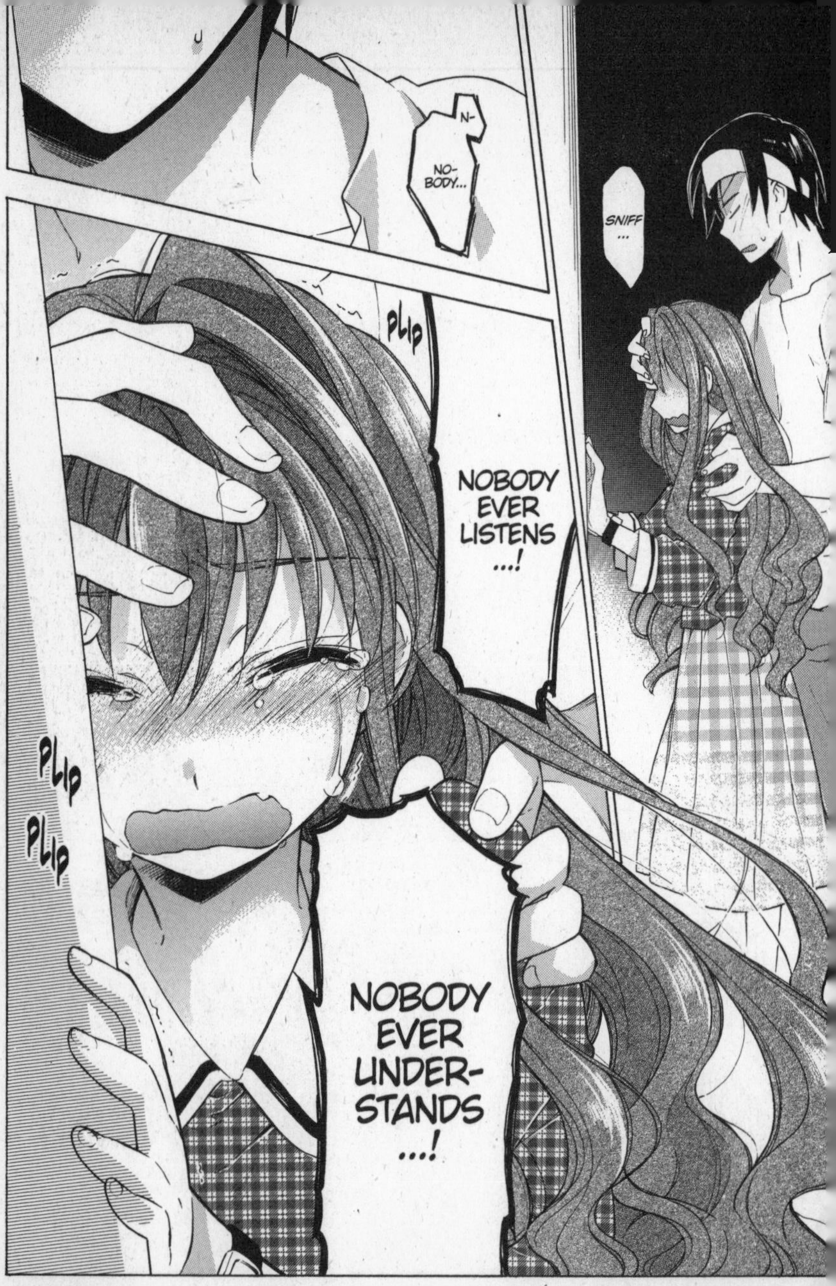
SNIFF ...
N- NO-BODY...
PLIP
NOBODY EVER LISTENS ...!
PLIP PLIP
NOBODY EVER UNDER-STANDS ...!

BAAAAGAAAN!!

Q1. what manga was
Haruda reading?

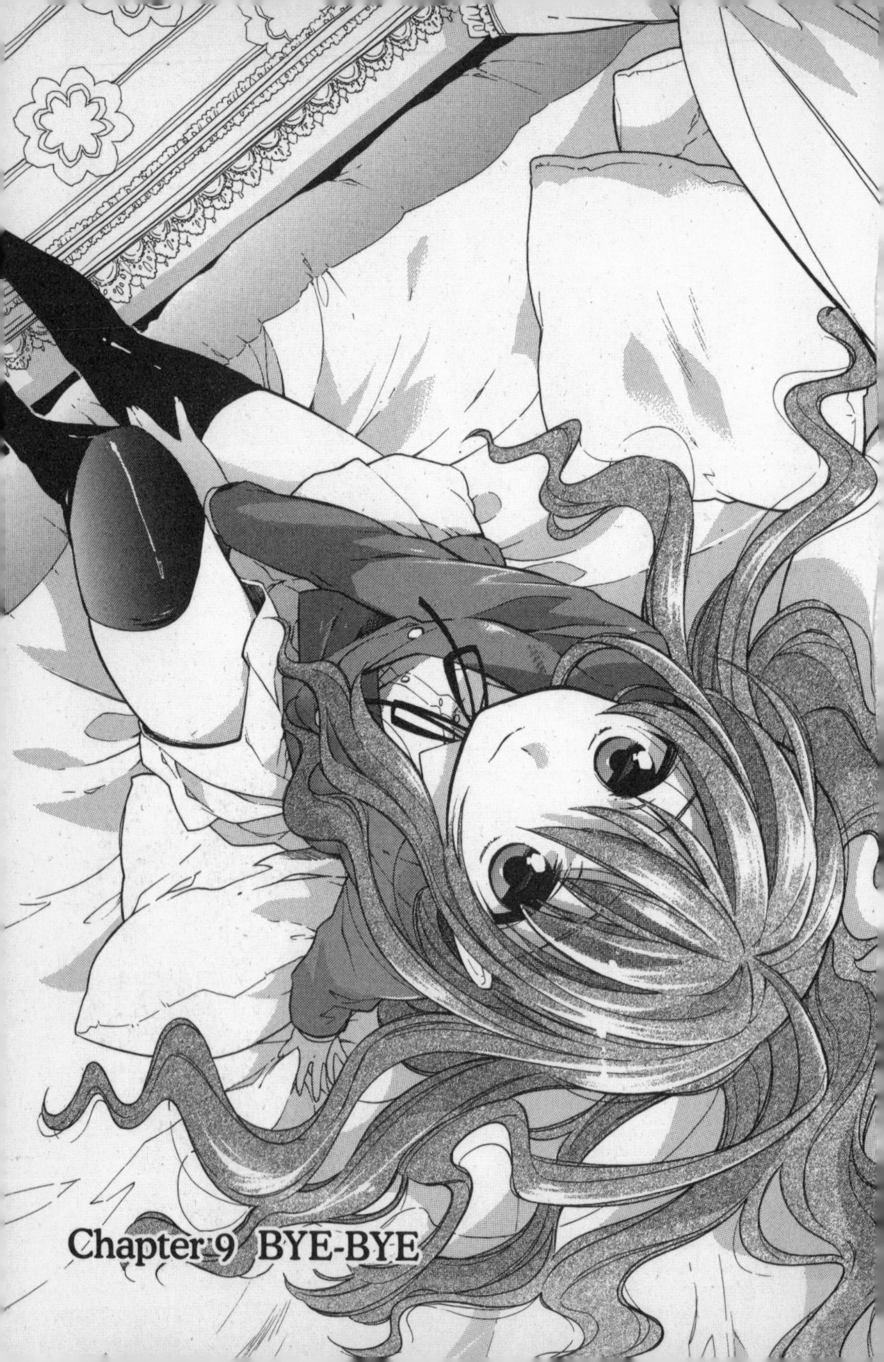

Chapter 9 BYE-BYE

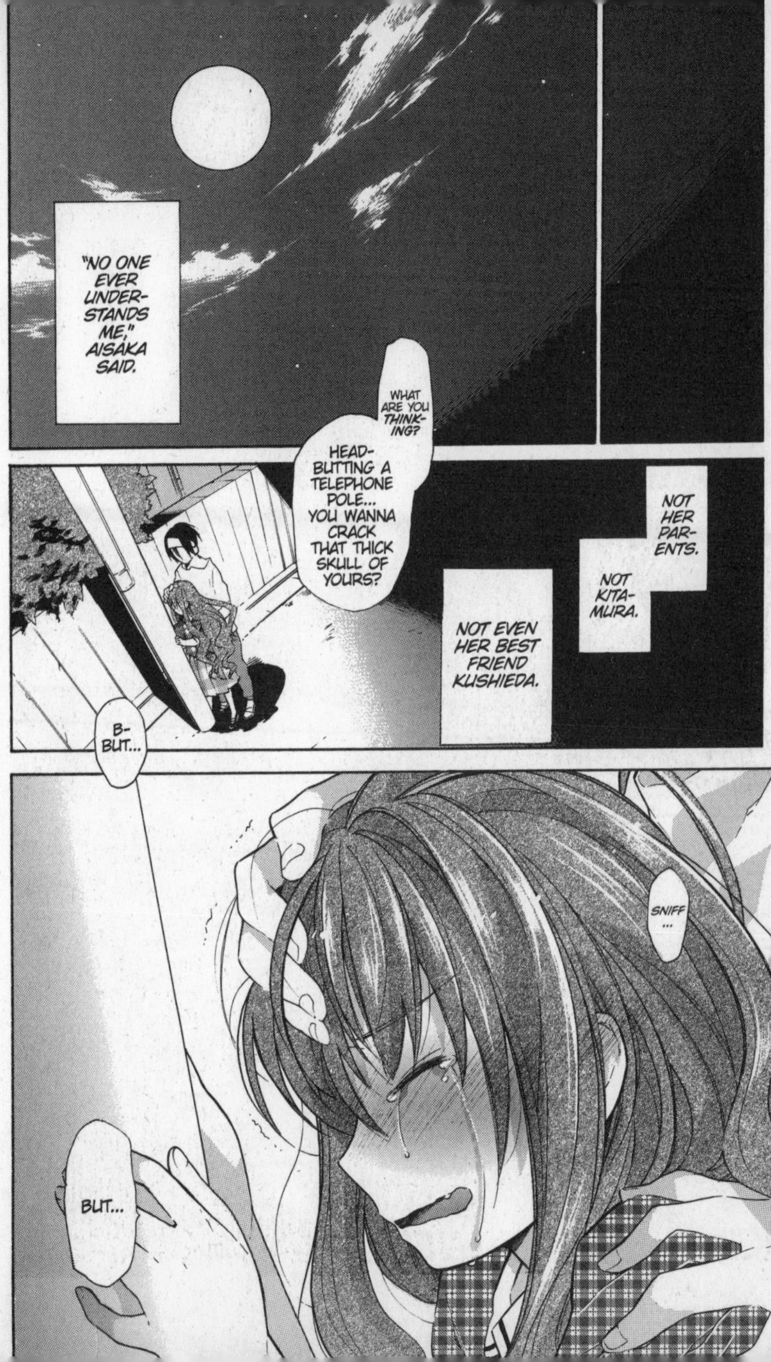
"NO ONE EVER UNDERSTANDS ME," AISAKA SAID.
NOT HER PARENTS.
NOT KITAMURA.
NOT EVEN HER BEST FRIEND KUSHIEDA.
WHAT ARE YOU THINKING?
HEAD-BUTTING A TELEPHONE POLE... YOU WANNA CRACK THAT THICK SKULL OF YOURS?
B-BUT...
SNIFF...
BUT...

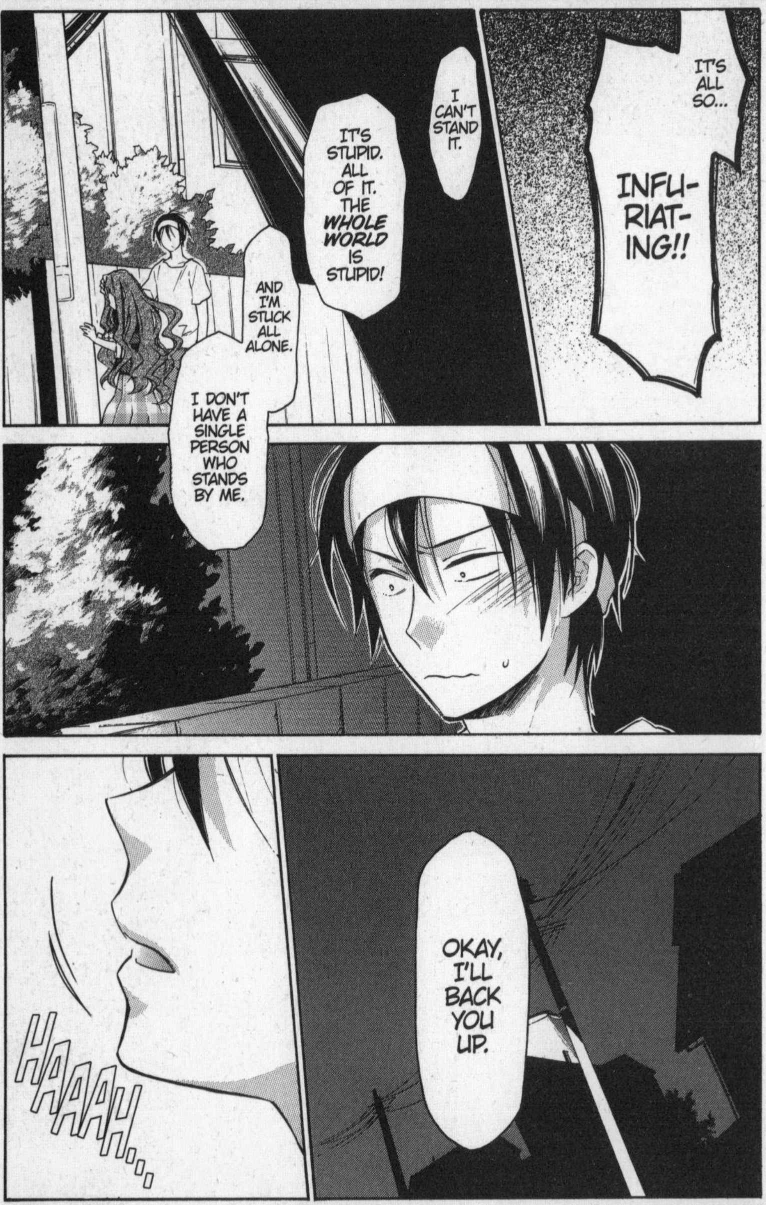
IT'S ALL SO...
INFURI-RIATING!!
I CAN'T STAND IT.
IT'S STUPID. ALL OF IT. THE *WHOLE WORLD* IS STUPID!
AND I'M STUCK ALL ALONE.
I DON'T HAVE A SINGLE PERSON WHO STANDS BY ME.
OKAY, I'LL BACK YOU UP.
HAAAH...

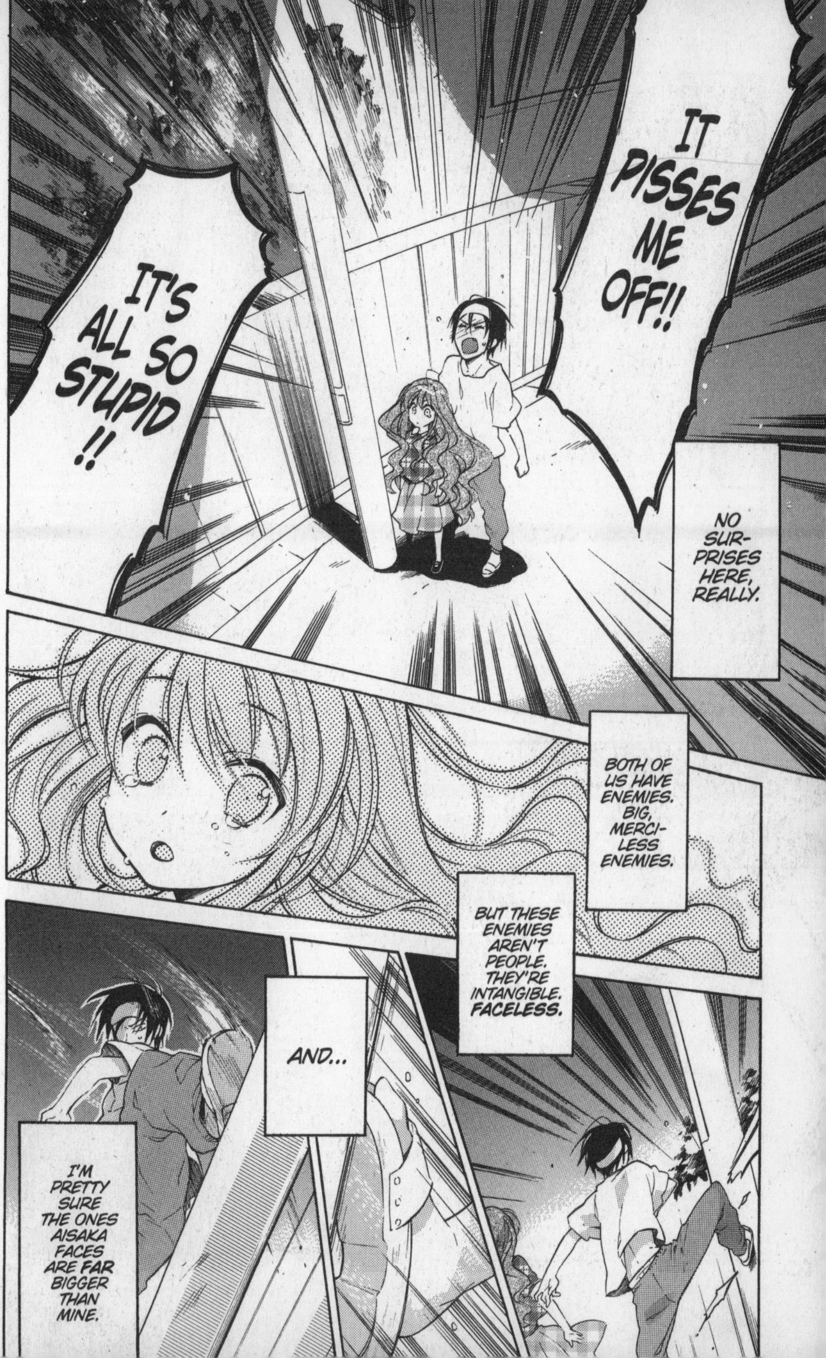
IT PISSES ME OFF!!
IT'S ALL SO STUPID!!
NO SUR-PRISES HERE, REALLY.
BOTH OF US HAVE ENEMIES. BIG, MERCI-LESS ENEMIES.
BUT THESE ENEMIES AREN'T PEOPLE. THEY'RE INTANGIBLE. FACELESS.
AND...
I'M PRETTY SURE THE ONES AISAKA FACES ARE FAR BIGGER THAN MINE.

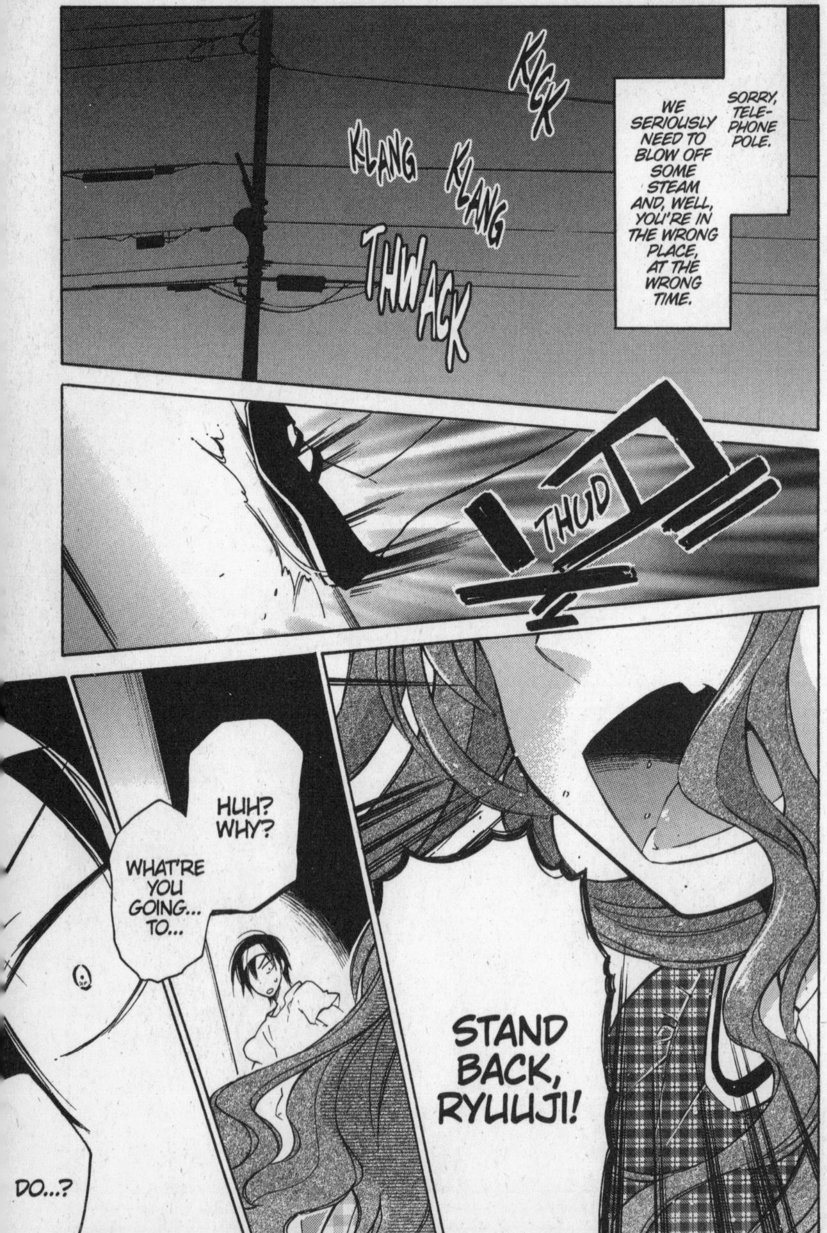
SORRY, TELE-PHONE POLE.
WE SERIOUSLY NEED TO BLOW OFF SOME STEAM AND, WELL, YOU'RE IN THE WRONG PLACE, AT THE WRONG TIME.
KICK
KLANG
KLANG
THWACK
THUD
STAND BACK, RYUUJI!
HUH? WHY?
WHAT'RE YOU GOING... TO...
DO...?

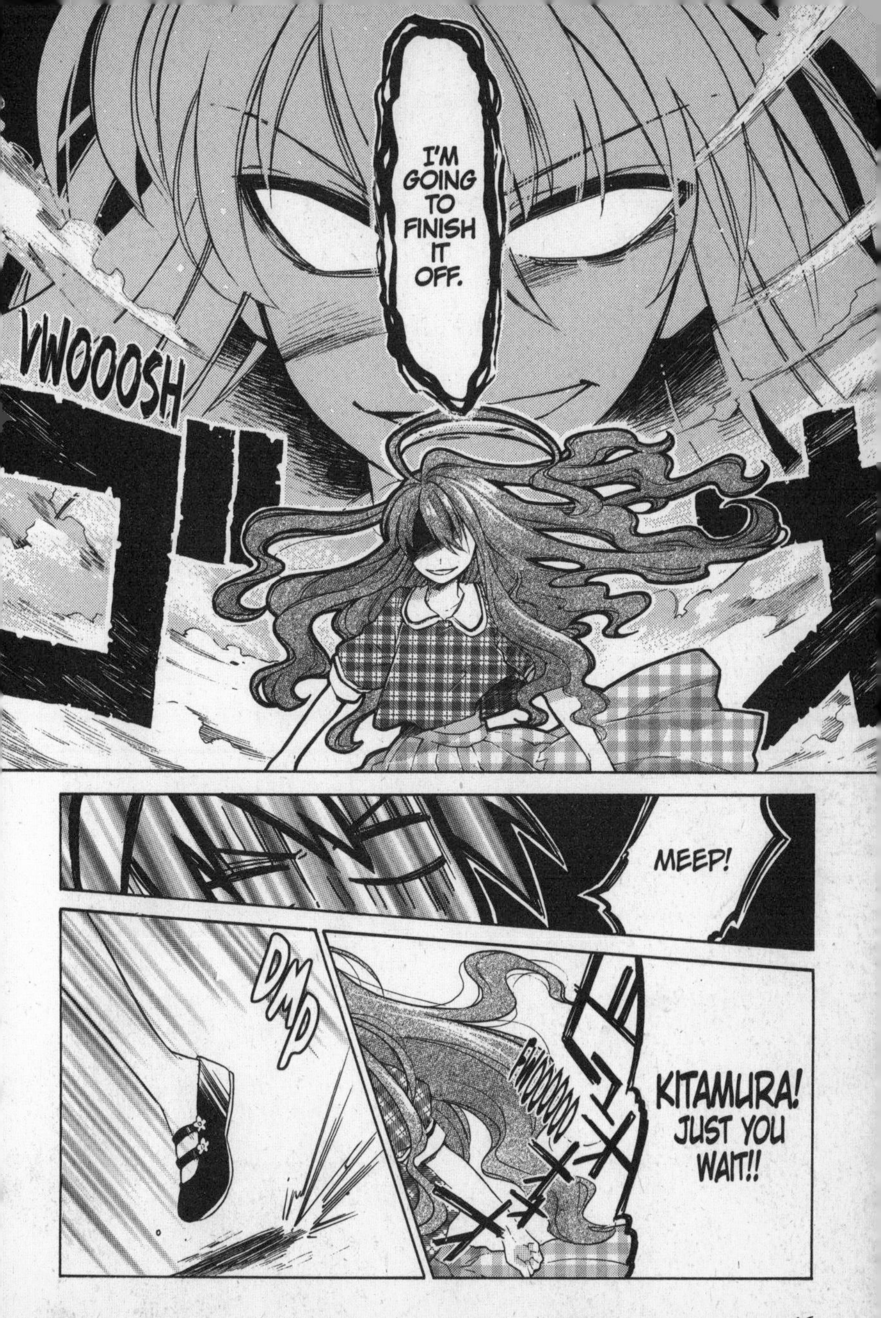
I'M GOING TO FINISH IT OFF.
VWOOOSH
MEEP!
KITAMURA! JUST YOU WAIT!!
DMP

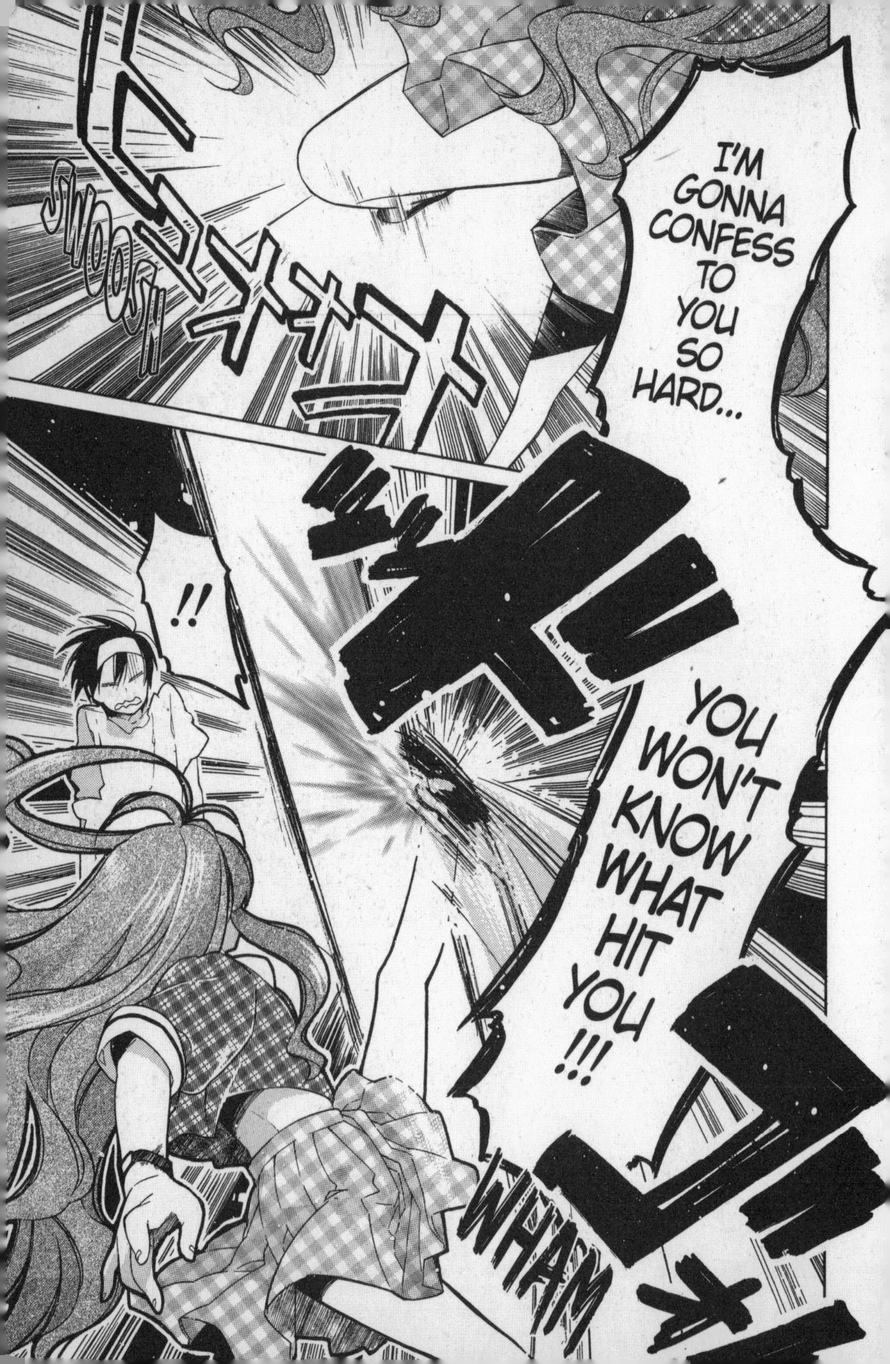
I'M GONNA CONFESS TO YOU SO HARD...
SWOOSH
YOU WON'T KNOW WHAT HIT YOU!!!
!!
WHAM

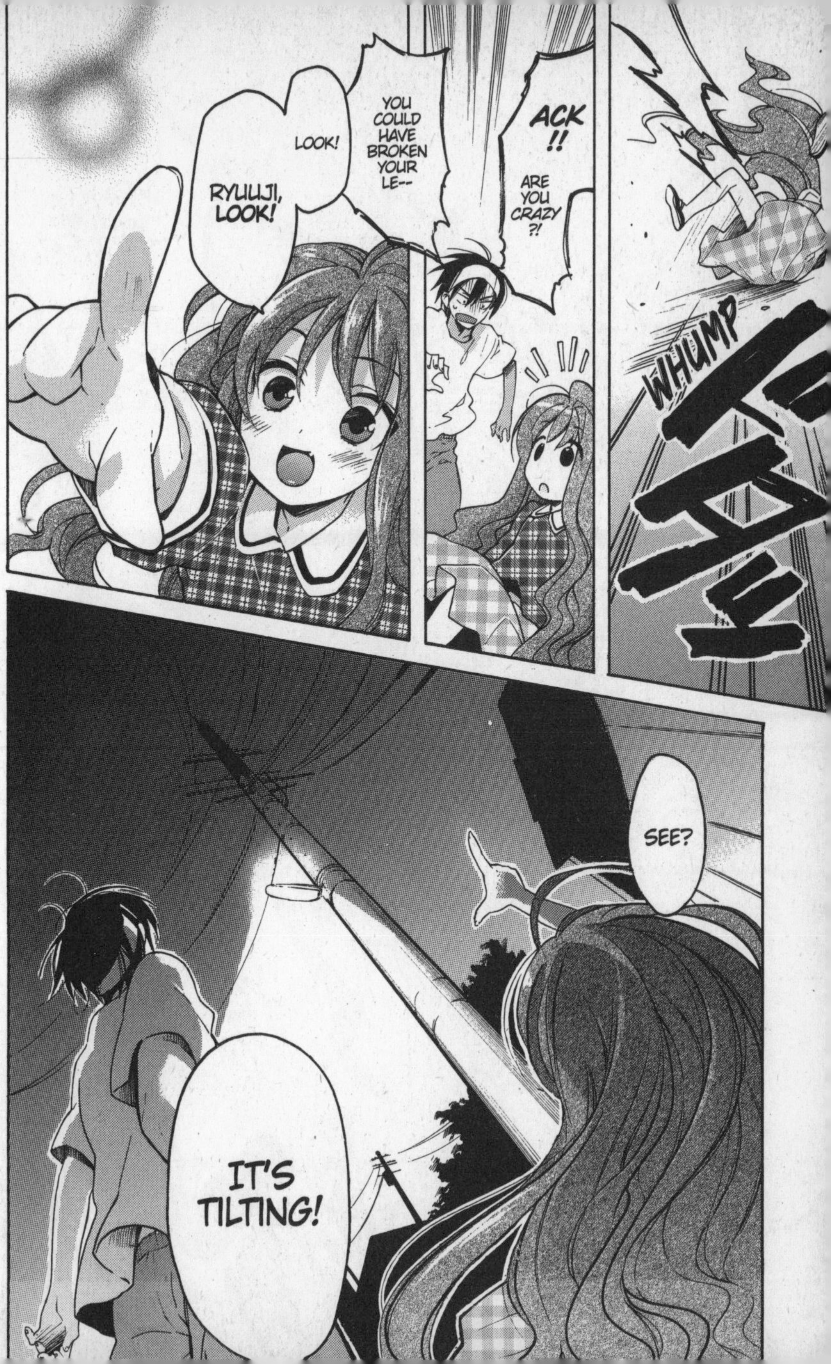
WHUMP
ACK!!
ARE YOU CRAZY?!
YOU COULD HAVE BROKEN YOUR LE--
LOOK!
RYUUJI, LOOK!
SEE?
IT'S TILTING!

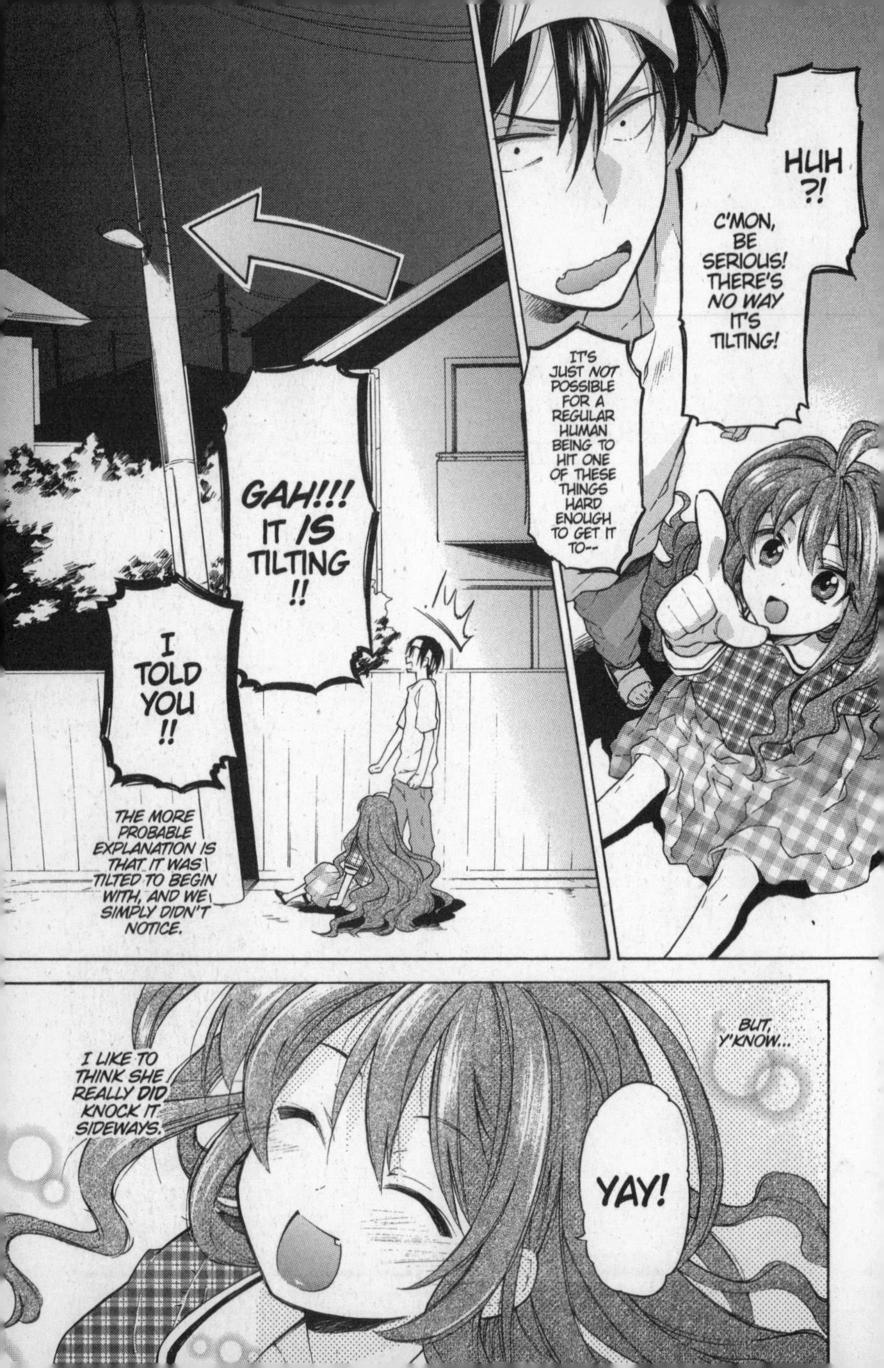
HUH ?!
C'MON, BE SERIOUS! THERE'S *NO WAY* IT'S TILTING!
IT'S JUST *NOT* POSSIBLE FOR A REGULAR HUMAN BEING TO HIT ONE OF THESE THINGS HARD ENOUGH TO GET IT TO--
GAH!!! IT *IS* TILTING !!
I TOLD YOU !!
THE MORE PROBABLE EXPLANATION IS THAT IT WAS TILTED TO BEGIN WITH, AND WE SIMPLY DIDN'T NOTICE.
BUT, Y'KNOW...
I LIKE TO THINK SHE REALLY DID KNOCK IT SIDEWAYS.
YAY!

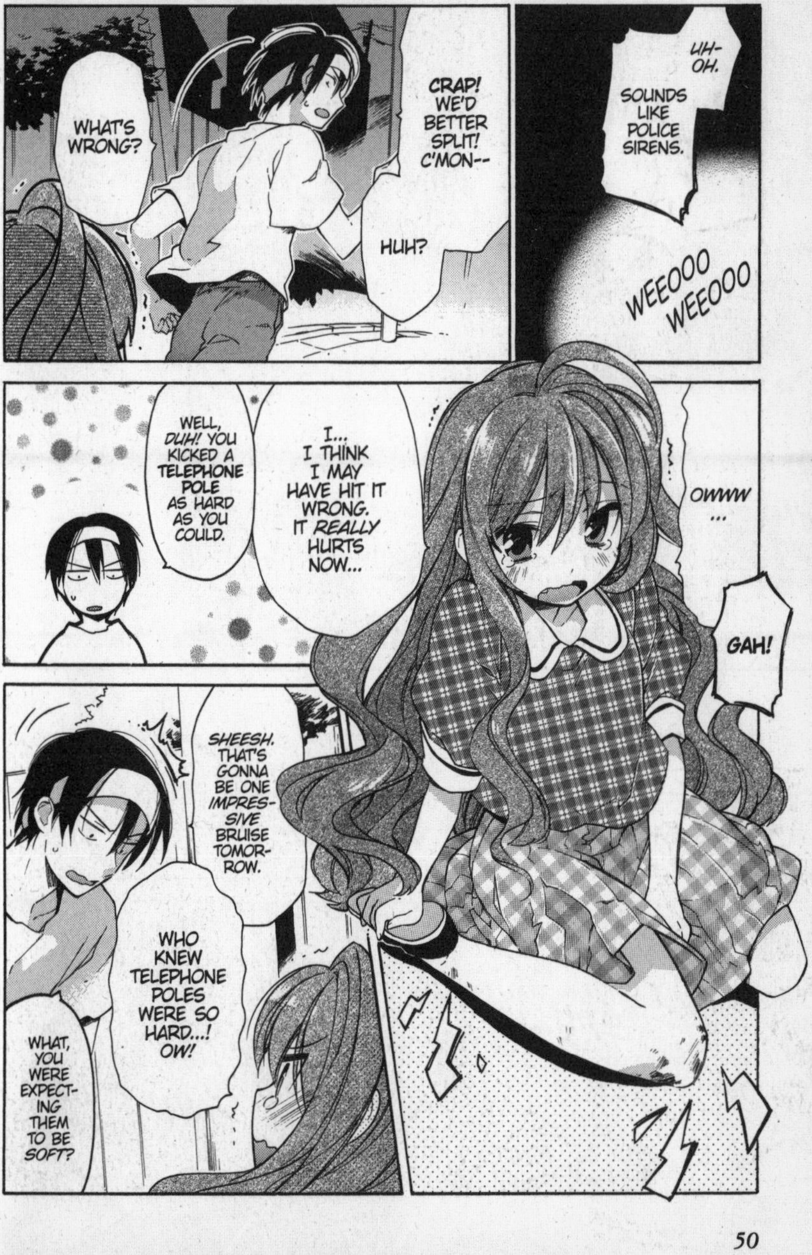
UH-OH.
SOUNDS LIKE POLICE SIRENS.
WEEOOO WEEOOO
CRAP! WE'D BETTER SPLIT! C'MON--
HUH?
WHAT'S WRONG?
OWWW...
GAH!
I... I THINK I MAY HAVE HIT IT WRONG. IT *REALLY* HURTS NOW...
WELL, *DUH!* YOU KICKED A TELEPHONE POLE AS HARD AS YOU COULD.
SHEESH. THAT'S GONNA BE ONE *IMPRESSIVE* BRUISE TOMORROW.
WHO KNEW TELEPHONE POLES WERE SO HARD...! OW!
WHAT, YOU WERE EXPECTING THEM TO BE *SOFT?*

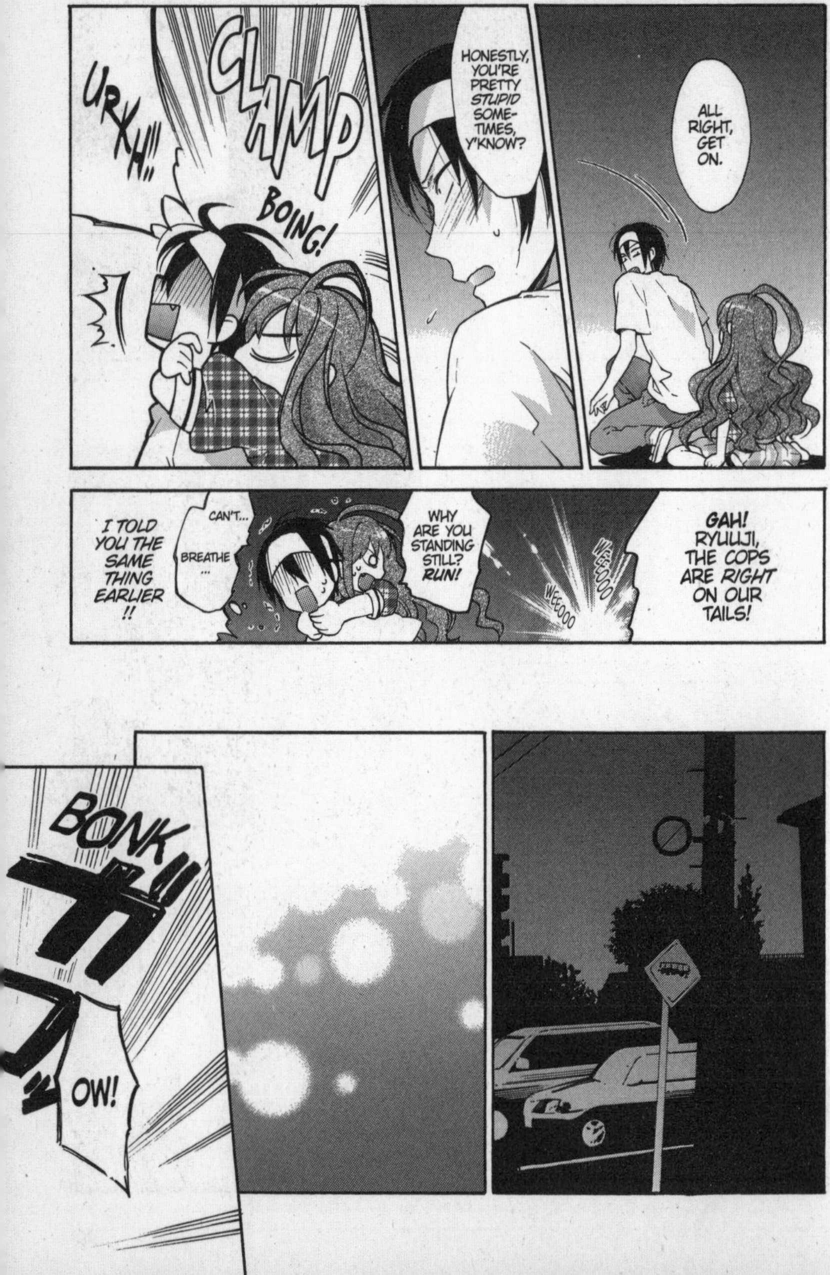
ALL RIGHT, GET ON.
HONESTLY, YOU'RE PRETTY STUPID SOMETIMES, Y'KNOW?
CLAMP
BOING!
URKH!!
GAH! RYUUJI, THE COPS ARE RIGHT ON OUR TAILS!
WEEOOO
WEEOOO
WHY ARE YOU STANDING STILL? RUN!
CAN'T... BREATHE...
I TOLD YOU THE SAME THING EARLIER!!
BONK!!
OW!

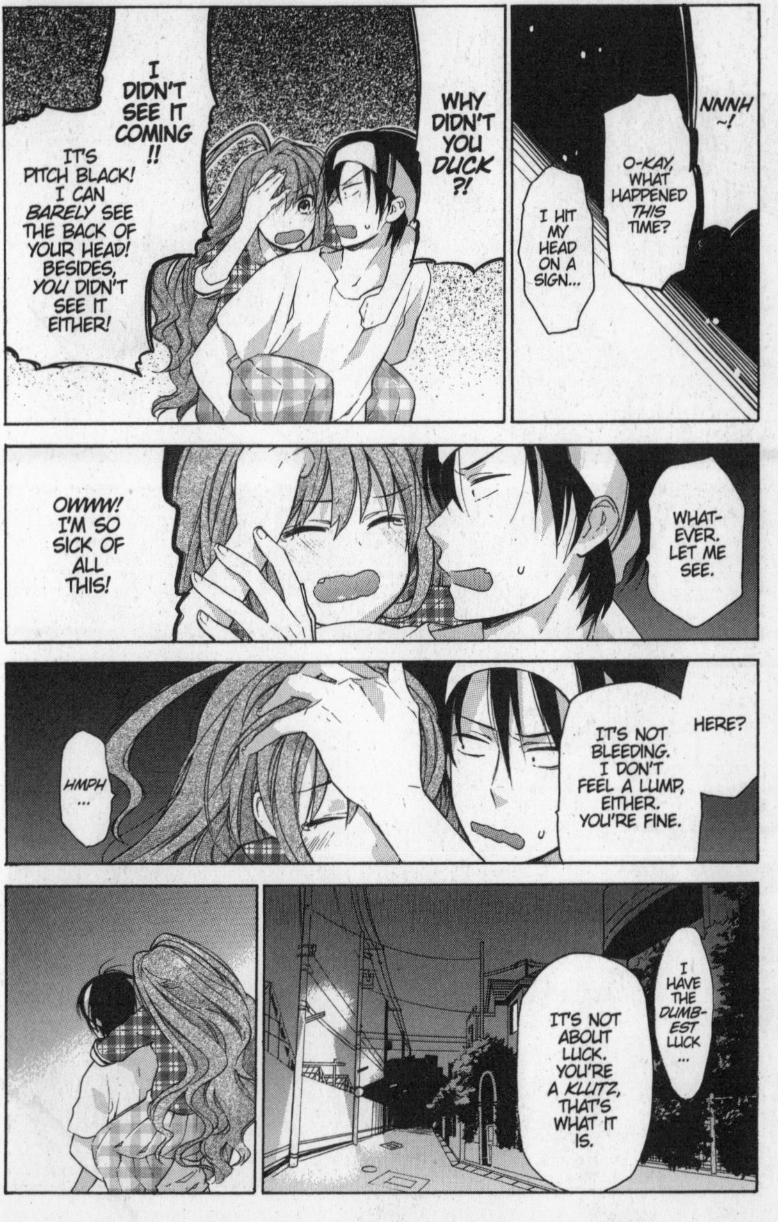
NNNH ~!
O-KAY, WHAT HAPPENED *THIS* TIME?
I HIT MY HEAD ON A SIGN...
WHY DIDN'T YOU DUCK ?!
I DIDN'T SEE IT COMING !!
IT'S PITCH BLACK! I CAN *BARELY* SEE THE BACK OF YOUR HEAD! BESIDES, *YOU* DIDN'T SEE IT EITHER!
WHAT-EVER. LET ME SEE.
OWWW! I'M SO SICK OF ALL THIS!
HERE?
IT'S NOT BLEEDING. I DON'T FEEL A LUMP, EITHER. YOU'RE FINE.
HMPH ...
I HAVE THE *DUMB-EST* LUCK ...
IT'S NOT ABOUT LUCK. YOU'RE A *KLUTZ*, THAT'S WHAT IT IS.

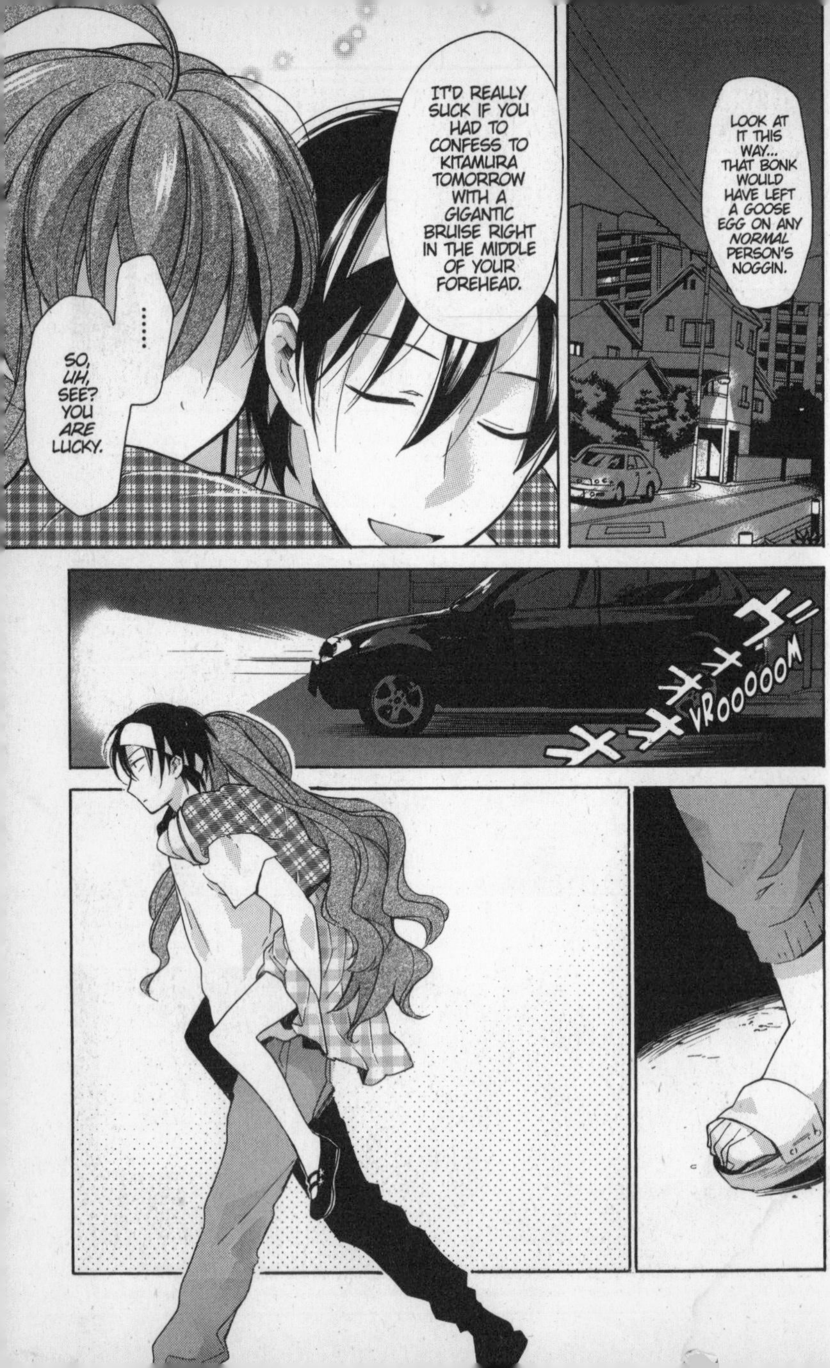
LOOK AT IT THIS WAY... THAT BONK WOULD HAVE LEFT A GOOSE EGG ON ANY *NORMAL* PERSON'S NOGGIN.
IT'D REALLY SUCK IF YOU HAD TO CONFESS TO KITAMURA TOMORROW WITH A GIGANTIC BRUISE RIGHT IN THE MIDDLE OF YOUR FOREHEAD.
......
SO, UH, SEE? YOU *ARE* LUCKY.
VROOOOOM

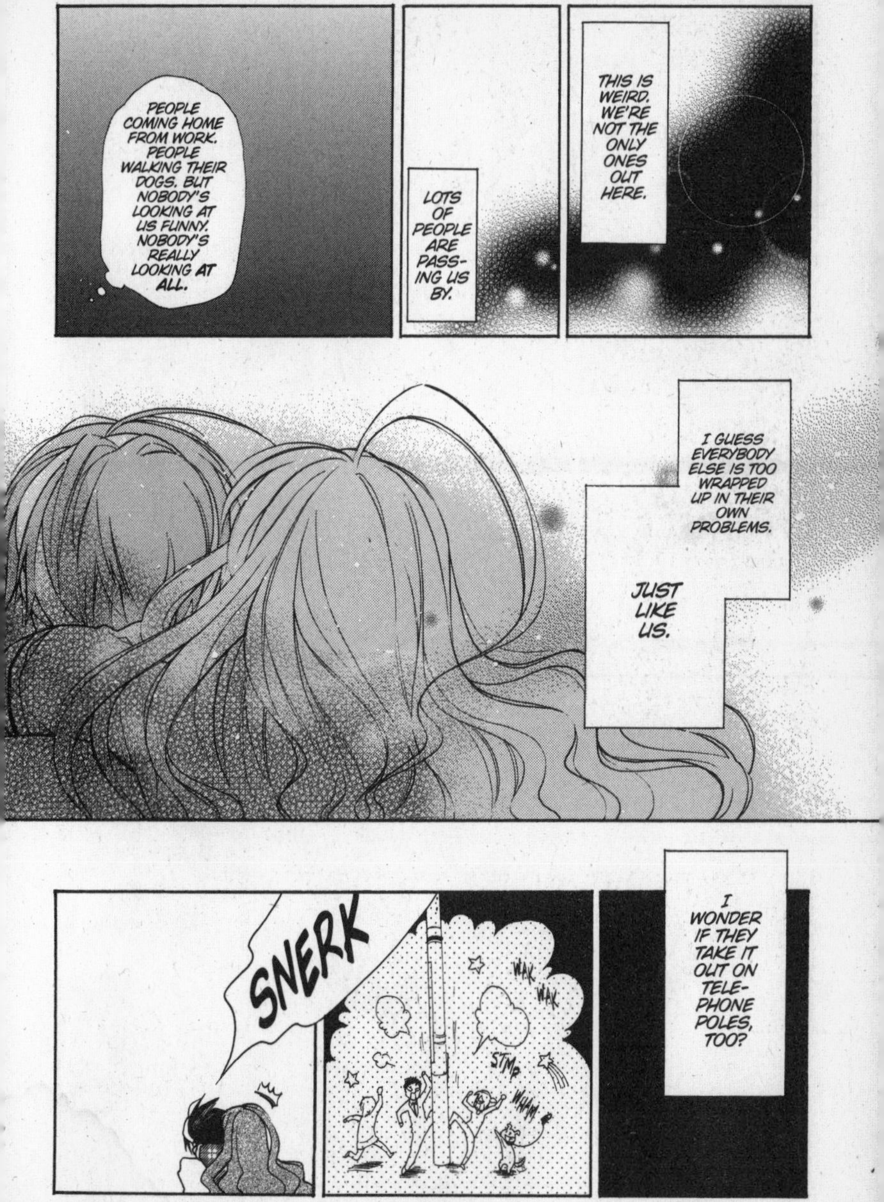
THIS IS WEIRD. WE'RE NOT THE ONLY ONES OUT HERE.
LOTS OF PEOPLE ARE PASSING US BY.
PEOPLE COMING HOME FROM WORK. PEOPLE WALKING THEIR DOGS. BUT NOBODY'S LOOKING AT US FUNNY. NOBODY'S REALLY LOOKING AT ALL.
I GUESS EVERYBODY ELSE IS TOO WRAPPED UP IN THEIR OWN PROBLEMS.
JUST LIKE US.
I WONDER IF THEY TAKE IT OUT ON TELEPHONE POLES, TOO?
WAK WAK
STMP
WHAM
SNERK

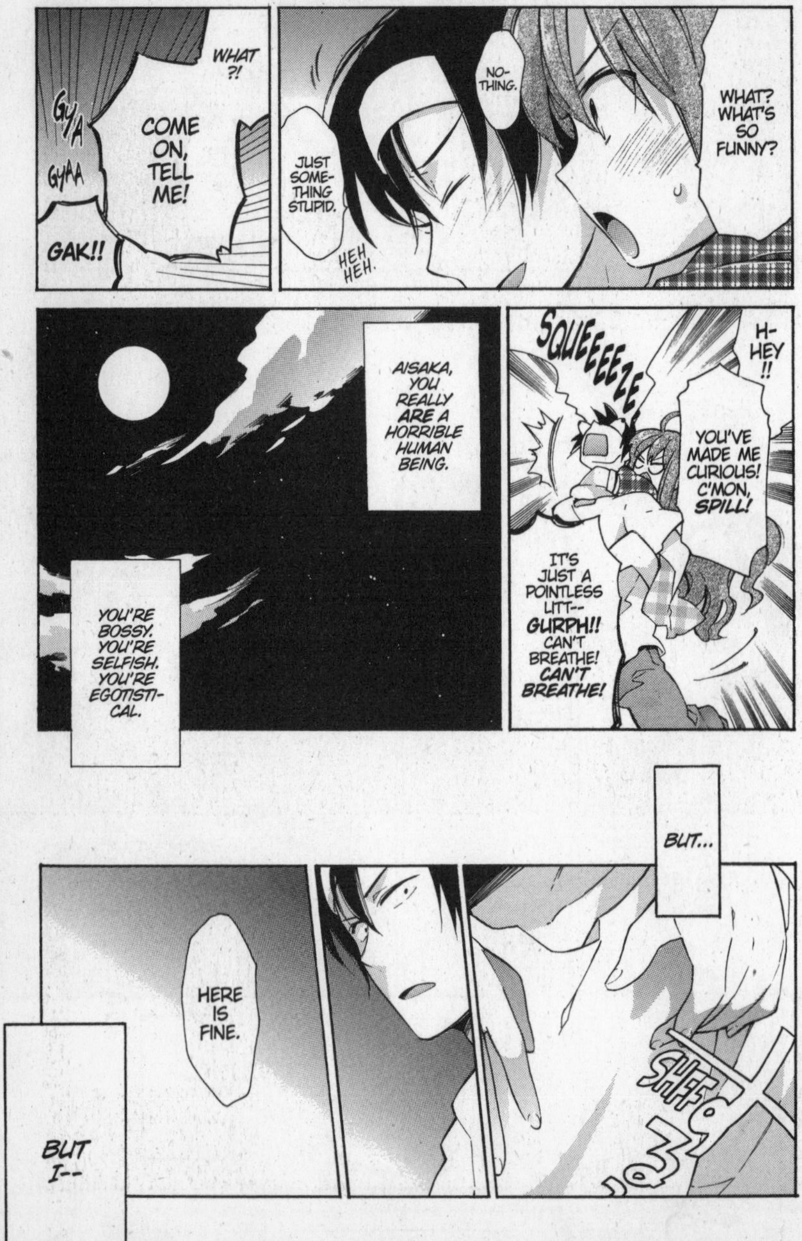
WHAT? WHAT'S SO FUNNY?
NO-THING.
JUST SOME-THING STUPID.
HEH HEH.
WHAT ?!
COME ON, TELL ME!
GYA GYAA
GAK!!
SQUEEEEEZE
H-HEY !!
YOU'VE MADE ME CURIOUS! C'MON, SPILL!
IT'S JUST A POINTLESS LITT-- GURPH!! CAN'T BREATHE! CAN'T BREATHE!
AISAKA, YOU REALLY ARE A HORRIBLE HUMAN BEING.
YOU'RE BOSSY. YOU'RE SELFISH. YOU'RE EGOTISTI-CAL.
BUT...
HERE IS FINE.
BUT I--

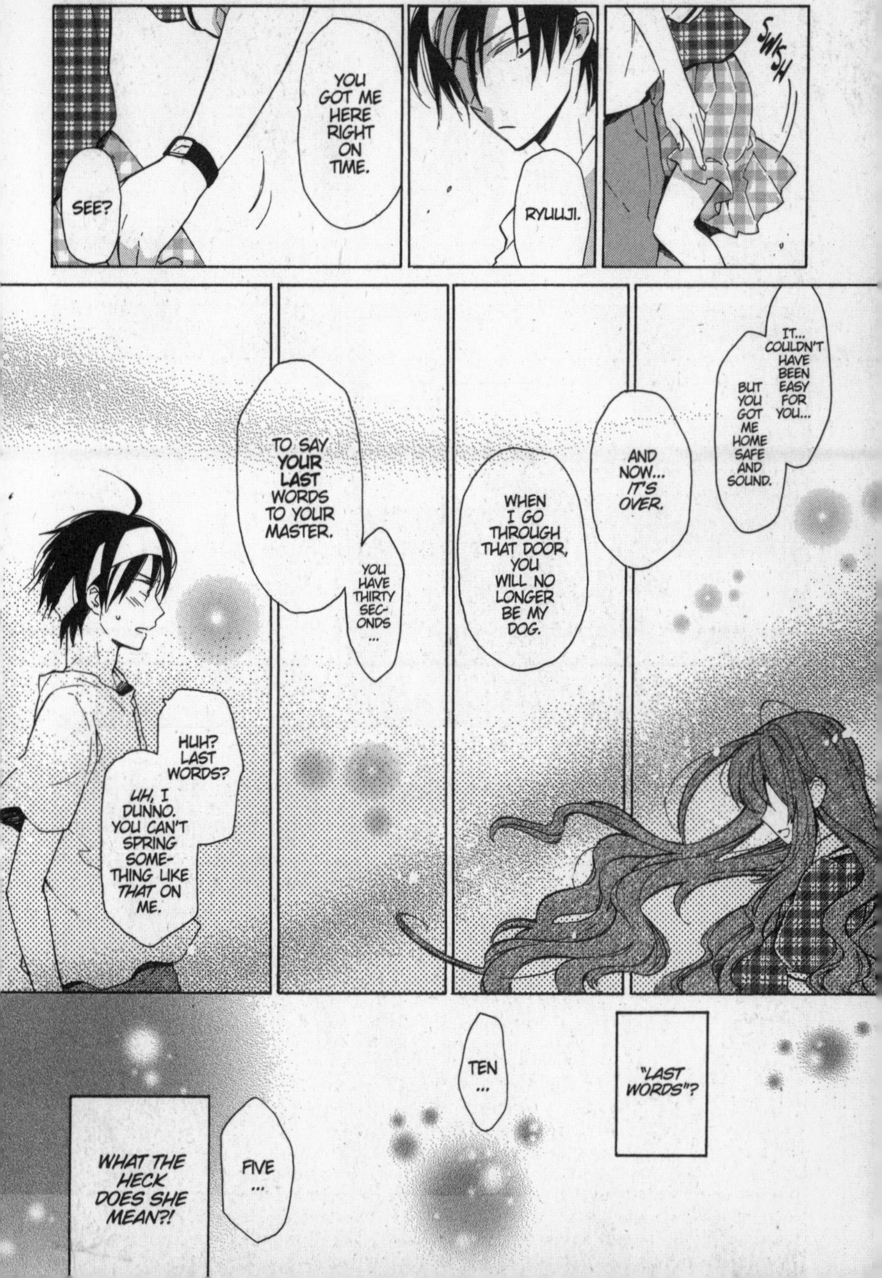
SWISH
RYUUJI.
YOU GOT ME HERE RIGHT ON TIME.
SEE?
IT... COULDN'T HAVE BEEN EASY FOR YOU...
BUT YOU GOT ME HOME SAFE AND SOUND.
AND NOW... IT'S OVER.
WHEN I GO THROUGH THAT DOOR, YOU WILL NO LONGER BE MY DOG.
YOU HAVE THIRTY SECONDS...
TO SAY YOUR LAST WORDS TO YOUR MASTER.
HUH? LAST WORDS?
UH, I DUNNO. YOU CAN'T SPRING SOME-THING LIKE THAT ON ME.
"LAST WORDS"?
TEN...
FIVE...
WHAT THE HECK DOES SHE MEAN?!

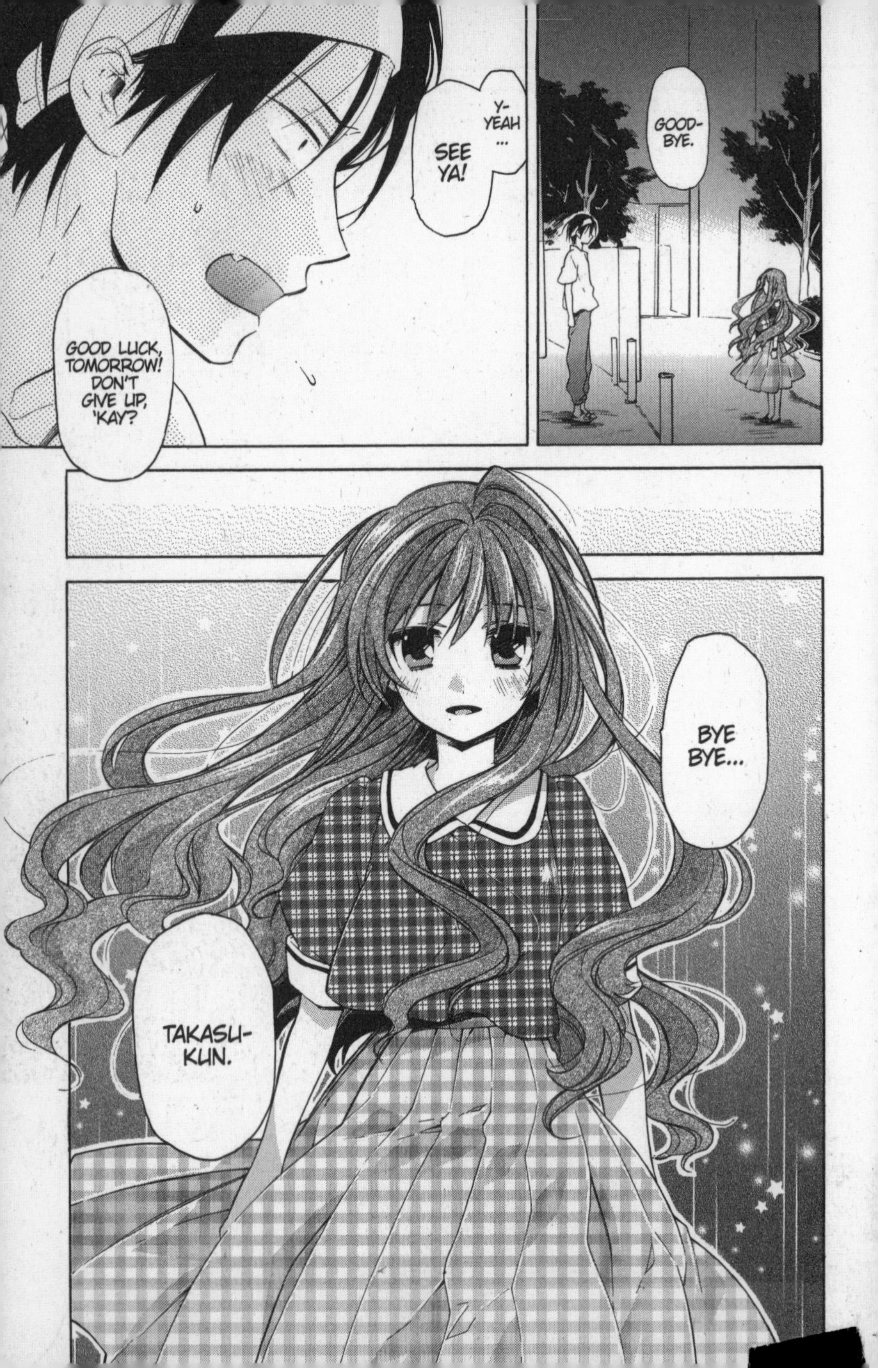
GOOD-BYE.
Y-YEAH ...
SEE YA!
GOOD LUCK, TOMORROW! DON'T GIVE UP, 'KAY?
BYE BYE...
TAKASU-KUN.

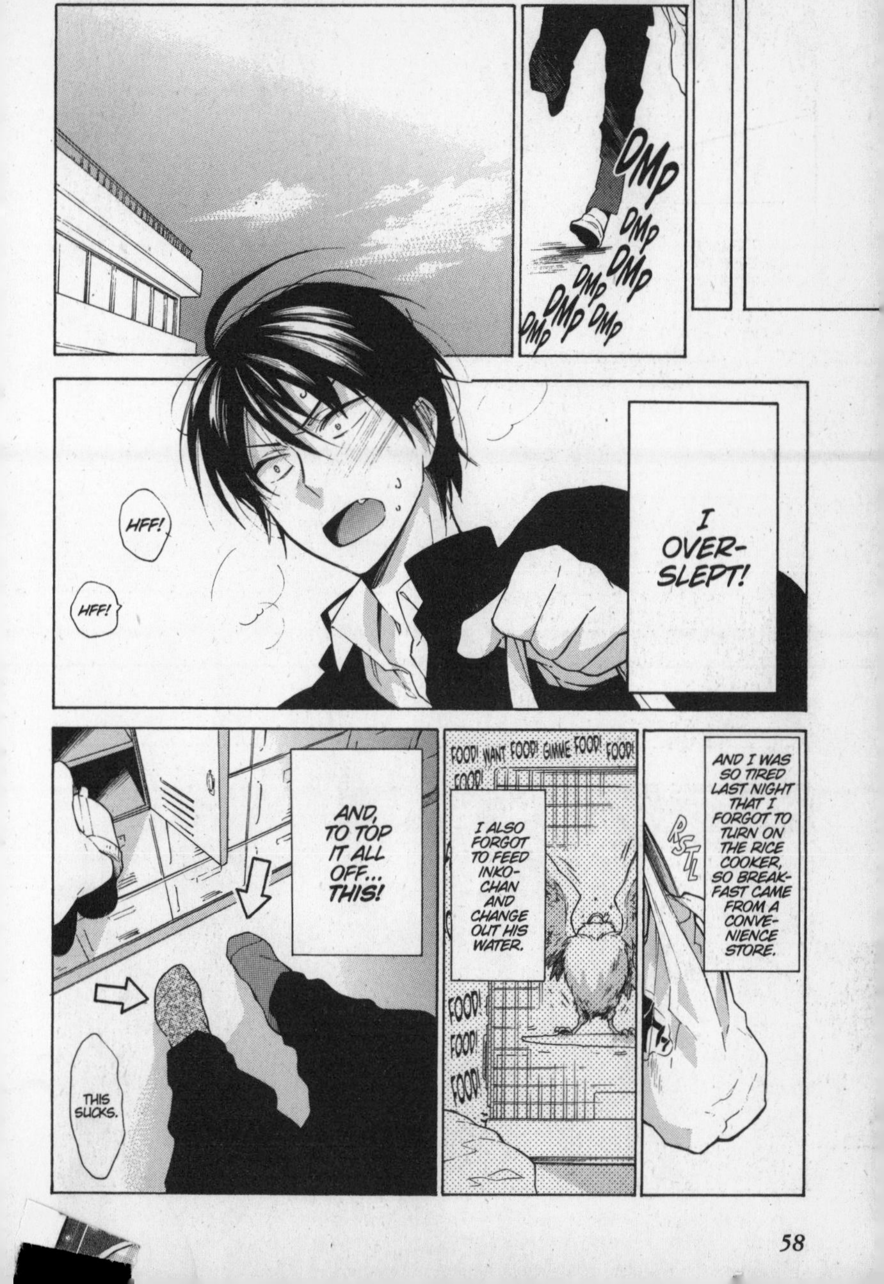
DMP DMP DMP DMP DMP DMP DMP
I OVER-SLEPT!
HFF!
HFF!
AND I WAS SO TIRED LAST NIGHT THAT I FORGOT TO TURN ON THE RICE COOKER, SO BREAK-FAST CAME FROM A CONVE-NIENCE STORE.
RSTL
FOOD! WANT FOOD! GIMME FOOD! FOOD! FOOD!
I ALSO FORGOT TO FEED INKO-CHAN AND CHANGE OUT HIS WATER.
FOOD! FOOD! FOOD!
AND, TO TOP IT ALL OFF... THIS!
THIS SUCKS.

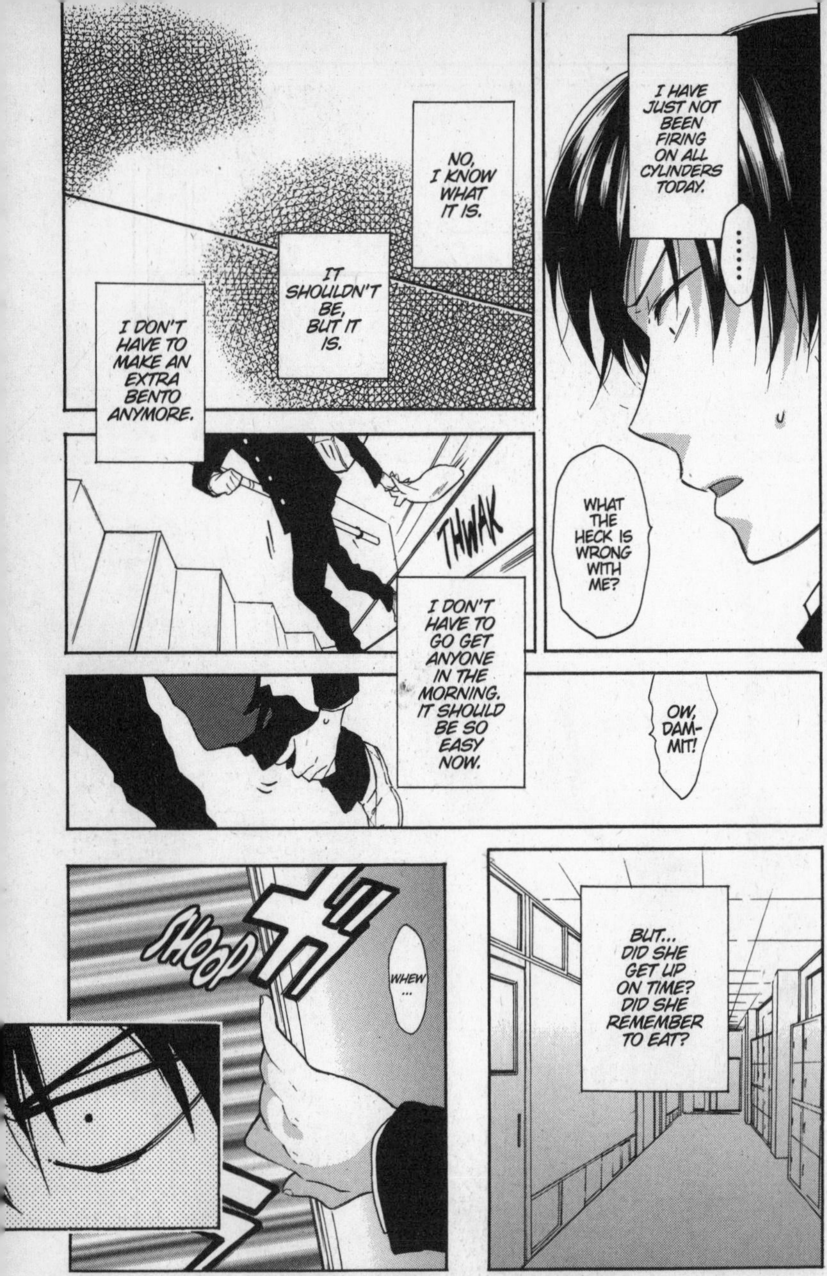
I HAVE JUST NOT BEEN FIRING ON ALL CYLINDERS TODAY.
......
WHAT THE HECK IS WRONG WITH ME?
NO, I KNOW WHAT IT IS.
IT SHOULDN'T BE, BUT IT IS.
I DON'T HAVE TO MAKE AN EXTRA BENTO ANYMORE.
THWAK
I DON'T HAVE TO GO GET ANYONE IN THE MORNING. IT SHOULD BE SO EASY NOW.
OW, DAM-MIT!
BUT... DID SHE GET UP ON TIME? DID SHE REMEMBER TO EAT?
SHOOP
WHEW...

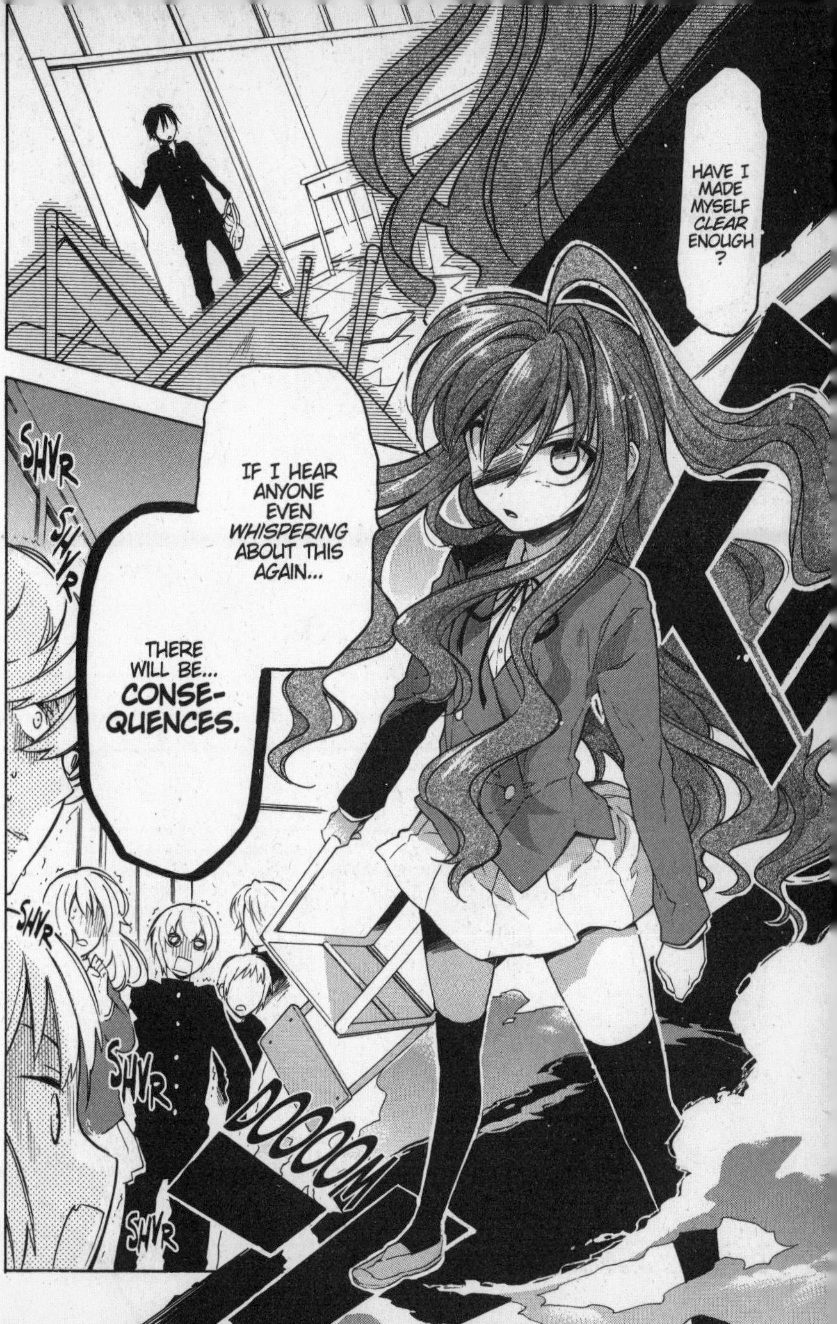

HAVE I MADE MYSELF CLEAR ENOUGH ?
IF I HEAR ANYONE EVEN WHISPERING ABOUT THIS AGAIN...
THERE WILL BE... CONSE- QUENCES.
SHVR
SHVR
SHVR
SHVR
SHVR
DOOOOM

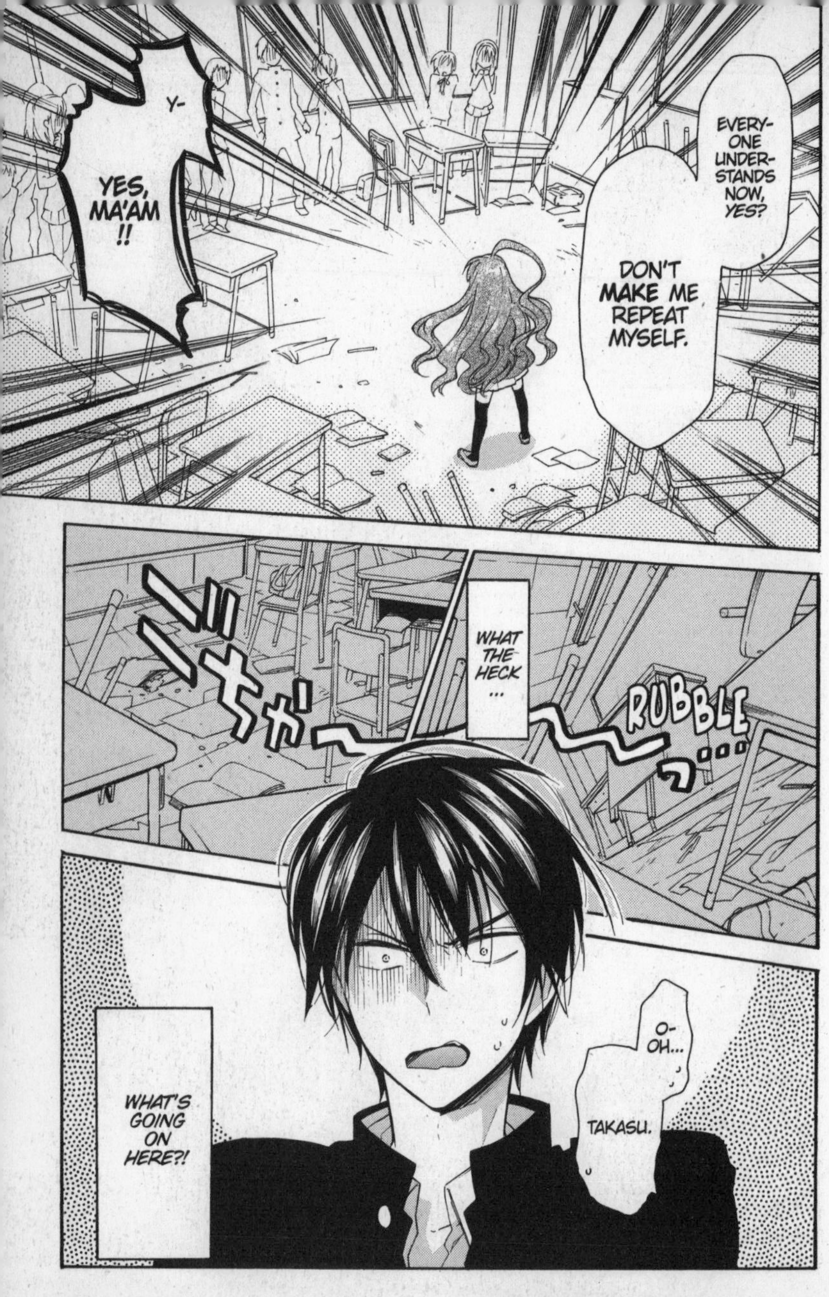

EVERY-ONE UNDER-STANDS NOW, YES?
DON'T MAKE ME REPEAT MYSELF.
Y-
YES, MA'AM!!
RUBBLE
WHAT THE HECK...
O-OH...
TAKASU.
WHAT'S GOING ON HERE?!

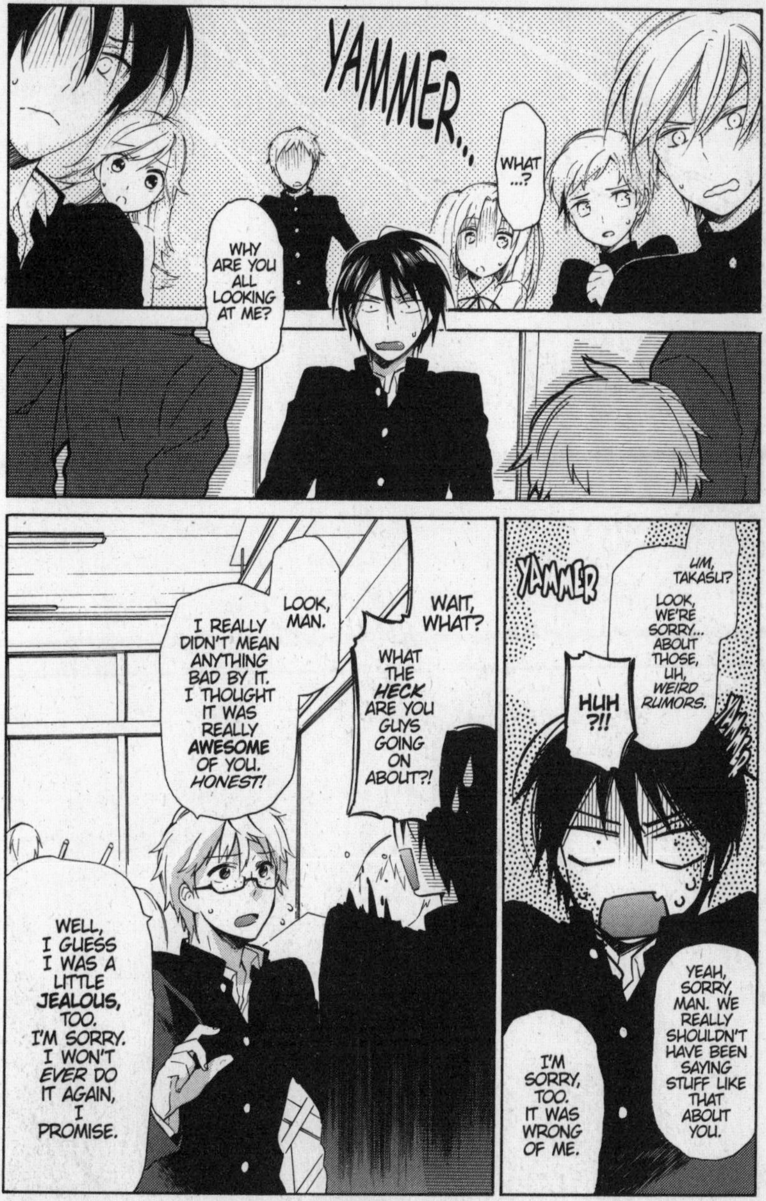
YAMMER...
WHAT ...?
WHY ARE YOU ALL LOOKING AT ME?
YAMMER
UM, TAKASU?
LOOK, WE'RE SORRY... ABOUT THOSE, UH, WEIRD RUMORS.
HUH ?!!
YEAH, SORRY, MAN. WE REALLY SHOULDN'T HAVE BEEN SAYING STUFF LIKE THAT ABOUT YOU.
I'M SORRY, TOO. IT WAS WRONG OF ME.
WAIT, WHAT?
WHAT THE HECK ARE YOU GUYS GOING ON ABOUT?!
LOOK, MAN.
I REALLY DIDN'T MEAN ANYTHING BAD BY IT. I THOUGHT IT WAS REALLY AWESOME OF YOU. HONEST!
WELL, I GUESS I WAS A LITTLE JEALOUS, TOO. I'M SORRY. I WON'T EVER DO IT AGAIN, I PROMISE.

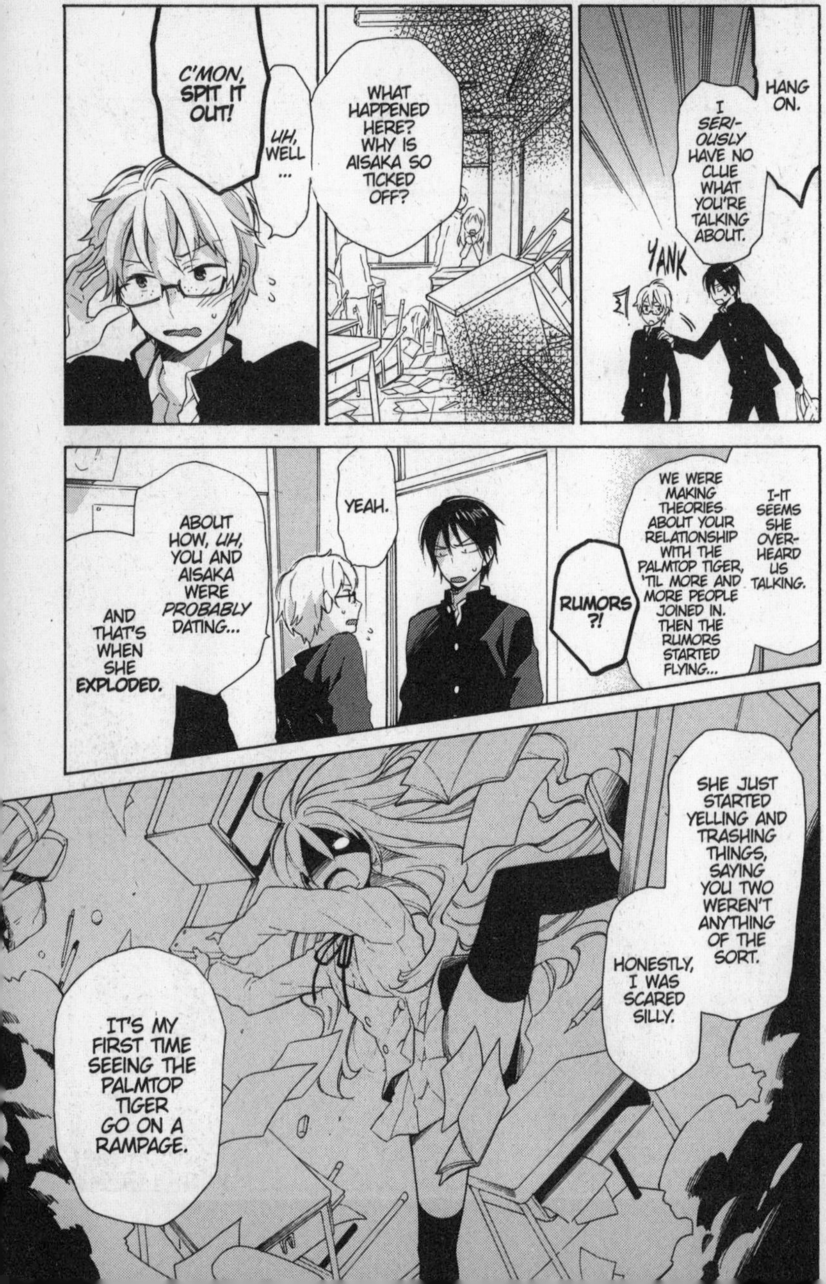
HANG ON.
I SERI-OUSLY HAVE NO CLUE WHAT YOU'RE TALKING ABOUT.
YANK
WHAT HAPPENED HERE? WHY IS AISAKA SO TICKED OFF?
C'MON, SPIT IT OUT!
UH, WELL ...
I-IT SEEMS SHE OVER-HEARD US TALKING.
WE WERE MAKING THEORIES ABOUT YOUR RELATIONSHIP WITH THE PALMTOP TIGER, 'TIL MORE AND MORE PEOPLE JOINED IN. THEN THE RUMORS STARTED FLYING...
RUMORS ?!
YEAH.
ABOUT HOW, *UH,* YOU AND AISAKA WERE *PROBABLY* DATING...
AND THAT'S WHEN SHE EXPLODED.
SHE JUST STARTED YELLING AND TRASHING THINGS, SAYING YOU TWO WEREN'T ANYTHING OF THE SORT.
HONESTLY, I WAS SCARED SILLY.
IT'S MY FIRST TIME SEEING THE PALMTOP TIGER GO ON A RAMPAGE.

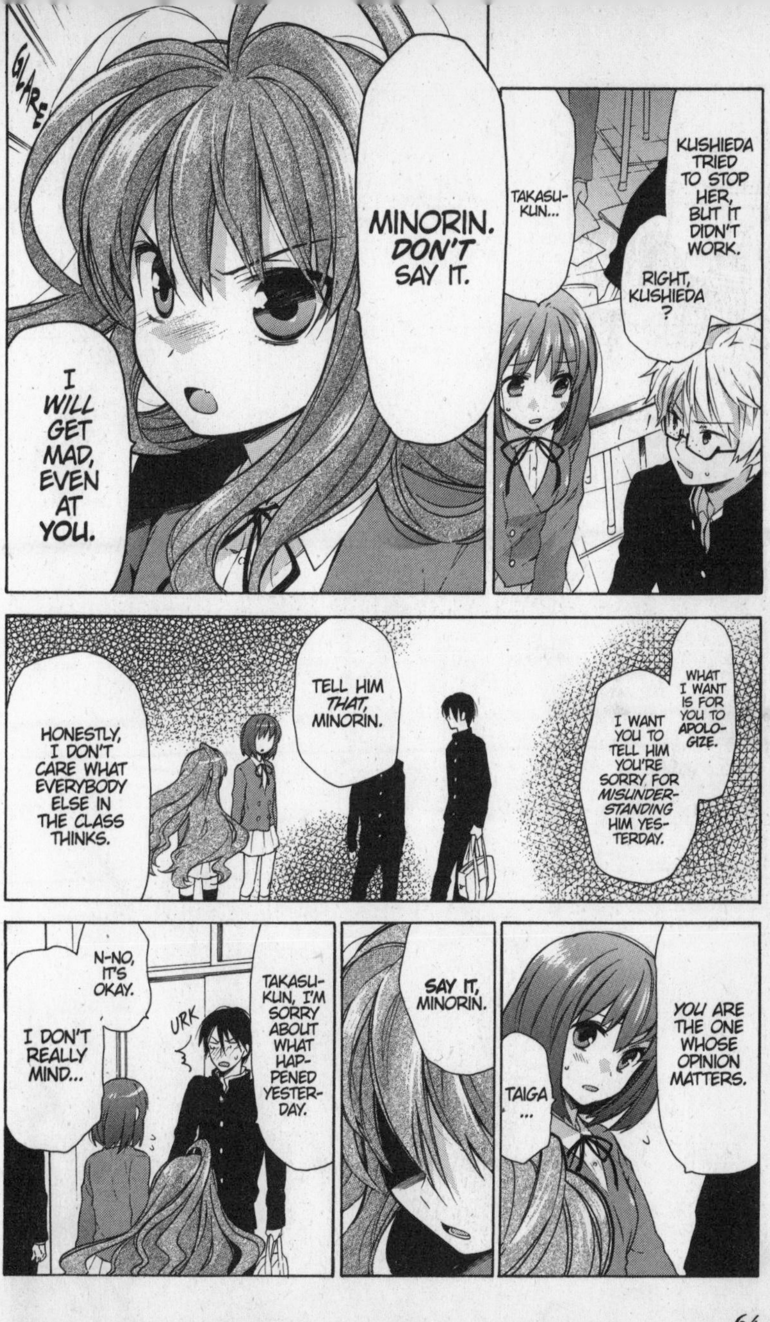
KUSHIEDA TRIED TO STOP HER, BUT IT DIDN'T WORK.
TAKASU-KUN...
RIGHT, KUSHIEDA?
GLARE
MINORIN. DON'T SAY IT.
I WILL GET MAD, EVEN AT YOU.
WHAT I WANT IS FOR YOU TO APOLOGIZE.
I WANT YOU TO TELL HIM YOU'RE SORRY FOR MISUNDERSTANDING HIM YESTERDAY.
TELL HIM THAT, MINORIN.
HONESTLY, I DON'T CARE WHAT EVERYBODY ELSE IN THE CLASS THINKS.
YOU ARE THE ONE WHOSE OPINION MATTERS.
TAIGA...
SAY IT, MINORIN.
TAKASU-KUN, I'M SORRY ABOUT WHAT HAPPENED YESTERDAY.
N-NO, IT'S OKAY.
URK
I DON'T REALLY MIND...

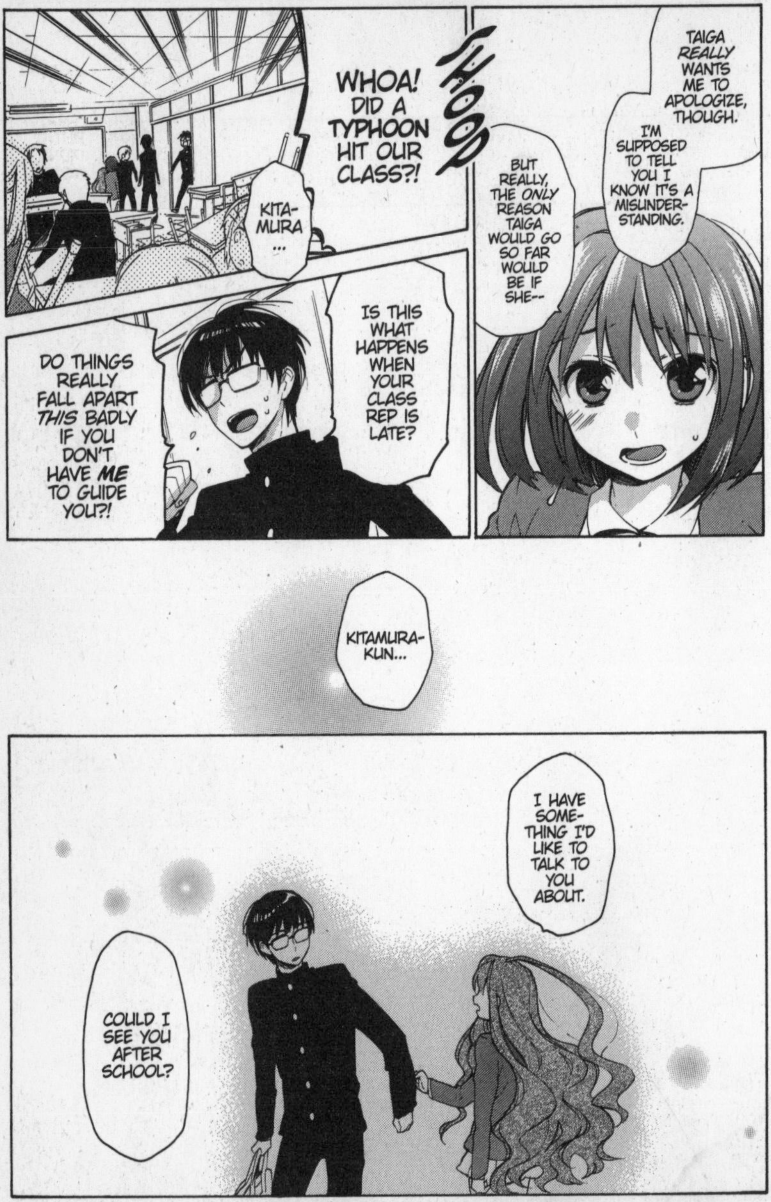
TAIGA REALLY WANTS ME TO APOLOGIZE, THOUGH.
I'M SUPPOSED TO TELL YOU I KNOW IT'S A MISUNDER-STANDING.
BUT REALLY, THE ONLY REASON TAIGA WOULD GO SO FAR WOULD BE IF SHE--
SHOOP
WHOA! DID A TYPHOON HIT OUR CLASS?!
KITA-MURA...
IS THIS WHAT HAPPENS WHEN YOUR CLASS REP IS LATE?
DO THINGS REALLY FALL APART THIS BADLY IF YOU DON'T HAVE ME TO GUIDE YOU?!
KITAMURA-KUN...
I HAVE SOME-THING I'D LIKE TO TALK TO YOU ABOUT.
COULD I SEE YOU AFTER SCHOOL?

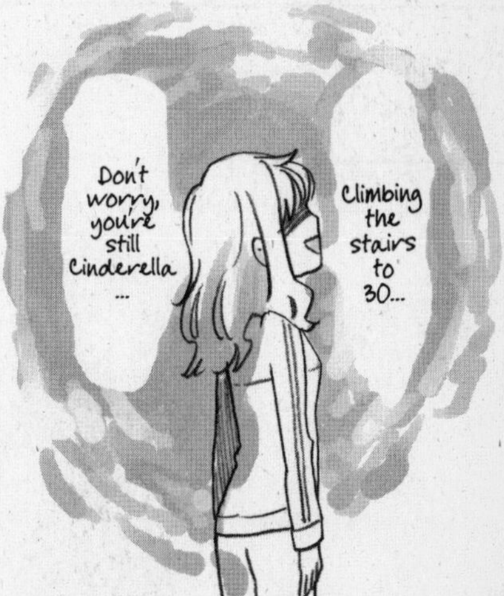
Climbing the stairs to 30...
Don't worry, you're still Cinderella ...

Chapter 10 WHITHER THE CONFESSION

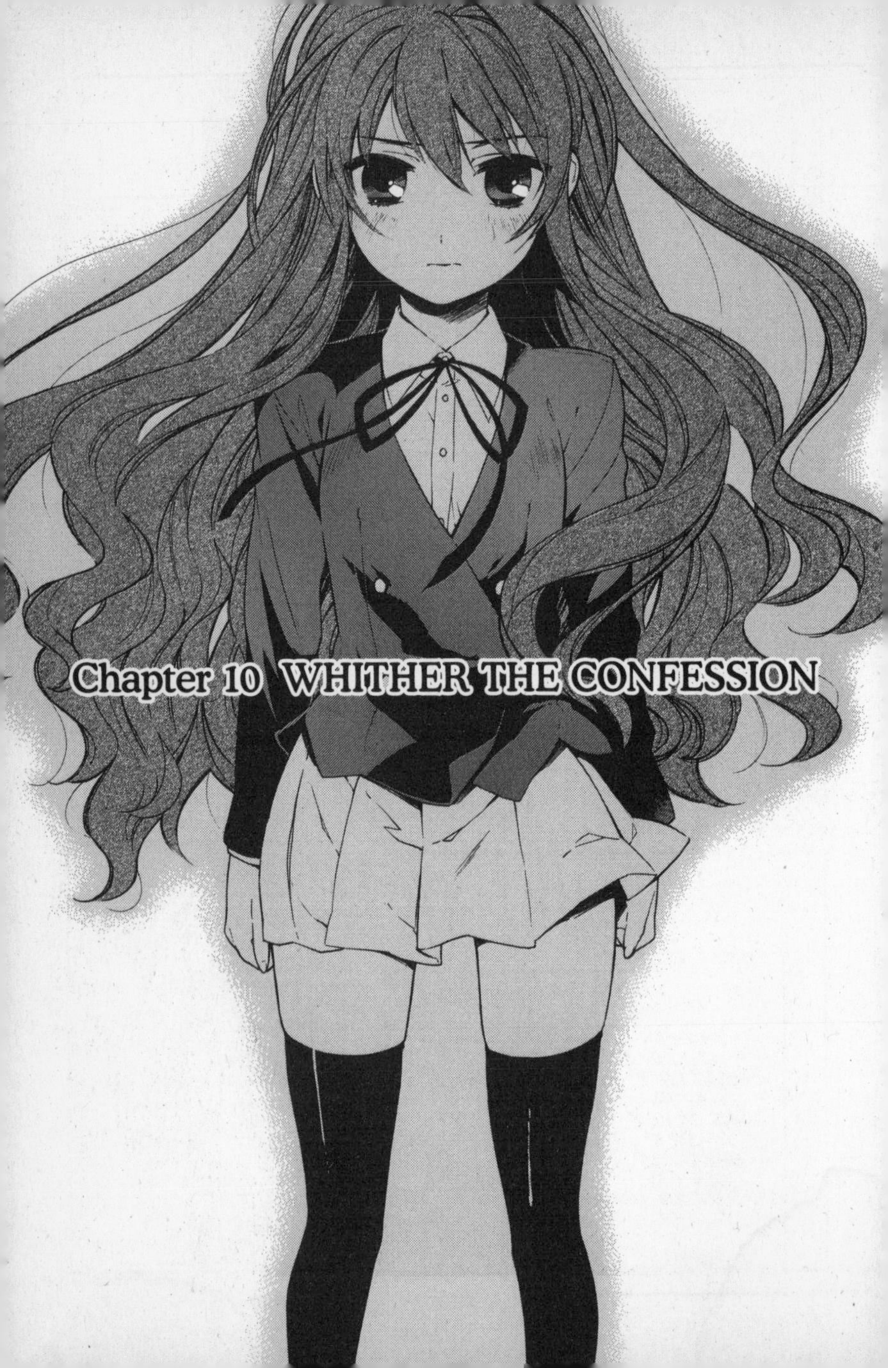

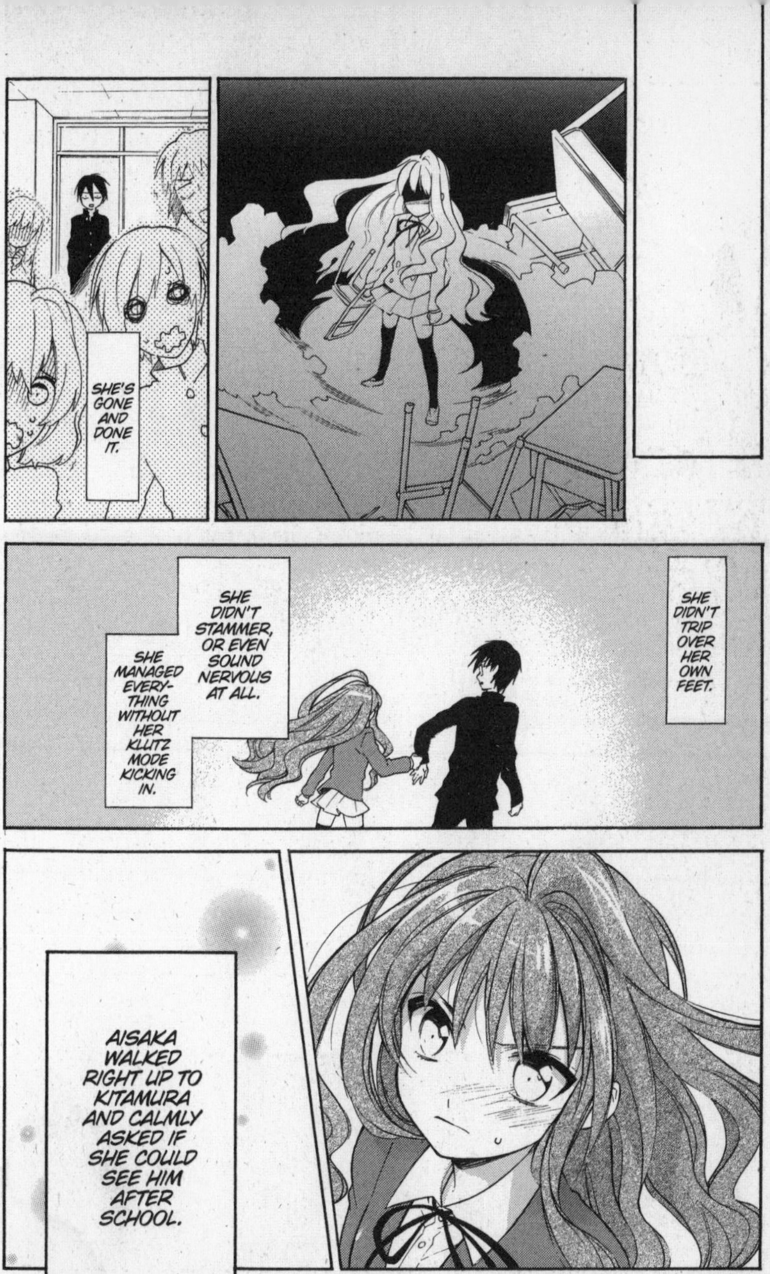
SHE'S GONE AND DONE IT.
SHE DIDN'T TRIP OVER HER OWN FEET.
SHE DIDN'T STAMMER, OR EVEN SOUND NERVOUS AT ALL.
SHE MANAGED EVERYTHING WITHOUT HER KLUTZ MODE KICKING IN.
AISAKA WALKED RIGHT UP TO KITAMURA AND CALMLY ASKED IF SHE COULD SEE HIM AFTER SCHOOL.

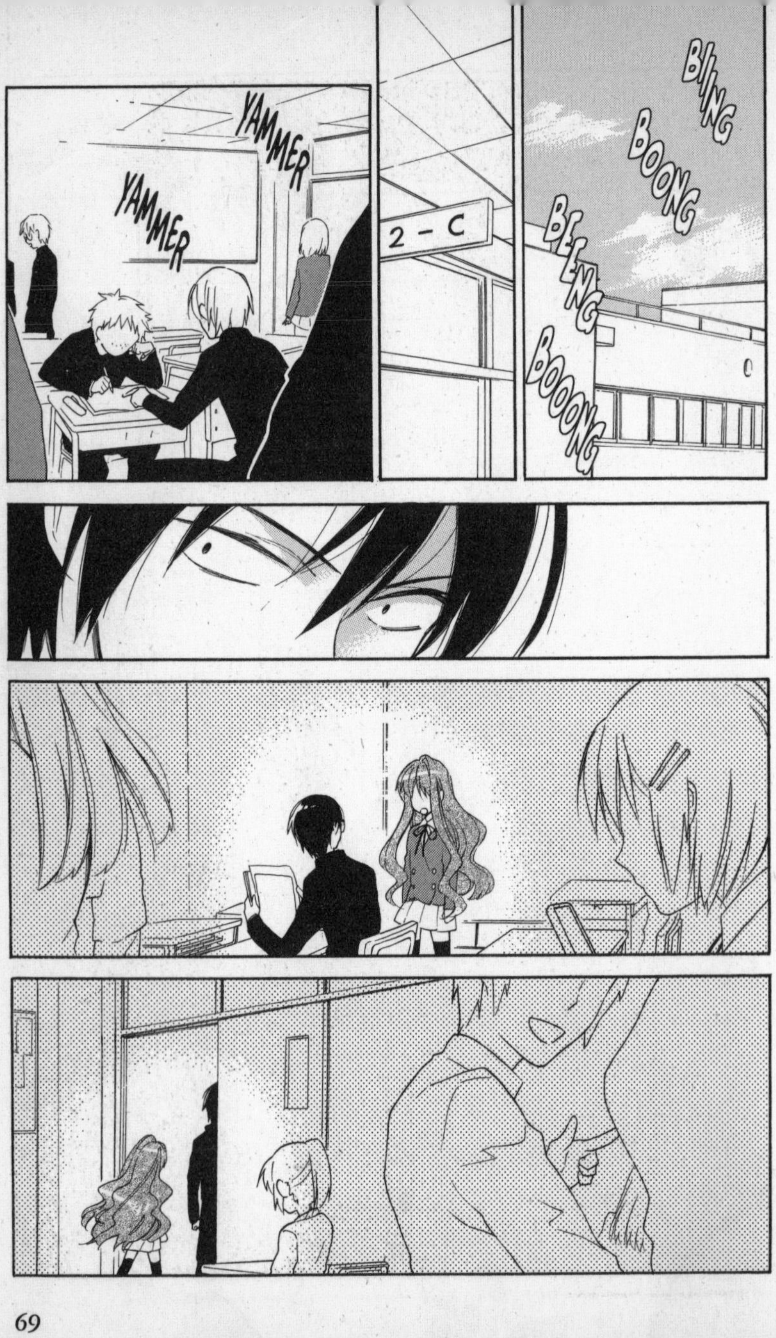
BIING BOONG
BEENG BOOONG
2 – C
YAMMER
YAMMER

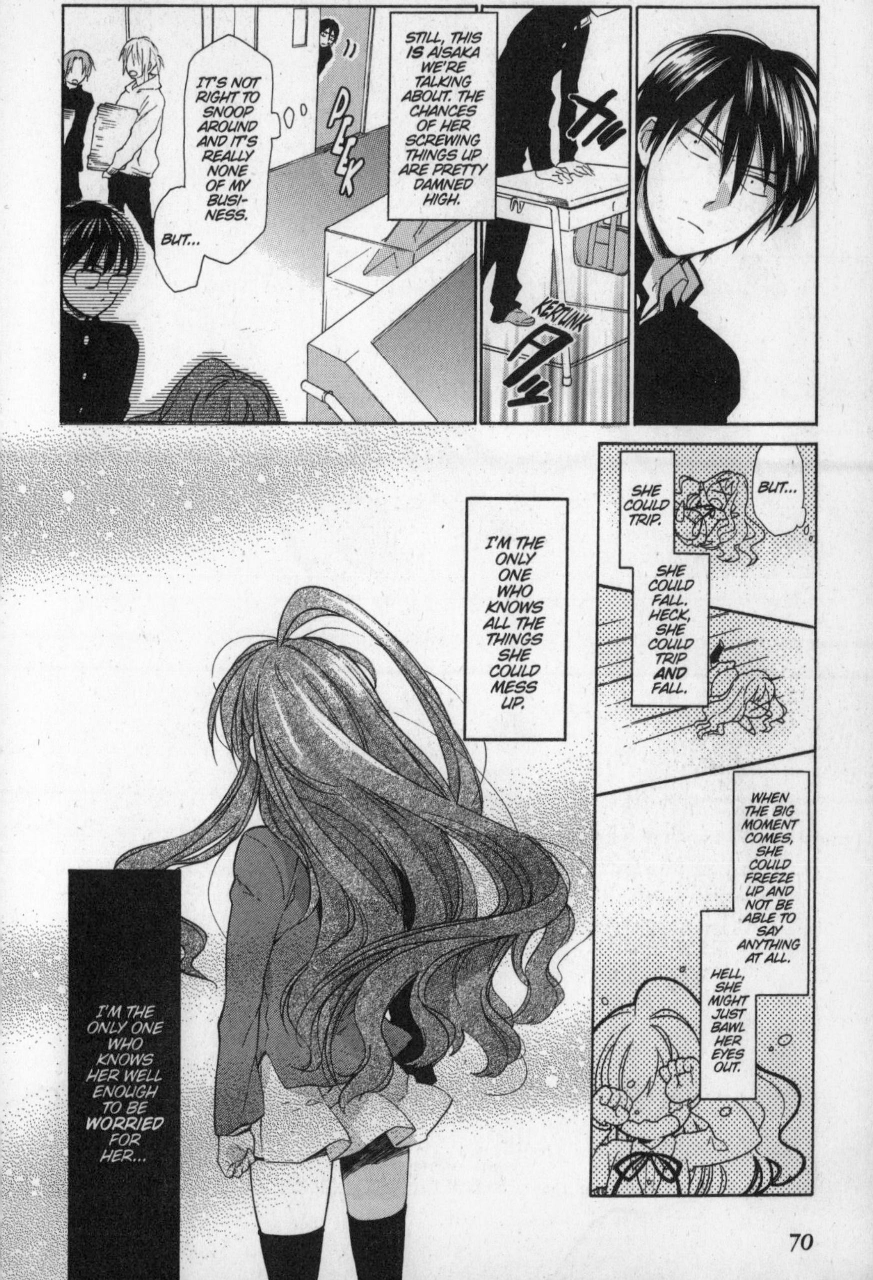
STILL, THIS IS AISAKA WE'RE TALKING ABOUT. THE CHANCES OF HER SCREWING THINGS UP ARE PRETTY DAMNED HIGH.
KERTUNK
IT'S NOT RIGHT TO SNOOP AROUND AND IT'S REALLY NONE OF MY BUSI-NESS.
BUT...
PEEK
BUT...
SHE COULD TRIP.
SHE COULD FALL. HECK, SHE COULD TRIP AND FALL.
WHEN THE BIG MOMENT COMES, SHE COULD FREEZE UP AND NOT BE ABLE TO SAY ANYTHING AT ALL.
HELL, SHE MIGHT JUST BAWL HER EYES OUT.
I'M THE ONLY ONE WHO KNOWS ALL THE THINGS SHE COULD MESS UP.
I'M THE ONLY ONE WHO KNOWS HER WELL ENOUGH TO BE WORRIED FOR HER...

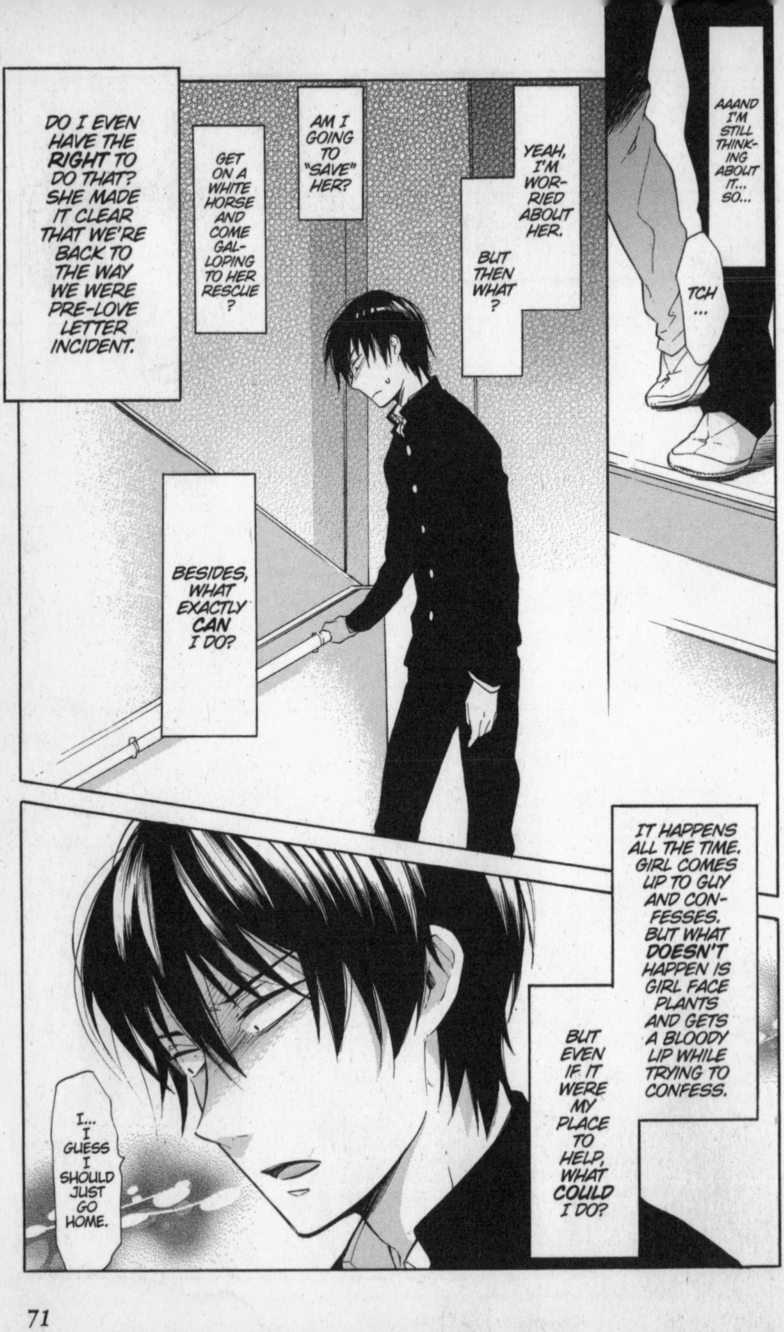
AAAND I'M STILL THINKING ABOUT IT... SO...
TCH...
YEAH, I'M WORRIED ABOUT HER.
BUT THEN WHAT?
AM I GOING TO "SAVE" HER?
GET ON A WHITE HORSE AND COME GALLOPING TO HER RESCUE?
DO I EVEN HAVE THE RIGHT TO DO THAT? SHE MADE IT CLEAR THAT WE'RE BACK TO THE WAY WE WERE PRE-LOVE LETTER INCIDENT.
BESIDES, WHAT EXACTLY CAN I DO?
IT HAPPENS ALL THE TIME. GIRL COMES UP TO GUY AND CONFESSES. BUT WHAT DOESN'T HAPPEN IS GIRL FACE PLANTS AND GETS A BLOODY LIP WHILE TRYING TO CONFESS.
BUT EVEN IF IT WERE MY PLACE TO HELP, WHAT COULD I DO?
I... I GUESS I SHOULD JUST GO HOME.

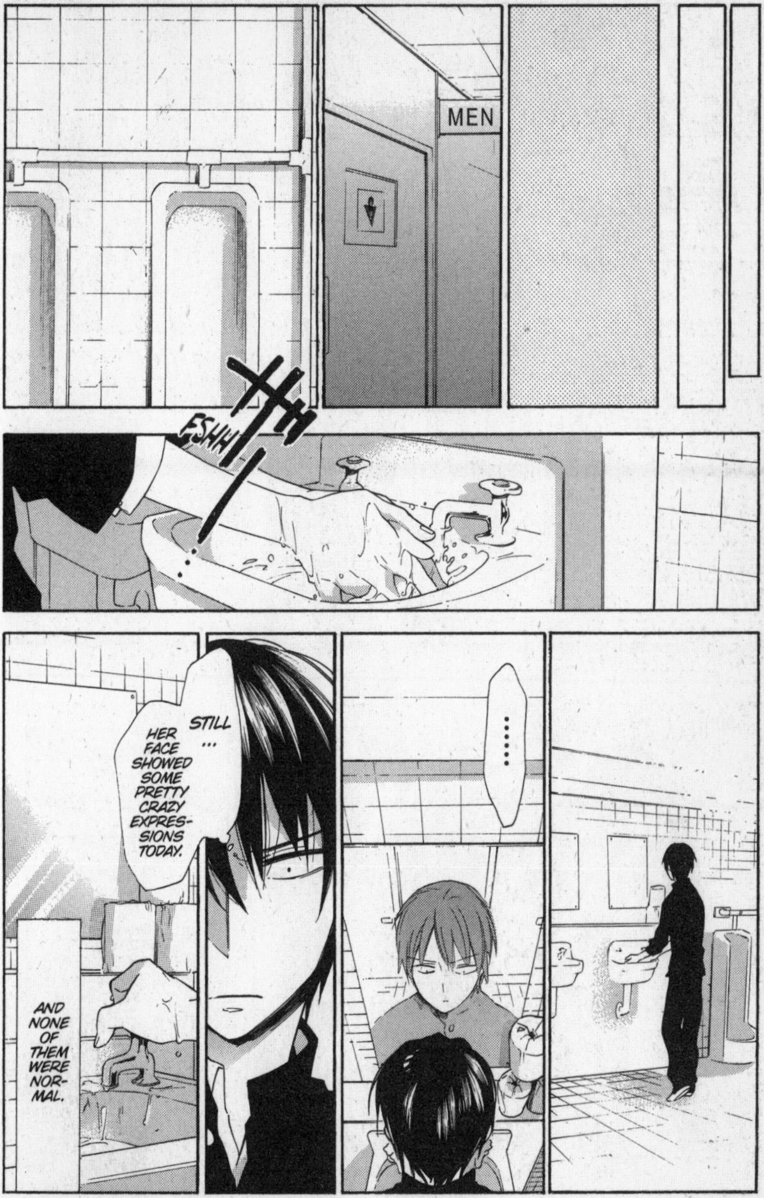
MEN
FSHH
......
STILL...
HER FACE SHOWED SOME PRETTY CRAZY EXPRESSIONS TODAY.
AND NONE OF THEM WERE NORMAL.

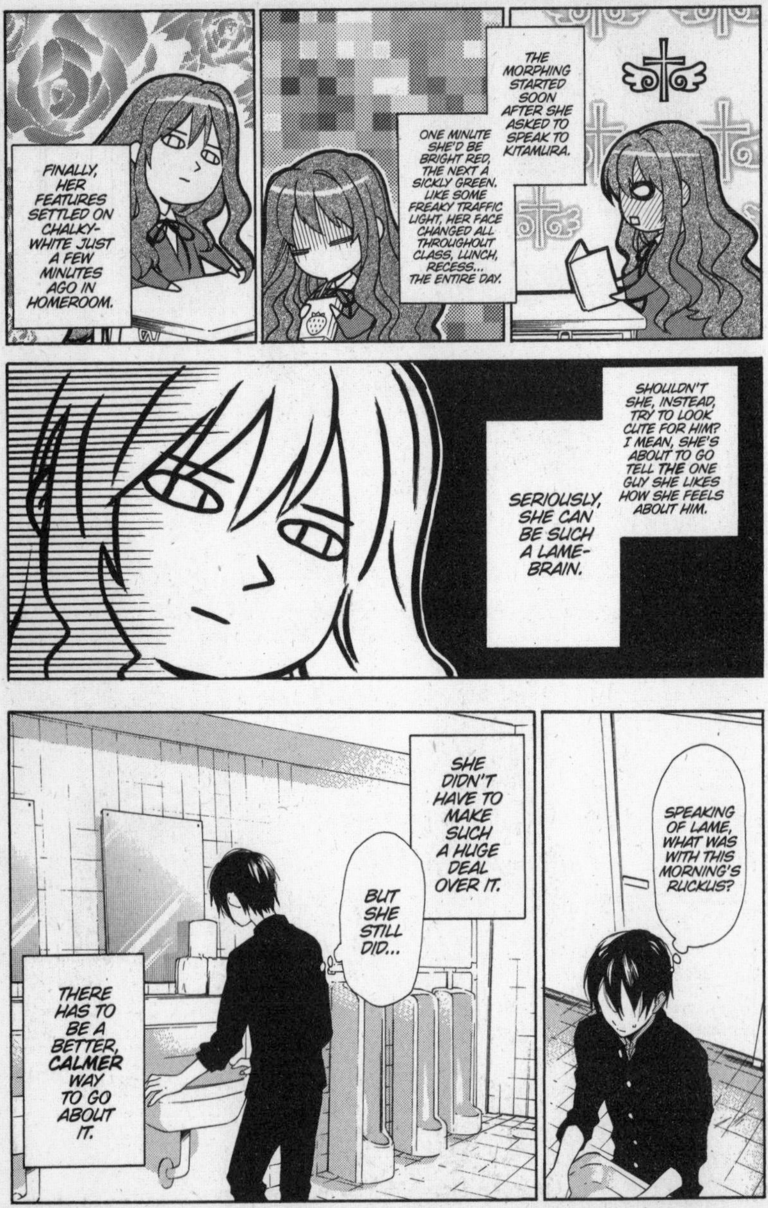
THE MORPHING STARTED SOON AFTER SHE ASKED TO SPEAK TO KITAMURA.
ONE MINUTE SHE'D BE BRIGHT RED, THE NEXT A SICKLY GREEN. LIKE SOME FREAKY TRAFFIC LIGHT, HER FACE CHANGED ALL THROUGHOUT CLASS, LUNCH, RECESS... THE ENTIRE DAY.
FINALLY, HER FEATURES SETTLED ON CHALKY-WHITE JUST A FEW MINUTES AGO IN HOMEROOM.
SHOULDN'T SHE, INSTEAD, TRY TO LOOK CUTE FOR HIM? I MEAN, SHE'S ABOUT TO GO TELL THE ONE GUY SHE LIKES HOW SHE FEELS ABOUT HIM.
SERIOUSLY, SHE CAN BE SUCH A LAME-BRAIN.
SPEAKING OF LAME, WHAT WAS WITH THIS MORNING'S RUCKUS?
SHE DIDN'T HAVE TO MAKE SUCH A HUGE DEAL OVER IT.
BUT SHE STILL DID...
THERE HAS TO BE A BETTER, CALMER WAY TO GO ABOUT IT.

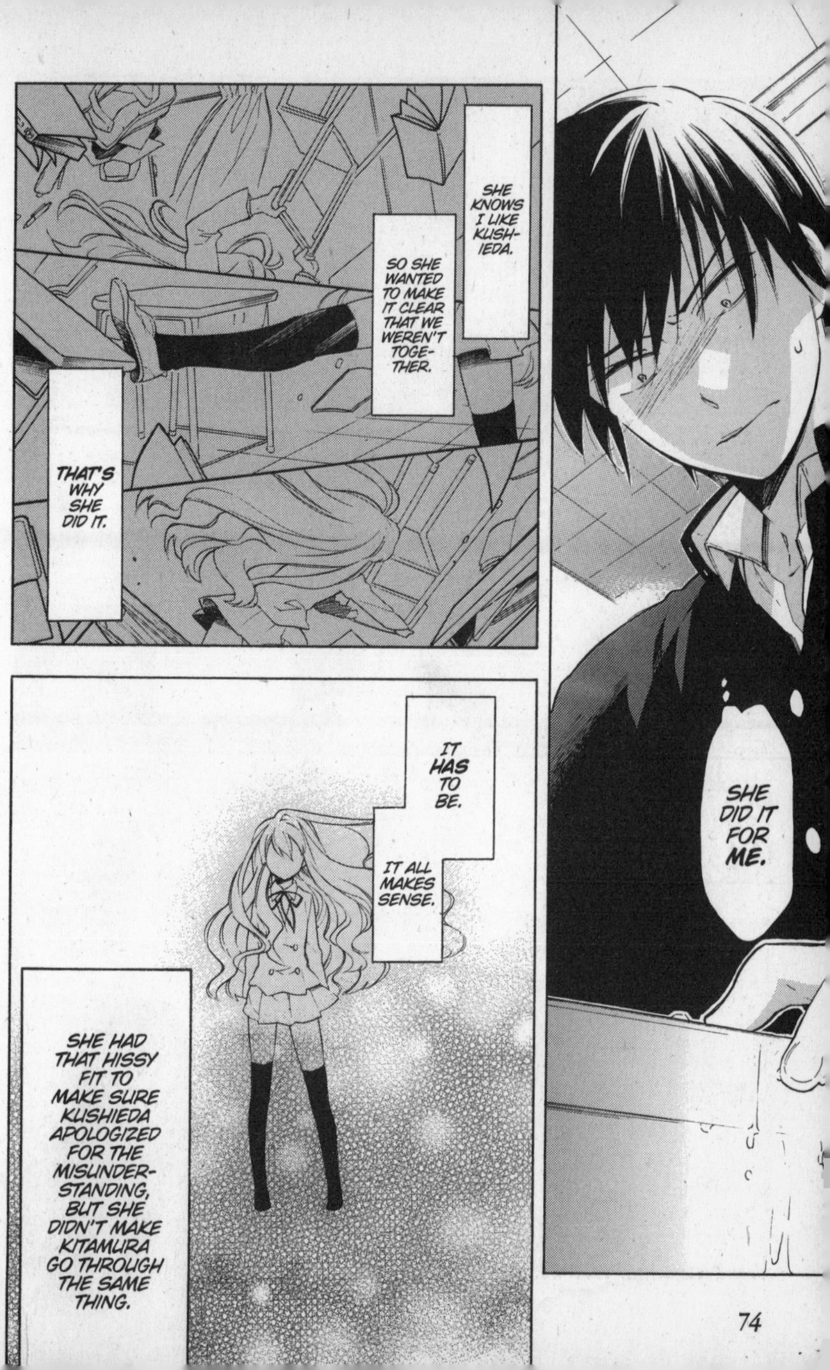
SHE DID IT FOR ME.
SHE KNOWS I LIKE KUSH-IEDA.
SO SHE WANTED TO MAKE IT CLEAR THAT WE WEREN'T TOGE-THER.
THAT'S WHY SHE DID IT.
IT HAS TO BE.
IT ALL MAKES SENSE.
SHE HAD THAT HISSY FIT TO MAKE SURE KUSHIEDA APOLOGIZED FOR THE MISUNDER-STANDING, BUT SHE DIDN'T MAKE KITAMURA GO THROUGH THE SAME THING.

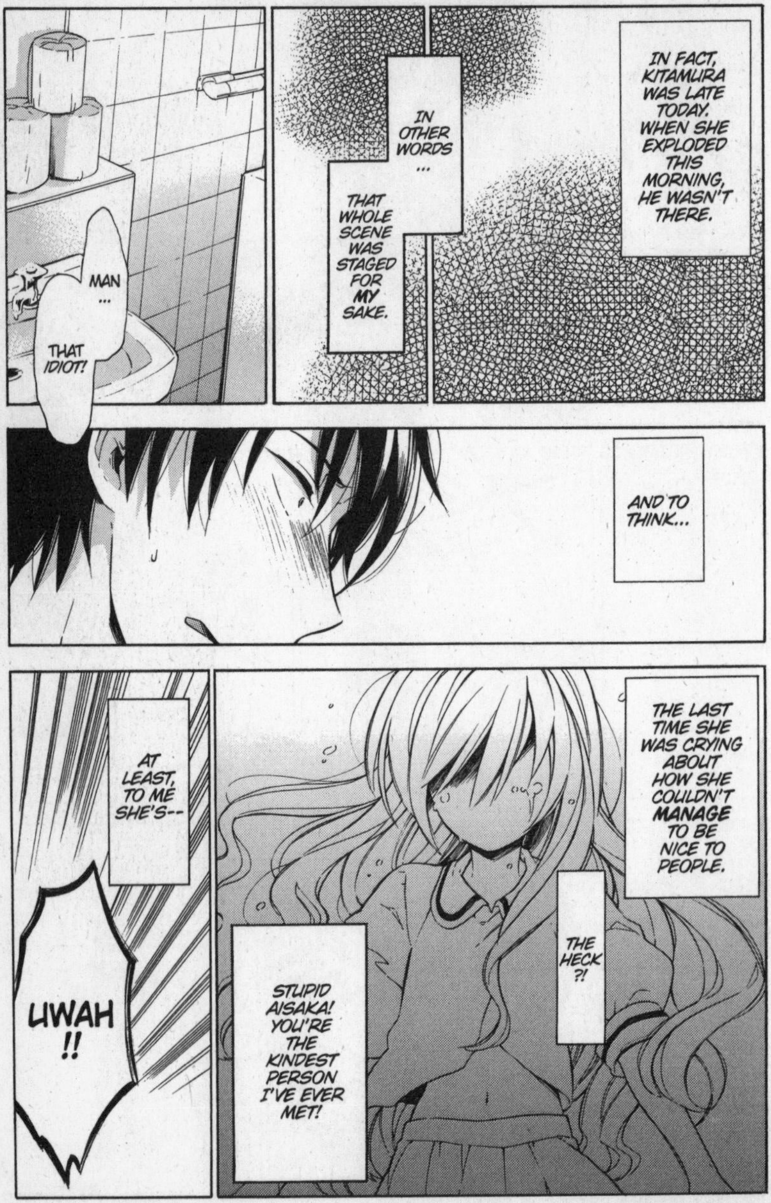
IN FACT, KITAMURA WAS LATE TODAY. WHEN SHE EXPLODED THIS MORNING, HE WASN'T THERE.
IN OTHER WORDS...
THAT WHOLE SCENE WAS STAGED FOR MY SAKE.
MAN...
THAT IDIOT!
AND TO THINK...
THE LAST TIME SHE WAS CRYING ABOUT HOW SHE COULDN'T MANAGE TO BE NICE TO PEOPLE.
THE HECK?!
STUPID AISAKA! YOU'RE THE KINDEST PERSON I'VE EVER MET!
AT LEAST, TO ME SHE'S--
UWAH!!

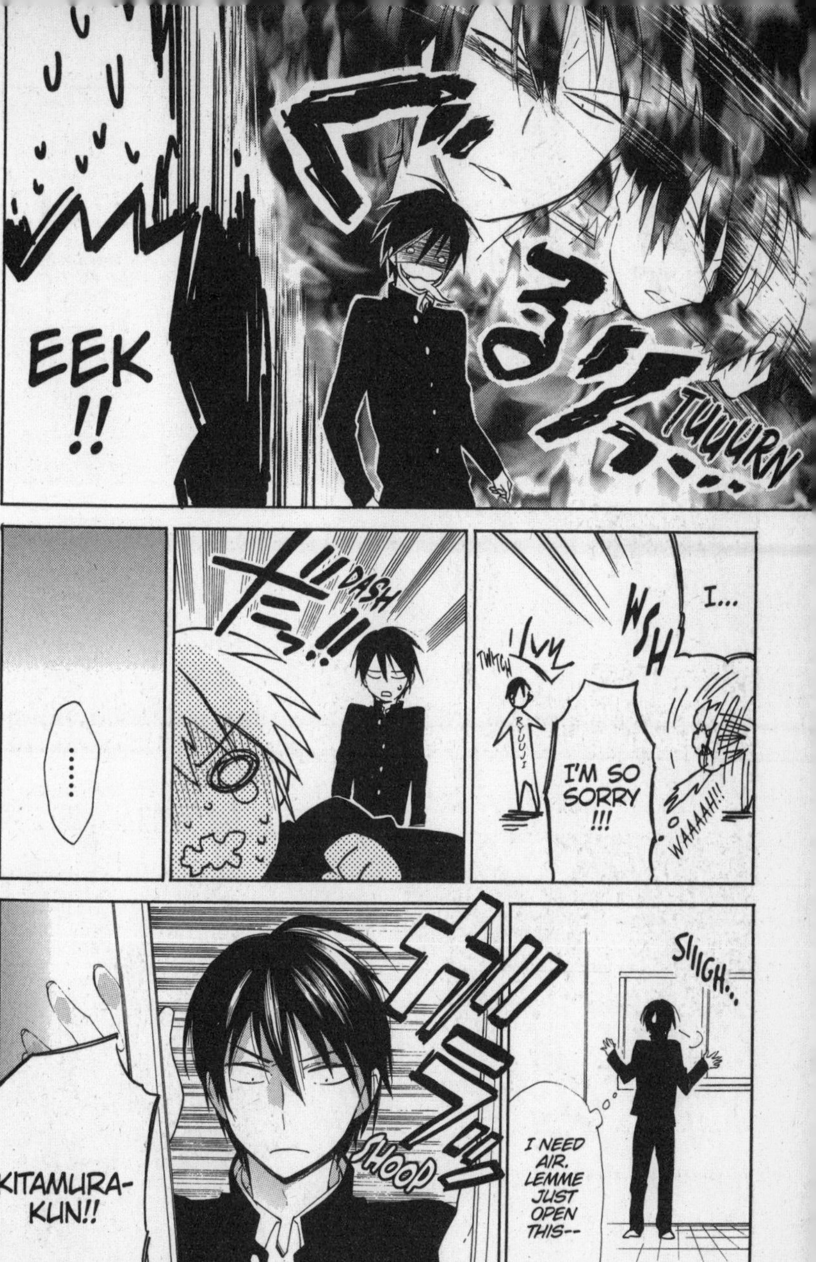
TUUURN...
EEK!!
I...
WSH
TWITCH
RYUUJI
I'M SO SORRY!!!
WAAAAH!!!
DASH
......
SIIIGH...
I NEED AIR. LEMME JUST OPEN THIS--
SHOOP
KITAMURA-KUN!!

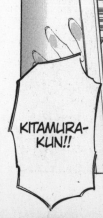

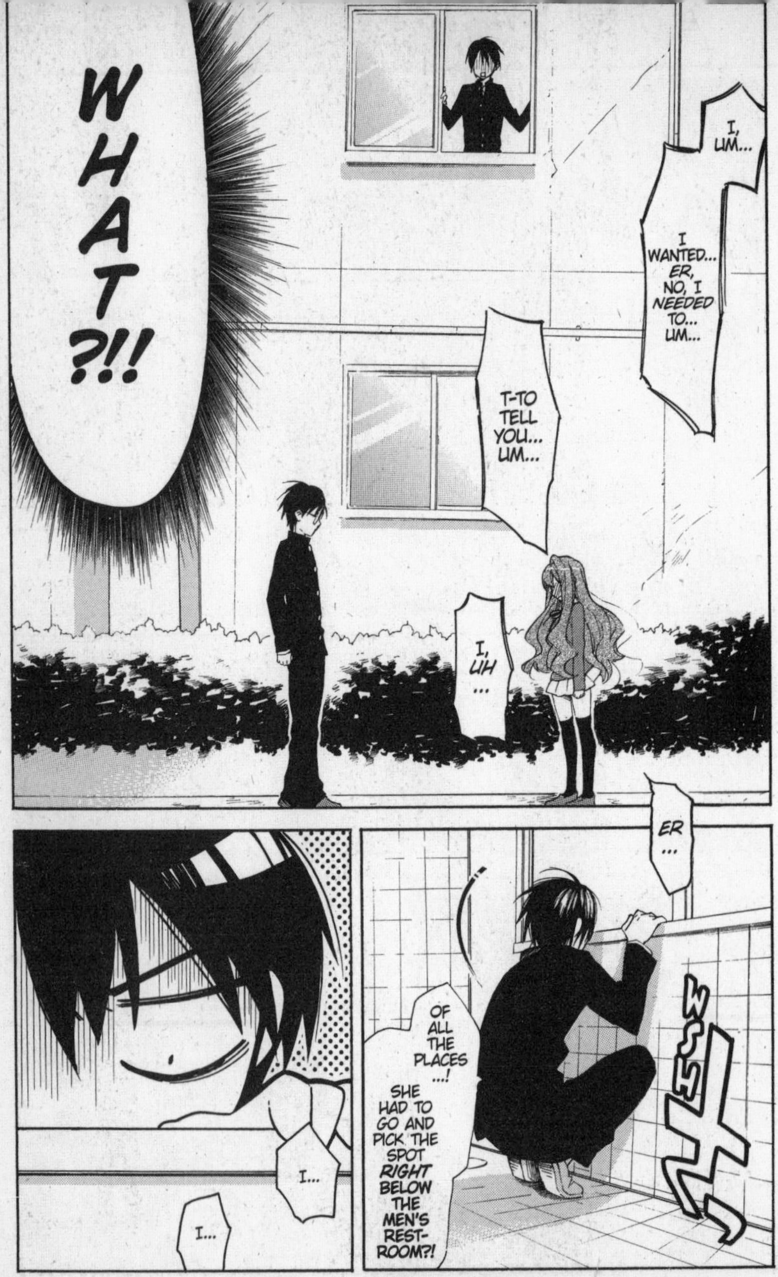
I, UM...
I WANTED... ER, NO, I NEEDED TO... UM...
T-TO TELL YOU... UM...
I, UH ...
WHAT ?!!
ER ...
WSH
OF ALL THE PLACES ...! SHE HAD TO GO AND PICK THE SPOT RIGHT BELOW THE MEN'S REST-ROOM?!
I...
I...

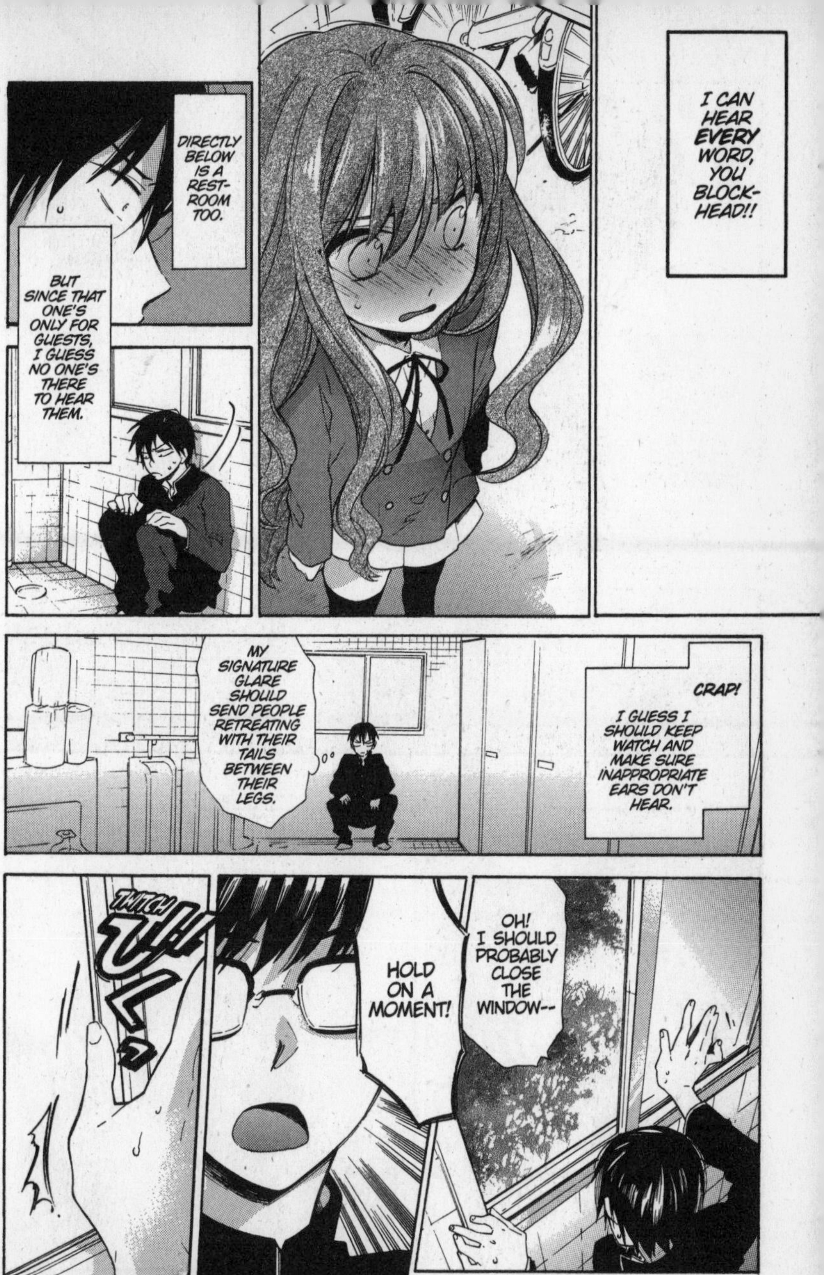
I CAN HEAR EVERY WORD, YOU BLOCKHEAD!!
DIRECTLY BELOW IS A RESTROOM TOO.
BUT SINCE THAT ONE'S ONLY FOR GUESTS, I GUESS NO ONE'S THERE TO HEAR THEM.
CRAP!
I GUESS I SHOULD KEEP WATCH AND MAKE SURE INAPPROPRIATE EARS DON'T HEAR.
MY SIGNATURE GLARE SHOULD SEND PEOPLE RETREATING WITH THEIR TAILS BETWEEN THEIR LEGS.
OH! I SHOULD PROBABLY CLOSE THE WINDOW--
HOLD ON A MOMENT!
TWITCH
UH!

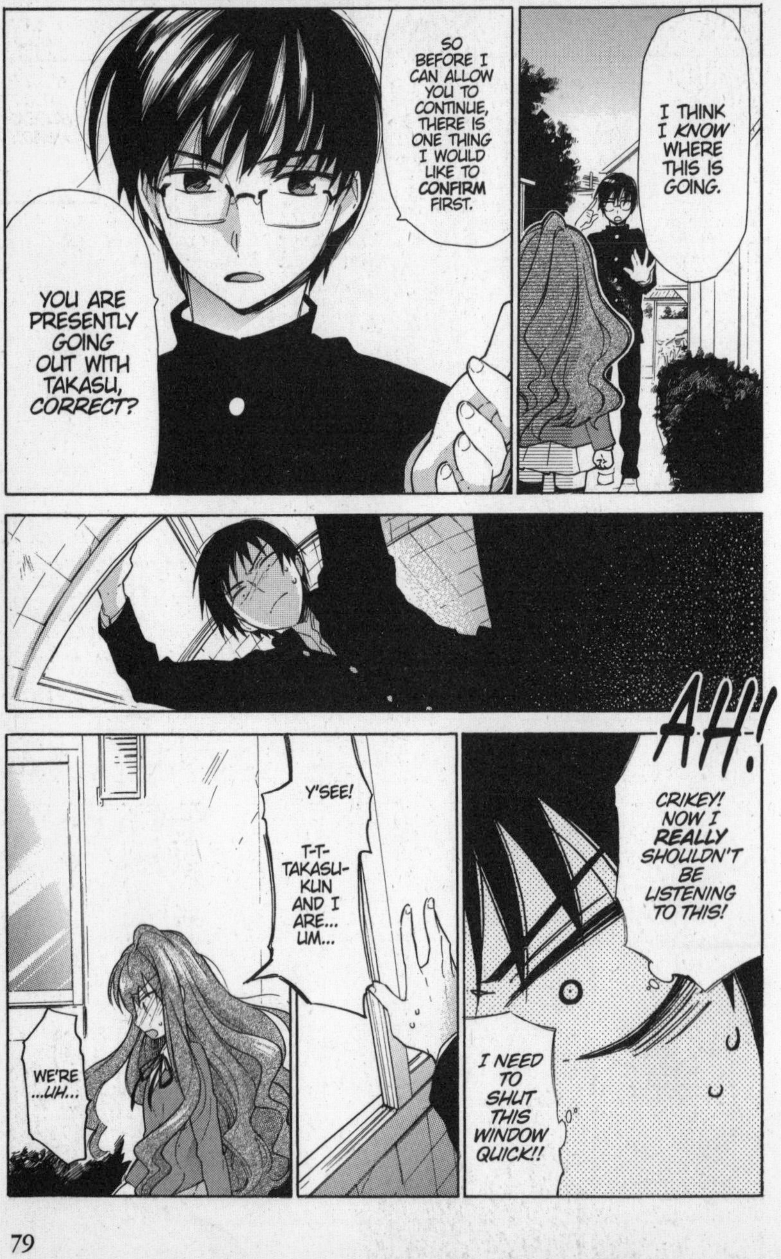
I THINK I KNOW WHERE THIS IS GOING.
SO BEFORE I CAN ALLOW YOU TO CONTINUE, THERE IS ONE THING I WOULD LIKE TO CONFIRM FIRST.
YOU ARE PRESENTLY GOING OUT WITH TAKASU, CORRECT?
AH!
CRIKEY! NOW I REALLY SHOULDN'T BE LISTENING TO THIS!
I NEED TO SHUT THIS WINDOW QUICK!!
Y'SEE!
T-T-TAKASU-KUN AND I ARE... UM...
WE'RE ...UH...

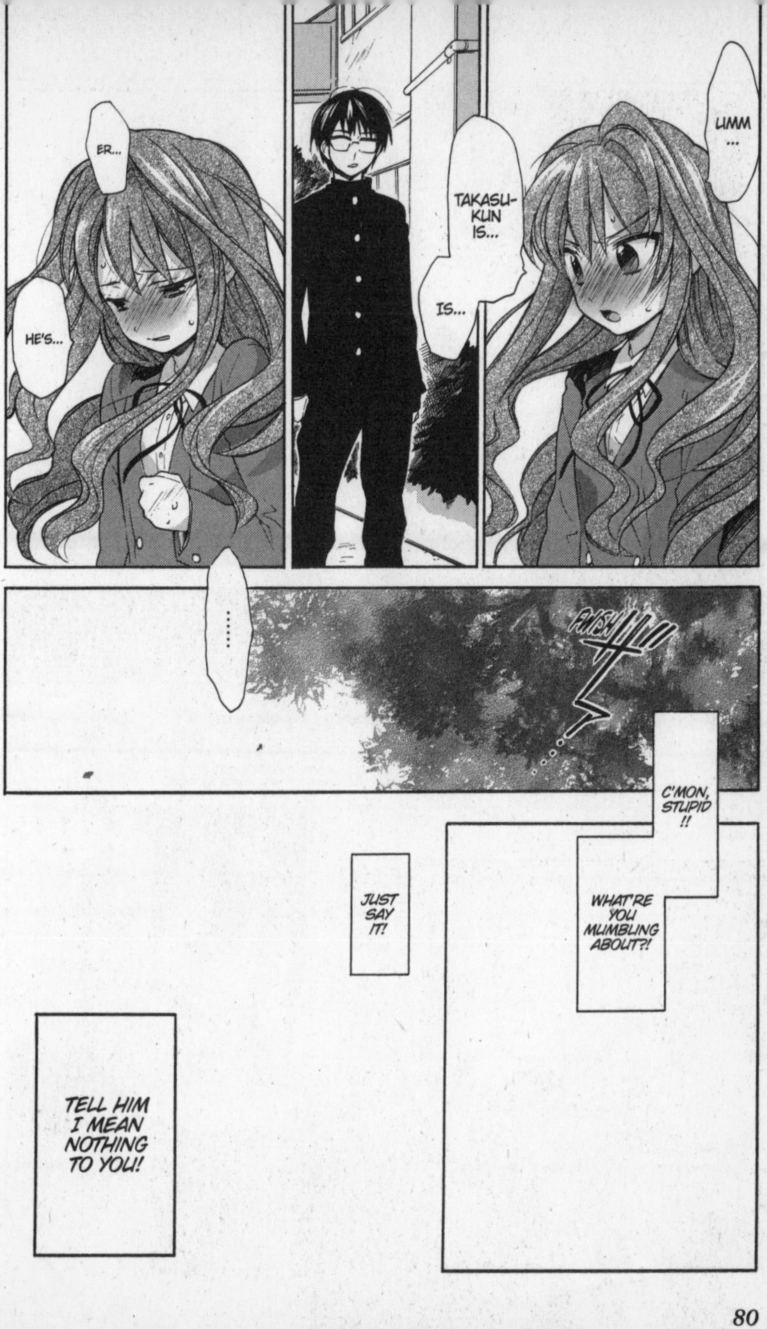
UMM ...
TAKASU-KUN IS...
IS...
ER...
HE'S...
FWISH
......
C'MON, STUPID!!
WHAT'RE YOU MUMBLING ABOUT?!
JUST SAY IT!
TELL HIM I MEAN NOTHING TO YOU!

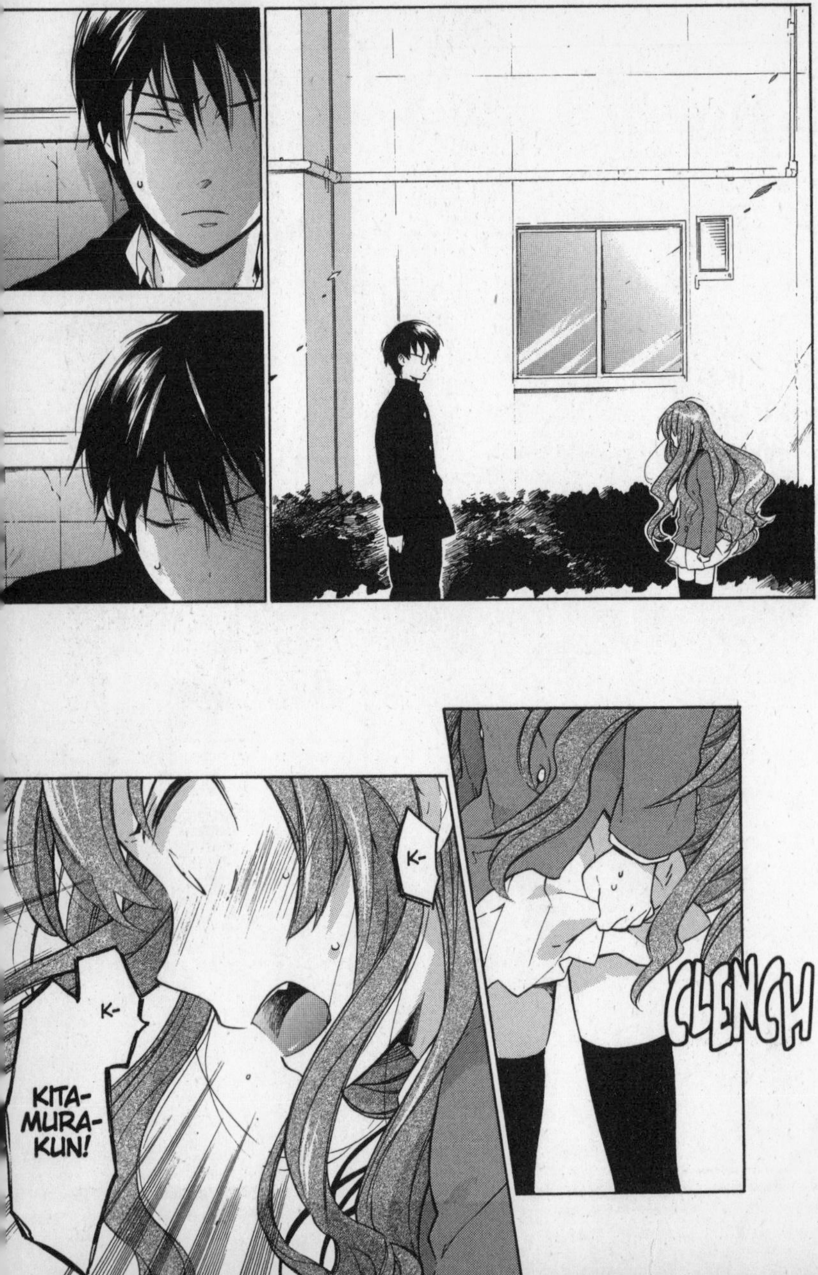
CLENCH
K-
K-
KITA-
MURA-
KUN!

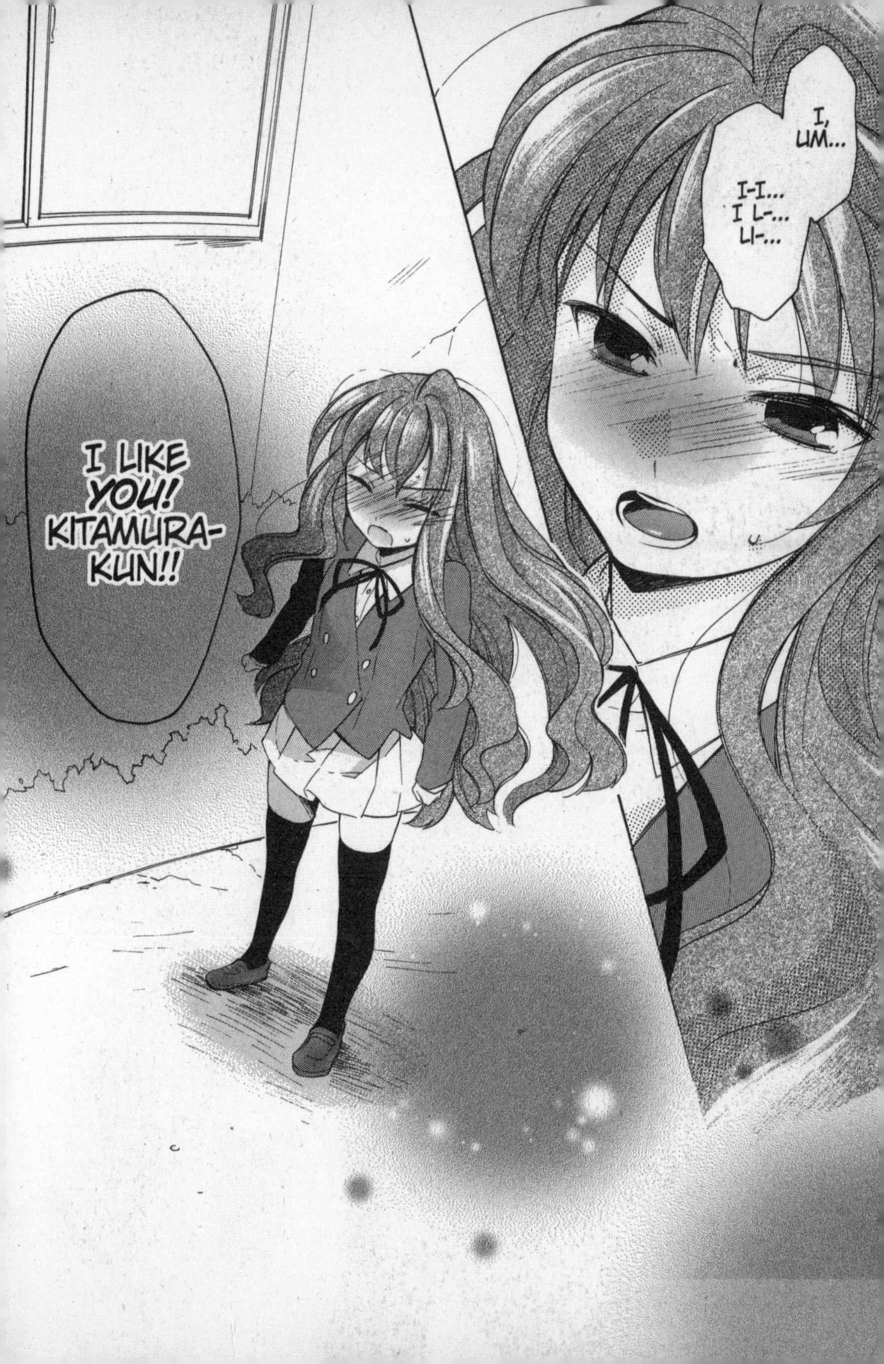
I, UM...
I-I... I L-... LI-...
I LIKE YOU! KITAMURA-KUN!!

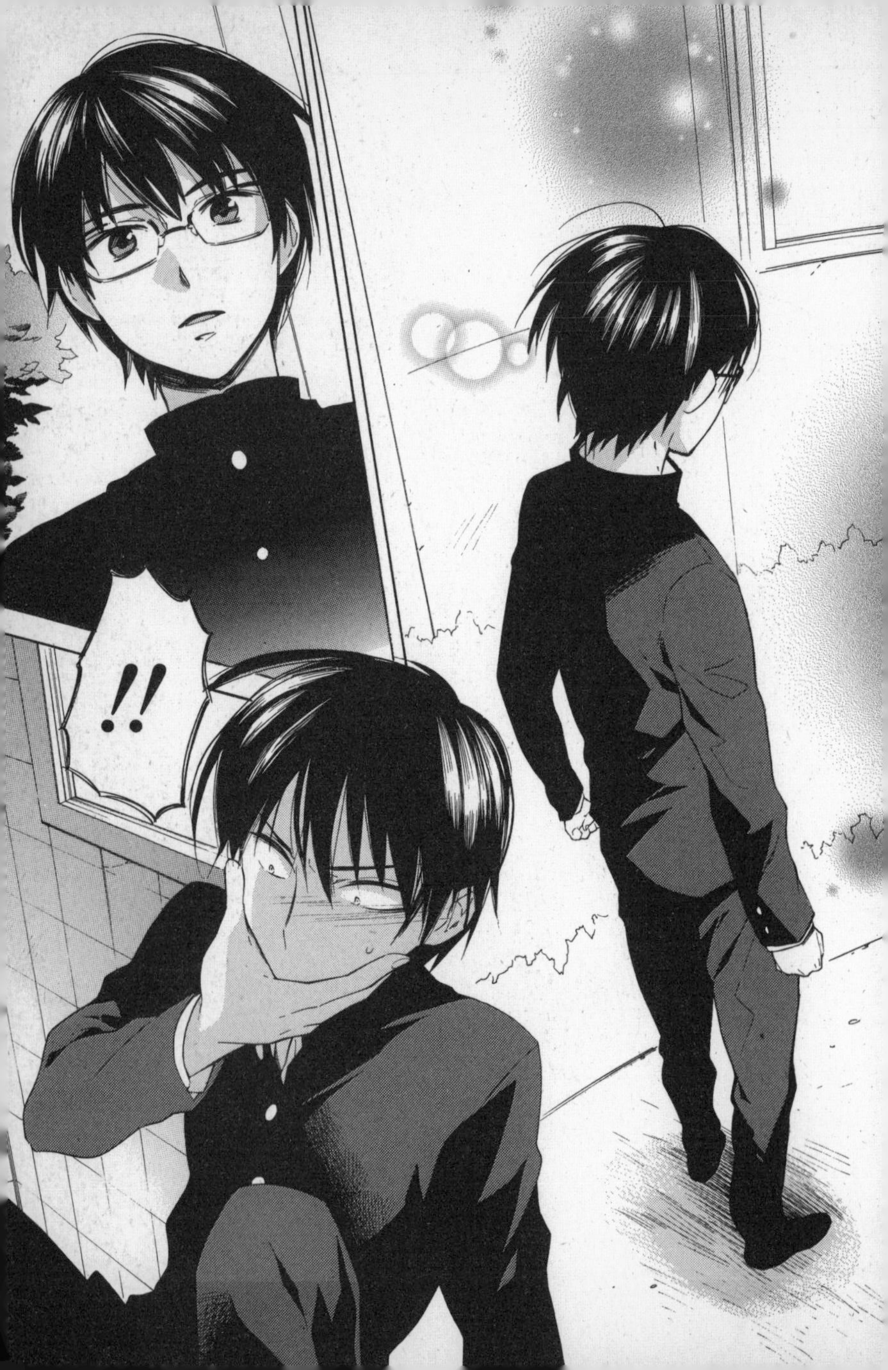
!!

MILITARY CRAWL
Third Stance

SHUFFLE

TWITCH

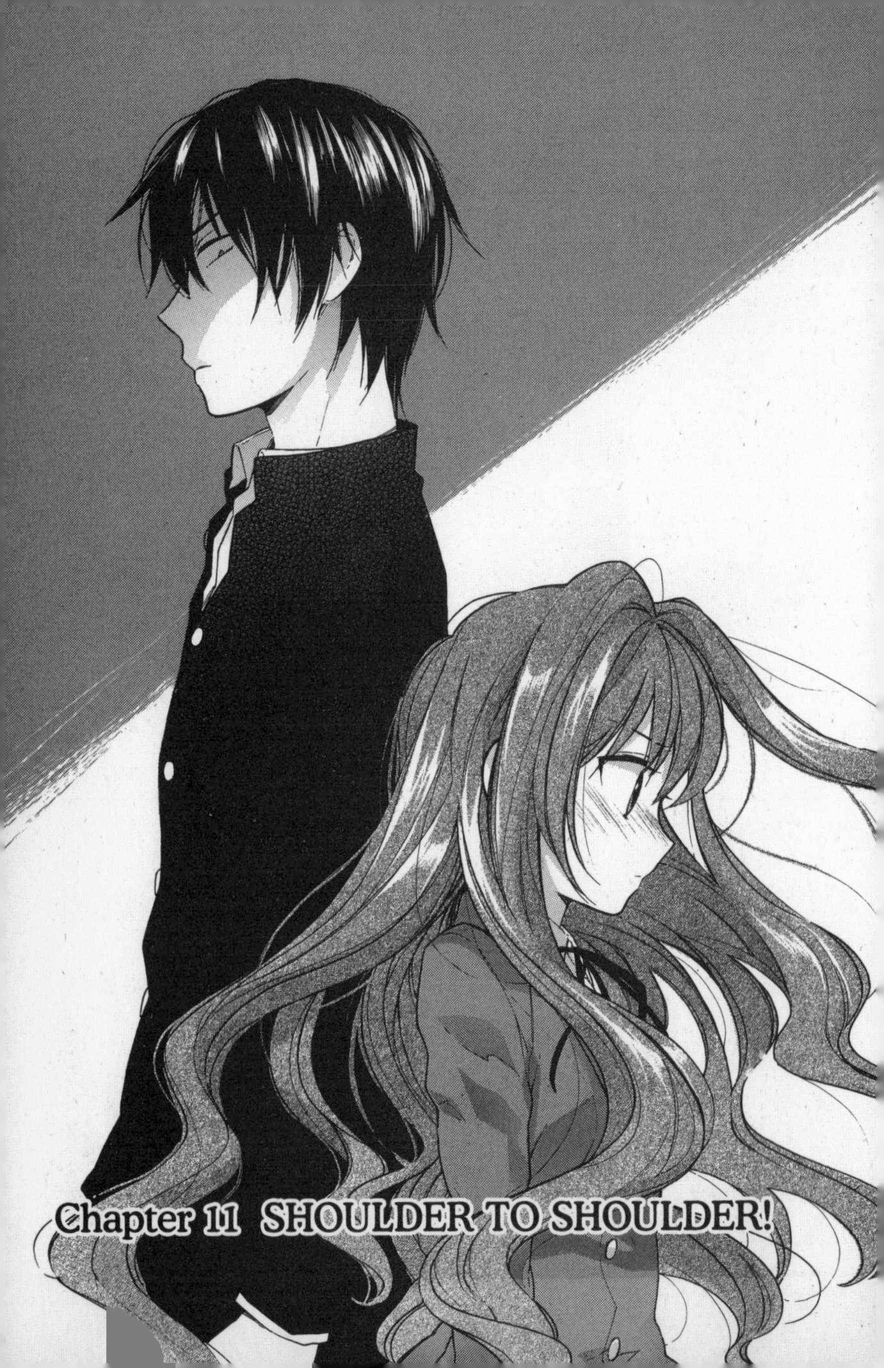
Chapter 11 SHOULDER TO SHOULDER!

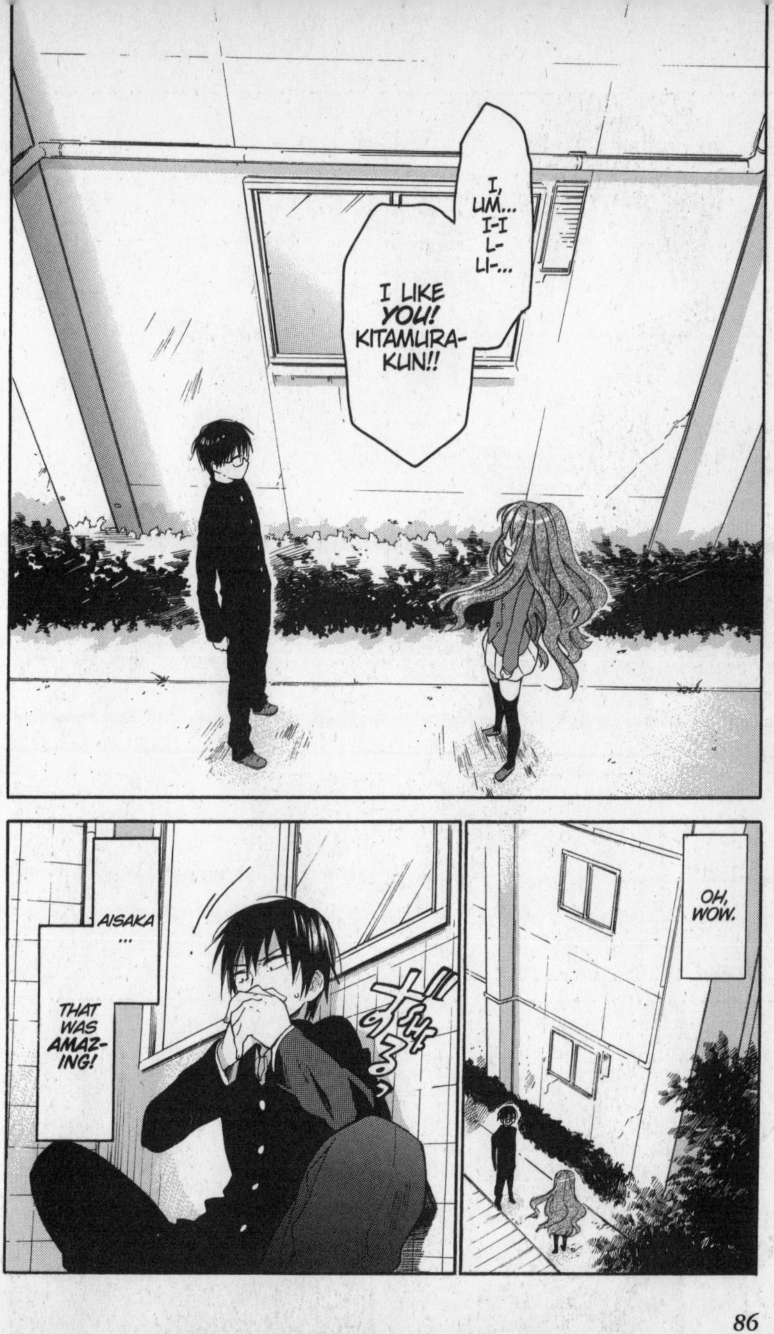
I, UM... I-I L- LI-...
I LIKE *YOU!* KITAMURA-KUN!!
OH, WOW.
AISAKA ...
THAT WAS AMAZ-ING!

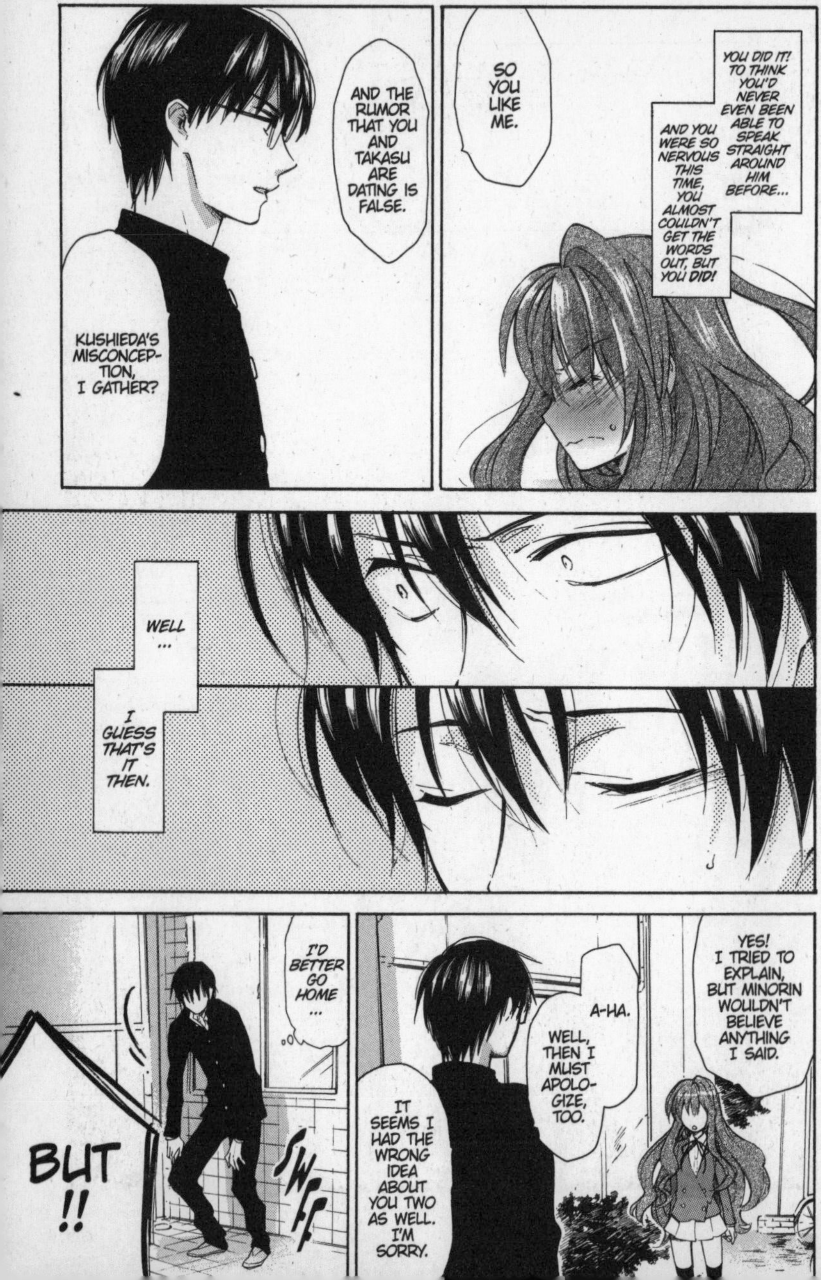
YOU DID IT! TO THINK YOU'D NEVER EVEN BEEN ABLE TO SPEAK STRAIGHT AROUND HIM BEFORE...
AND YOU WERE SO NERVOUS THIS TIME, YOU ALMOST COULDN'T GET THE WORDS OUT, BUT YOU DID!
SO YOU LIKE ME.
AND THE RUMOR THAT YOU AND TAKASU ARE DATING IS FALSE.
KUSHIEDA'S MISCONCEPTION, I GATHER?
WELL ...
I GUESS THAT'S IT THEN.
YES! I TRIED TO EXPLAIN, BUT MINORIN WOULDN'T BELIEVE ANYTHING I SAID.
A-HA.
WELL, THEN I MUST APOLOGIZE, TOO.
IT SEEMS I HAD THE WRONG IDEA ABOUT YOU TWO AS WELL. I'M SORRY.
I'D BETTER GO HOME ...
SWFF
BUT !!

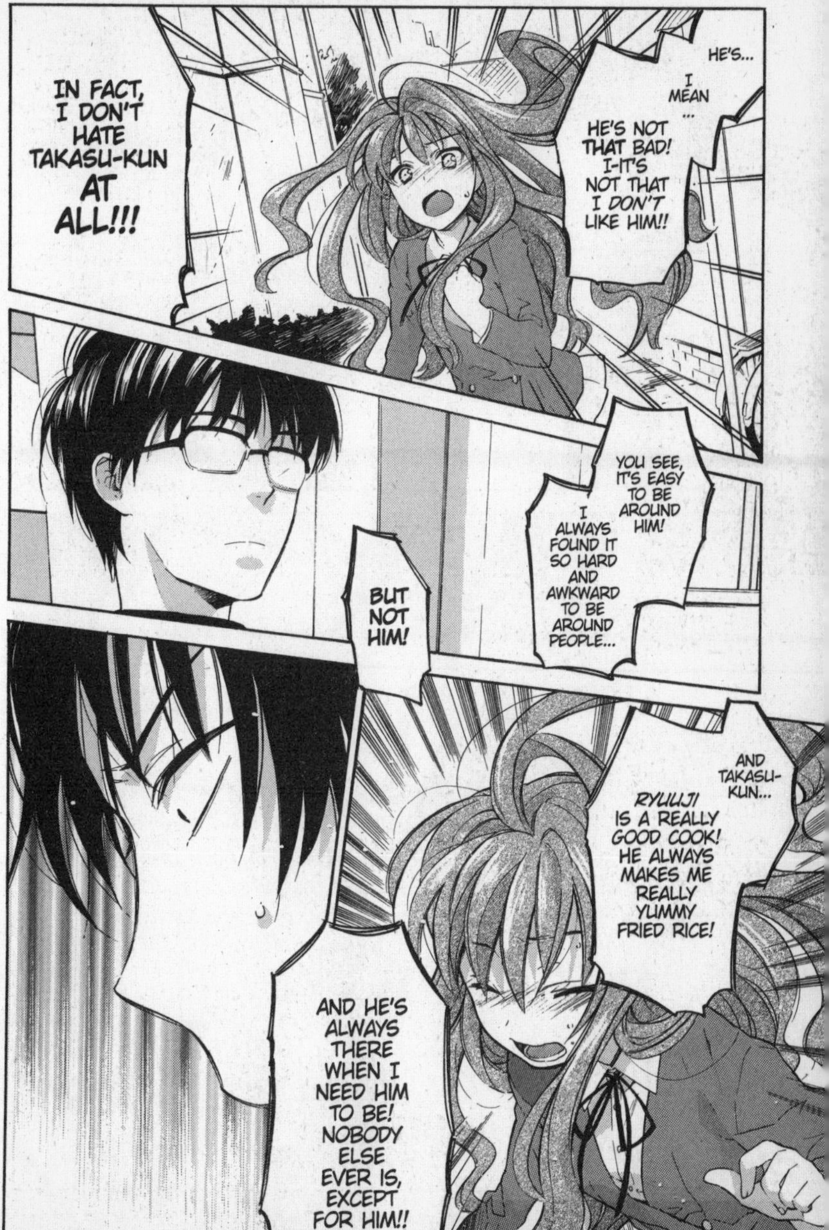
HE'S...
I MEAN ...
HE'S NOT THAT BAD! I-IT'S NOT THAT I *DON'T* LIKE HIM!!
IN FACT, I DON'T HATE TAKASU-KUN AT ALL!!!
YOU SEE, IT'S EASY TO BE AROUND HIM!
I ALWAYS FOUND IT SO HARD AND AWKWARD TO BE AROUND PEOPLE...
BUT NOT HIM!
AND TAKASU-KUN...
RYUUJI IS A REALLY GOOD COOK! HE ALWAYS MAKES ME REALLY YUMMY FRIED RICE!
AND HE'S ALWAYS THERE WHEN I NEED HIM TO BE! NOBODY ELSE EVER IS, EXCEPT FOR HIM!!

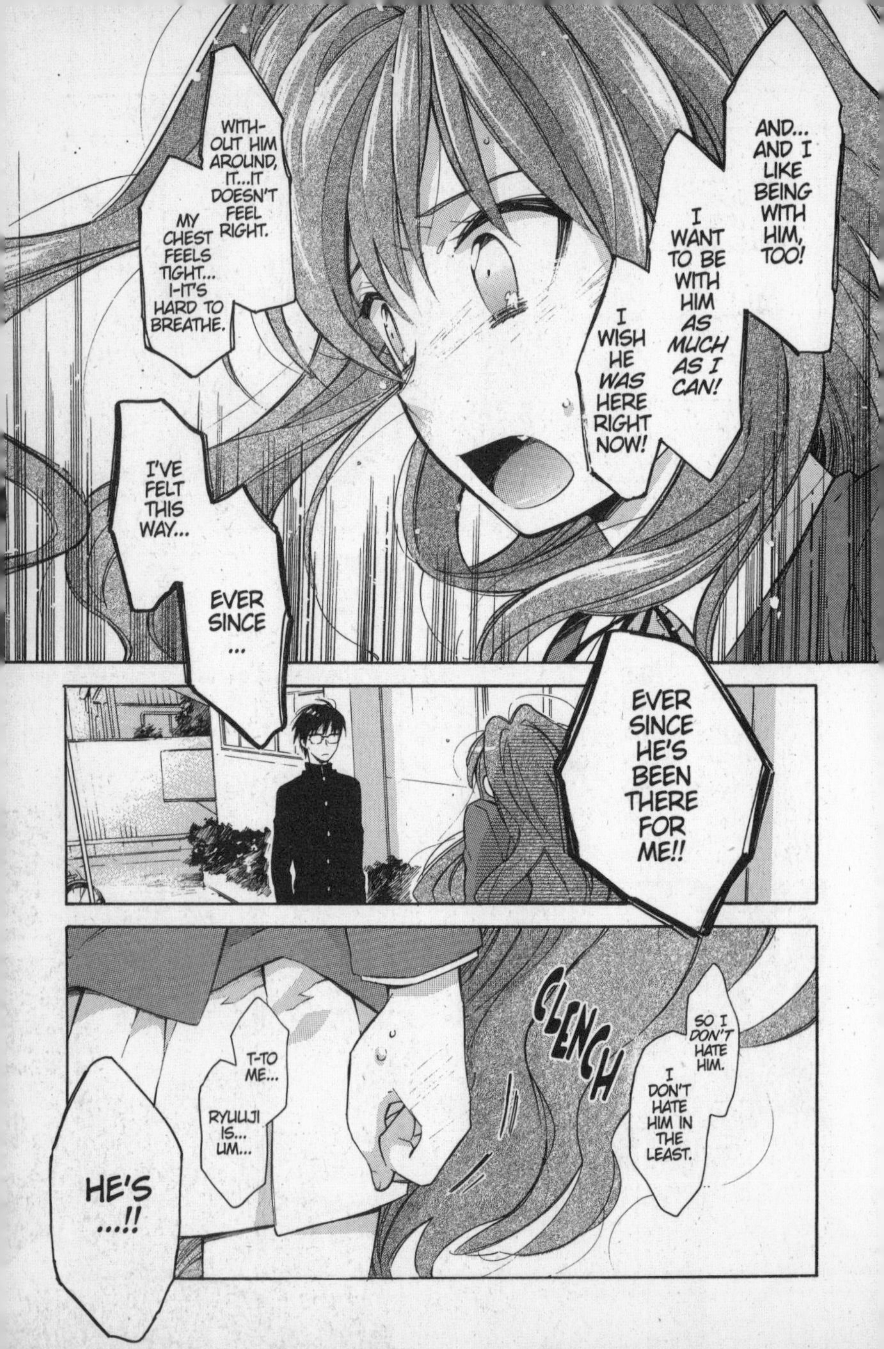
AND... AND I LIKE BEING WITH HIM, TOO!
I WANT TO BE WITH HIM AS MUCH AS I CAN!
I WISH HE WAS HERE RIGHT NOW!
WITH-OUT HIM AROUND, IT...IT DOESN'T FEEL RIGHT.
MY CHEST FEELS TIGHT... I-IT'S HARD TO BREATHE.
I'VE FELT THIS WAY...
EVER SINCE ...
EVER SINCE HE'S BEEN THERE FOR ME!!
CLENCH
SO I DON'T HATE HIM.
I DON'T HATE HIM IN THE LEAST.
T-TO ME...
RYUUJI IS... UM...
HE'S ...!!

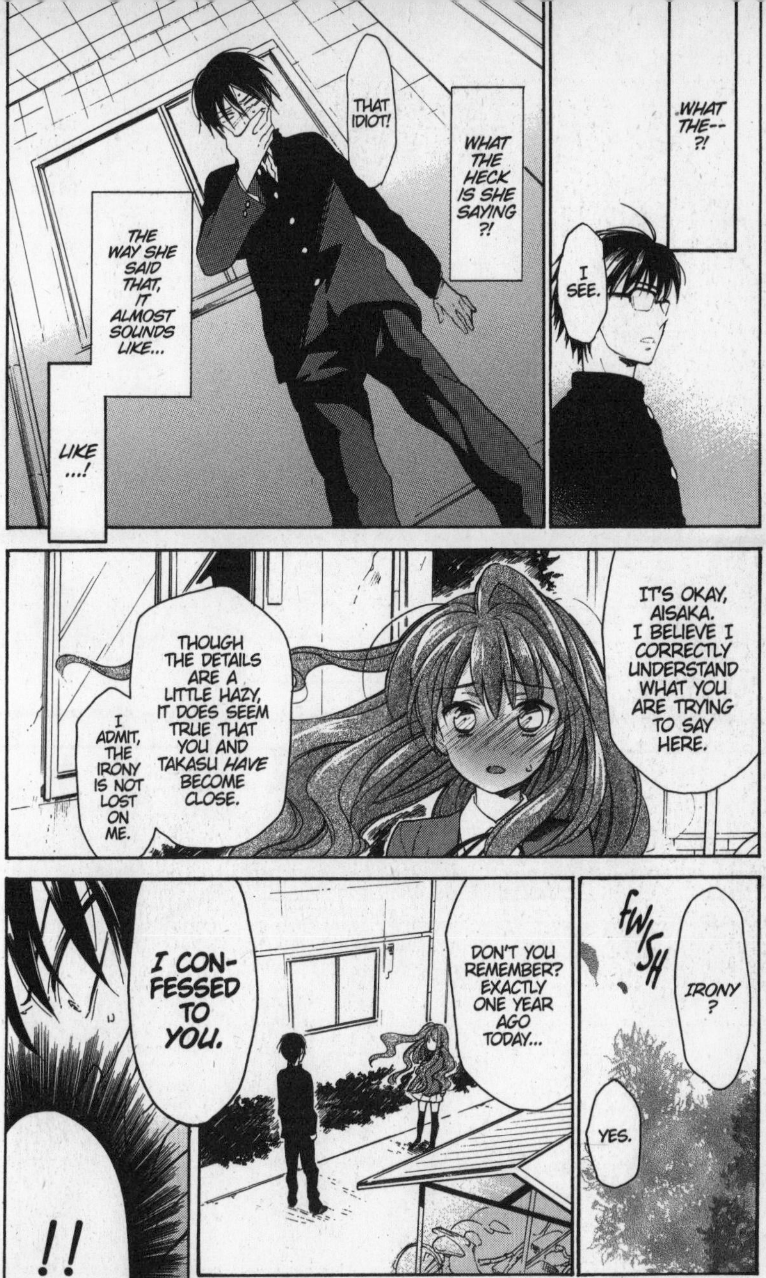
WHAT THE--?!
I SEE.
WHAT THE HECK IS SHE SAYING?!
THAT IDIOT!
THE WAY SHE SAID THAT, IT ALMOST SOUNDS LIKE...
LIKE...!
IT'S OKAY, AISAKA. I BELIEVE I CORRECTLY UNDERSTAND WHAT YOU ARE TRYING TO SAY HERE.
THOUGH THE DETAILS ARE A LITTLE HAZY, IT DOES SEEM TRUE THAT YOU AND TAKASU *HAVE* BECOME CLOSE.
I ADMIT, THE IRONY IS NOT LOST ON ME.
FWISH
IRONY?
YES.
DON'T YOU REMEMBER? EXACTLY ONE YEAR AGO TODAY...
I CON-FESSED TO YOU.
!!

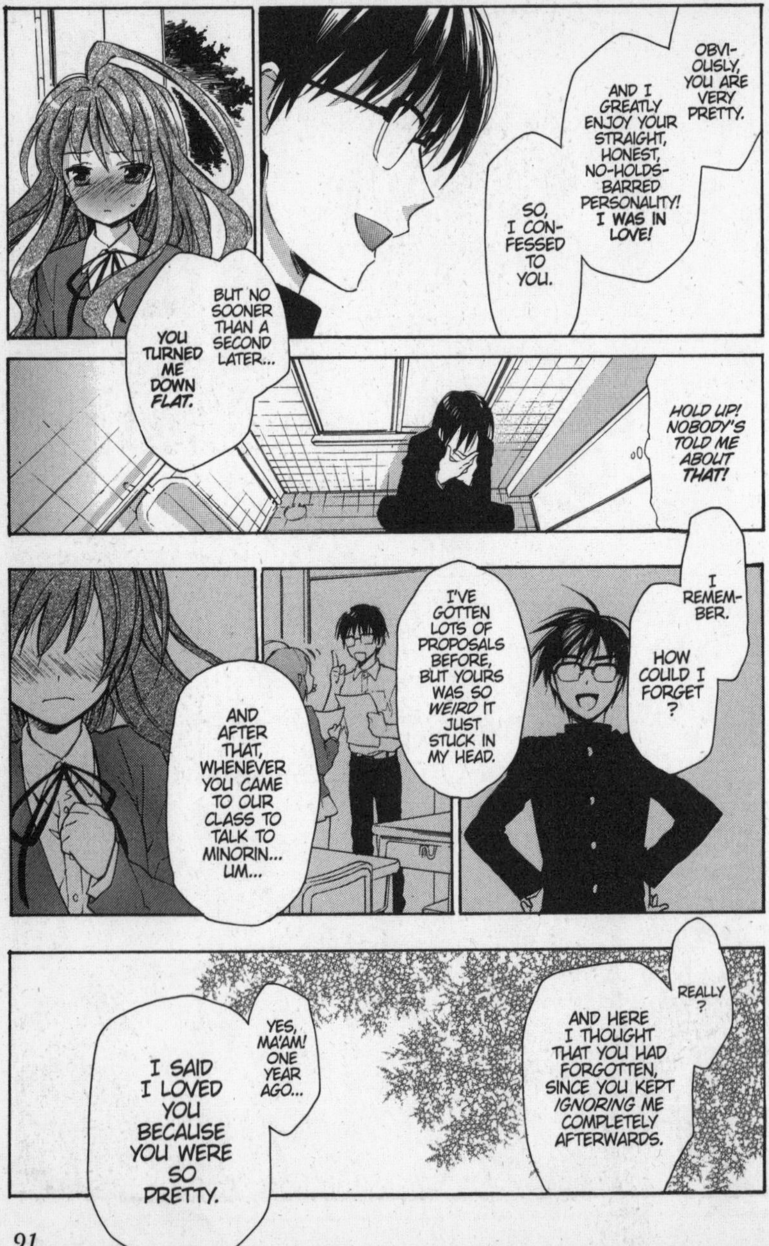
OBVIOUSLY, YOU ARE VERY PRETTY.
AND I GREATLY ENJOY YOUR STRAIGHT, HONEST, NO-HOLDS-BARRED PERSONALITY! I WAS IN LOVE!
SO, I CONFESSED TO YOU.
BUT NO SOONER THAN A SECOND LATER...
YOU TURNED ME DOWN *FLAT.*
*HOLD UP! NOBODY'S TOLD ME ABOUT **THAT!***
I REMEMBER.
HOW COULD I FORGET?
I'VE GOTTEN LOTS OF PROPOSALS BEFORE, BUT YOURS WAS SO *WEIRD* IT JUST STUCK IN MY HEAD.
AND AFTER THAT, WHENEVER YOU CAME TO OUR CLASS TO TALK TO MINORIN... UM...
REALLY?
AND HERE I THOUGHT THAT YOU HAD FORGOTTEN, SINCE YOU KEPT *IGNORING* ME COMPLETELY AFTERWARDS.
YES, MA'AM! ONE YEAR AGO...
I SAID I LOVED YOU BECAUSE YOU WERE SO PRETTY.

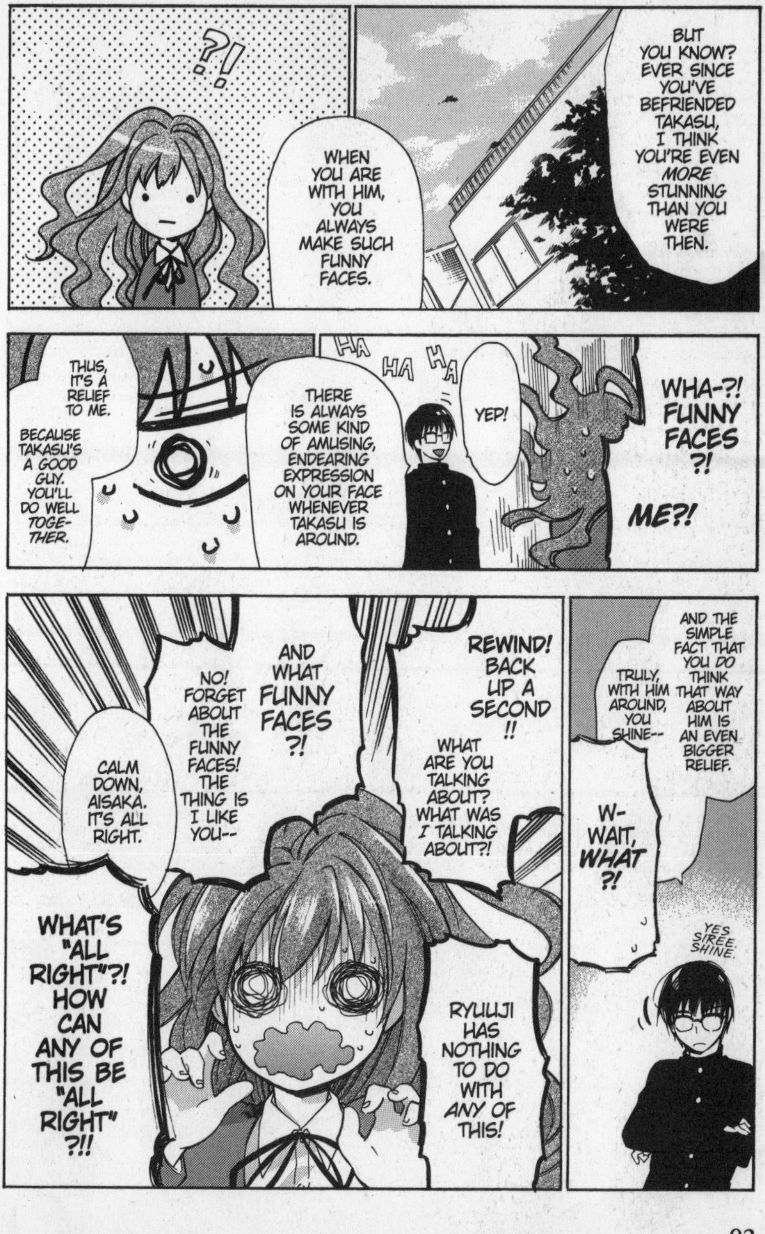
BUT YOU KNOW? EVER SINCE YOU'VE BEFRIENDED TAKASU, I THINK YOU'RE EVEN *MORE* STUNNING THAN YOU WERE THEN.
WHEN YOU ARE WITH HIM, YOU ALWAYS MAKE SUCH FUNNY FACES.
?!
WHA-?! FUNNY FACES ?!
ME?!
HA HA HA
YEP!
THERE IS ALWAYS SOME KIND OF AMUSING, ENDEARING EXPRESSION ON YOUR FACE WHENEVER TAKASU IS AROUND.
THUS, IT'S A RELIEF TO ME.
BECAUSE TAKASU'S A GOOD GUY. YOU'LL DO WELL *TOGE-THER.*
AND THE SIMPLE FACT THAT YOU *DO* THINK THAT WAY ABOUT HIM IS AN EVEN BIGGER RELIEF.
TRULY, WITH HIM AROUND, YOU SHINE--
W-WAIT, *WHAT* ?!
YES SIREE. SHINE.
REWIND! BACK UP A SECOND !!
WHAT ARE YOU TALKING ABOUT? WHAT WAS I TALKING ABOUT?!
AND WHAT FUNNY FACES ?!
NO! FORGET ABOUT THE FUNNY FACES! THE THING IS I LIKE YOU--
CALM DOWN, AISAKA. IT'S ALL RIGHT.
RYUUJI HAS NOTHING TO DO WITH *ANY* OF THIS!
WHAT'S "ALL RIGHT"?! HOW CAN ANY OF THIS BE "ALL RIGHT" ?!!

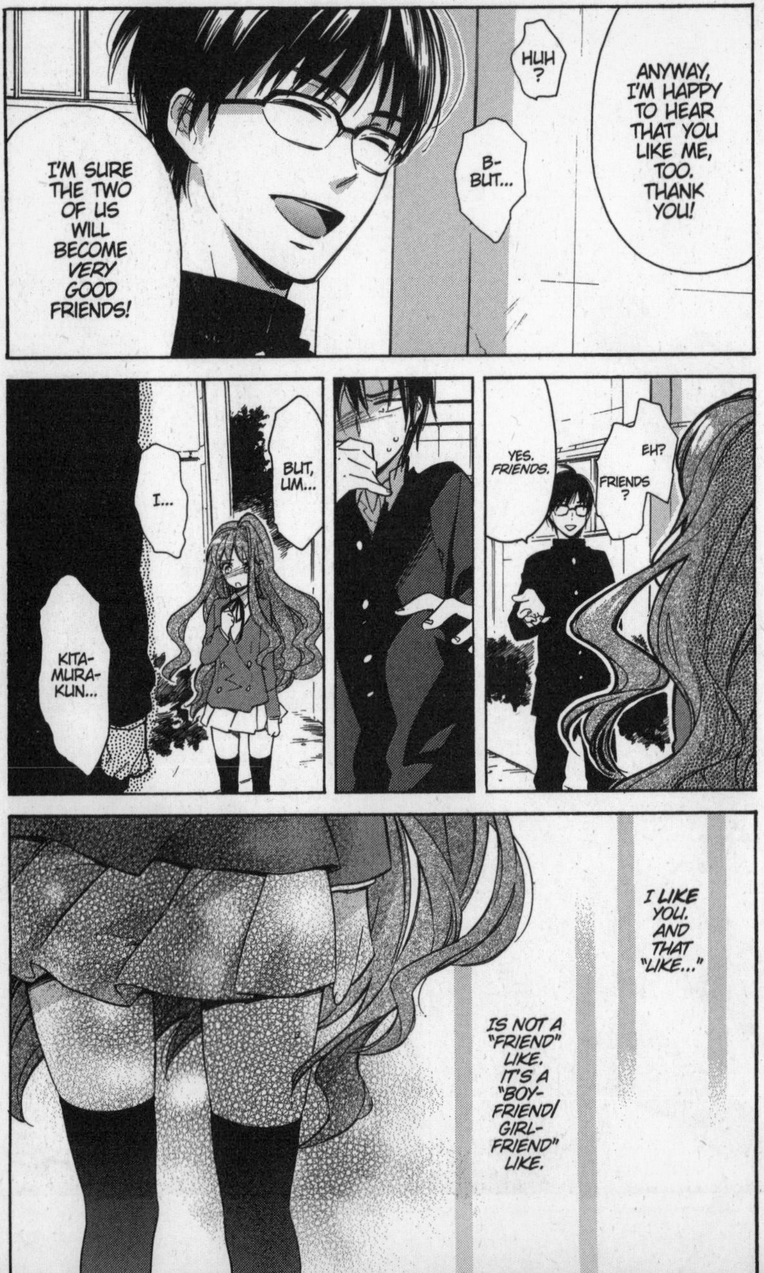
ANYWAY, I'M HAPPY TO HEAR THAT YOU LIKE ME, TOO. THANK YOU!
HUH?
B-BUT...
I'M SURE THE TWO OF US WILL BECOME VERY GOOD FRIENDS!
EH?
FRIENDS?
YES. FRIENDS.
BUT, UM...
I...
KITA-MURA-KUN...
I LIKE YOU. AND THAT "LIKE..."
IS NOT A "FRIEND" LIKE. IT'S A "BOY-FRIEND/GIRL-FRIEND" LIKE.

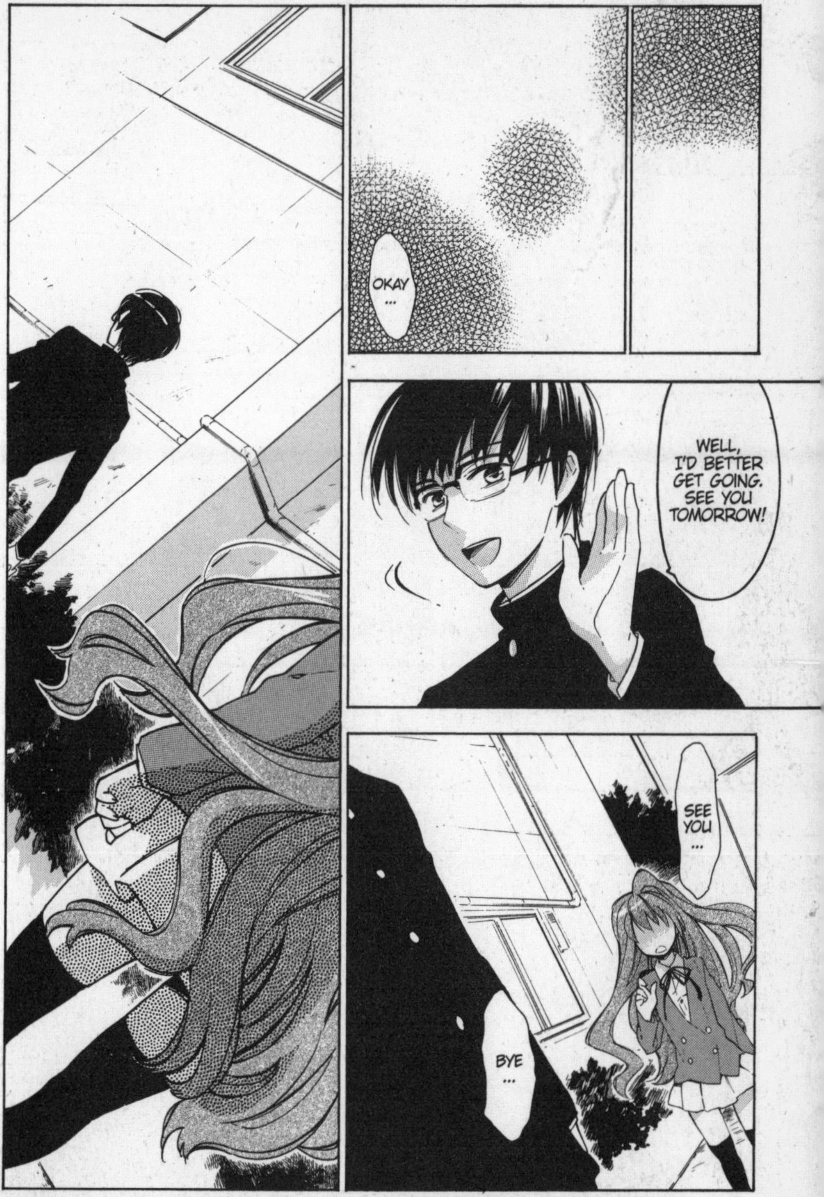
OKAY ...
WELL, I'D BETTER GET GOING. SEE YOU TOMORROW!
SEE YOU ...
BYE ...

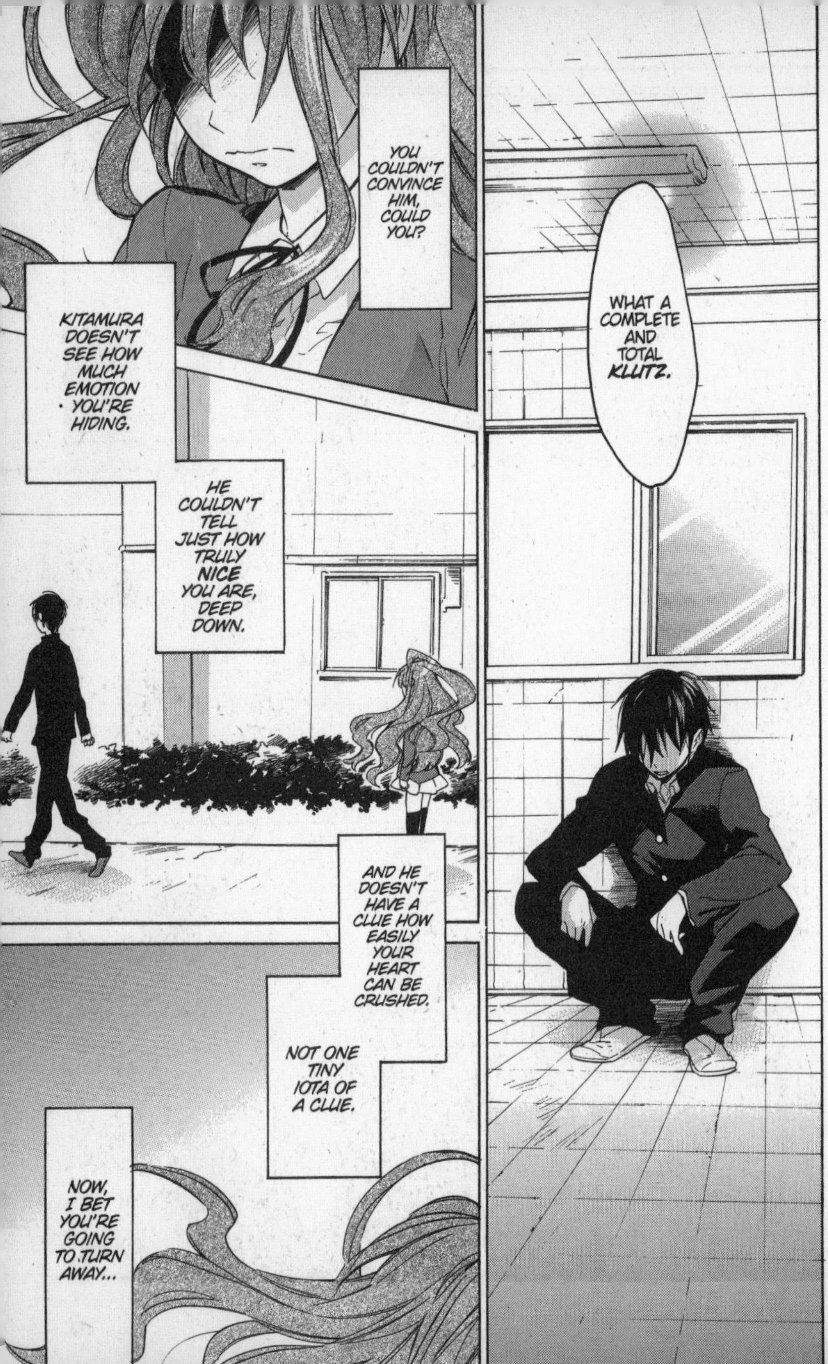
WHAT A COMPLETE AND TOTAL KLUTZ.
YOU COULDN'T CONVINCE HIM, COULD YOU?
KITAMURA DOESN'T SEE HOW MUCH EMOTION YOU'RE HIDING.
HE COULDN'T TELL JUST HOW TRULY NICE YOU ARE, DEEP DOWN.
AND HE DOESN'T HAVE A CLUE HOW EASILY YOUR HEART CAN BE CRUSHED.
NOT ONE TINY IOTA OF A CLUE.
NOW, I BET YOU'RE GOING TO TURN AWAY...

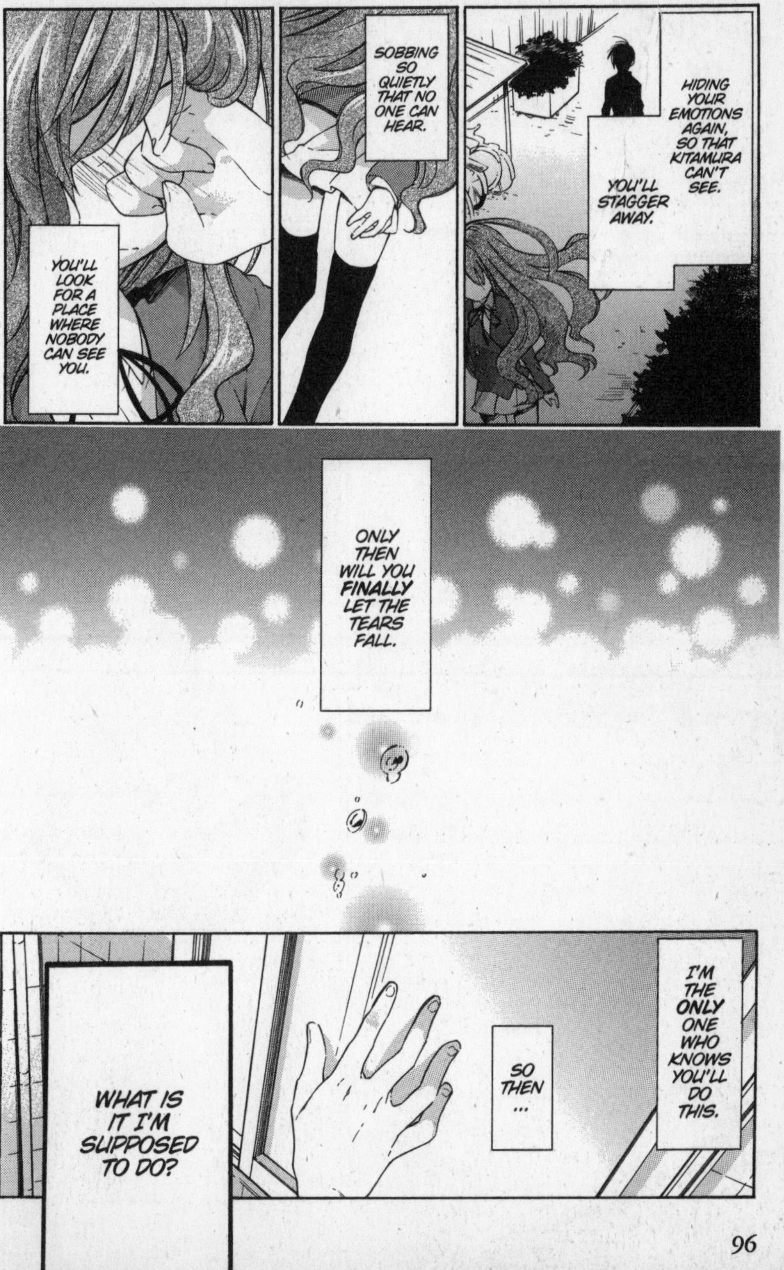
HIDING YOUR EMOTIONS AGAIN, SO THAT KITAMURA CAN'T SEE.
YOU'LL STAGGER AWAY.
SOBBING SO QUIETLY THAT NO ONE CAN HEAR.
YOU'LL LOOK FOR A PLACE WHERE NOBODY CAN SEE YOU.
ONLY THEN WILL YOU **FINALLY** LET THE TEARS FALL.
I'M THE **ONLY** ONE WHO KNOWS YOU'LL DO THIS.
SO THEN ...
WHAT IS IT I'M SUPPOSED TO DO?

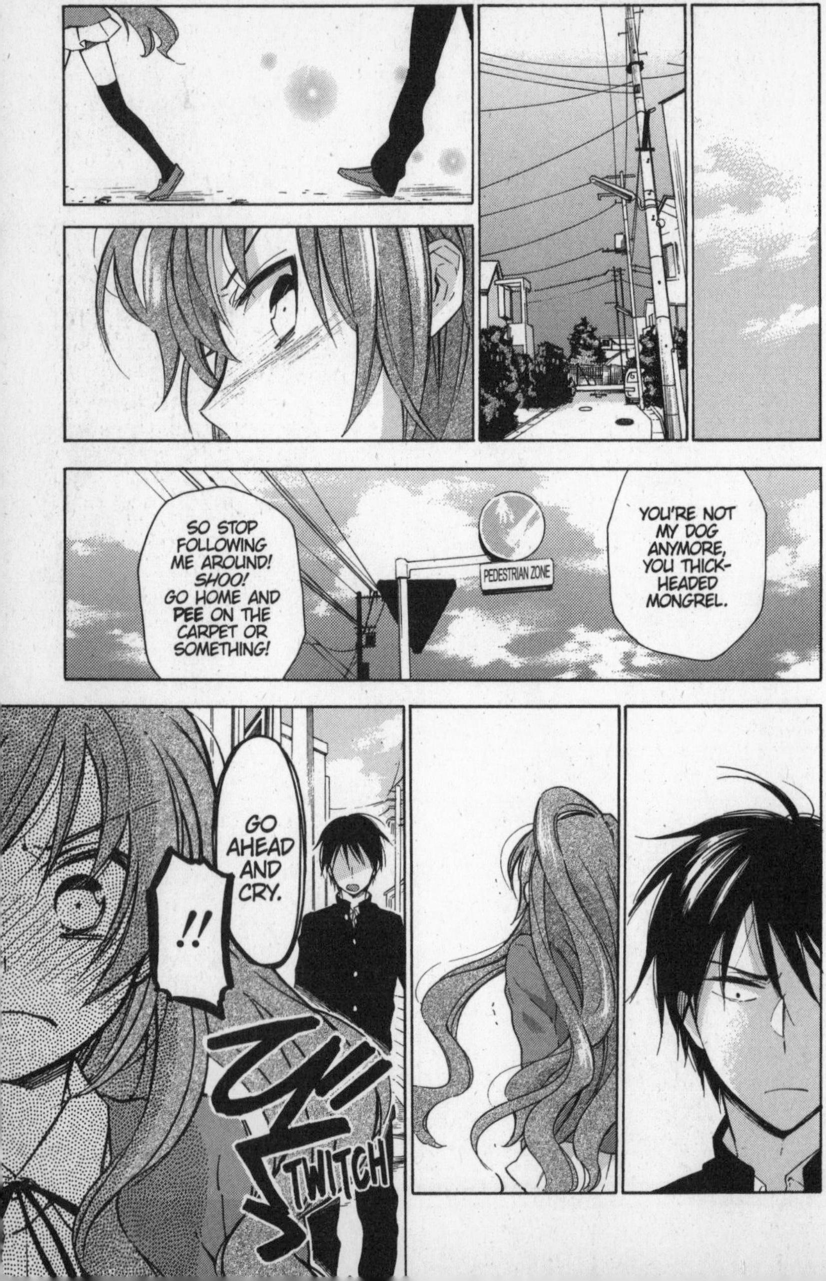
YOU'RE NOT MY DOG ANYMORE, YOU THICK-HEADED MONGREL.
PEDESTRIAN ZONE
SO STOP FOLLOWING ME AROUND! SHOO! GO HOME AND PEE ON THE CARPET OR SOMETHING!
GO AHEAD AND CRY.
!!
TWITCH

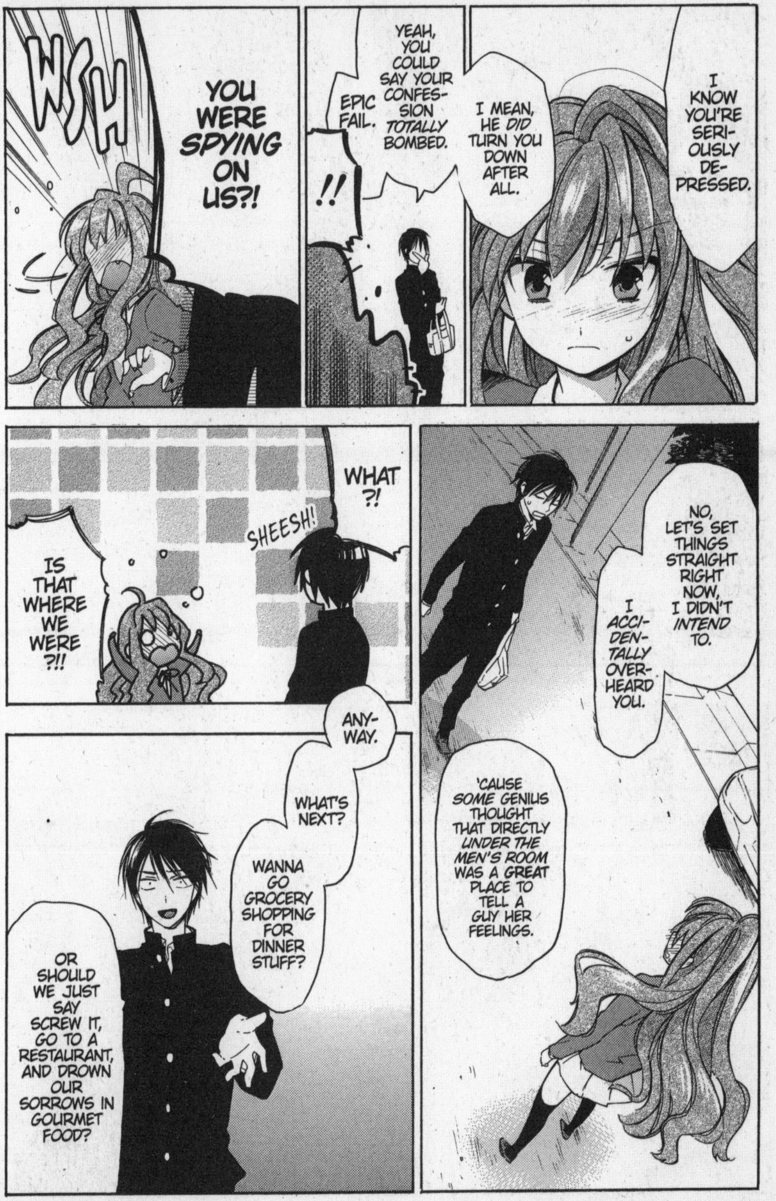
I KNOW YOU'RE SERIOUSLY DEPRESSED.
I MEAN, HE DID TURN YOU DOWN AFTER ALL.
YEAH, YOU COULD SAY YOUR CONFESSION TOTALLY BOMBED.
EPIC FAIL.
!!
WSH
YOU WERE SPYING ON US?!
NO, LET'S SET THINGS STRAIGHT RIGHT NOW, I DIDN'T INTEND TO.
I ACCIDENTALLY OVERHEARD YOU.
'CAUSE SOME GENIUS THOUGHT THAT DIRECTLY UNDER THE MEN'S ROOM WAS A GREAT PLACE TO TELL A GUY HER FEELINGS.
WHAT?!
SHEESH!
IS THAT WHERE WE WERE?!!
ANYWAY.
WHAT'S NEXT?
WANNA GO GROCERY SHOPPING FOR DINNER STUFF?
OR SHOULD WE JUST SAY SCREW IT, GO TO A RESTAURANT, AND DROWN OUR SORROWS IN GOURMET FOOD?

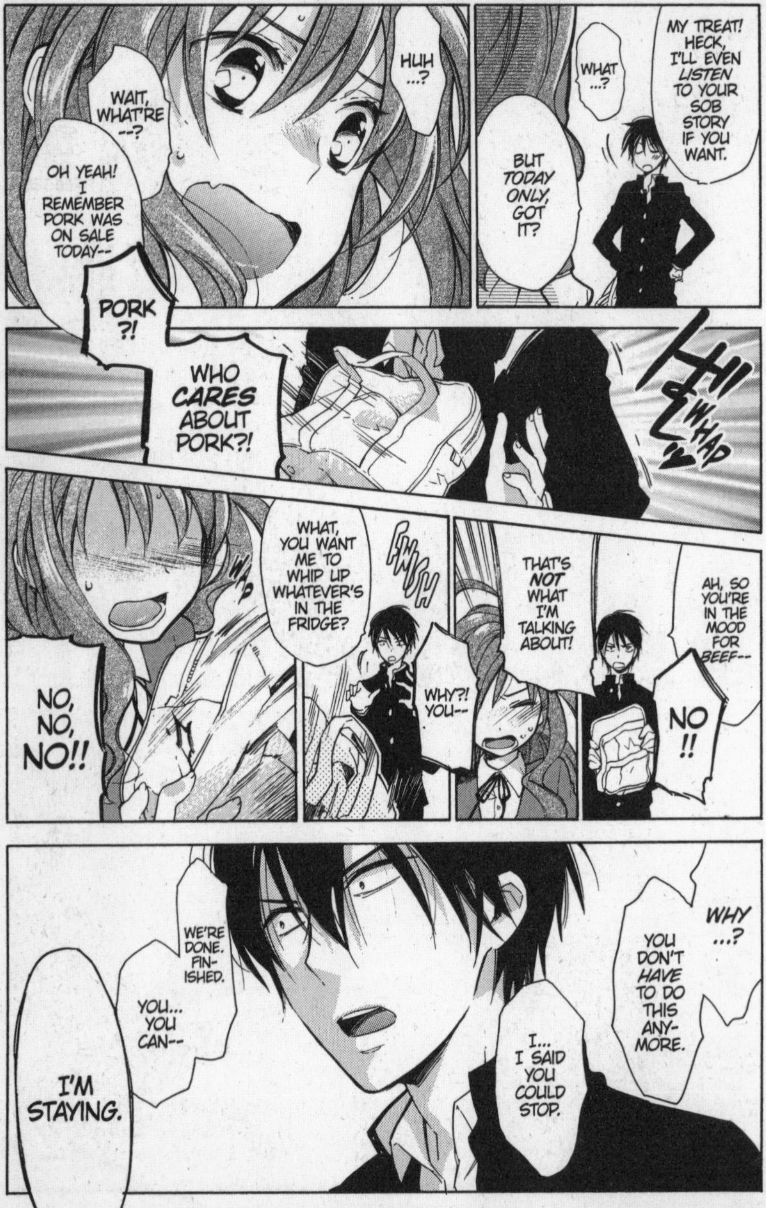
MY TREAT! HECK, I'LL EVEN *LISTEN* TO YOUR SOB STORY IF YOU WANT.
WHAT ...?
BUT *TODAY ONLY,* GOT IT?
HUH ...?
WAIT, WHAT'RE --?
OH YEAH! I REMEMBER PORK WAS ON SALE TODAY--
PORK ?!
WHO *CARES* ABOUT PORK?!
AH, SO YOU'RE IN THE MOOD FOR *BEEF*--
NO !!
THAT'S *NOT* WHAT I'M TALKING ABOUT!
WHY?! YOU--
WHAT, YOU WANT ME TO WHIP UP WHATEVER'S IN THE FRIDGE?
NO, NO, NO!!
WHY ...?
YOU DON'T *HAVE* TO DO THIS ANY-MORE.
I... I SAID YOU COULD STOP.
WE'RE DONE. FIN-ISHED.
YOU... YOU CAN--
I'M STAYING.

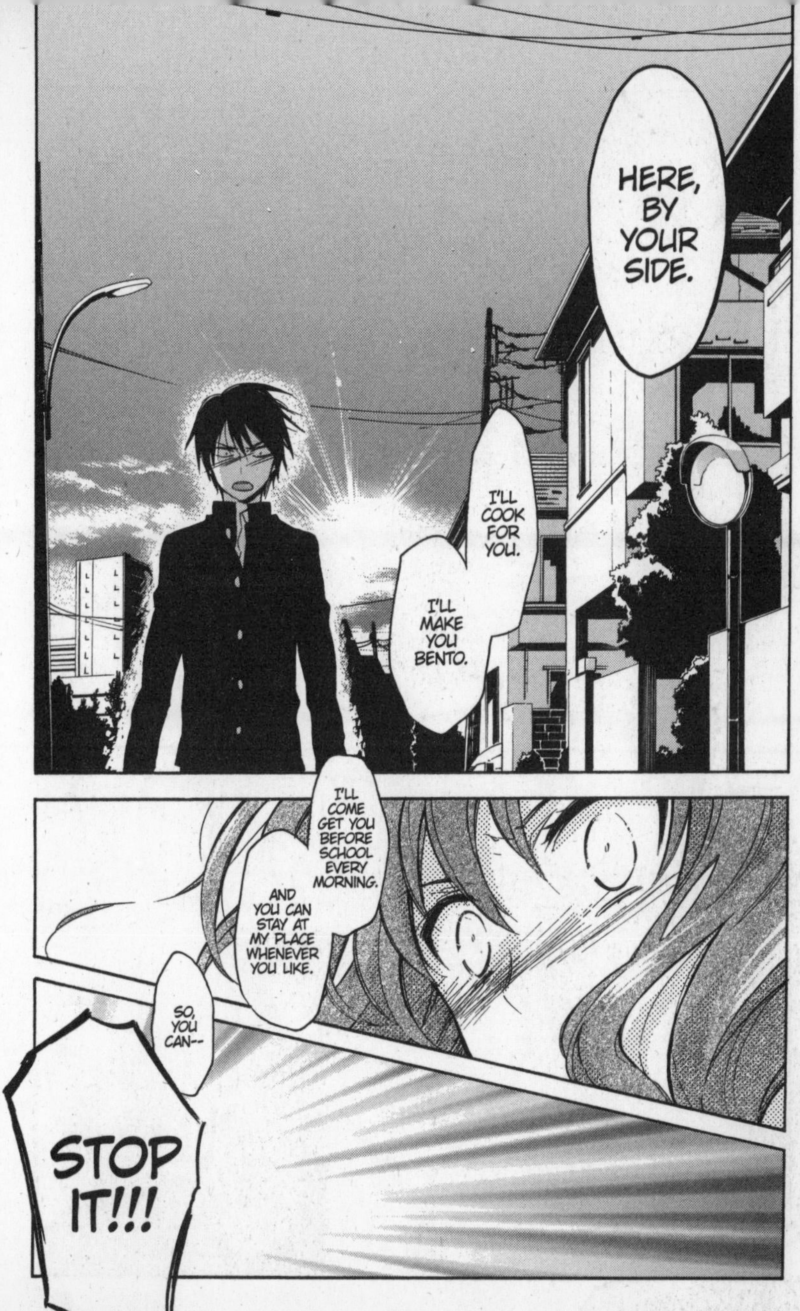
HERE, BY YOUR SIDE.
I'LL COOK FOR YOU.
I'LL MAKE YOU BENTO.
I'LL COME GET YOU BEFORE SCHOOL EVERY MORNING.
AND YOU CAN STAY AT MY PLACE WHENEVER YOU LIKE.
SO, YOU CAN--
STOP IT!!!

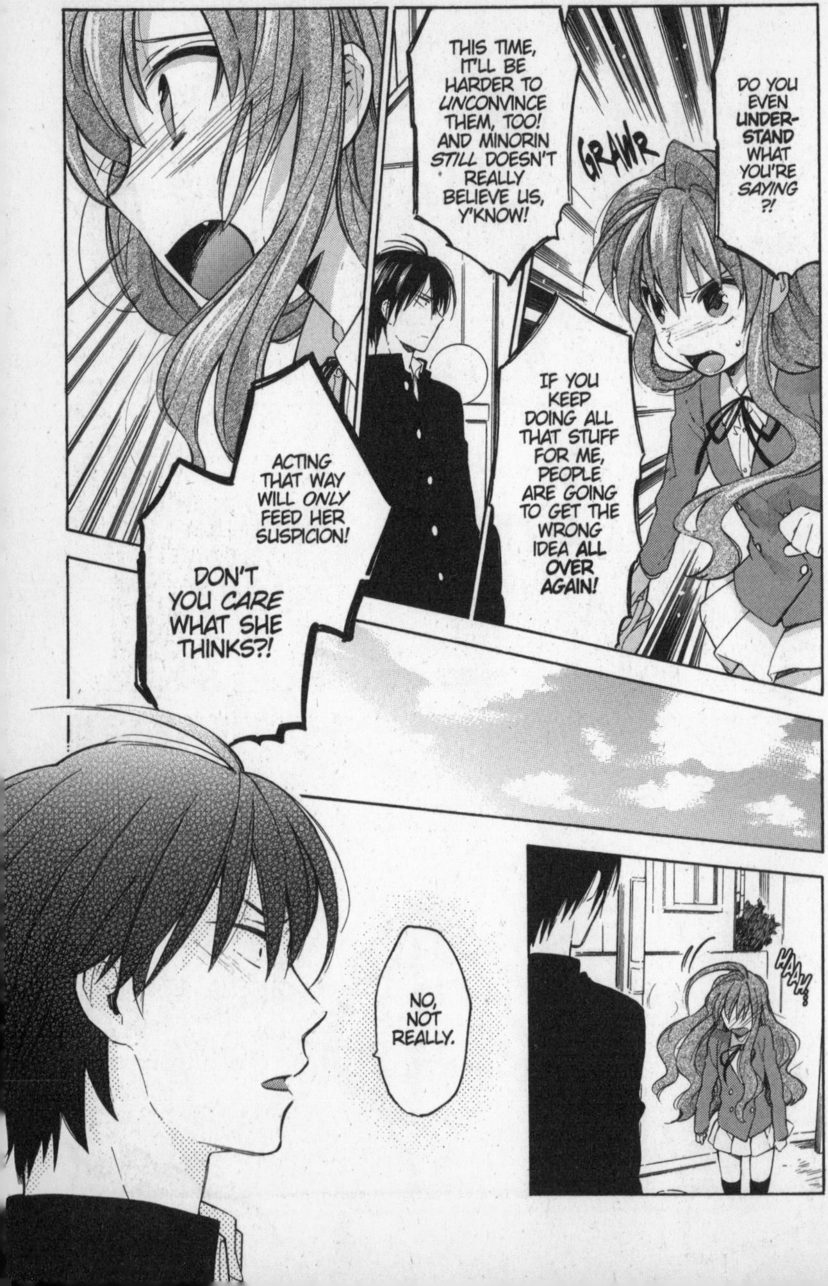
DO YOU EVEN UNDERSTAND WHAT YOU'RE SAYING ?!
GRAWR
THIS TIME, IT'LL BE HARDER TO UNCONVINCE THEM, TOO! AND MINORIN STILL DOESN'T REALLY BELIEVE US, Y'KNOW!
IF YOU KEEP DOING ALL THAT STUFF FOR ME, PEOPLE ARE GOING TO GET THE WRONG IDEA ALL OVER AGAIN!
ACTING THAT WAY WILL ONLY FEED HER SUSPICION!
DON'T YOU CARE WHAT SHE THINKS?!
HAAH
NO, NOT REALLY.

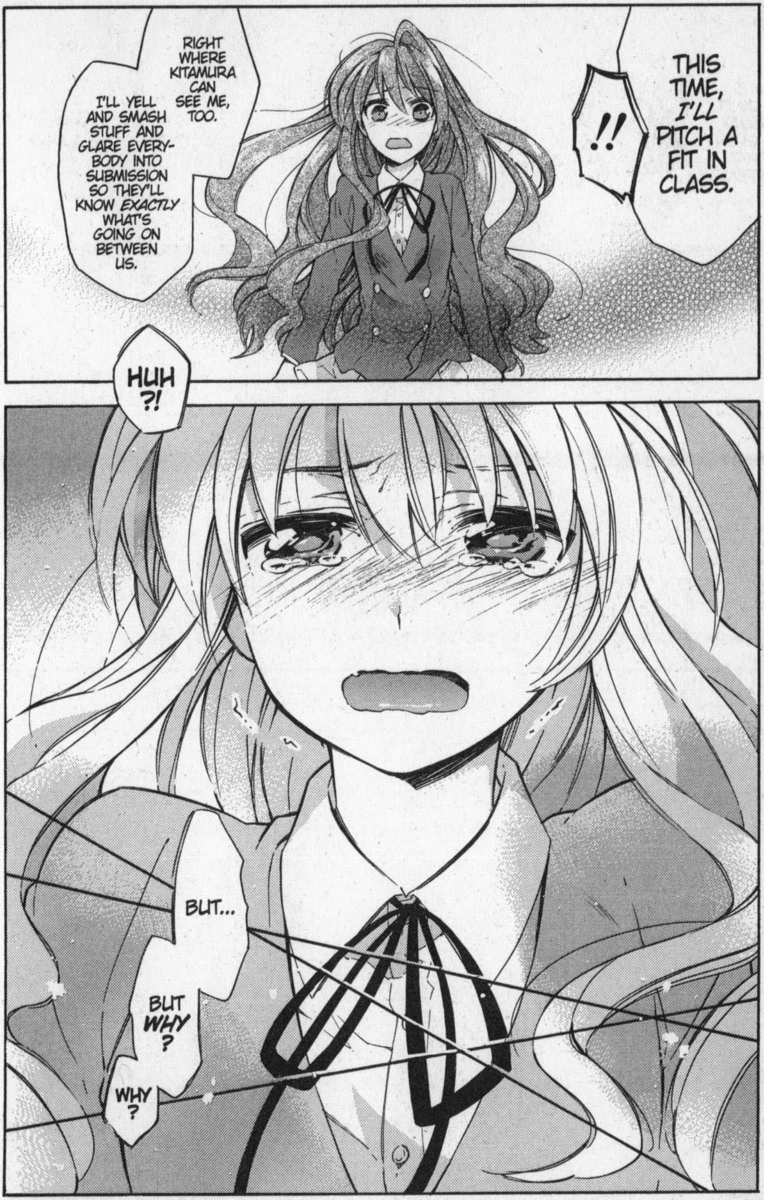
THIS TIME, I'LL PITCH A FIT IN CLASS.
!!
RIGHT WHERE KITAMURA CAN SEE ME, TOO.
I'LL YELL AND SMASH STUFF AND GLARE EVERY-BODY INTO SUBMISSION SO THEY'LL KNOW EXACTLY WHAT'S GOING ON BETWEEN US.
HUH?!
BUT...
BUT WHY?
WHY?

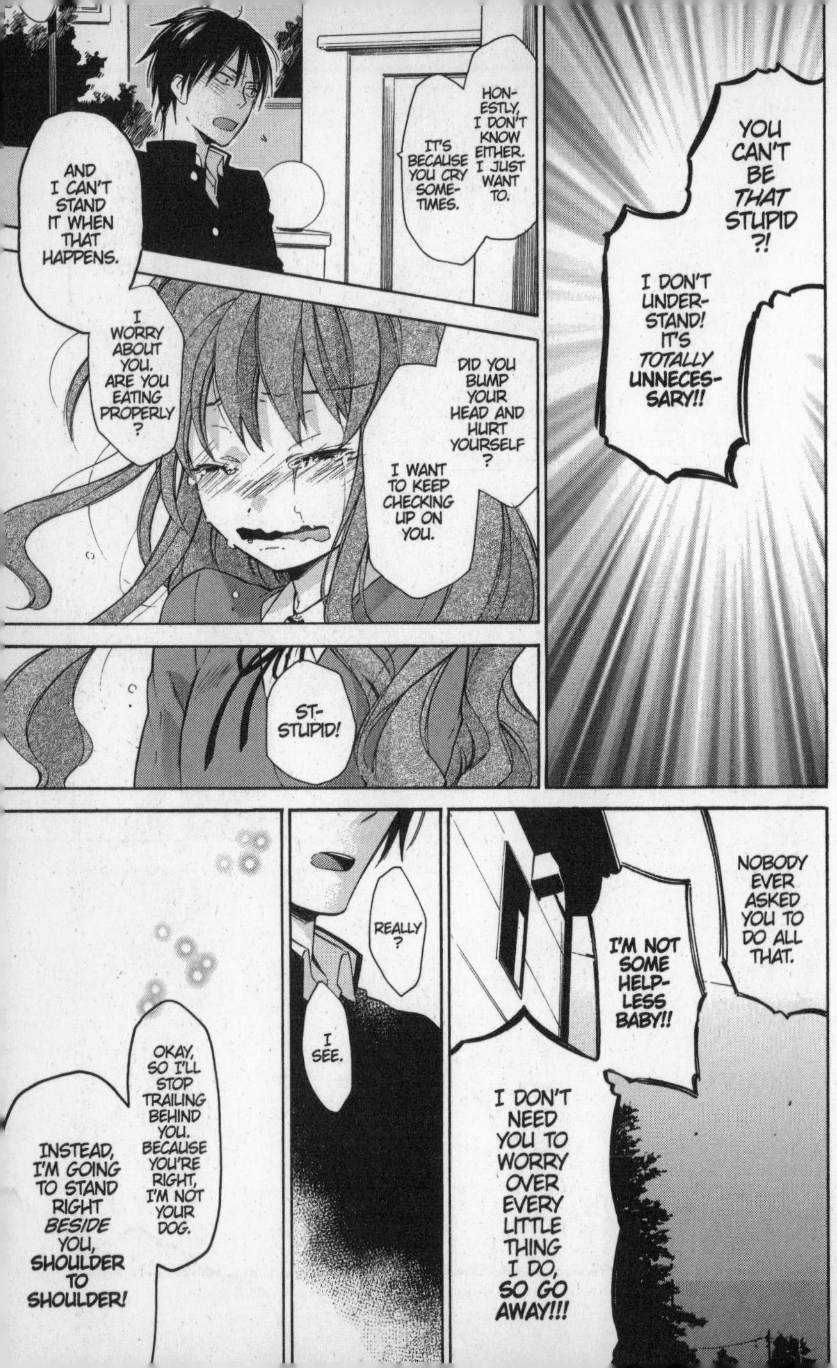

YOU CAN'T BE *THAT* STUPID?!
I DON'T UNDERSTAND! IT'S *TOTALLY* UNNECESSARY!!
HONESTLY, I DON'T KNOW EITHER. I JUST WANT TO.
IT'S BECAUSE YOU CRY SOMETIMES.
AND I CAN'T STAND IT WHEN THAT HAPPENS.
DID YOU BUMP YOUR HEAD AND HURT YOURSELF?
I WANT TO KEEP CHECKING UP ON YOU.
I WORRY ABOUT YOU. ARE YOU EATING PROPERLY?
ST-STUPID!
NOBODY EVER ASKED YOU TO DO ALL THAT.
I'M NOT SOME HELPLESS BABY!!
I DON'T NEED YOU TO WORRY OVER EVERY LITTLE THING I DO, SO GO AWAY!!!
REALLY?
I SEE.
OKAY, SO I'LL STOP TRAILING BEHIND YOU. BECAUSE YOU'RE RIGHT, I'M NOT YOUR DOG.
INSTEAD, I'M GOING TO STAND RIGHT *BESIDE* YOU, SHOULDER TO SHOULDER!

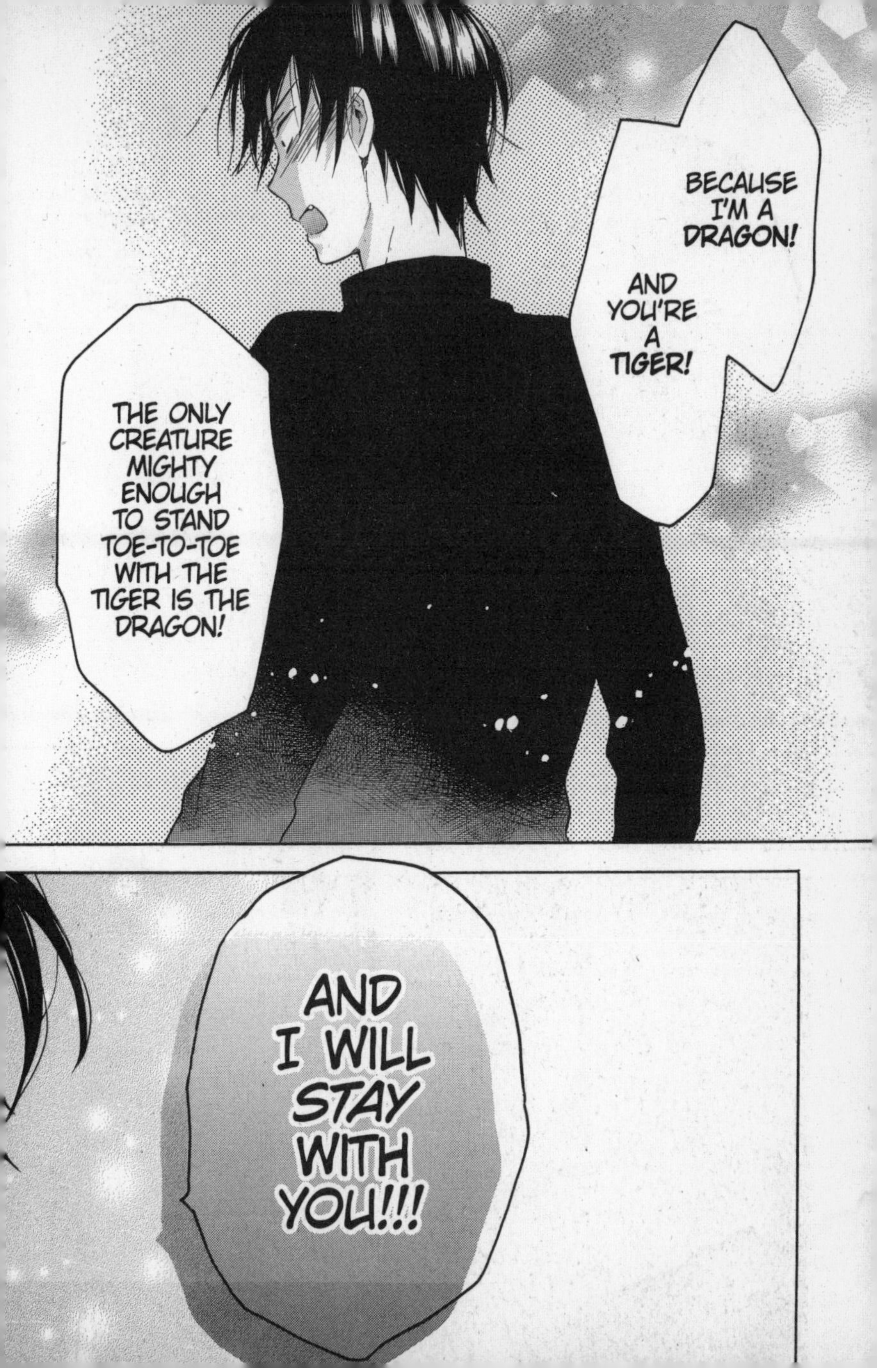
BECAUSE I'M A DRAGON!
AND YOU'RE A TIGER!
THE ONLY CREATURE MIGHTY ENOUGH TO STAND TOE-TO-TOE WITH THE TIGER IS THE DRAGON!
AND I WILL STAY WITH YOU!!!

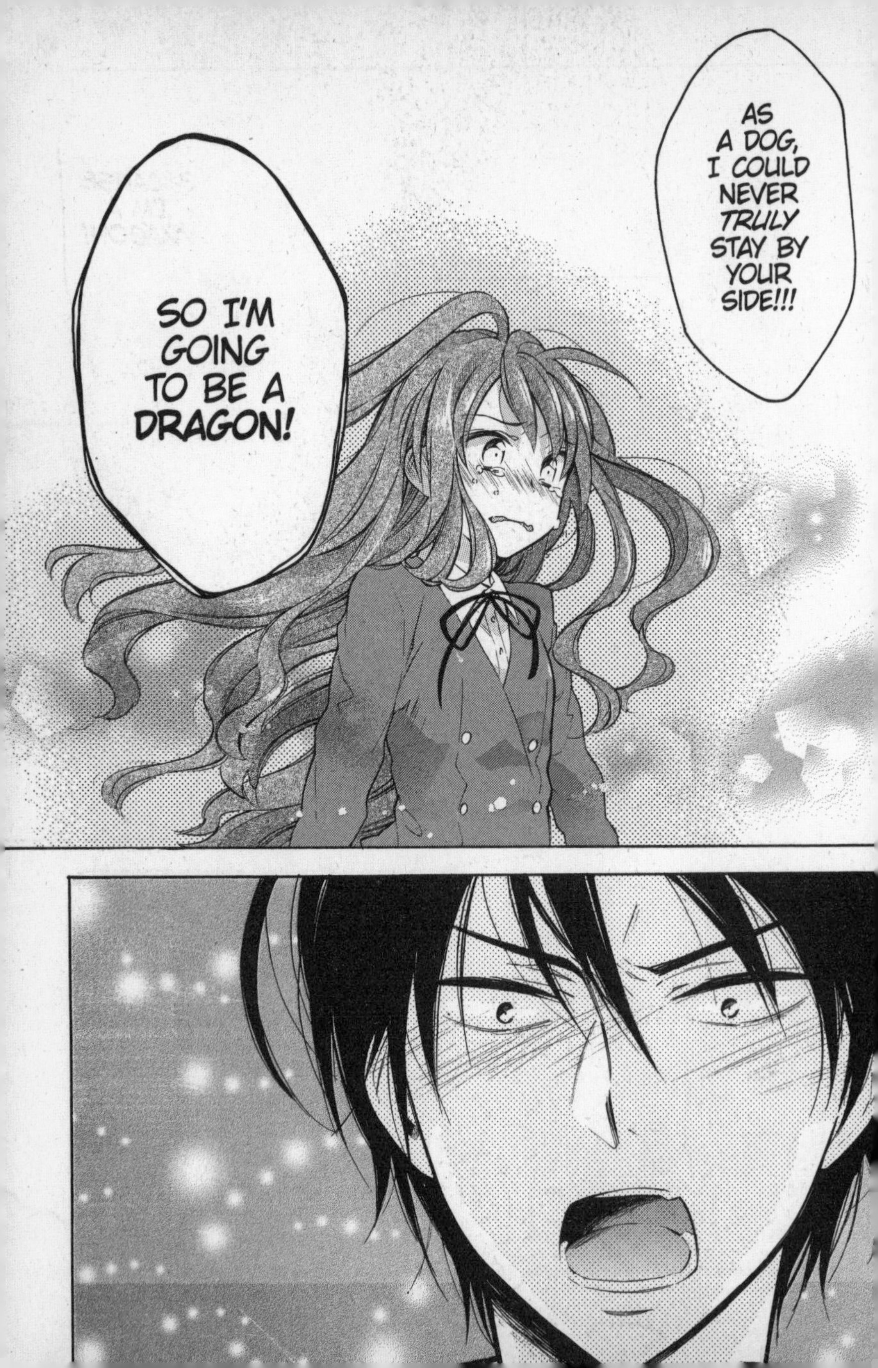
AS A DOG, I COULD NEVER TRULY STAY BY YOUR SIDE!!!
SO I'M GOING TO BE A DRAGON!

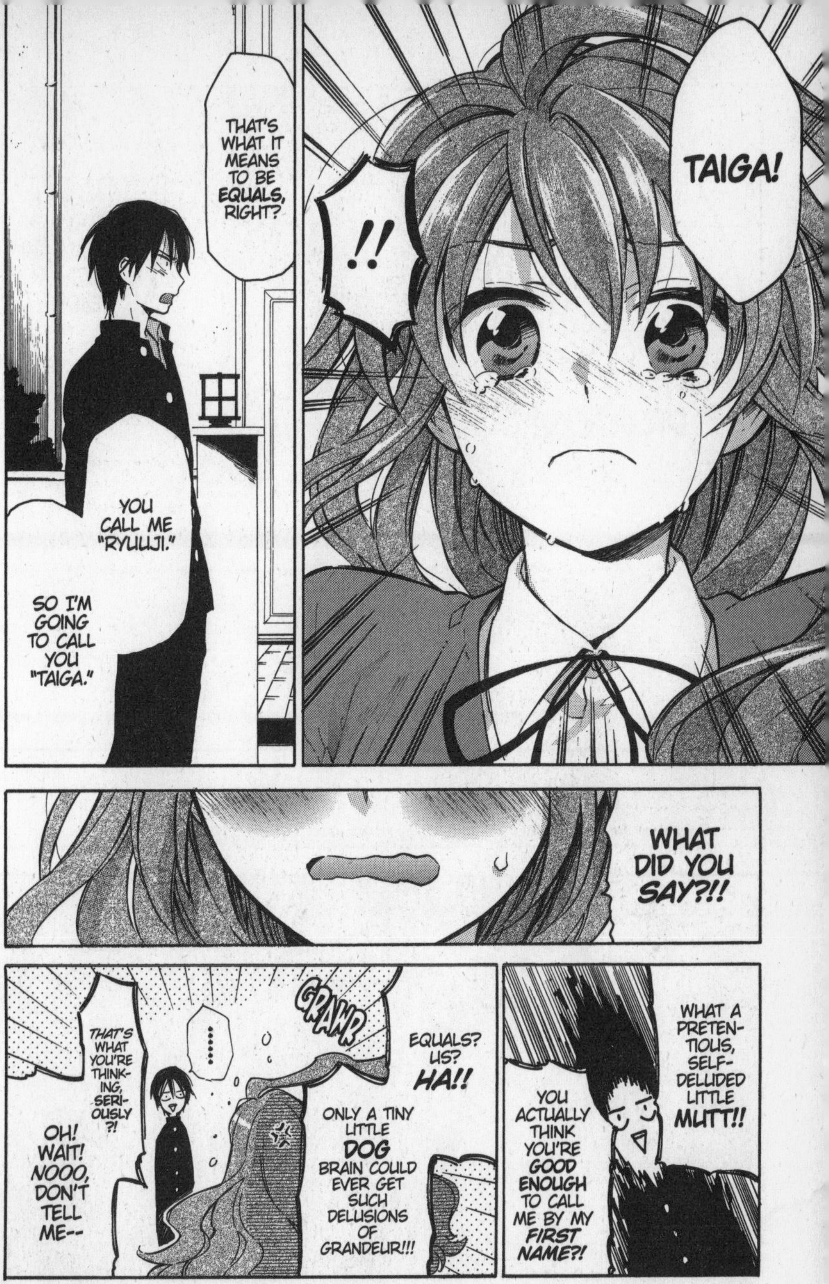
TAIGA!
!!
THAT'S WHAT IT MEANS TO BE EQUALS, RIGHT?
YOU CALL ME "RYUUJI."
SO I'M GOING TO CALL YOU "TAIGA."
WHAT DID YOU SAY?!!
WHAT A PRETEN-TIOUS, SELF-DELUDED LITTLE MUTT!!
YOU ACTUALLY THINK YOU'RE GOOD ENOUGH TO CALL ME BY MY FIRST NAME?!
EQUALS? US? HA!!
GRAWR
ONLY A TINY LITTLE DOG BRAIN COULD EVER GET SUCH DELUSIONS OF GRANDEUR!!!
......
THAT'S WHAT YOU'RE THINK-ING, SERI-OUSLY?!
OH! WAIT! NOOO, DON'T TELL ME--

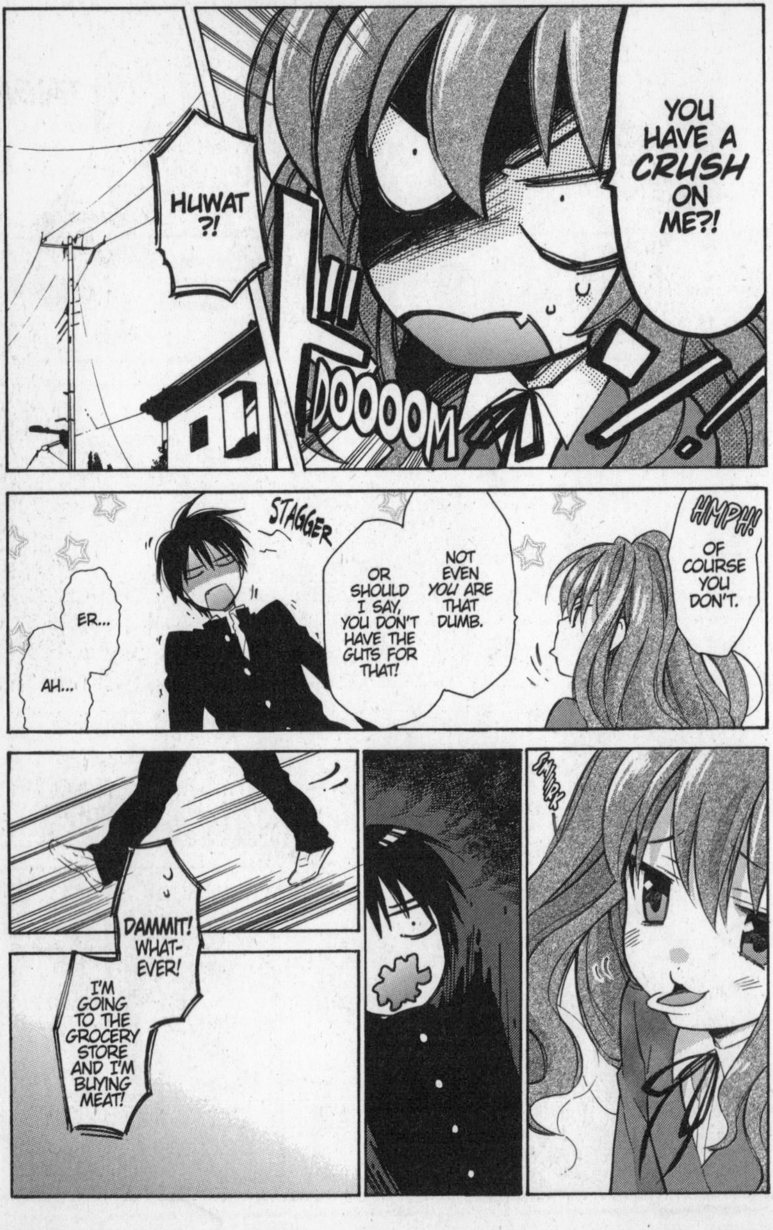
YOU HAVE A CRUSH ON ME?!
HUWAT?!
DOOOOM
HMPH!
OF COURSE YOU DON'T.
NOT EVEN YOU ARE THAT DUMB.
OR SHOULD I SAY, YOU DON'T HAVE THE GUTS FOR THAT!
STAGGER
ER...
AH...
SMIRK
DAMMIT! WHAT-EVER!
I'M GOING TO THE GROCERY STORE AND I'M BUYING MEAT!

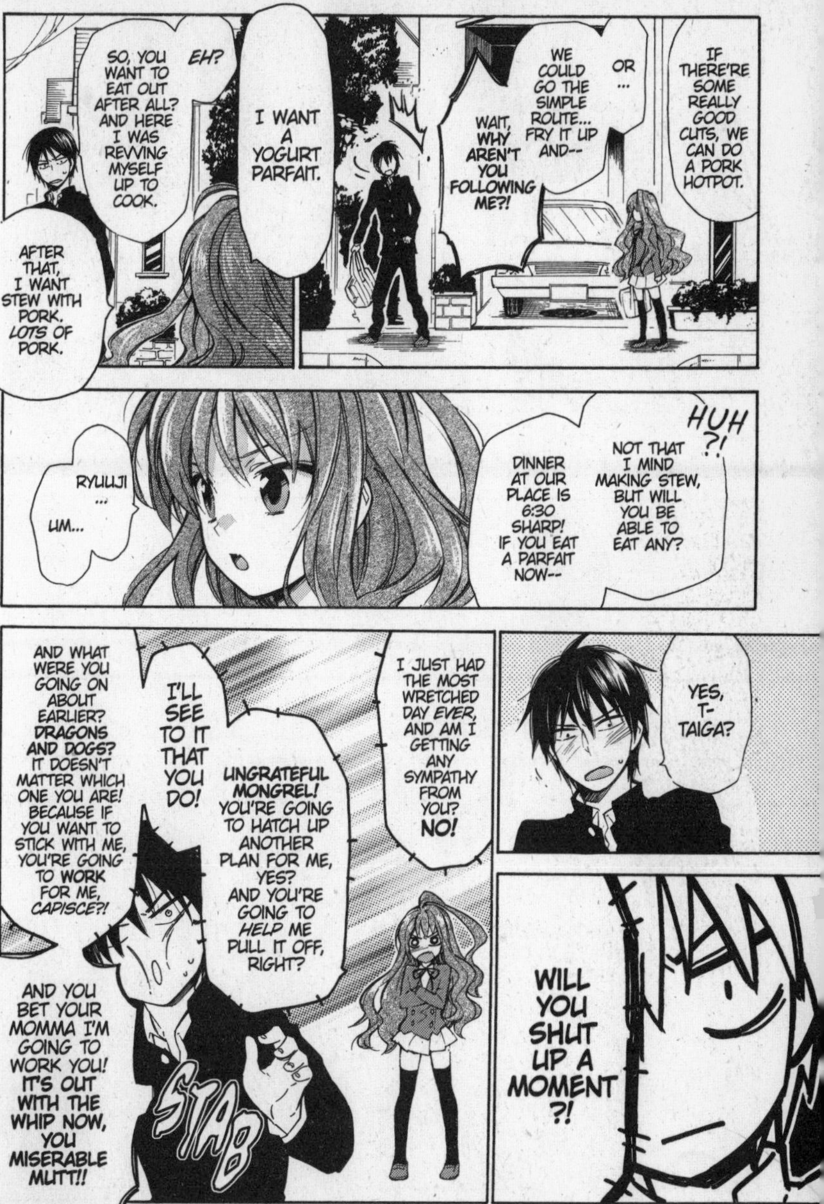
IF THERE'RE SOME REALLY GOOD CUTS, WE CAN DO A PORK HOTPOT.
OR ... WE COULD GO THE SIMPLE ROUTE... FRY IT UP AND--
WAIT, WHY AREN'T YOU FOLLOWING ME?!
I WANT A YOGURT PARFAIT.
EH?
SO, YOU WANT TO EAT OUT AFTER ALL? AND HERE I WAS REVVING MYSELF UP TO COOK.
AFTER THAT, I WANT STEW WITH PORK. *LOTS OF PORK.*
HUH?!
NOT THAT I MIND MAKING STEW, BUT WILL YOU BE ABLE TO EAT ANY?
DINNER AT OUR PLACE IS 6:30 SHARP! IF YOU EAT A PARFAIT NOW--
RYUUJI ... UM...
YES, T-TAIGA?
WILL YOU SHUT UP A MOMENT?!
I JUST HAD THE MOST WRETCHED DAY *EVER*, AND AM I GETTING ANY SYMPATHY FROM YOU? **NO!**
UNGRATEFUL MONGREL! YOU'RE GOING TO HATCH UP ANOTHER PLAN FOR ME, YES? AND YOU'RE GOING TO *HELP ME* PULL IT OFF, RIGHT?
I'LL SEE TO IT THAT YOU DO!
AND WHAT WERE YOU GOING ON ABOUT EARLIER? **DRAGONS AND DOGS?** IT DOESN'T MATTER WHICH ONE YOU ARE! BECAUSE IF YOU WANT TO STICK WITH ME, YOU'RE GOING TO **WORK** FOR ME, *CAPISCE?!*
STAB
AND YOU BET YOUR MOMMA I'M GOING TO WORK YOU! IT'S OUT WITH THE WHIP NOW, YOU MISERABLE MUTT!!

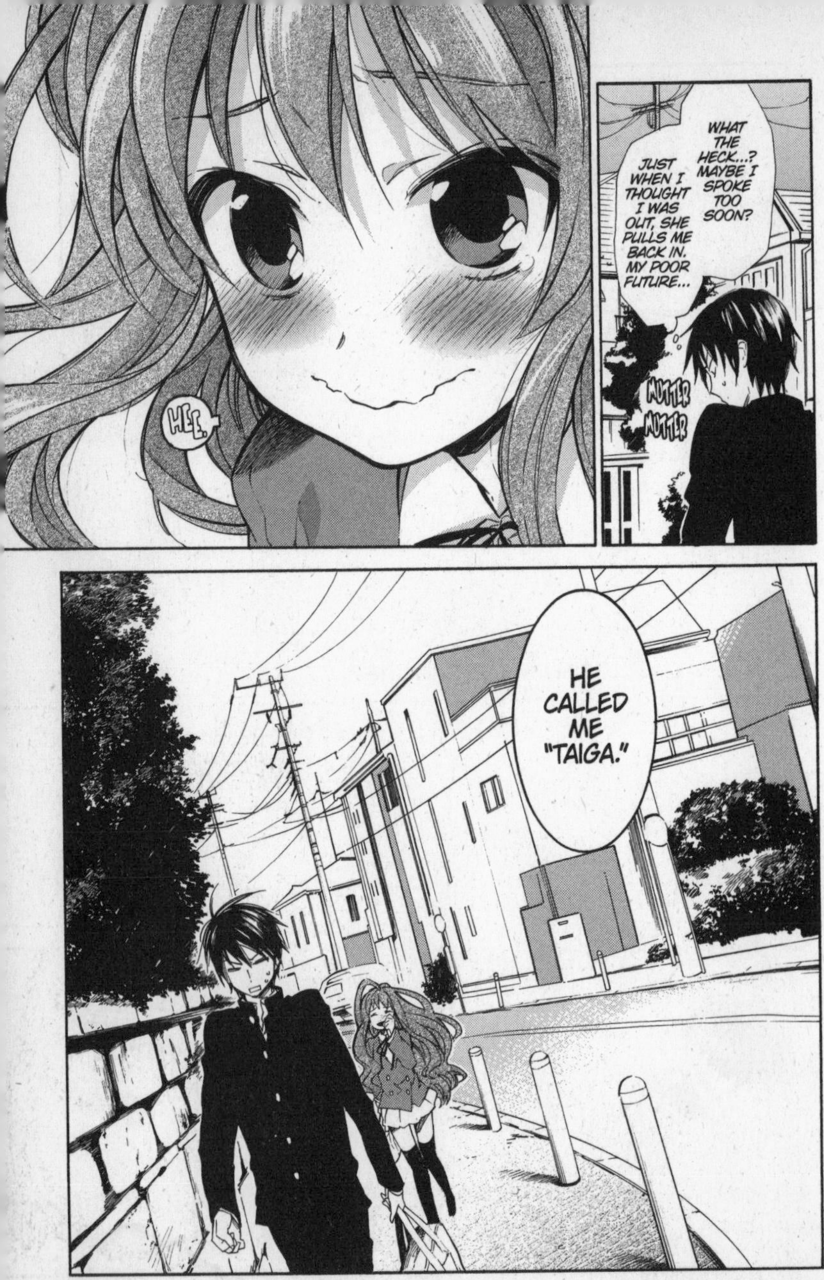
WHAT THE HECK...? MAYBE I SPOKE TOO SOON?
JUST WHEN I THOUGHT I WAS OUT, SHE PULLS ME BACK IN. MY POOR FUTURE...
MUTTER MUTTER
HEE.
HE CALLED ME "TAIGA."

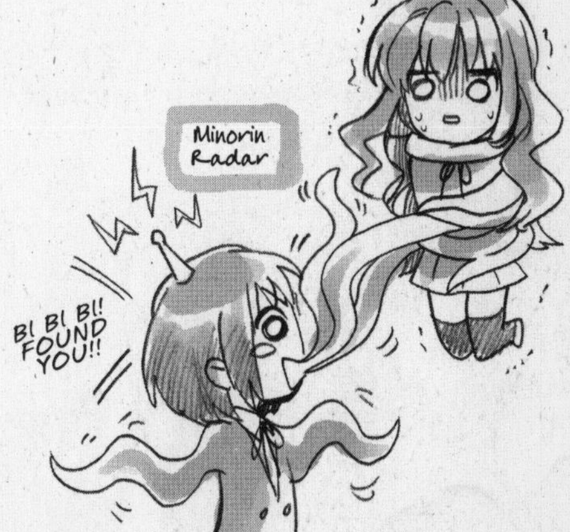
Minorin Radar
BI BI BI! FOUND YOU!!

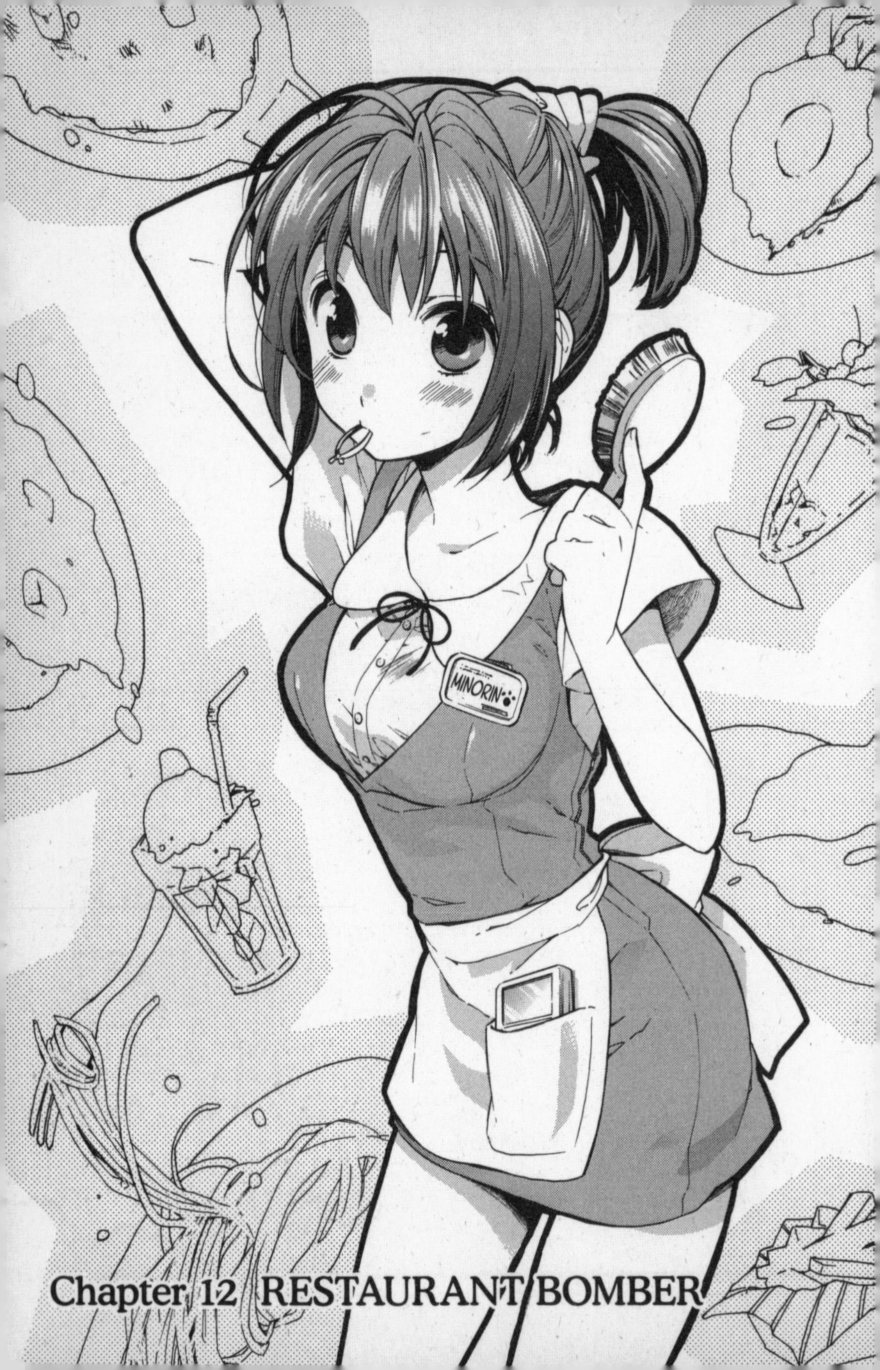
MINORIN

Chapter 12 RESTAURANT BOMBER

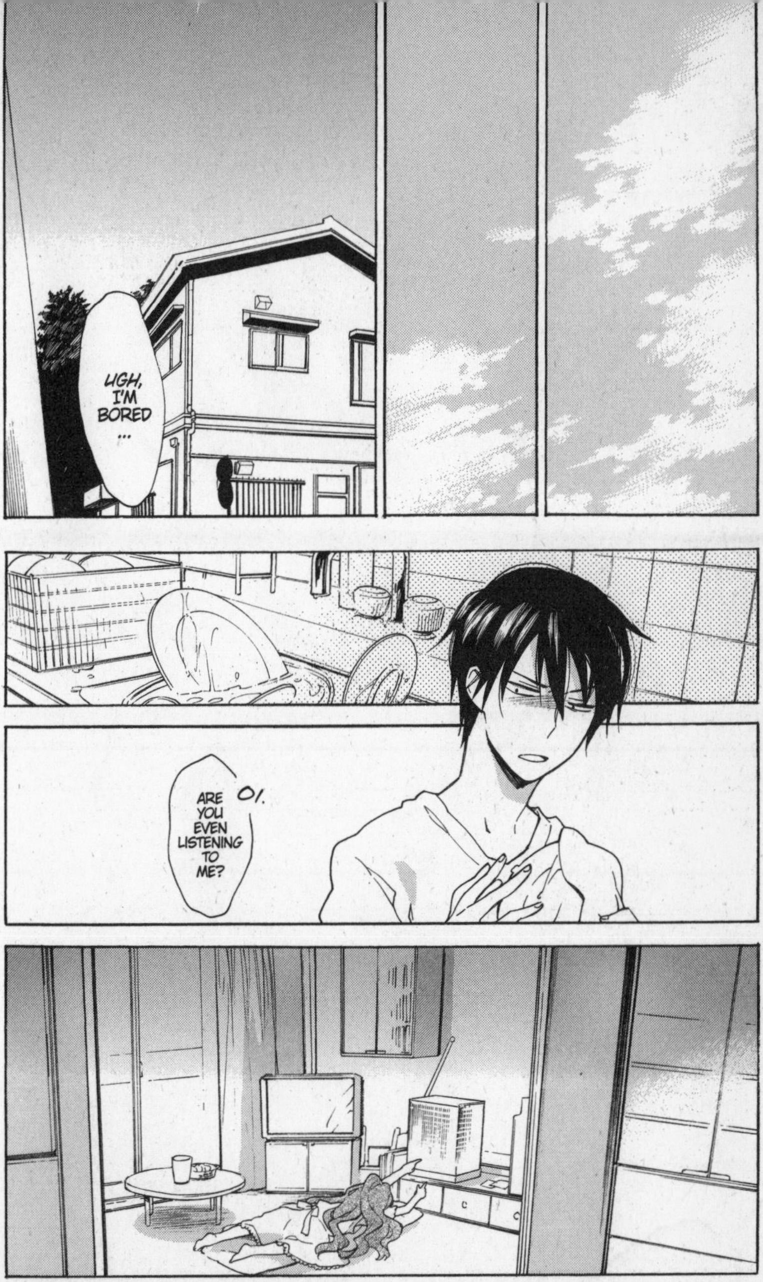
UGH, I'M BORED ...
OI.
ARE YOU EVEN LISTENING TO ME?

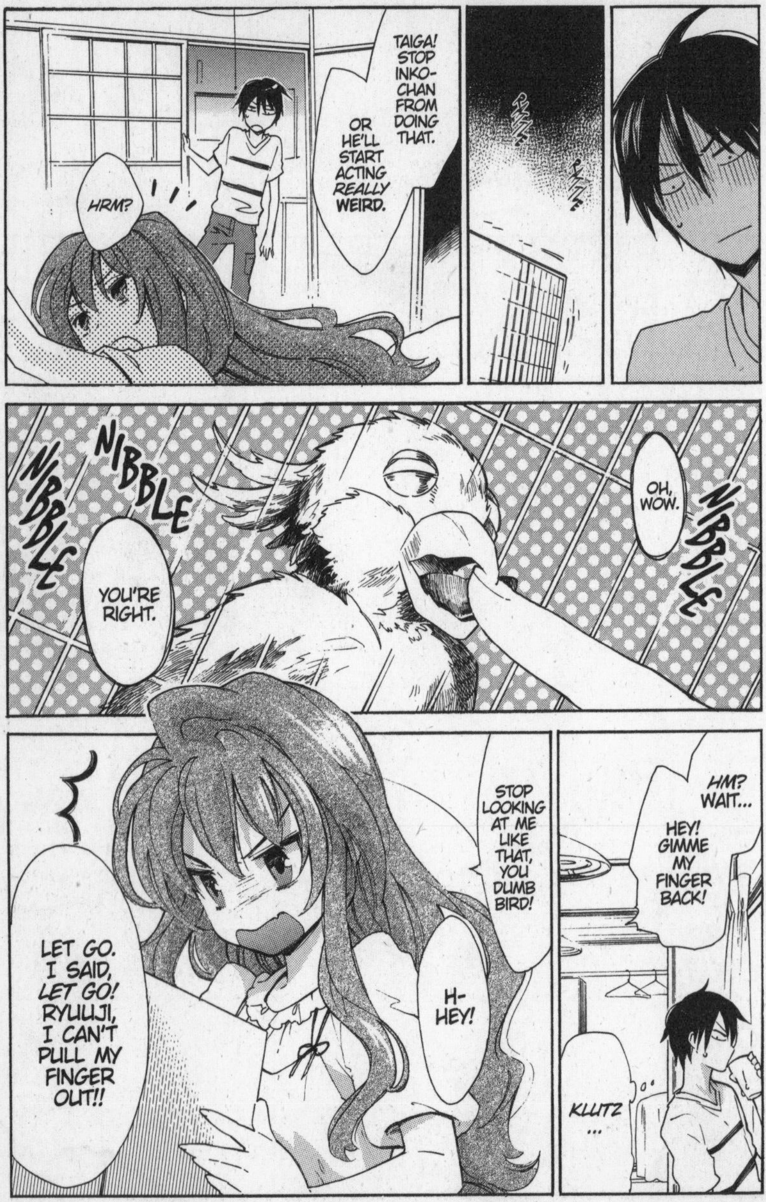
TAIGA! STOP INKO-CHAN FROM DOING THAT.
OR HE'LL START ACTING *REALLY* WEIRD.
HRM?
OH, WOW.
NIBBLE
NIBBLE
NIBBLE
YOU'RE RIGHT.
HM? WAIT...
HEY! GIMME MY FINGER BACK!
KLUTZ ...
STOP LOOKING AT ME LIKE THAT, YOU DUMB BIRD!
H-HEY!
LET GO. I SAID, *LET GO!* RYUUJI, I CAN'T PULL MY FINGER OUT!!

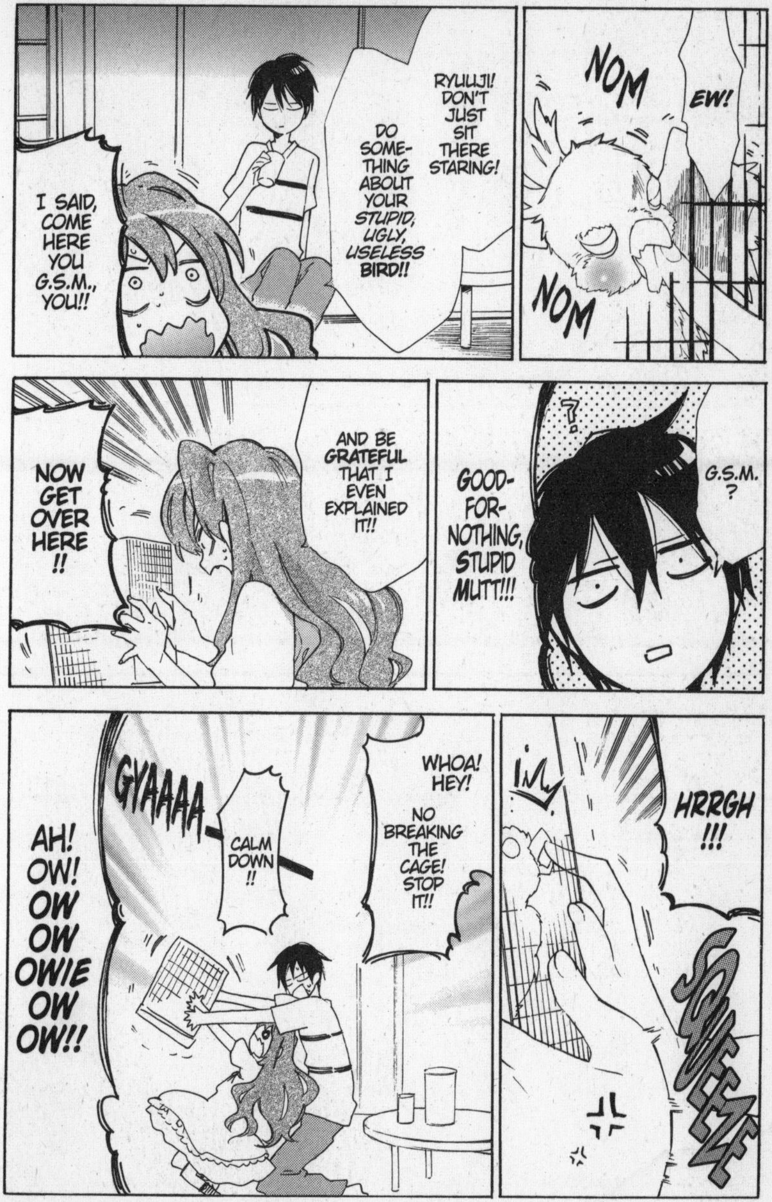
NOM
EW!
NOM
RYUUJI! DON'T JUST SIT THERE STARING!
DO SOME-THING ABOUT YOUR STUPID, UGLY, USELESS BIRD!!
I SAID, COME HERE YOU G.S.M., YOU!!
?!
G.S.M. ?
GOOD-FOR-NOTHING, STUPID MUTT!!!
AND BE GRATEFUL THAT I EVEN EXPLAINED IT!!
NOW GET OVER HERE !!
HRRGH !!!
SQUEEEZE
WHOA! HEY!
NO BREAKING THE CAGE! STOP IT!!
CALM DOWN !!
GYAAAA
AH! OW! OW OW OWIE OW OW!!

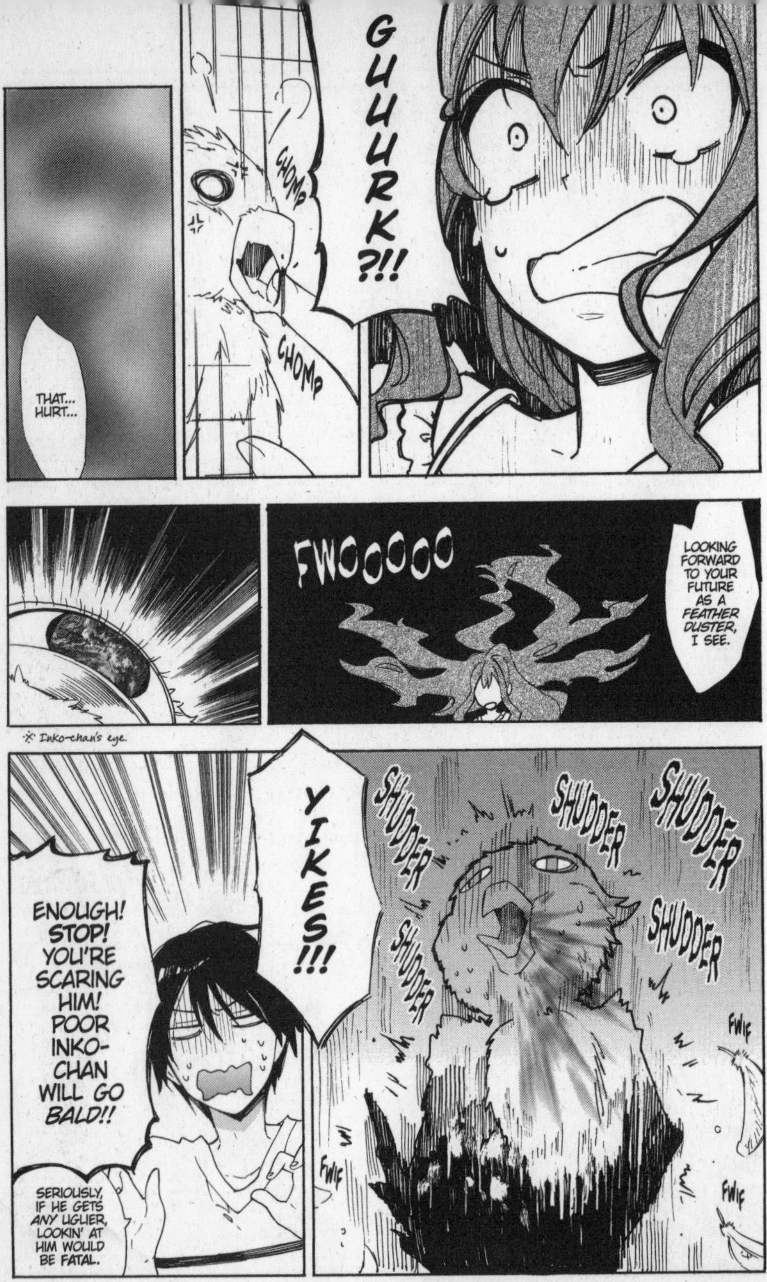
GUUURK?!!
CHOMP
CHOMP
THAT... HURT...
FWOOOOO
LOOKING FORWARD TO YOUR FUTURE AS A FEATHER DUSTER, I SEE.
※ Inko-chan's eye.
SHUDDER
SHUDDER
SHUDDER
SHUDDER
SHUDDER
FWIP
FWIP
FWIP
YIKES!!!
ENOUGH! STOP! YOU'RE SCARING HIM! POOR INKO-CHAN WILL GO BALD!!
SERIOUSLY, IF HE GETS ANY UGLIER, LOOKIN' AT HIM WOULD BE FATAL.

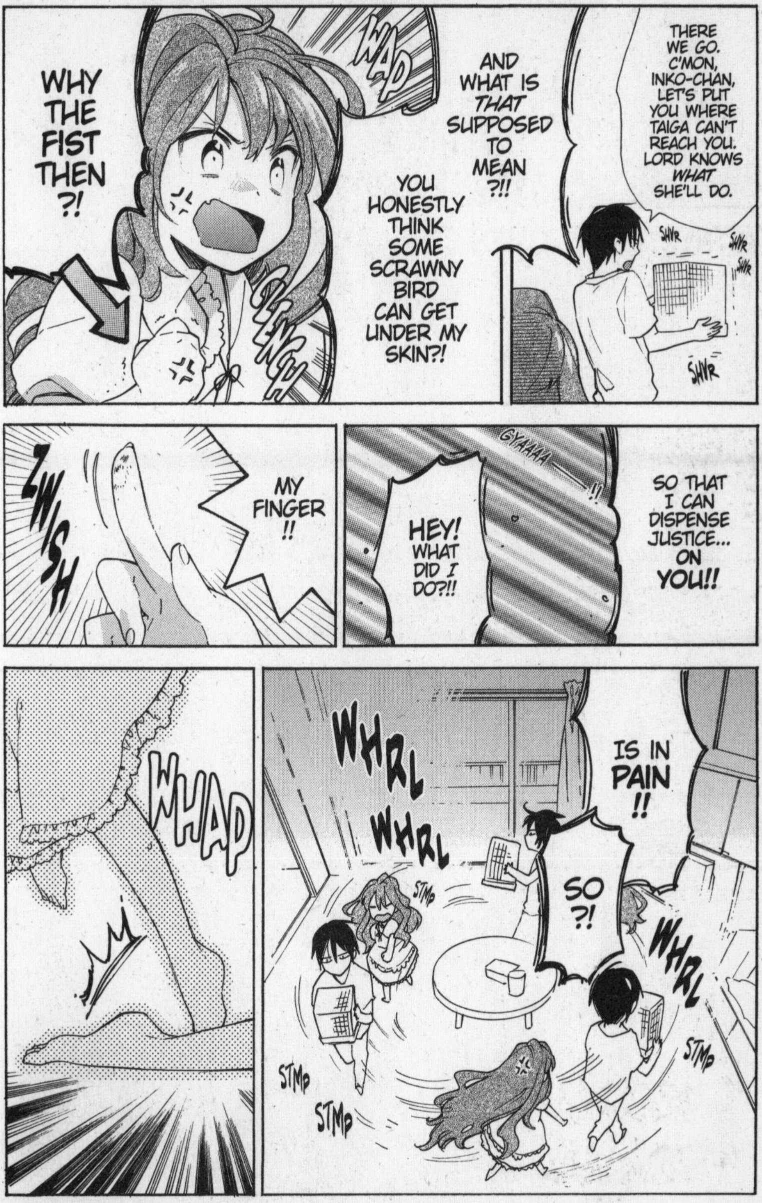
THERE WE GO. C'MON, INKO-CHAN, LET'S PUT YOU WHERE TAIGA CAN'T REACH YOU. LORD KNOWS WHAT SHE'LL DO.
SHVR
SHVR
SHVR
SHVR
AND WHAT IS THAT SUPPOSED TO MEAN ?!!
WAP
YOU HONESTLY THINK SOME SCRAWNY BIRD CAN GET UNDER MY SKIN?!
CLENCH
WHY THE FIST THEN ?!
SO THAT I CAN DISPENSE JUSTICE... ON YOU!!
GYAAAA
!!
HEY! WHAT DID I DO?!!
MY FINGER !!
ZWISH
IS IN PAIN !!
SO ?!
WHRL
WHRL
STMP
WHRL
STMP
STMP
STMP
WHAP

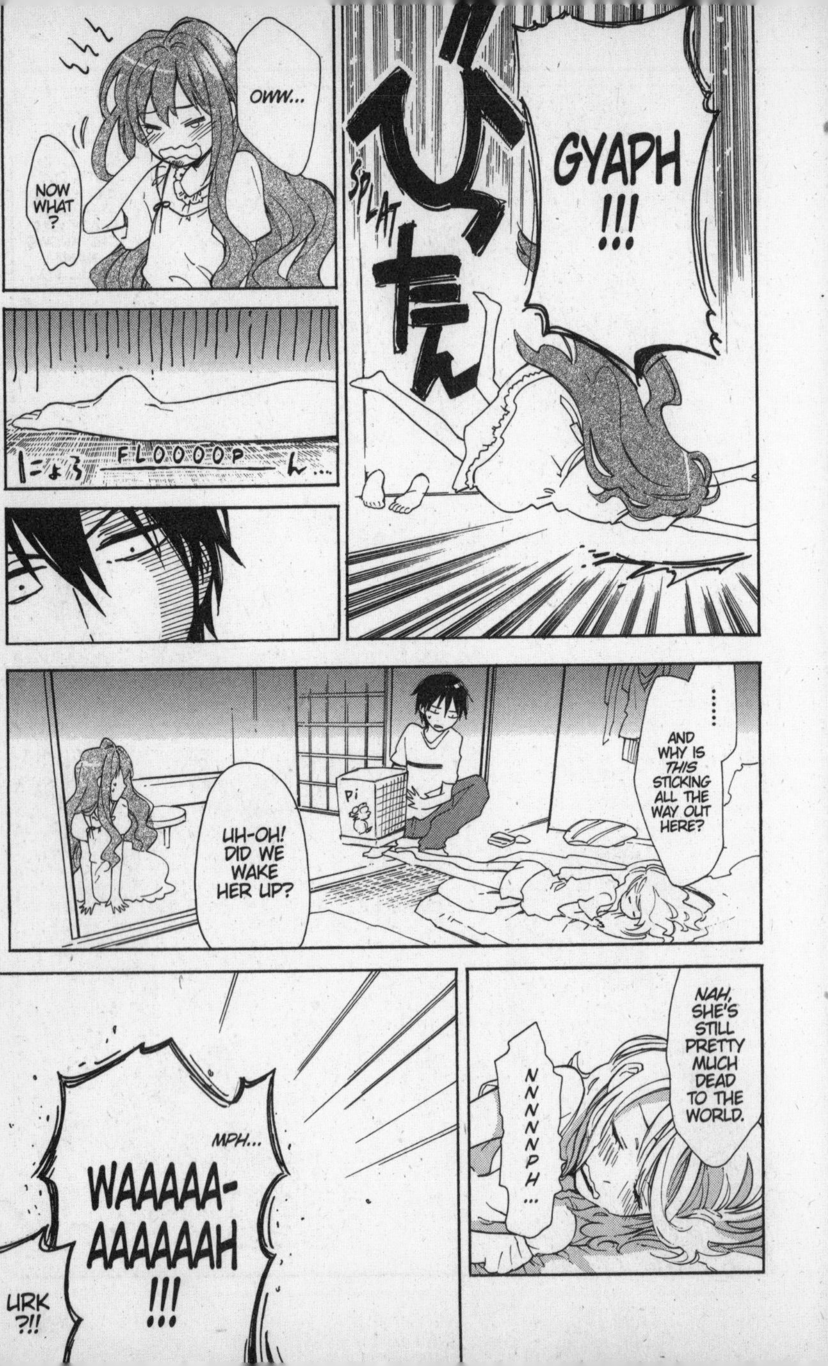

GYAPH !!!
SPLAT
OWW...
NOW WHAT?
にょろ FLOOOOP ん...
......
AND WHY IS *THIS* STICKING ALL THE WAY OUT HERE?
UH-OH! DID WE WAKE HER UP?
NAH, SHE'S STILL PRETTY MUCH DEAD TO THE WORLD.
NNNNNPH...
MPH...
WAAAAA-AAAAAAH !!!
URK ?!!

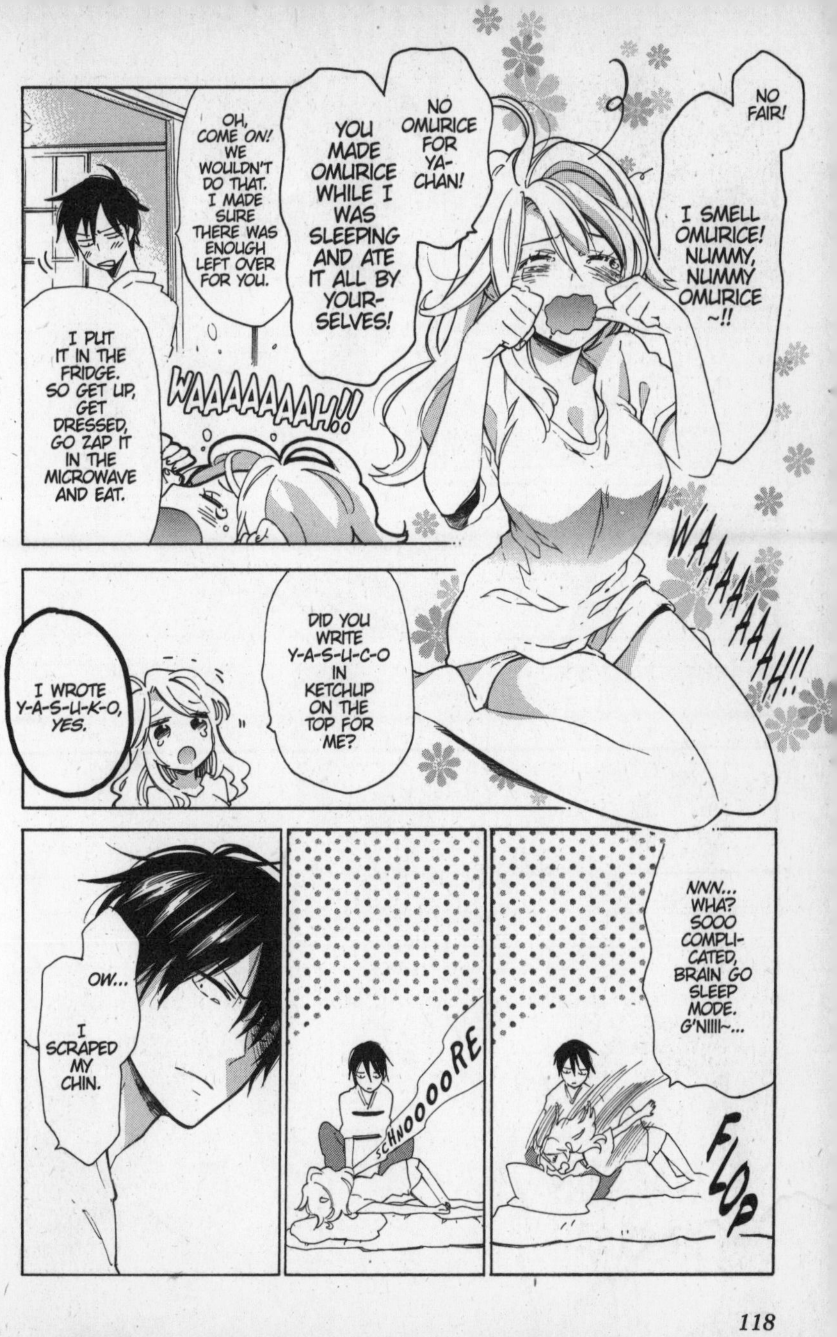
NO FAIR!
I SMELL OMURICE! NUMMY, NUMMY OMURICE ~!!
NO OMURICE FOR YA-CHAN!
YOU MADE OMURICE WHILE I WAS SLEEPING AND ATE IT ALL BY YOUR-SELVES!
WAAAAAAAAH!!
OH, COME ON! WE WOULDN'T DO THAT. I MADE SURE THERE WAS ENOUGH LEFT OVER FOR YOU.
I PUT IT IN THE FRIDGE. SO GET UP, GET DRESSED, GO ZAP IT IN THE MICROWAVE AND EAT.
WAAAAAAAH!!
DID YOU WRITE Y-A-S-U-C-O IN KETCHUP ON THE TOP FOR ME?
I WROTE Y-A-S-U-K-O, YES.
NNN... WHA? SOOO COMPLI-CATED, BRAIN GO SLEEP MODE. G'NIIII~...
FLOP
SCHNOOOOORE
OW...
I SCRAPED MY CHIN.

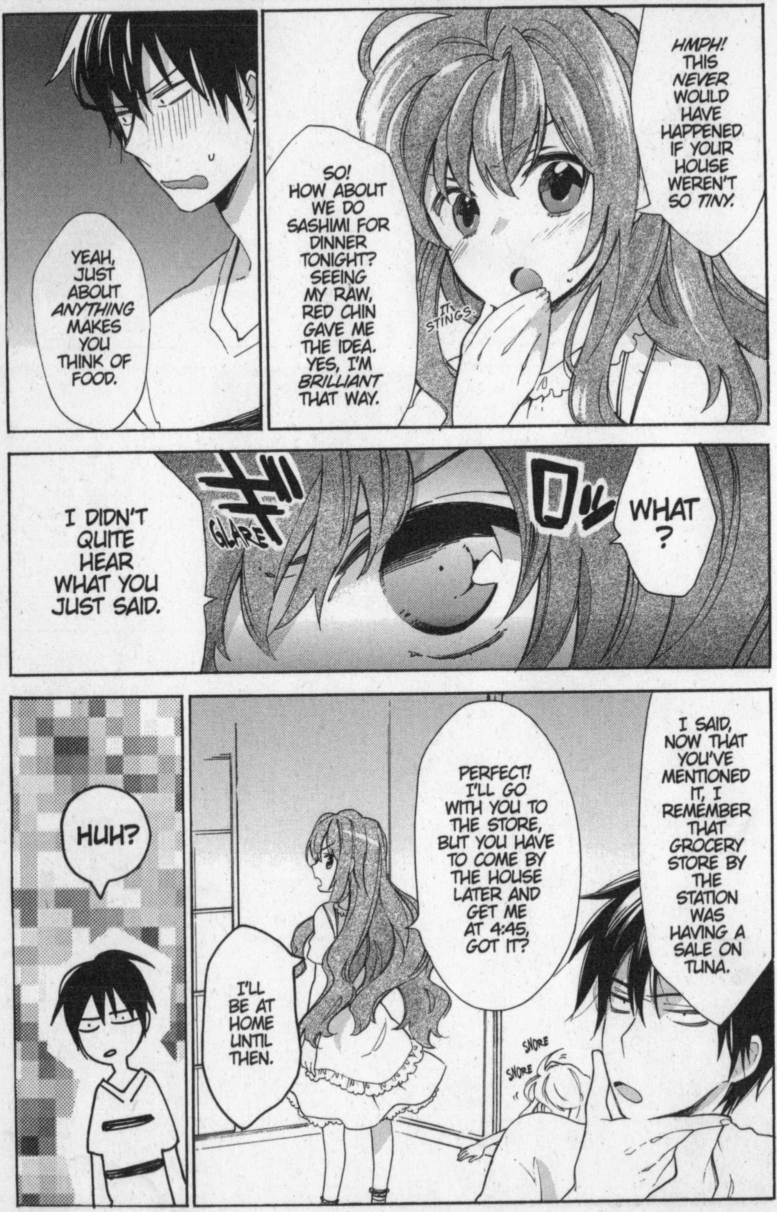
HMPH! THIS NEVER WOULD HAVE HAPPENED IF YOUR HOUSE WEREN'T SO TINY.
IT STINGS
SO! HOW ABOUT WE DO SASHIMI FOR DINNER TONIGHT? SEEING MY RAW, RED CHIN GAVE ME THE IDEA. YES, I'M BRILLIANT THAT WAY.
YEAH, JUST ABOUT ANYTHING MAKES YOU THINK OF FOOD.
WHAT?
GLARE
I DIDN'T QUITE HEAR WHAT YOU JUST SAID.
I SAID, NOW THAT YOU'VE MENTIONED IT, I REMEMBER THAT GROCERY STORE BY THE STATION WAS HAVING A SALE ON TUNA.
PERFECT! I'LL GO WITH YOU TO THE STORE, BUT YOU HAVE TO COME BY THE HOUSE LATER AND GET ME AT 4:45, GOT IT?
SNORE
SNORE
I'LL BE AT HOME UNTIL THEN.
HUH?

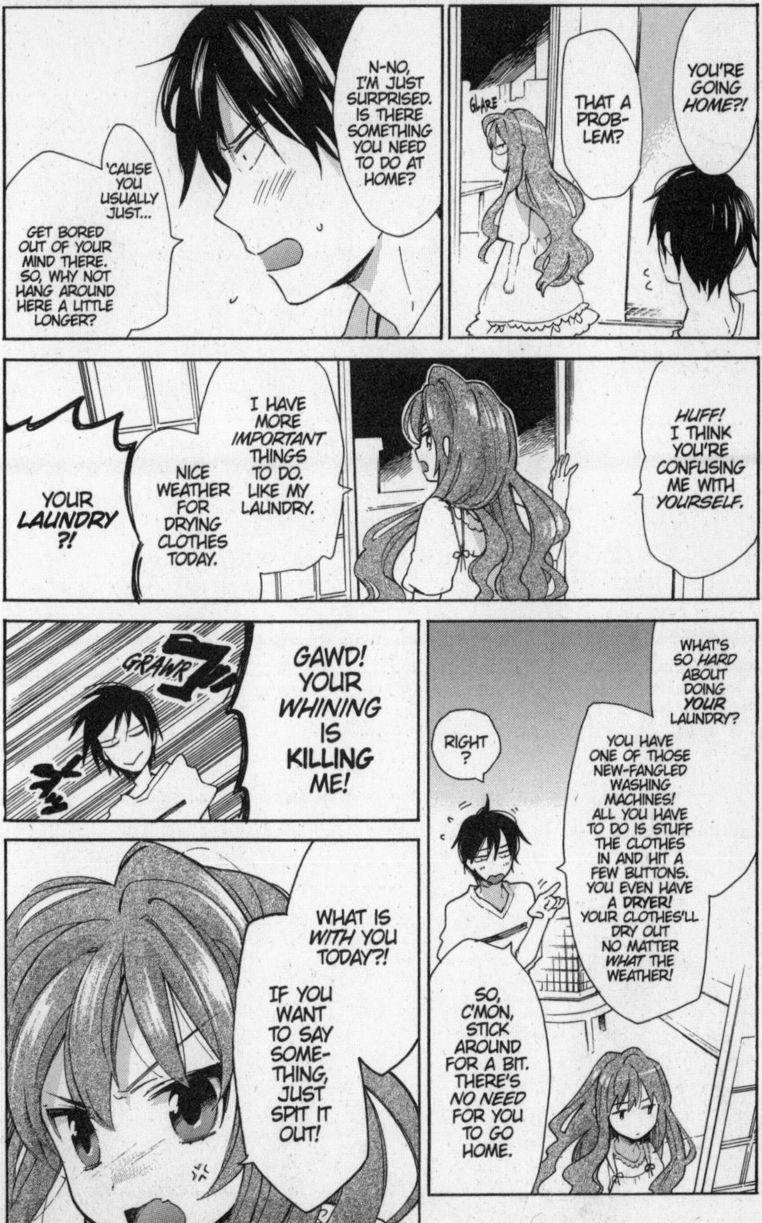
YOU'RE GOING *HOME*?!
THAT A PROB-LEM?
GLARE
N-NO, I'M JUST SURPRISED. IS THERE SOMETHING YOU NEED TO DO AT HOME?
'CAUSE YOU USUALLY JUST...
GET BORED OUT OF YOUR MIND THERE. SO, WHY NOT HANG AROUND HERE A LITTLE LONGER?
HUFF! I THINK YOU'RE CONFUSING ME WITH *YOURSELF*.
I HAVE MORE *IMPORTANT* THINGS TO DO. LIKE MY LAUNDRY.
NICE WEATHER FOR DRYING CLOTHES TODAY.
YOUR *LAUNDRY* ?!
WHAT'S SO *HARD* ABOUT DOING *YOUR* LAUNDRY?
YOU HAVE ONE OF THOSE NEW-FANGLED WASHING MACHINES! ALL YOU HAVE TO DO IS STUFF THE CLOTHES IN AND HIT A FEW BUTTONS. YOU EVEN HAVE A **DRYER!** YOUR CLOTHES'LL DRY OUT NO MATTER *WHAT* THE WEATHER!
RIGHT ?
SO, C'MON, STICK AROUND FOR A BIT. THERE'S *NO NEED* FOR YOU TO GO HOME.
GRAWR
GAWD! YOUR *WHINING* IS **KILLING** ME!
WHAT IS *WITH* YOU TODAY?!
IF YOU WANT TO SAY SOME-THING, JUST SPIT IT OUT!

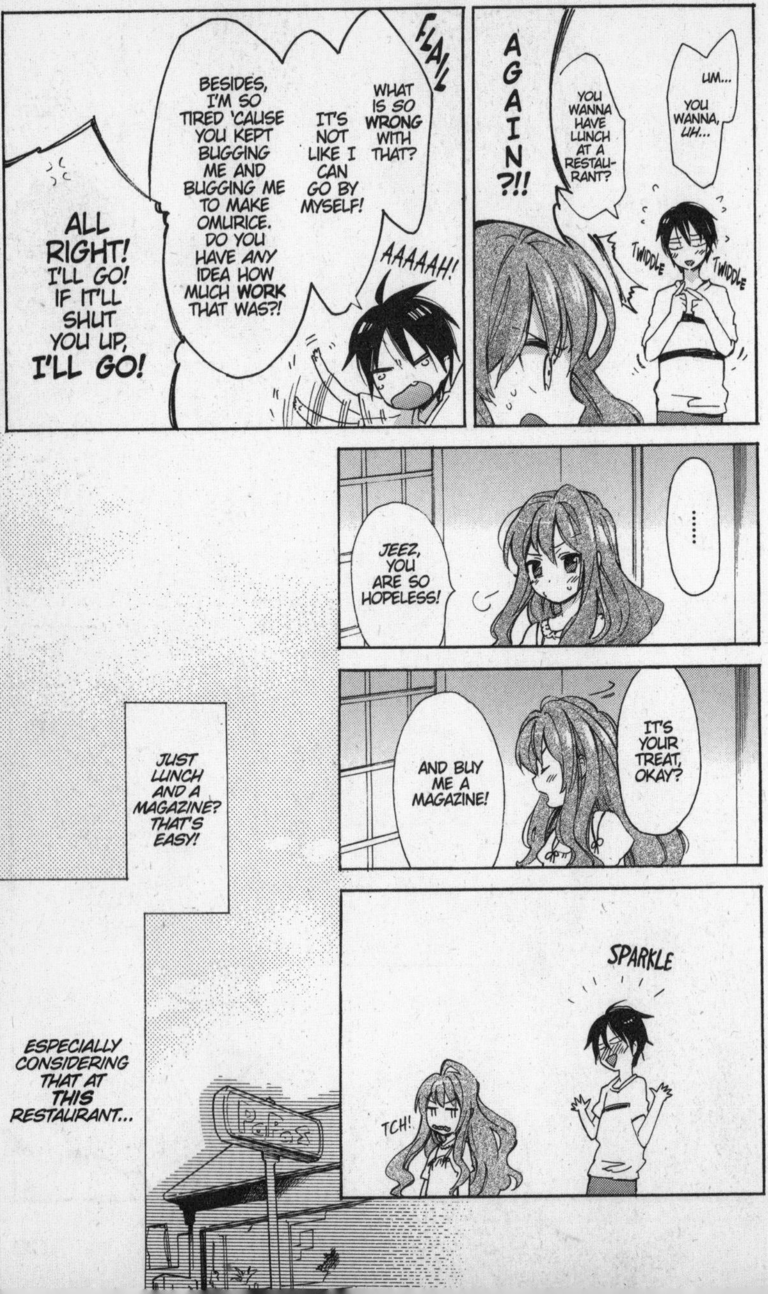
UM...
YOU WANNA, UH...
YOU WANNA HAVE LUNCH AT A RESTAURANT?
AGAIN?!!
TWIDDLE
TWIDDLE
FLAIL
WHAT IS SO WRONG WITH THAT?
IT'S NOT LIKE I CAN GO BY MYSELF!
BESIDES, I'M SO TIRED 'CAUSE YOU KEPT BUGGING ME AND BUGGING ME TO MAKE OMURICE. DO YOU HAVE ANY IDEA HOW MUCH WORK THAT WAS?!
AAAAAH!
ALL RIGHT! I'LL GO! IF IT'LL SHUT YOU UP, I'LL GO!
......
JEEZ, YOU ARE SO HOPELESS!
IT'S YOUR TREAT, OKAY?
AND BUY ME A MAGAZINE!
SPARKLE
TCH!
JUST LUNCH AND A MAGAZINE? THAT'S EASY!
ESPECIALLY CONSIDERING THAT AT THIS RESTAURANT...

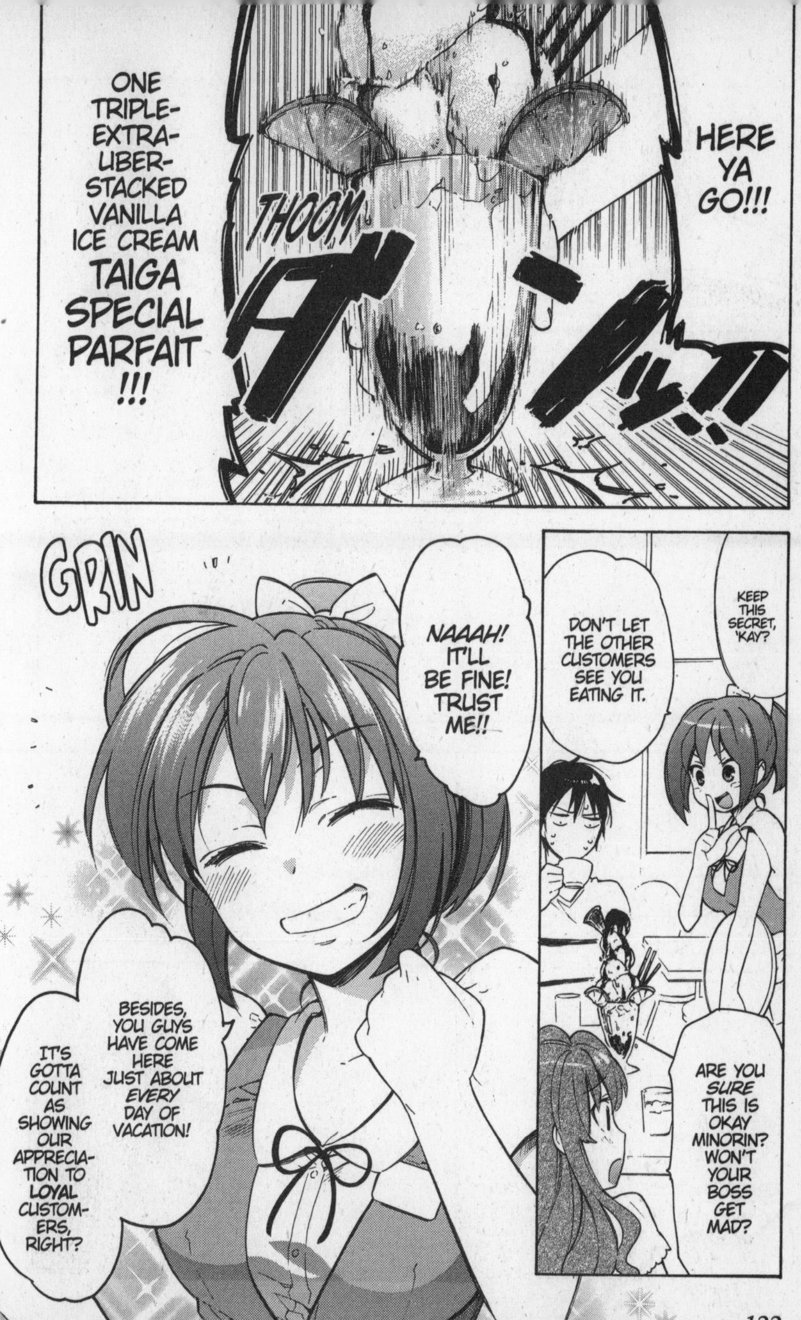
HERE YA GO!!!
THOOM
ONE TRIPLE-EXTRA-UBER-STACKED VANILLA ICE CREAM TAIGA SPECIAL PARFAIT!!!
KEEP THIS SECRET, 'KAY?
DON'T LET THE OTHER CUSTOMERS SEE YOU EATING IT.
ARE YOU *SURE* THIS IS OKAY MINORIN? WON'T YOUR BOSS GET MAD?
GRIN
NAAAH! IT'LL BE FINE! TRUST ME!!
BESIDES, YOU GUYS HAVE COME HERE JUST ABOUT *EVERY* DAY OF VACATION!
IT'S GOTTA COUNT AS SHOWING OUR APPRECIATION TO LOYAL CUSTOMERS, RIGHT?

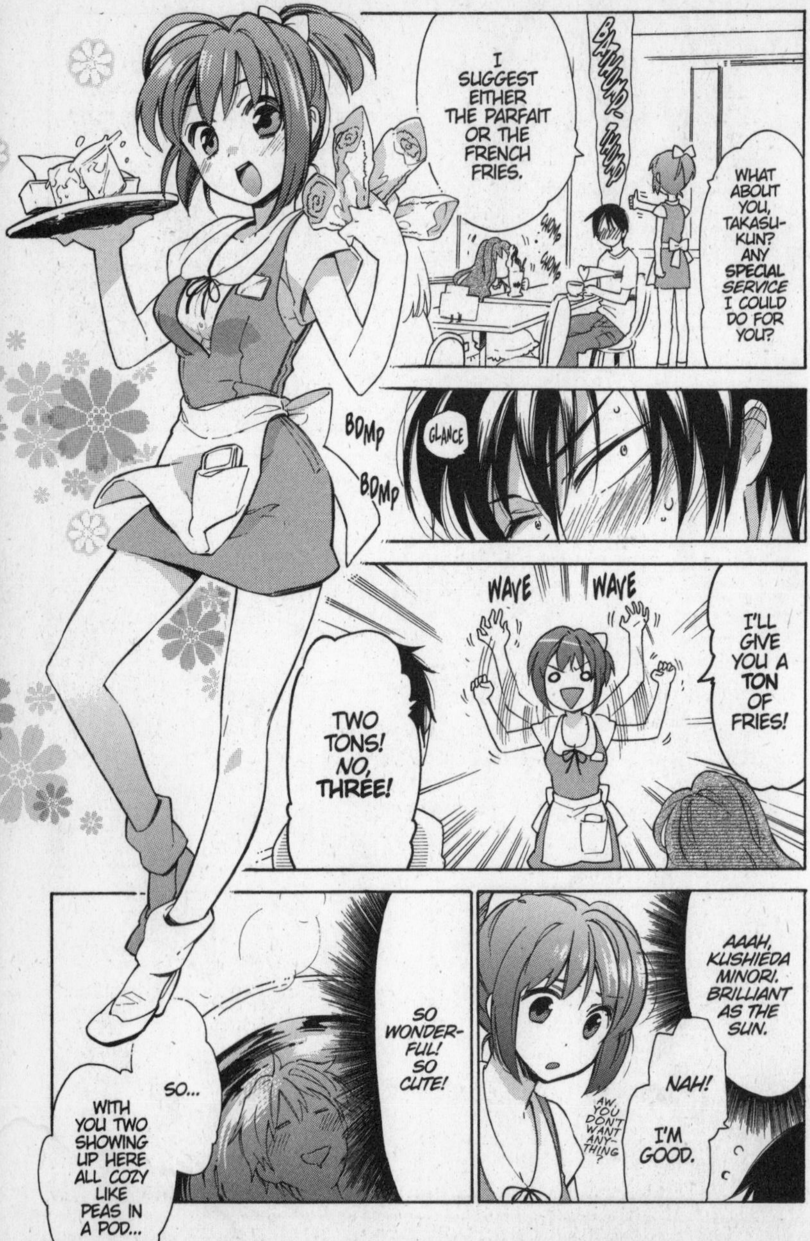
WHAT ABOUT YOU, TAKASU-KUN? ANY SPECIAL SERVICE I COULD DO FOR YOU?
I SUGGEST EITHER THE PARFAIT OR THE FRENCH FRIES.
CHOMP
CHOMP
GLANCE
BDMP
BDMP
I'LL GIVE YOU A TON OF FRIES!
WAVE WAVE
TWO TONS! NO, THREE!
AAAH, KUSHIEDA MINORI. BRILLIANT AS THE SUN.
NAH!
I'M GOOD.
AW, YOU DON'T WANT ANYTHING?
SO WONDER-FUL! SO CUTE!
SO...
WITH YOU TWO SHOWING UP HERE ALL COZY LIKE PEAS IN A POD...

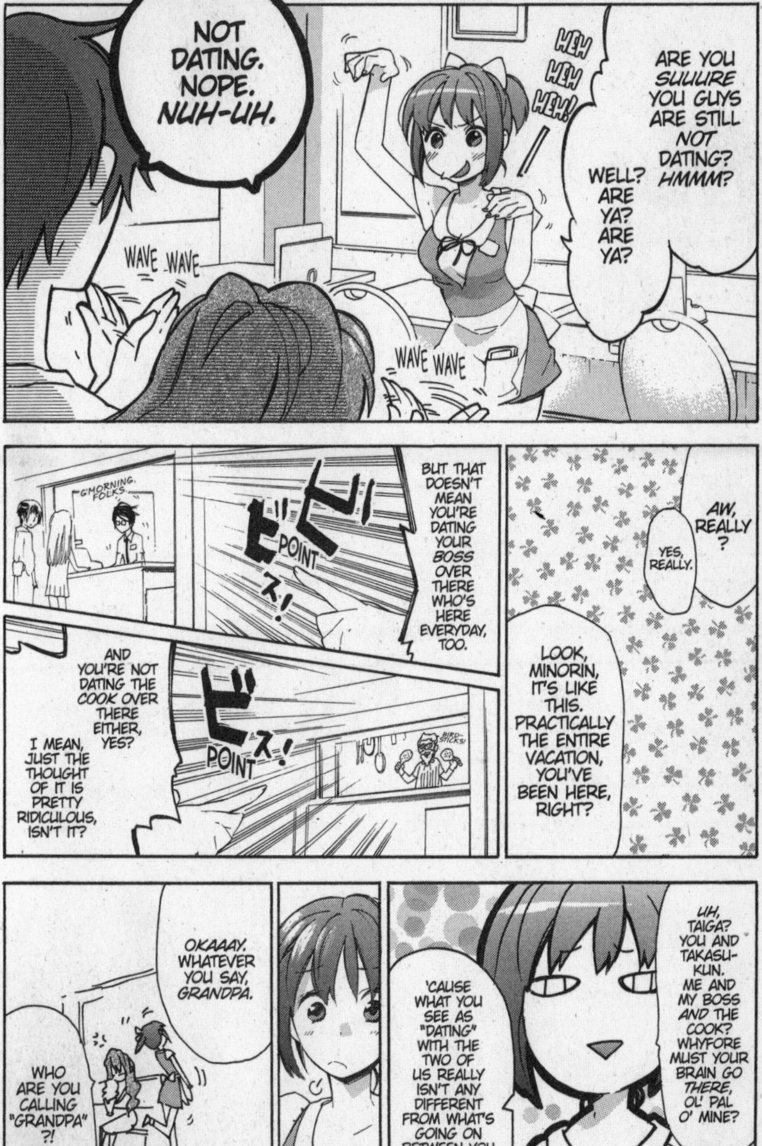
ARE YOU SUUURE YOU GUYS ARE STILL NOT DATING? HMMM?
HEH HEH HEH!
WELL? ARE YA? ARE YA?
NOT DATING. NOPE. NUH-UH.
WAVE WAVE
WAVE WAVE
AW, REALLY?
YES, REALLY.
LOOK, MINORIN, IT'S LIKE THIS. PRACTICALLY THE ENTIRE VACATION, YOU'VE BEEN HERE, RIGHT?
BUT THAT DOESN'T MEAN YOU'RE DATING YOUR BOSS OVER THERE WHO'S HERE EVERYDAY, TOO.
POINT
G'MORNING, FOLKS.
AND YOU'RE NOT DATING THE COOK OVER THERE EITHER, YES?
POINT
BIRD-STICKS!
I MEAN, JUST THE THOUGHT OF IT IS PRETTY RIDICULOUS, ISN'T IT?
UH, TAIGA? YOU AND TAKASU-KUN. ME AND MY BOSS AND THE COOK? WHYFORE MUST YOUR BRAIN GO THERE, OL' PAL O' MINE?
'CAUSE WHAT YOU SEE AS "DATING" WITH THE TWO OF US REALLY ISN'T ANY DIFFERENT FROM WHAT'S GOING ON BETWEEN YOU AND THEM.
OKAAAY. WHATEVER YOU SAY, GRANDPA.
WHO ARE YOU CALLING "GRANDPA"?!

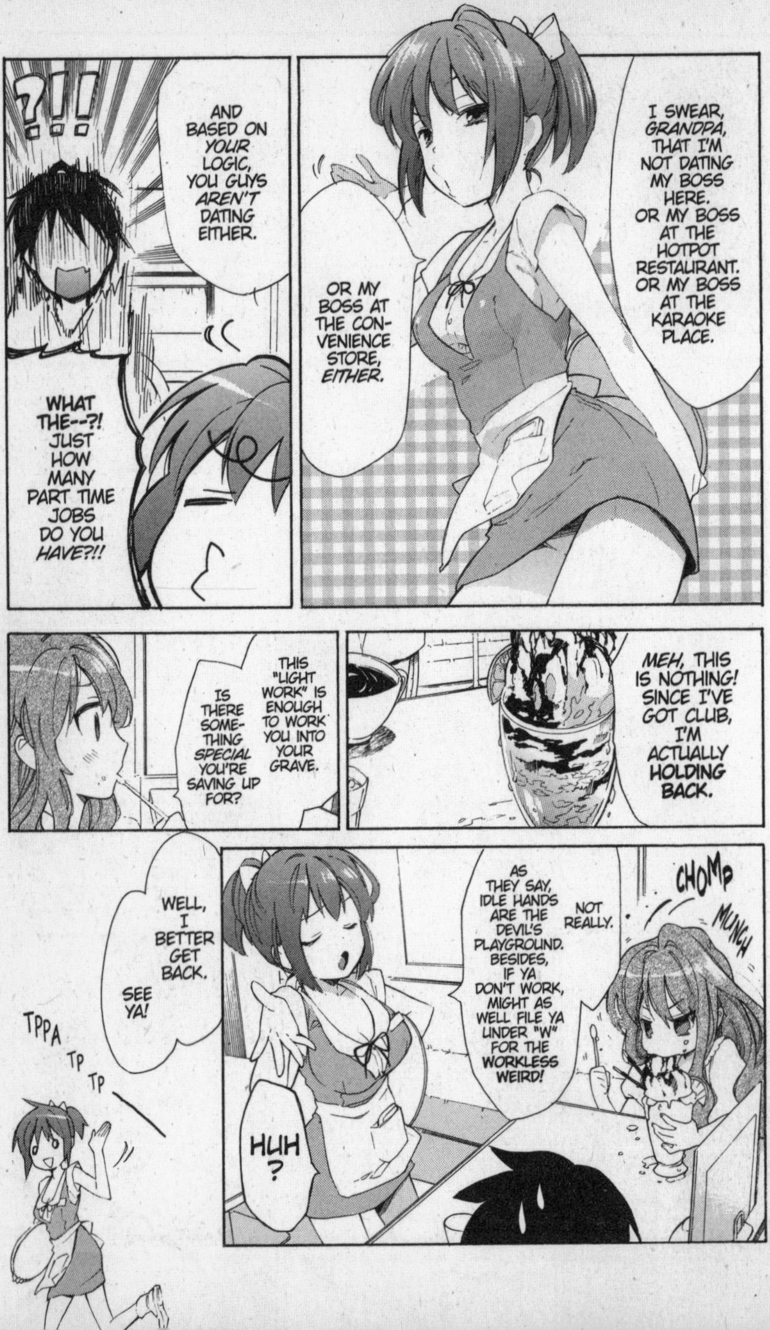
I SWEAR, GRANDPA, THAT I'M NOT DATING MY BOSS HERE. OR MY BOSS AT THE HOTPOT RESTAURANT. OR MY BOSS AT THE KARAOKE PLACE.
OR MY BOSS AT THE CON-VENIENCE STORE, EITHER.
AND BASED ON YOUR LOGIC, YOU GUYS AREN'T DATING EITHER.
?!!!
WHAT THE--?! JUST HOW MANY PART TIME JOBS DO YOU HAVE?!!
MEH, THIS IS NOTHING! SINCE I'VE GOT CLUB, I'M ACTUALLY HOLDING BACK.
THIS "LIGHT WORK" IS ENOUGH TO WORK YOU INTO YOUR GRAVE.
IS THERE SOME-THING SPECIAL YOU'RE SAVING UP FOR?
CHOMP
MUNCH
NOT REALLY.
AS THEY SAY, IDLE HANDS ARE THE DEVIL'S PLAYGROUND. BESIDES, IF YA DON'T WORK, MIGHT AS WELL FILE YA UNDER "W" FOR THE WORKLESS WEIRD!
HUH?
WELL, I BETTER GET BACK.
SEE YA!
TPPA
TP
TP

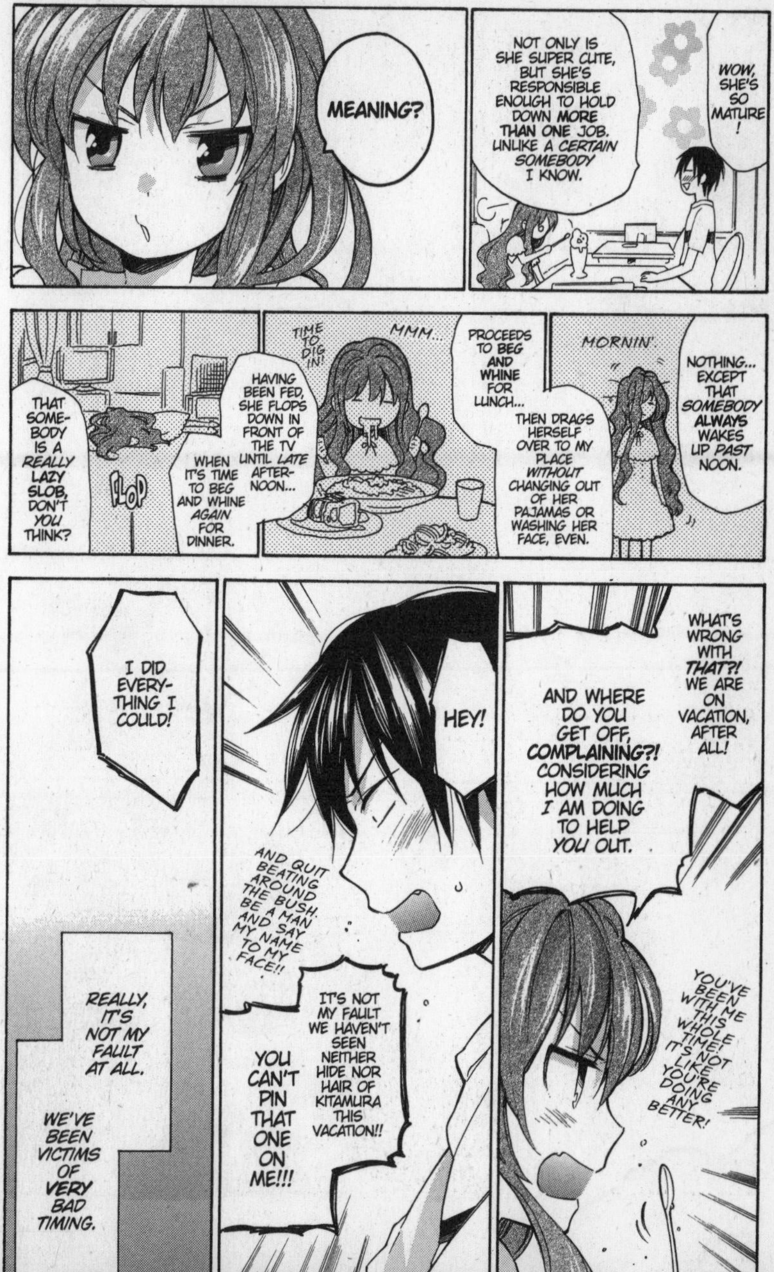
WOW, SHE'S SO MATURE!
NOT ONLY IS SHE SUPER CUTE, BUT SHE'S RESPONSIBLE ENOUGH TO HOLD DOWN MORE THAN ONE JOB. UNLIKE A CERTAIN SOMEBODY I KNOW.
MEANING?
MORNIN'
NOTHING... EXCEPT THAT SOMEBODY ALWAYS WAKES UP PAST NOON.
PROCEEDS TO BEG AND WHINE FOR LUNCH...
THEN DRAGS HERSELF OVER TO MY PLACE WITHOUT CHANGING OUT OF HER PAJAMAS OR WASHING HER FACE, EVEN.
MMM...
TIME TO DIG IN!
HAVING BEEN FED, SHE FLOPS DOWN IN FRONT OF THE TV UNTIL LATE AFTER-NOON...
WHEN IT'S TIME TO BEG AND WHINE AGAIN FOR DINNER.
THAT SOME-BODY IS A REALLY LAZY SLOB, DON'T YOU THINK?
FLOP
WHAT'S WRONG WITH THAT?! WE ARE ON VACATION, AFTER ALL!
AND WHERE DO YOU GET OFF, COMPLAINING?! CONSIDERING HOW MUCH I AM DOING TO HELP YOU OUT.
YOU'VE BEEN WITH ME THIS WHOLE TIME! IT'S NOT LIKE YOU'RE DOING ANY BETTER!
HEY!
AND QUIT BEATING AROUND THE BUSH. BE A MAN AND SAY MY NAME TO MY FACE!!
IT'S NOT MY FAULT WE HAVEN'T SEEN NEITHER HIDE NOR HAIR OF KITAMURA THIS VACATION!!
YOU CAN'T PIN THAT ONE ON ME!!!
I DID EVERY-THING I COULD!
REALLY, IT'S NOT MY FAULT AT ALL.
WE'VE BEEN VICTIMS OF VERY BAD TIMING.

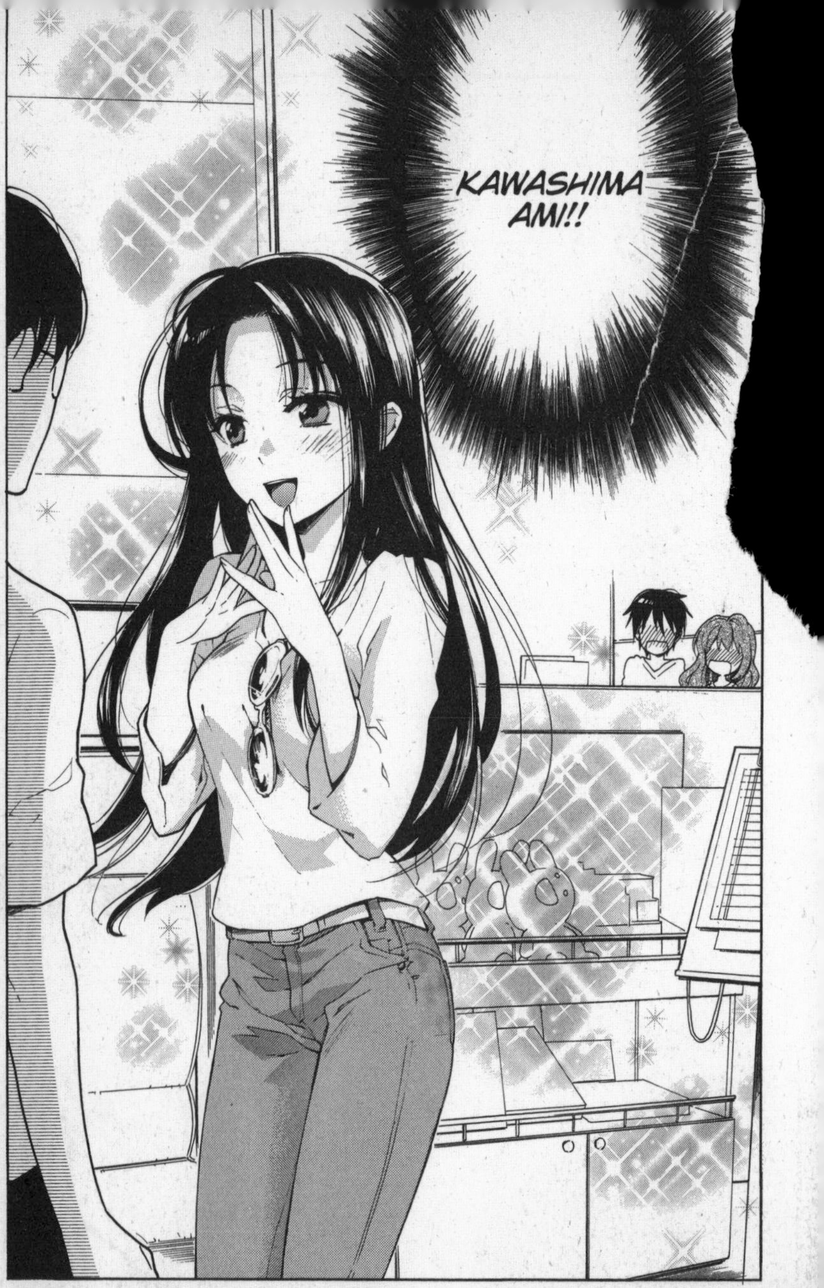
KAWASHIMA AMI!!

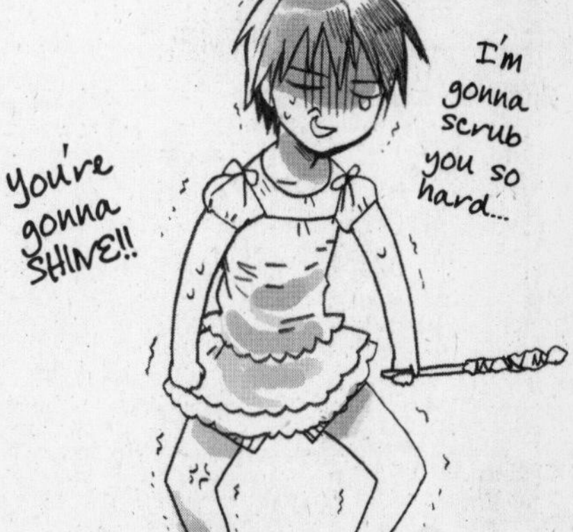
I'm gonna scrub you so hard...
You're gonna SHINE!!

Chapter 13 SEDUCTIVE MODEL GIRL

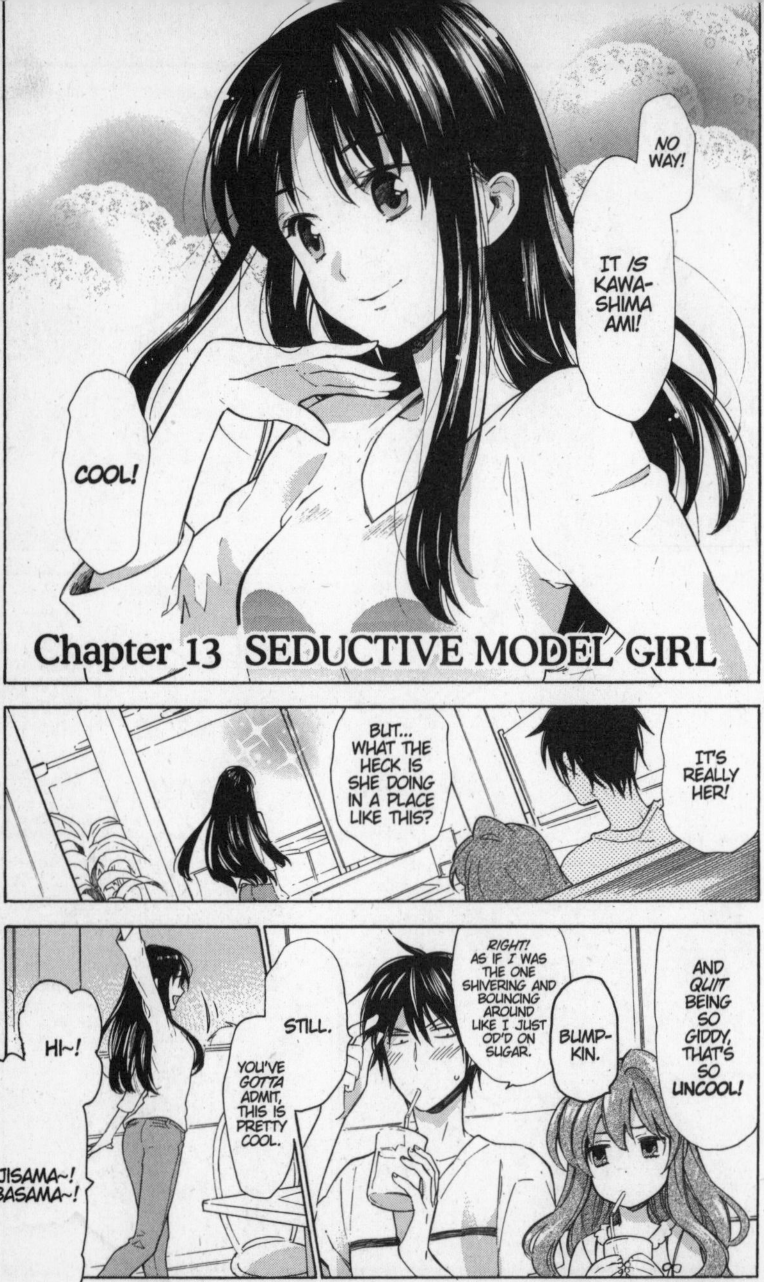
NO WAY!
IT IS KAWASHIMA AMI!
COOL!
IT'S REALLY HER!
BUT... WHAT THE HECK IS SHE DOING IN A PLACE LIKE THIS?
AND *QUIT* BEING SO GIDDY, THAT'S SO UNCOOL!
BUMP-KIN.
RIGHT! AS IF *I* WAS THE ONE SHIVERING AND BOUNCING AROUND LIKE I JUST OD'D ON SUGAR.
STILL.
YOU'VE *GOTTA* ADMIT, THIS IS PRETTY COOL.
HI~!
OJISAMA~! OBASAMA~!

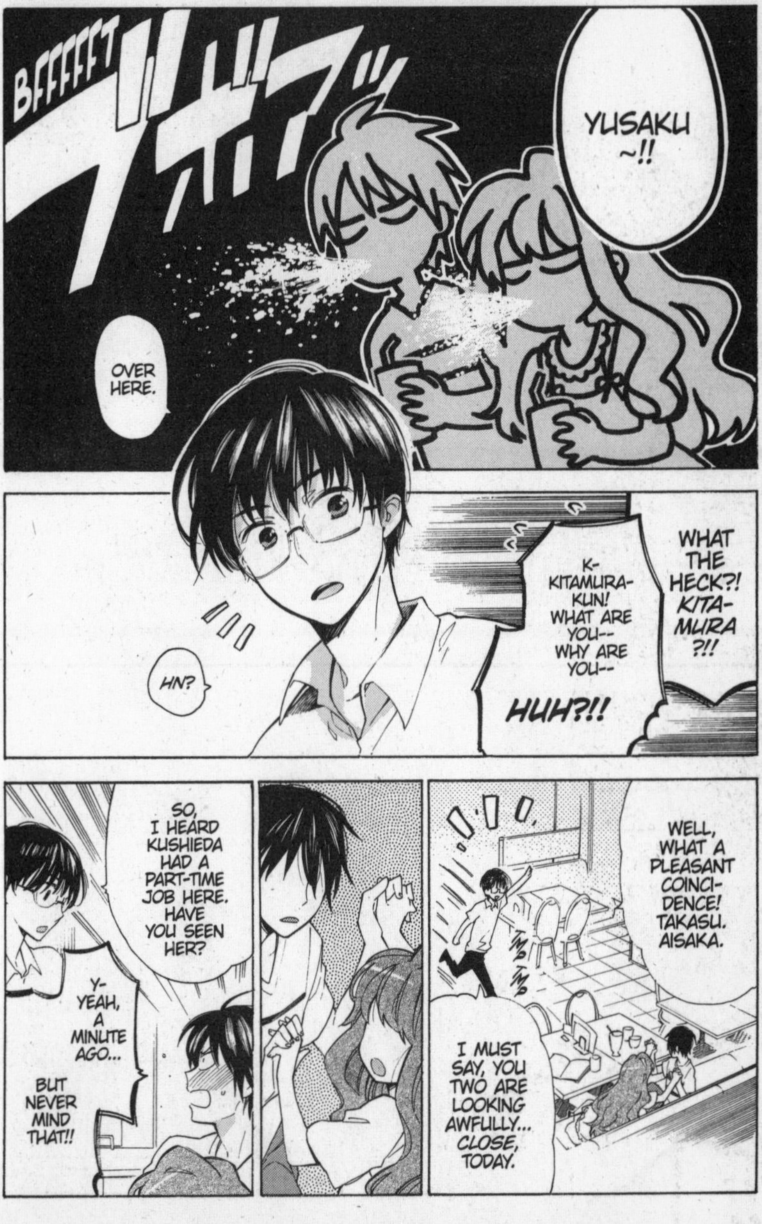
YUSAKU ~!!
BFFFFFT
OVER HERE.
WHAT THE HECK?! KITAMURA?!!
K-KITAMURA-KUN! WHAT ARE YOU-- WHY ARE YOU--
HUH?!!
HN?
WELL, WHAT A PLEASANT COINCIDENCE! TAKASU. AISAKA.
I MUST SAY, YOU TWO ARE LOOKING AWFULLY... CLOSE, TODAY.
TMP TMP
SO, I HEARD KUSHIEDA HAD A PART-TIME JOB HERE. HAVE YOU SEEN HER?
Y-YEAH, A MINUTE AGO...
BUT NEVER MIND THAT!!

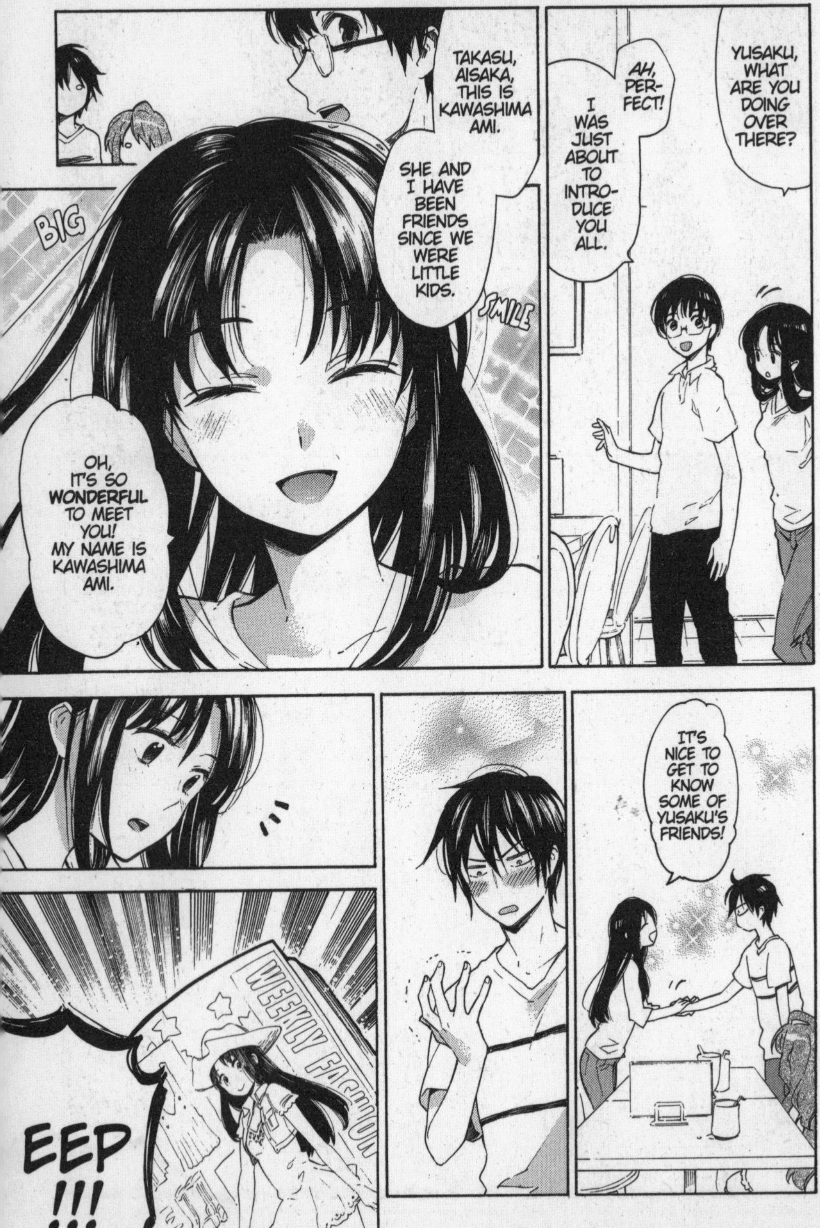
YUSAKU, WHAT ARE YOU DOING OVER THERE?
AH, PERFECT!
I WAS JUST ABOUT TO INTRODUCE YOU ALL.
TAKASU, AISAKA, THIS IS KAWASHIMA AMI.
SHE AND I HAVE BEEN FRIENDS SINCE WE WERE LITTLE KIDS.
SMILE
BIG
OH, IT'S SO WONDERFUL TO MEET YOU! MY NAME IS KAWASHIMA AMI.
IT'S NICE TO GET TO KNOW SOME OF YUSAKU'S FRIENDS!
...
WEEKLY FASHION
EEP!!!

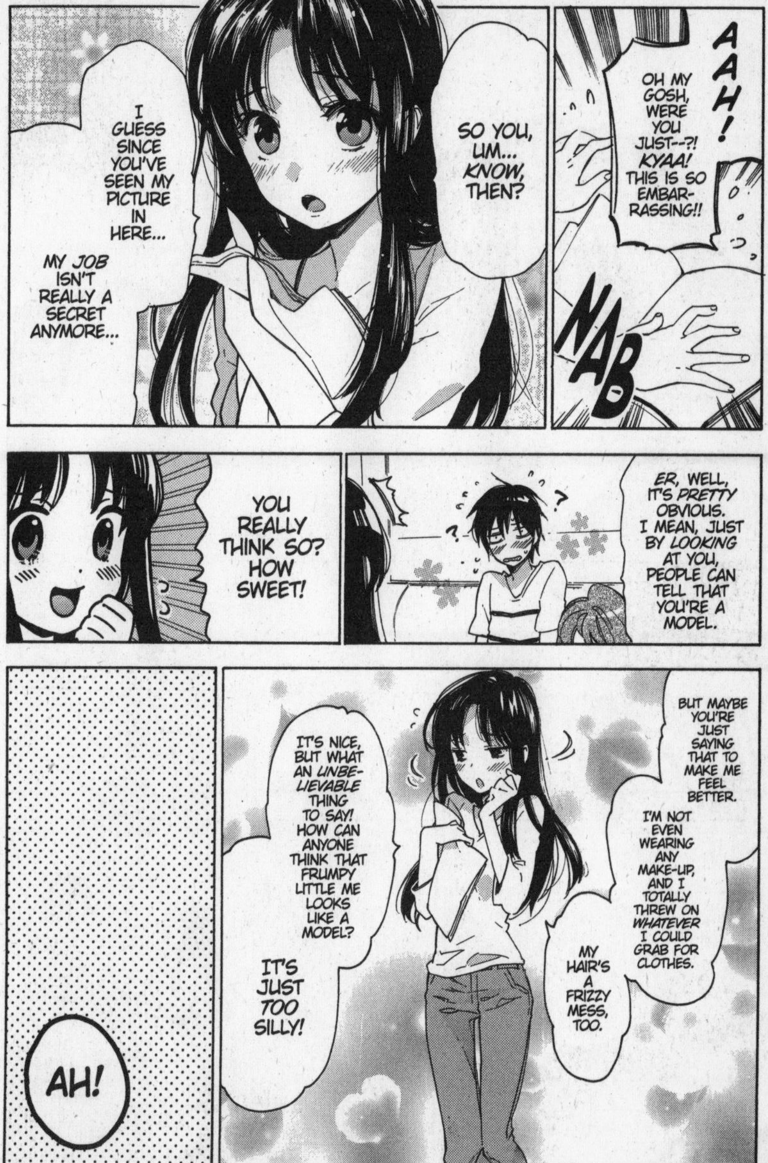
AAAH!
OH MY GOSH, WERE YOU JUST--?! KYAA! THIS IS SO EMBARRASSING!!
NAB
SO YOU, UM... KNOW, THEN?
I GUESS SINCE YOU'VE SEEN MY PICTURE IN HERE...
MY JOB ISN'T REALLY A SECRET ANYMORE...
ER, WELL, IT'S PRETTY OBVIOUS. I MEAN, JUST BY LOOKING AT YOU, PEOPLE CAN TELL THAT YOU'RE A MODEL.
YOU REALLY THINK SO? HOW SWEET!
BUT MAYBE YOU'RE JUST SAYING THAT TO MAKE ME FEEL BETTER.
I'M NOT EVEN WEARING ANY MAKE-UP, AND I TOTALLY THREW ON WHATEVER I COULD GRAB FOR CLOTHES.
MY HAIR'S A FRIZZY MESS, TOO.
IT'S NICE, BUT WHAT AN UNBELIEVABLE THING TO SAY! HOW CAN ANYONE THINK THAT FRUMPY LITTLE ME LOOKS LIKE A MODEL?
IT'S JUST TOO SILLY!
AH!

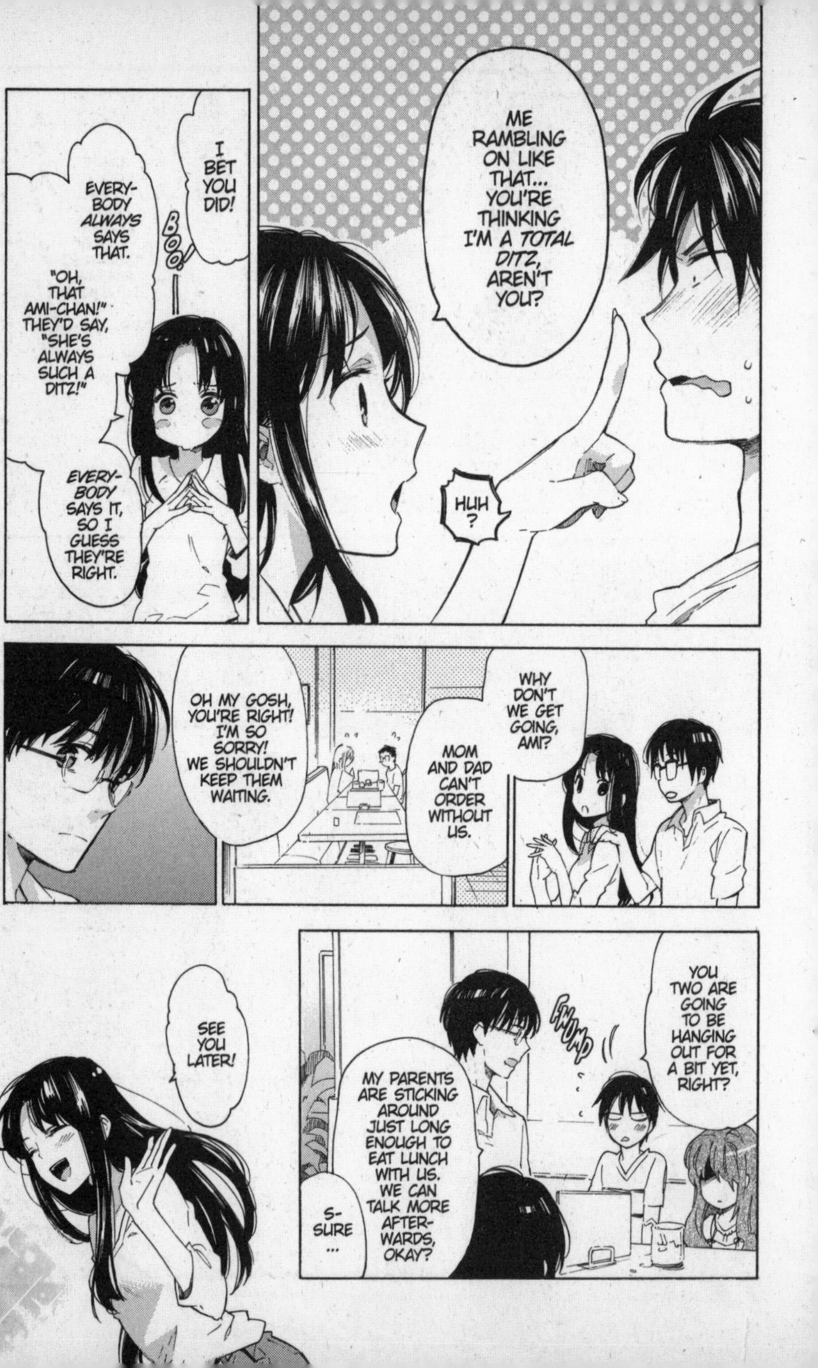
ME RAMBLING ON LIKE THAT... YOU'RE THINKING I'M A *TOTAL* DITZ, AREN'T YOU?
HUH?
I BET YOU DID!
BOO!
EVERY-BODY *ALWAYS* SAYS THAT.
"OH, THAT AMI-CHAN!" THEY'D SAY, "SHE'S ALWAYS SUCH A DITZ!"
EVERY-BODY SAYS IT, SO I GUESS THEY'RE RIGHT.
WHY DON'T WE GET GOING, AMI?
MOM AND DAD CAN'T ORDER WITHOUT US.
OH MY GOSH, YOU'RE RIGHT! I'M SO SORRY! WE SHOULDN'T KEEP THEM WAITING.
YOU TWO ARE GOING TO BE HANGING OUT FOR A BIT YET, RIGHT?
FWUMP
MY PARENTS ARE STICKING AROUND JUST LONG ENOUGH TO EAT LUNCH WITH US. WE CAN TALK MORE AFTER-WARDS, OKAY?
S-SURE ...
SEE YOU LATER!

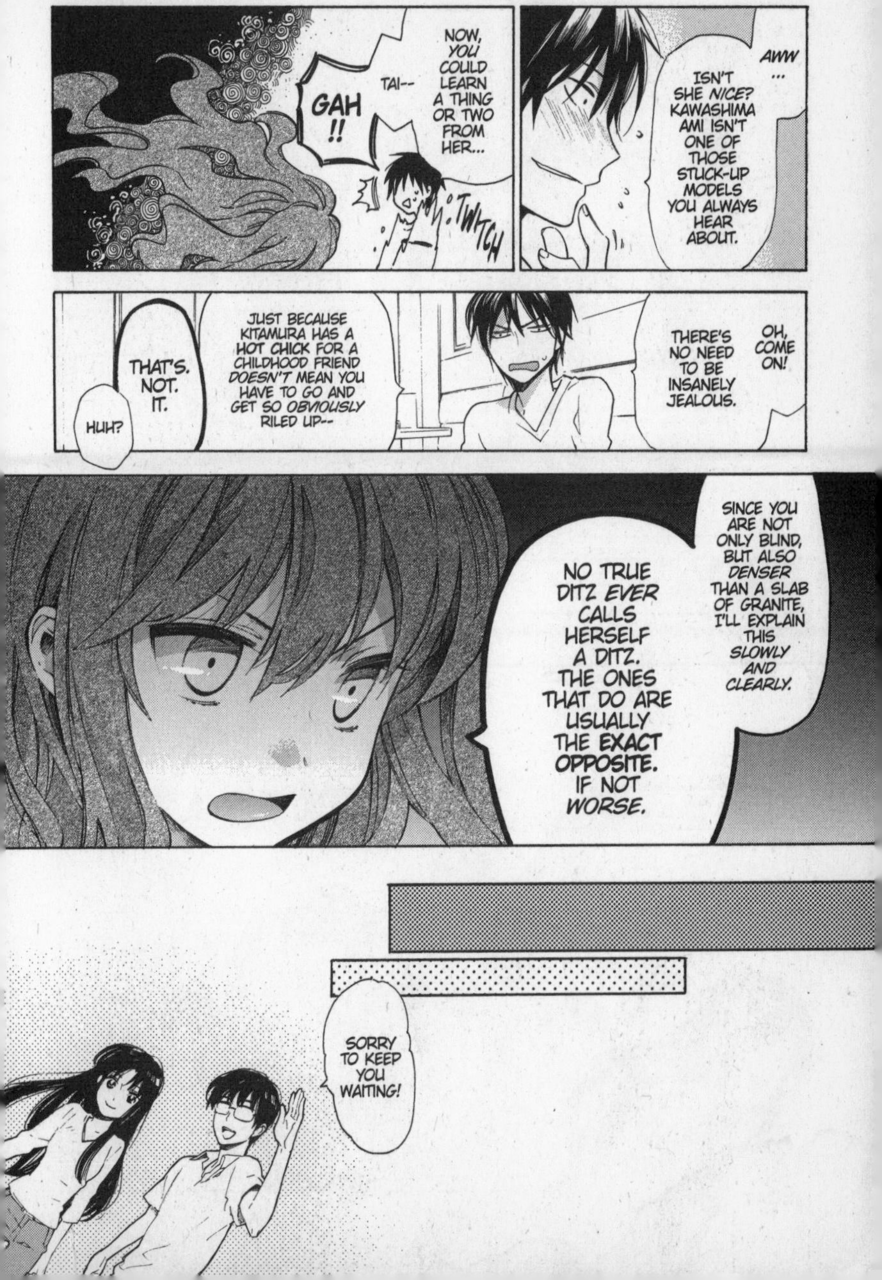
AWW...
ISN'T SHE NICE? KAWASHIMA AMI ISN'T ONE OF THOSE STUCK-UP MODELS YOU ALWAYS HEAR ABOUT.
NOW, YOU COULD LEARN A THING OR TWO FROM HER...
TAI--
GAH!!
TWITCH
OH, COME ON!
THERE'S NO NEED TO BE INSANELY JEALOUS.
JUST BECAUSE KITAMURA HAS A HOT CHICK FOR A CHILDHOOD FRIEND DOESN'T MEAN YOU HAVE TO GO AND GET SO OBVIOUSLY RILED UP--
THAT'S. NOT. IT.
HUH?
SINCE YOU ARE NOT ONLY BLIND, BUT ALSO DENSER THAN A SLAB OF GRANITE, I'LL EXPLAIN THIS SLOWLY AND CLEARLY.
NO TRUE DITZ EVER CALLS HERSELF A DITZ. THE ONES THAT DO ARE USUALLY THE EXACT OPPOSITE. IF NOT WORSE.
SORRY TO KEEP YOU WAITING!

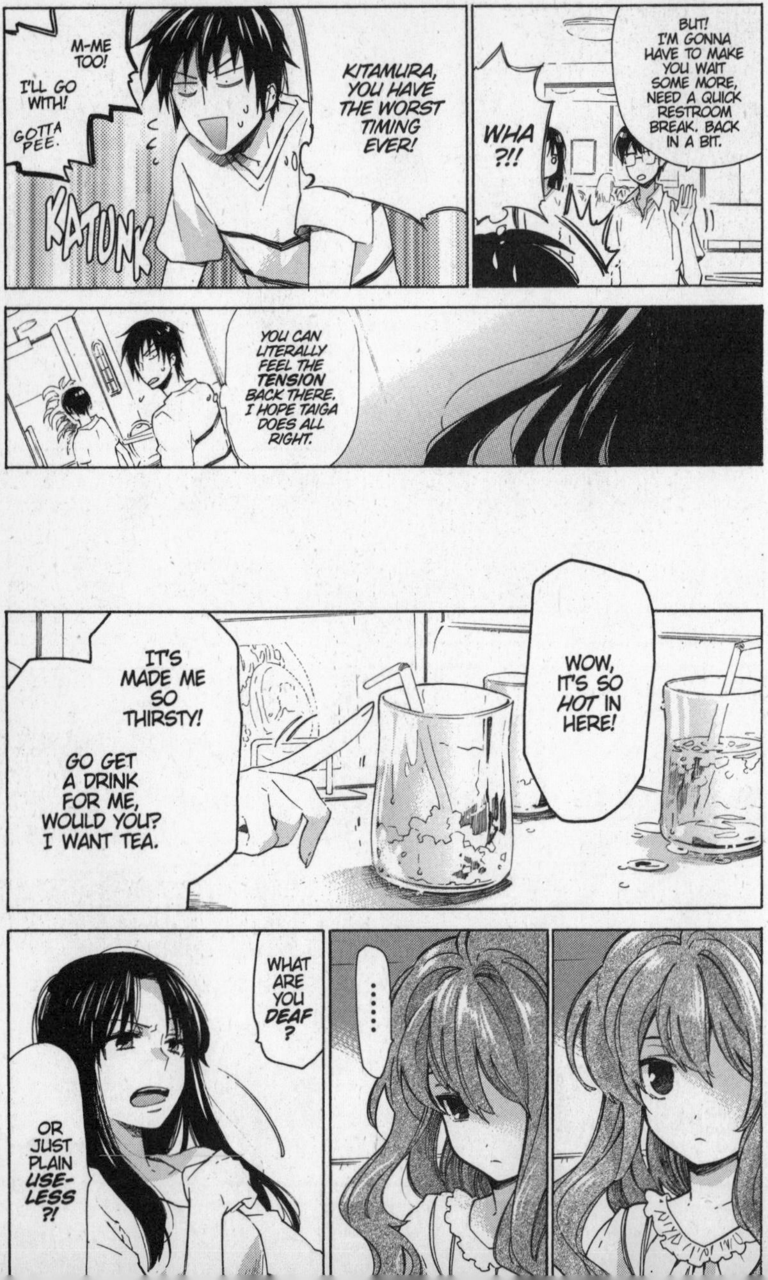
BUT! I'M GONNA HAVE TO MAKE YOU WAIT SOME MORE, NEED A QUICK RESTROOM BREAK. BACK IN A BIT.
WHA ?!!
KITAMURA, YOU HAVE THE WORST TIMING EVER!
M-ME TOO!
I'LL GO WITH!
GOTTA PEE.
KATUNK
YOU CAN LITERALLY FEEL THE TENSION BACK THERE. I HOPE TAIGA DOES ALL RIGHT.
WOW, IT'S SO HOT IN HERE!
IT'S MADE ME SO THIRSTY!
GO GET A DRINK FOR ME, WOULD YOU? I WANT TEA.
......
WHAT ARE YOU DEAF?
OR JUST PLAIN USE-LESS?!

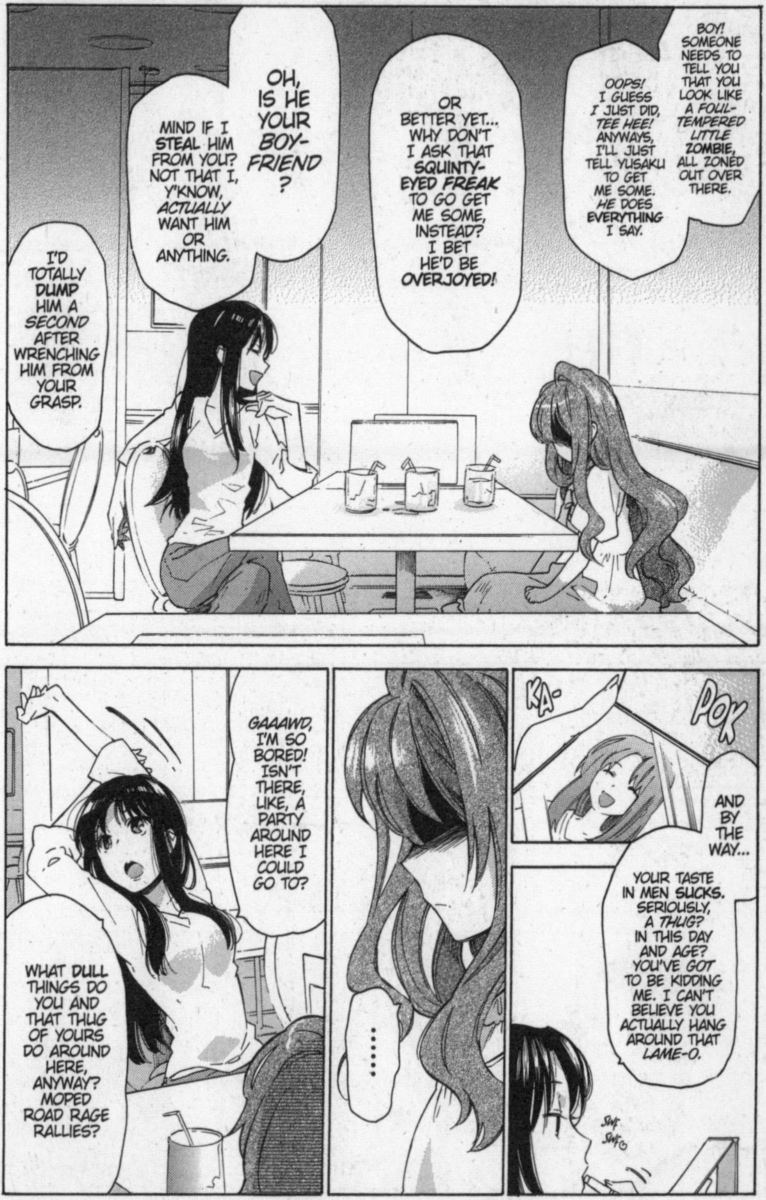
BOY! SOMEONE NEEDS TO TELL YOU THAT YOU LOOK LIKE A FOUL-TEMPERED LITTLE ZOMBIE, ALL ZONED OUT OVER THERE.
OOPS! I GUESS I JUST DID, TEE HEE! ANYWAYS, I'LL JUST TELL YUSAKU TO GET ME SOME. HE DOES EVERYTHING I SAY.
OR BETTER YET... WHY DON'T I ASK THAT SQUINTY-EYED FREAK TO GO GET ME SOME, INSTEAD? I BET HE'D BE OVERJOYED!
OH, IS HE YOUR BOY-FRIEND?
MIND IF I STEAL HIM FROM YOU? NOT THAT I, Y'KNOW, ACTUALLY WANT HIM OR ANYTHING.
I'D TOTALLY DUMP HIM A SECOND AFTER WRENCHING HIM FROM YOUR GRASP.
KA-POK
AND BY THE WAY...
YOUR TASTE IN MEN SUCKS. SERIOUSLY, A THUG? IN THIS DAY AND AGE? YOU'VE GOT TO BE KIDDING ME. I CAN'T BELIEVE YOU ACTUALLY HANG AROUND THAT LAME-O.
SWF SWF
......
GAAAWD, I'M SO BORED! ISN'T THERE, LIKE, A PARTY AROUND HERE I COULD GO TO?
WHAT DULL THINGS DO YOU AND THAT THUG OF YOURS DO AROUND HERE, ANYWAY? MOPED ROAD RAGE RALLIES?

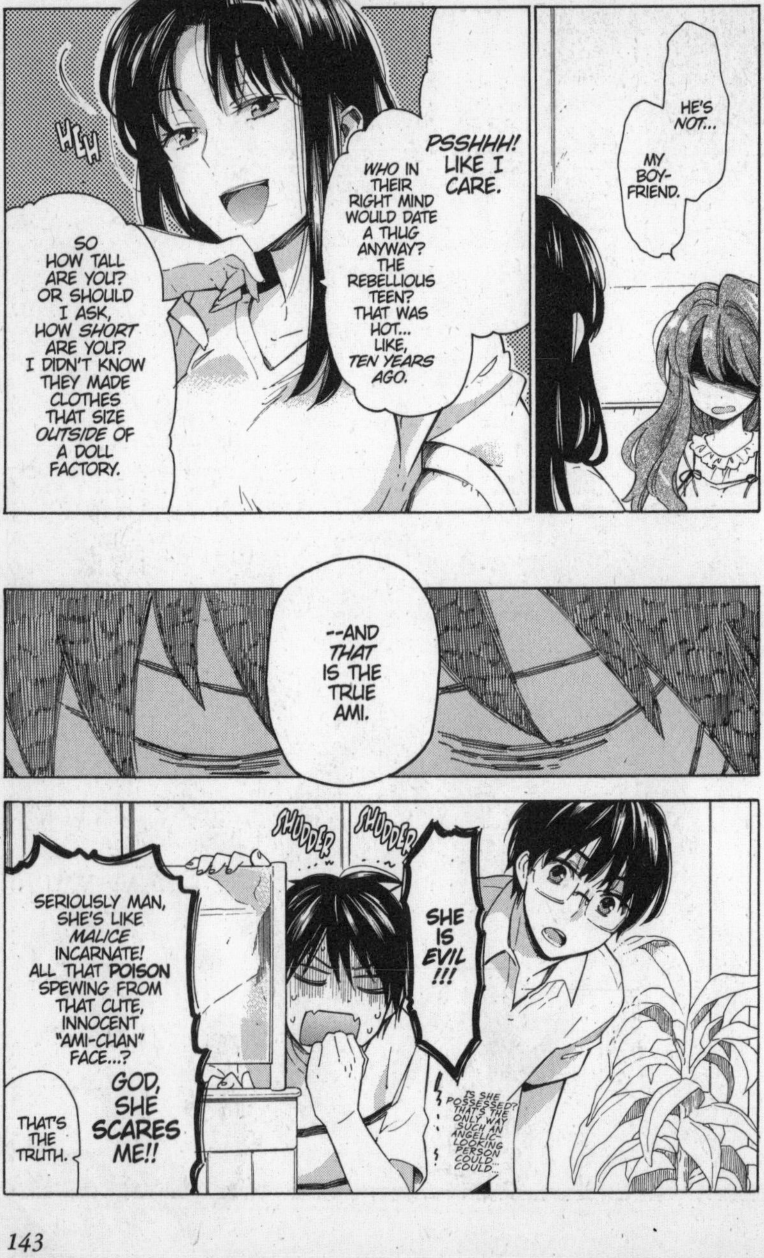
HE'S NOT... MY BOYFRIEND.
PSSHHH! LIKE I CARE.
WHO IN THEIR RIGHT MIND WOULD DATE A THUG ANYWAY? THE REBELLIOUS TEEN? THAT WAS HOT... LIKE, TEN YEARS AGO.
HEH
SO HOW TALL ARE YOU? OR SHOULD I ASK, HOW SHORT ARE YOU? I DIDN'T KNOW THEY MADE CLOTHES THAT SIZE OUTSIDE OF A DOLL FACTORY.
--AND THAT IS THE TRUE AMI.
SHUDDER
SHUDDER
SHE IS EVIL!!!
IS SHE POSSESSED? THAT'S THE ONLY WAY SUCH AN ANGELIC-LOOKING PERSON COULD... COULD...
SERIOUSLY MAN, SHE'S LIKE MALICE INCARNATE! ALL THAT POISON SPEWING FROM THAT CUTE, INNOCENT "AMI-CHAN" FACE...?
GOD, SHE SCARES ME!!
THAT'S THE TRUTH.

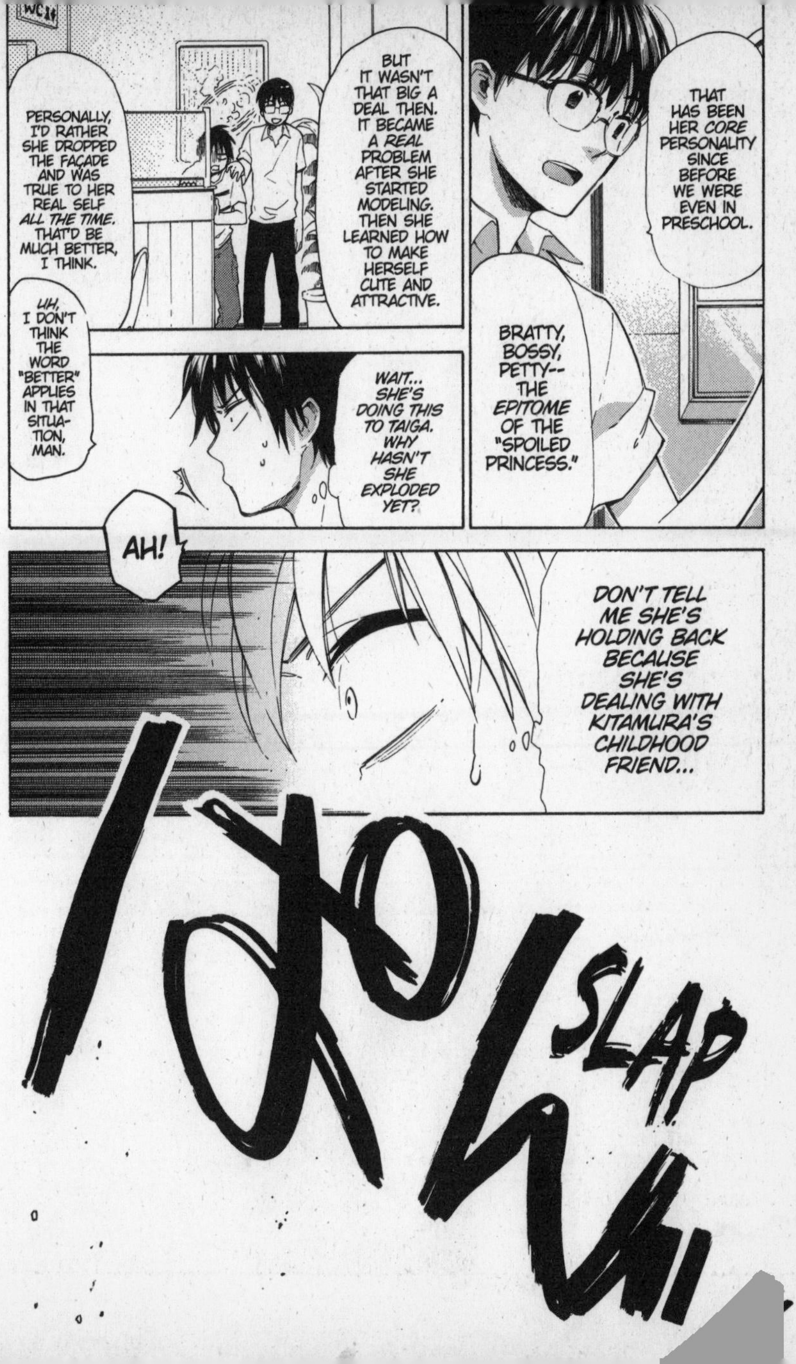
THAT HAS BEEN HER CORE PERSONALITY SINCE BEFORE WE WERE EVEN IN PRESCHOOL.
BRATTY, BOSSY, PETTY-- THE EPITOME OF THE "SPOILED PRINCESS."
BUT IT WASN'T THAT BIG A DEAL THEN. IT BECAME A REAL PROBLEM AFTER SHE STARTED MODELING. THEN SHE LEARNED HOW TO MAKE HERSELF CUTE AND ATTRACTIVE.
PERSONALLY, I'D RATHER SHE DROPPED THE FAÇADE AND WAS TRUE TO HER REAL SELF ALL THE TIME. THAT'D BE MUCH BETTER, I THINK.
UH, I DON'T THINK THE WORD "BETTER" APPLIES IN THAT SITUATION, MAN.
WAIT... SHE'S DOING THIS TO TAIGA. WHY HASN'T SHE EXPLODED YET?
AH!
DON'T TELL ME SHE'S HOLDING BACK BECAUSE SHE'S DEALING WITH KITAMURA'S CHILDHOOD FRIEND...
SLAP!

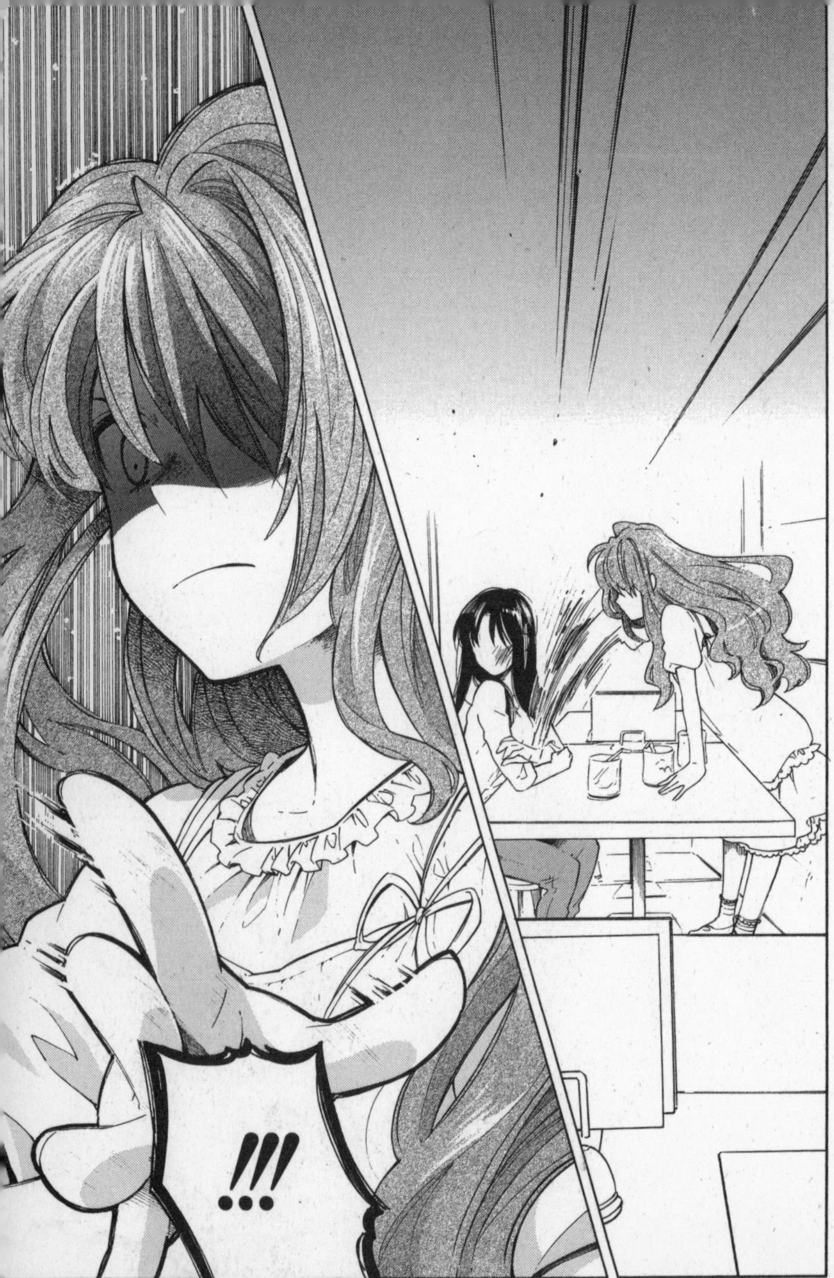
!!!

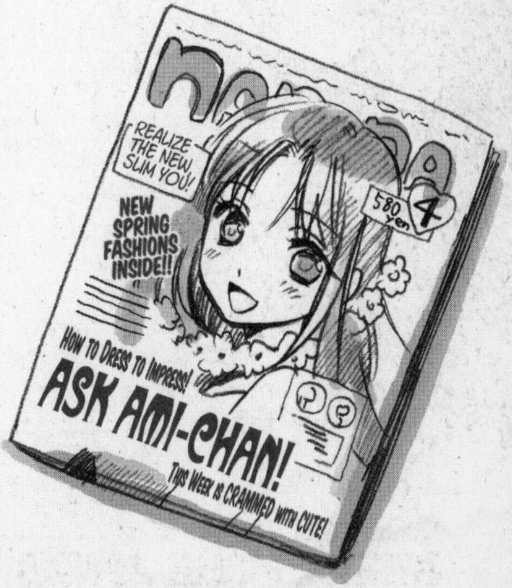
REALIZE THE NEW SLIM YOU!
580 yen
4
NEW SPRING FASHIONS INSIDE!!
How to Dress to Impress!
ASK AMI-CHAN!
This Week is CRAMMED with CUTE!

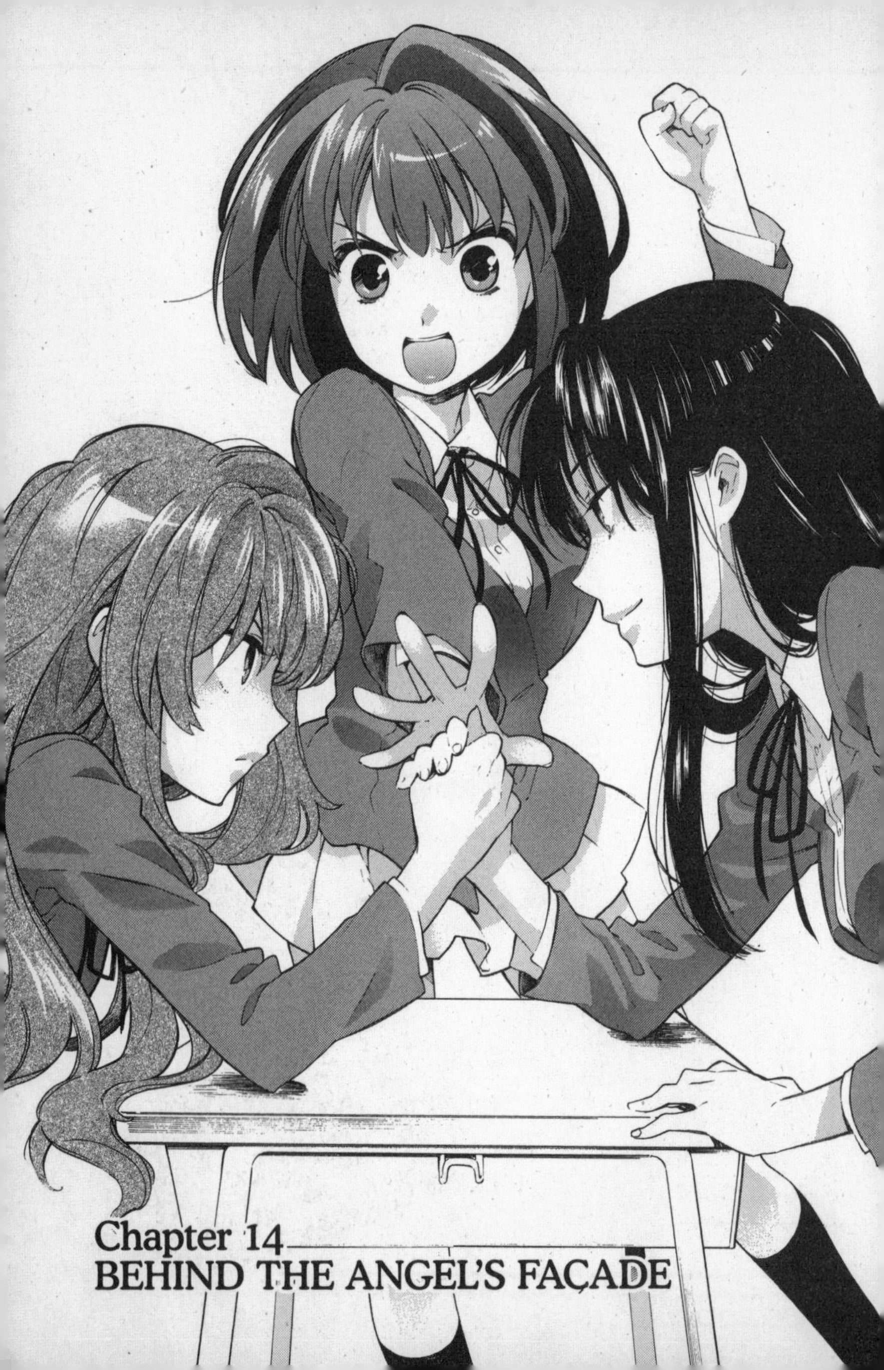

Chapter 14
BEHIND THE ANGEL'S FAÇADE

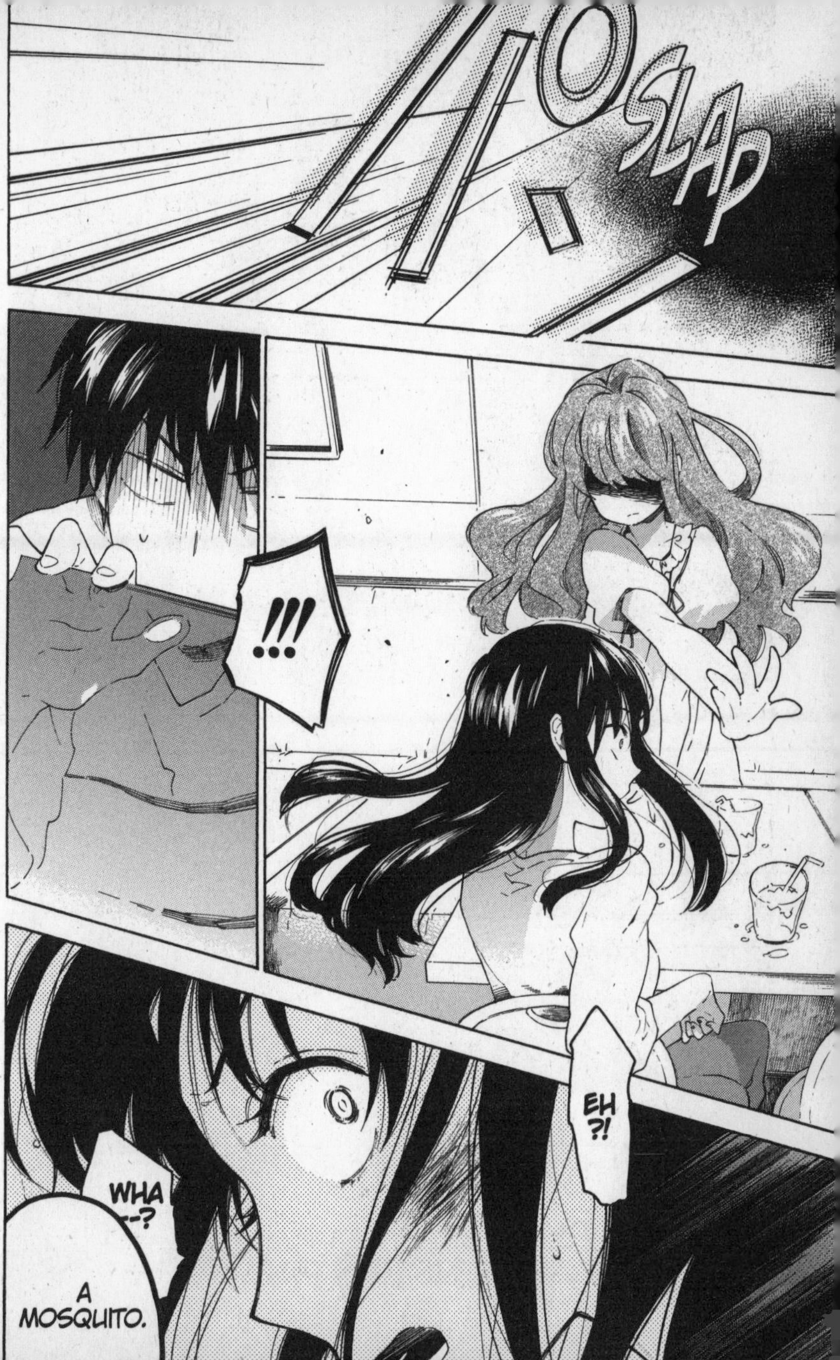
SLAP
EH?!
!!!
WHA--?
A MOSQUITO.

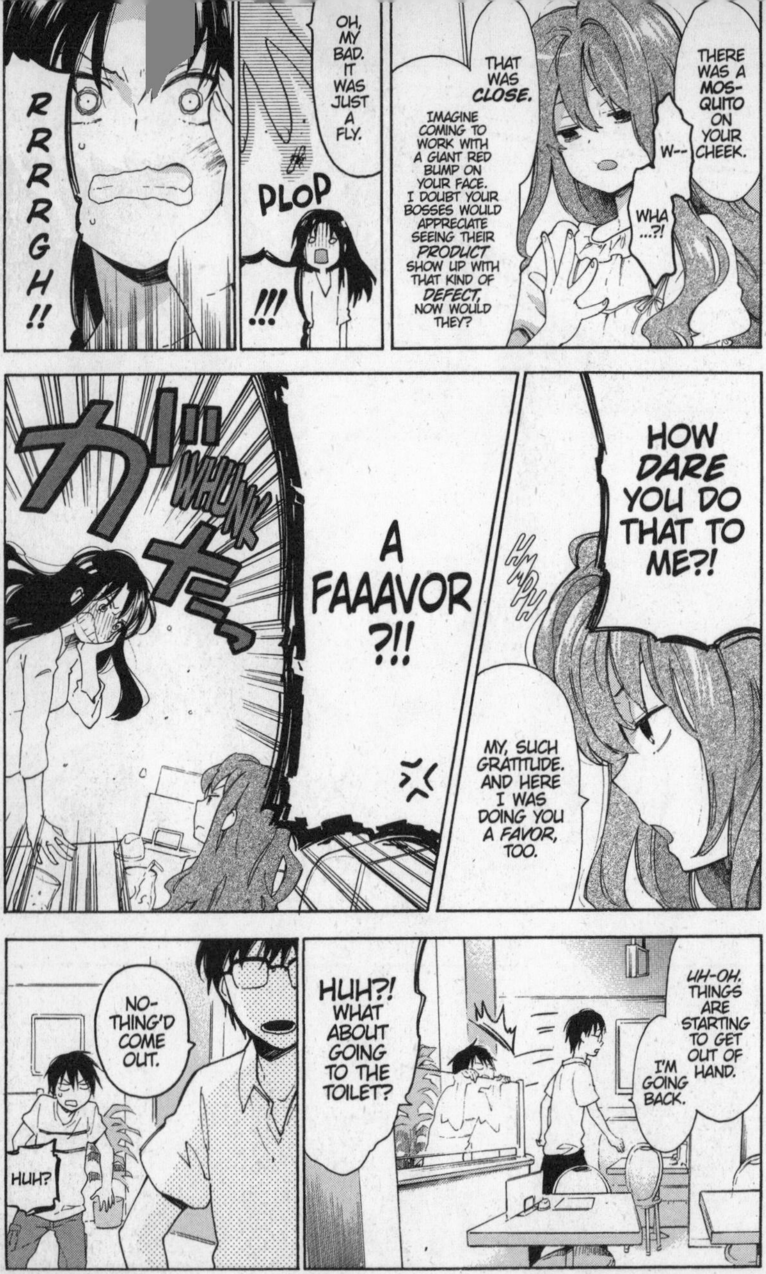
THERE WAS A MOS-QUITO ON YOUR CHEEK.
W--
WHA ...?!
THAT WAS CLOSE.
IMAGINE COMING TO WORK WITH A GIANT RED BUMP ON YOUR FACE. I DOUBT YOUR BOSSES WOULD APPRECIATE SEEING THEIR PRODUCT SHOW UP WITH THAT KIND OF DEFECT, NOW WOULD THEY?
OH, MY BAD. IT WAS JUST A FLY.
PLOP
!!!
RRRRRGH!!
HOW DARE YOU DO THAT TO ME?!
HMPH
MY, SUCH GRATITUDE. AND HERE I WAS DOING YOU A FAVOR, TOO.
A FAAAVOR ?!!
がたっ
WHUNK
UH-OH. THINGS ARE STARTING TO GET OUT OF HAND.
I'M GOING BACK.
HUH?! WHAT ABOUT GOING TO THE TOILET?
NO-THING'D COME OUT.
HUH?

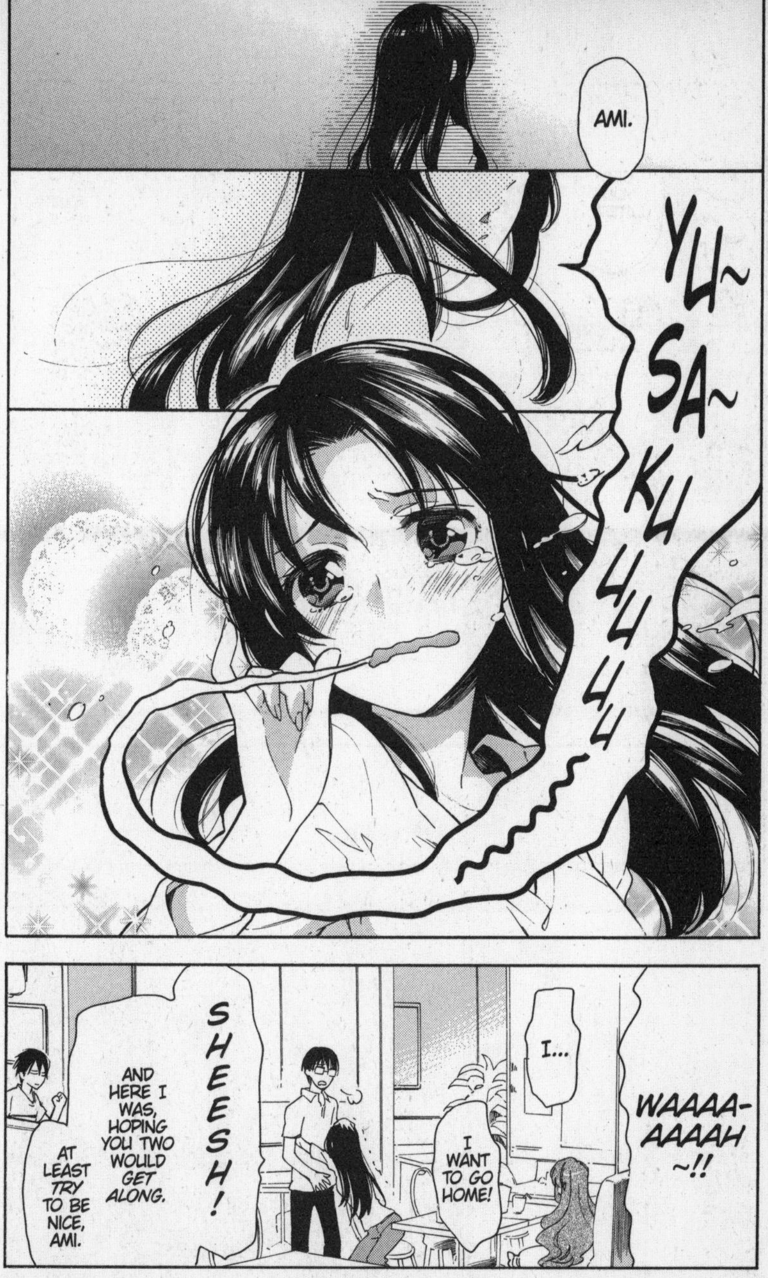
AMI.
YU~ SA~ KUUUUUU~
WAAAA-AAAAH~!!
I...
I WANT TO GO HOME!
SHEESH!
AND HERE I WAS, HOPING YOU TWO WOULD GET ALONG.
AT LEAST TRY TO BE NICE, AMI.

UH... 'KAY.

SEE YOU LATER!

WAH! WAH!

I'D BETTER TAKE THIS ONE HOME, NOW.

YOU TOO, TAKA-SU.

SORRY ABOUT ALL THE *FUSS,* AISAKA.

TAIGA...?

UM...

WAAAH...

・・・・・・

・・・・・・

・・・・・・

・・・・・・

・・・・・・

NOW, I WOULD SAY, "AND THAT WAS THE END OF IT," IF I COULD, BUT...

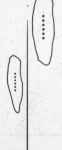

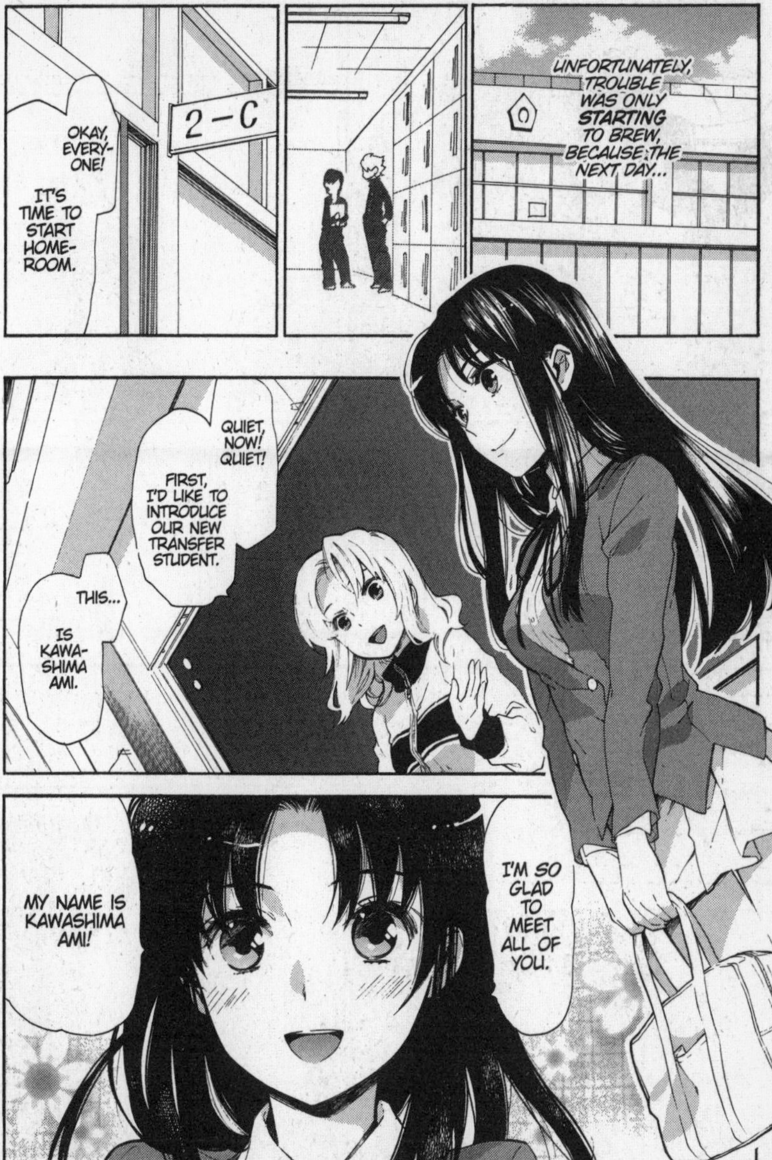
UNFORTUNATELY, TROUBLE WAS ONLY STARTING TO BREW, BECAUSE THE NEXT DAY...
2-C
OKAY, EVERYONE!
IT'S TIME TO START HOMEROOM.
QUIET, NOW! QUIET!
FIRST, I'D LIKE TO INTRODUCE OUR NEW TRANSFER STUDENT.
THIS...
IS KAWASHIMA AMI.
I'M SO GLAD TO MEET ALL OF YOU.
MY NAME IS KAWASHIMA AMI!

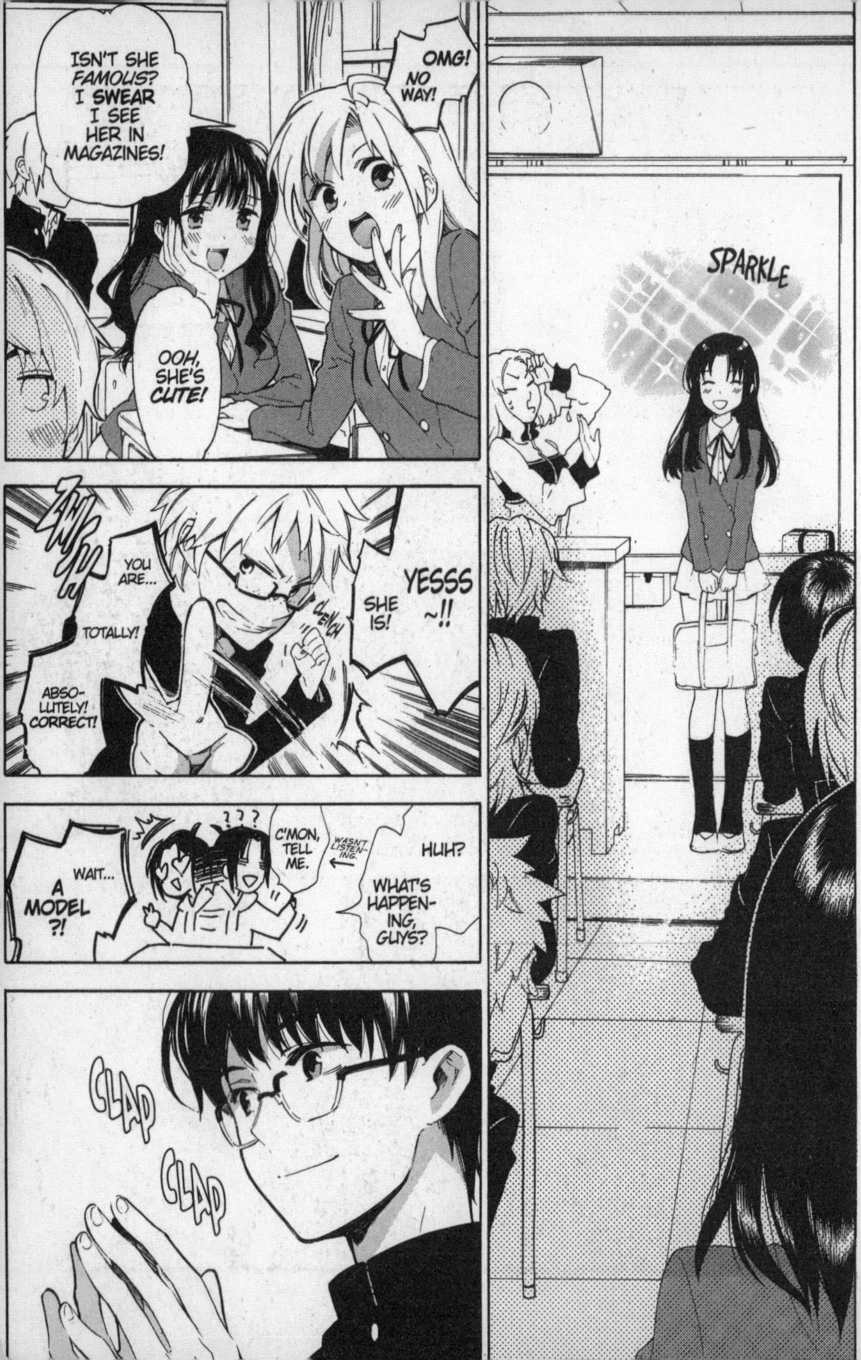
SPARKLE
OMG! NO WAY!
ISN'T SHE FAMOUS? I SWEAR I SEE HER IN MAGAZINES!
OOH, SHE'S CUTE!
YESSS ~!!
SHE IS!
CLENCH
YOU ARE...
TOTALLY!
ABSOLUTELY! CORRECT!
HUH?
WHAT'S HAPPENING, GUYS?
WASN'T LISTENING.
C'MON, TELL ME.
???
WAIT...
A MODEL ?!
CLAP
CLAP

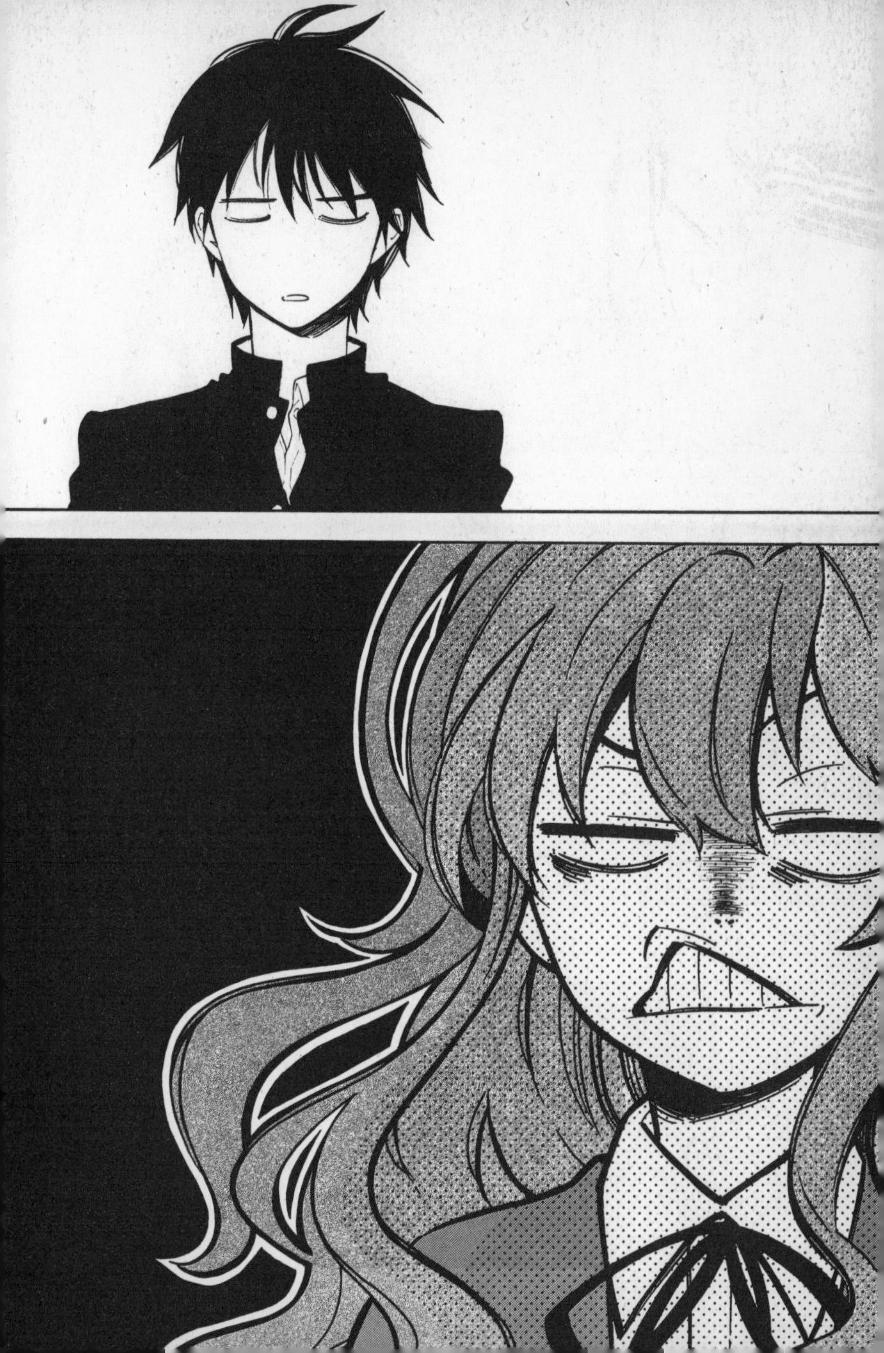

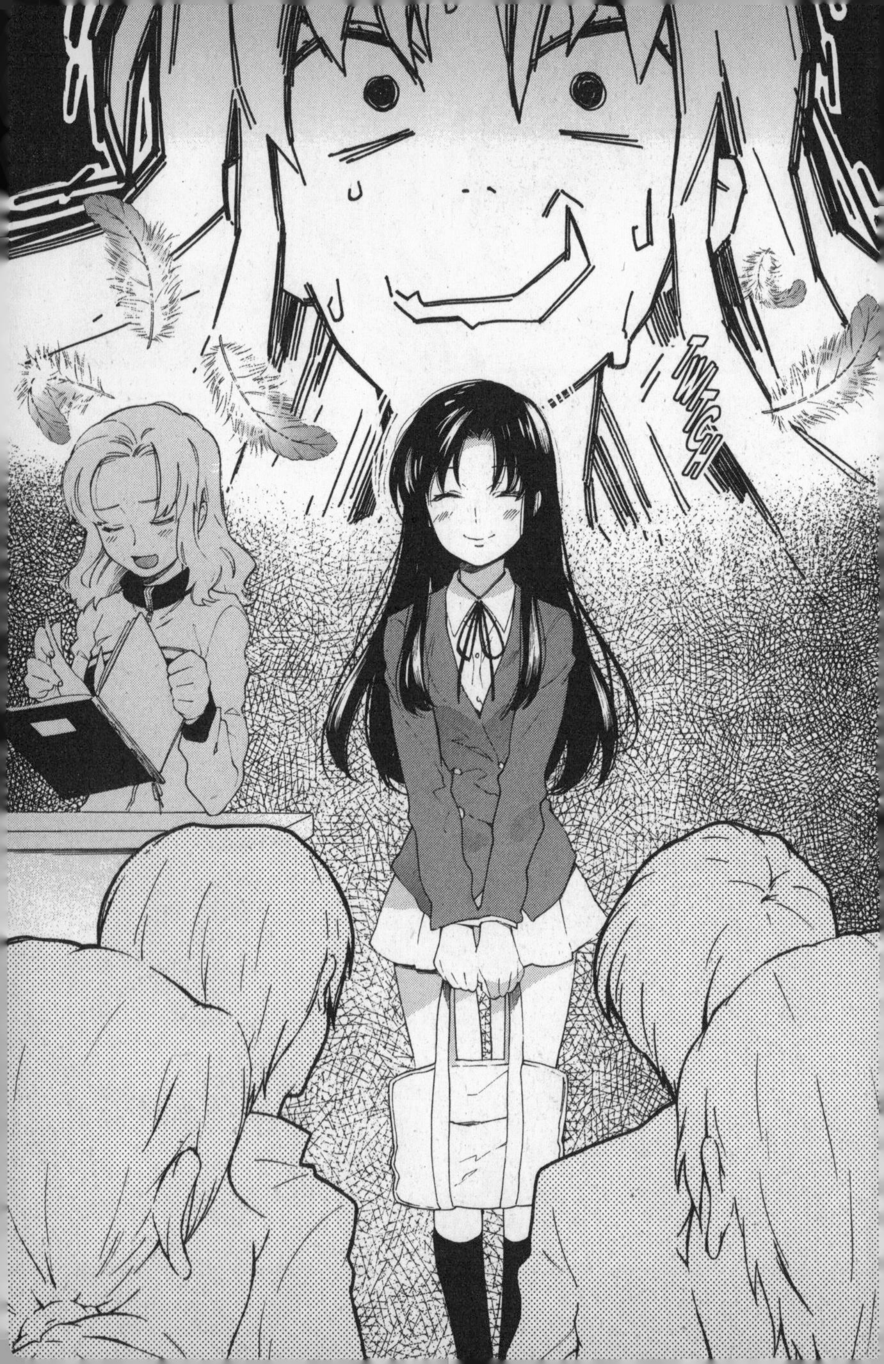
TWITCH

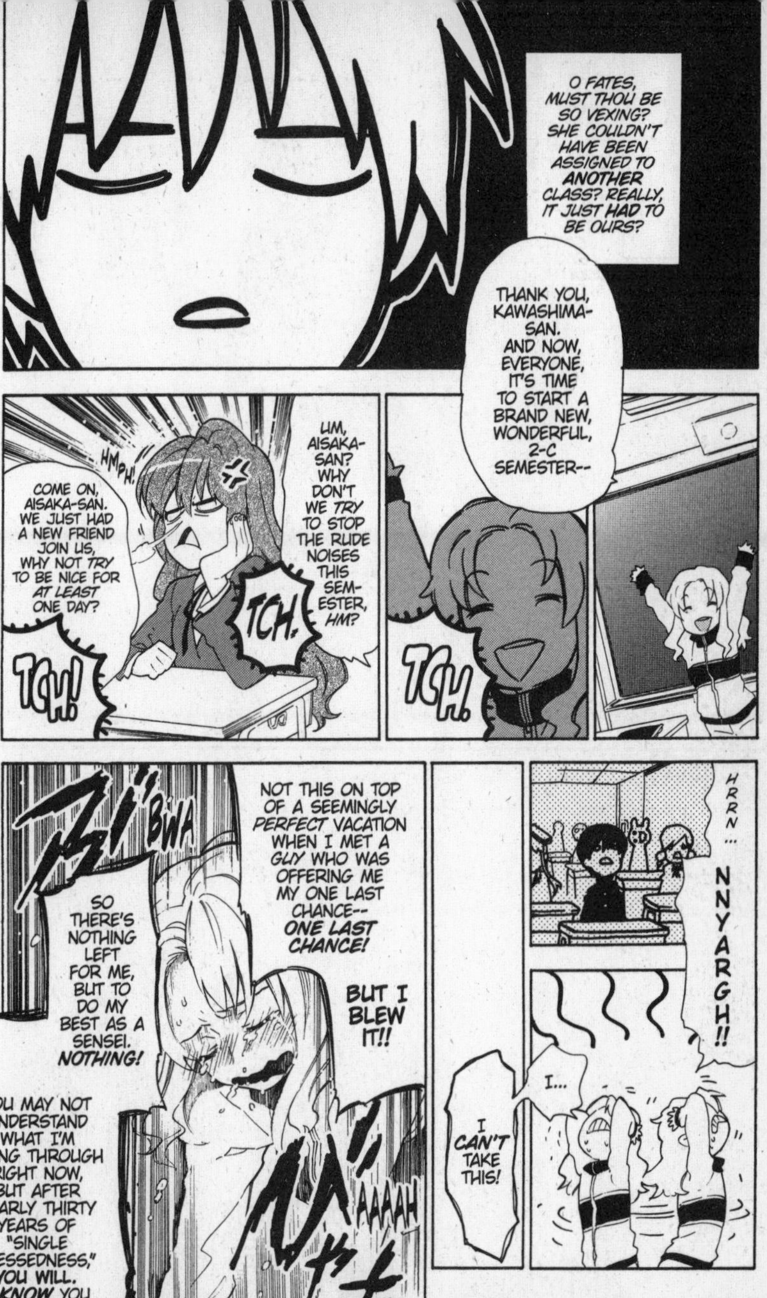

O FATES, MUST THOU BE SO VEXING? SHE COULDN'T HAVE BEEN ASSIGNED TO **ANOTHER** CLASS? REALLY, IT JUST **HAD** TO BE OURS?
THANK YOU, KAWASHIMA-SAN. AND NOW, EVERYONE, IT'S TIME TO START A BRAND NEW, WONDERFUL, 2-C SEMESTER--
UM, AISAKA-SAN? WHY DON'T WE *TRY* TO STOP THE RUDE NOISES THIS SEMESTER, *HM*?
TCH.
TCH.
HMPH!
COME ON, AISAKA-SAN. WE JUST HAD A NEW FRIEND JOIN US, WHY NOT *TRY* TO BE NICE FOR *AT LEAST* ONE DAY?
TCH!
HRRN...
NNYARGH!!
I...
I *CAN'T* TAKE THIS!
NOT THIS ON TOP OF A SEEMINGLY *PERFECT* VACATION WHEN I MET A *GUY* WHO WAS OFFERING ME MY ONE LAST CHANCE-- ***ONE LAST CHANCE!***
BUT I BLEW IT!!
BWA
SO THERE'S NOTHING LEFT FOR ME, BUT TO DO MY BEST AS A SENSEI. ***NOTHING!***
AAAAH
YOU MAY NOT UNDERSTAND WHAT I'M GOING THROUGH RIGHT NOW, BUT AFTER NEARLY THIRTY YEARS OF "SINGLE BLESSEDNESS," **YOU WILL.** I ***KNOW*** YOU WILL!

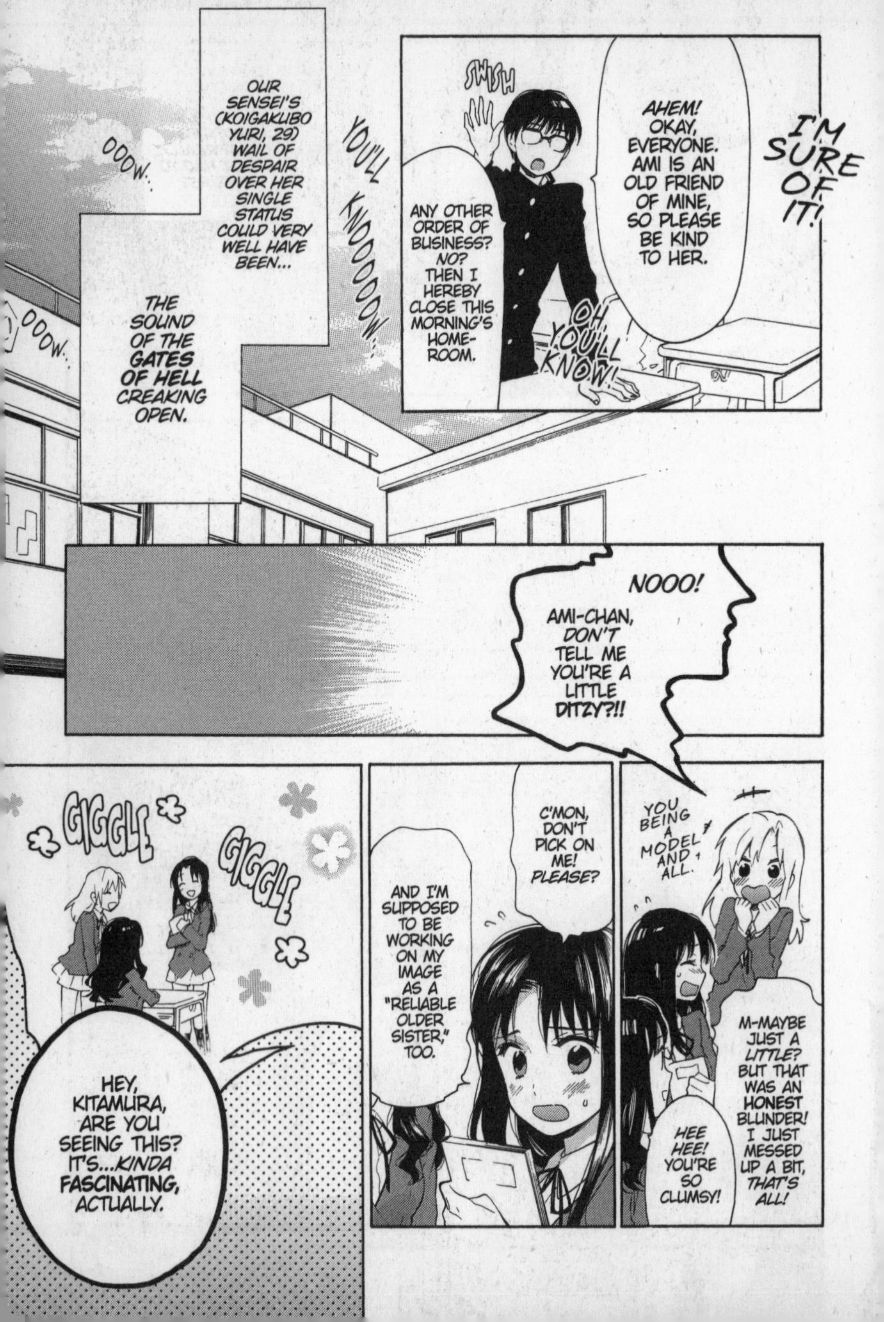
I'M SURE OF IT!
AHEM! OKAY, EVERYONE. AMI IS AN OLD FRIEND OF MINE, SO PLEASE BE KIND TO HER.
SWISH
ANY OTHER ORDER OF BUSINESS? NO? THEN I HEREBY CLOSE THIS MORNING'S HOME-ROOM.
OH, YOU'LL KNOW!
YOU'LL KNOOOOOOW...
OUR SENSEI'S (KOIGAKUBO YURI, 29) WAIL OF DESPAIR OVER HER SINGLE STATUS COULD VERY WELL HAVE BEEN...
OOOW...
THE SOUND OF THE GATES OF HELL CREAKING OPEN.
OOOW...
NOOO!
AMI-CHAN, DON'T TELL ME YOU'RE A LITTLE DITZY?!!
YOU BEING A MODEL AND ALL.
M-MAYBE JUST A LITTLE? BUT THAT WAS AN HONEST BLUNDER! I JUST MESSED UP A BIT, THAT'S ALL!
HEE HEE! YOU'RE SO CLUMSY!
C'MON, DON'T PICK ON ME! PLEASE?
AND I'M SUPPOSED TO BE WORKING ON MY IMAGE AS A "RELIABLE OLDER SISTER," TOO.
GIGGLE
GIGGLE
HEY, KITAMURA, ARE YOU SEEING THIS? IT'S...KINDA FASCINATING, ACTUALLY.

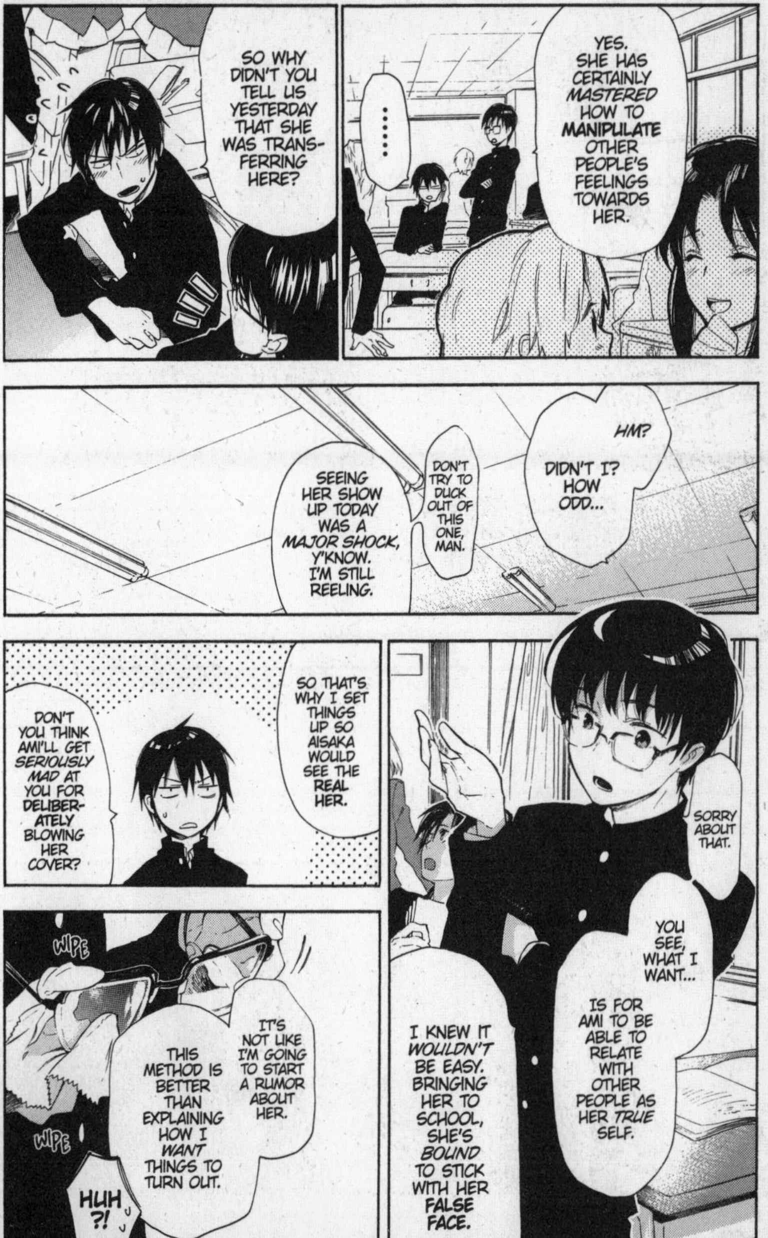
YES. SHE HAS CERTAINLY MASTERED HOW TO MANIPULATE OTHER PEOPLE'S FEELINGS TOWARDS HER.
......
SO WHY DIDN'T YOU TELL US YESTERDAY THAT SHE WAS TRANS-FERRING HERE?
HM?
DIDN'T I? HOW ODD...
DON'T TRY TO DUCK OUT OF THIS ONE, MAN.
SEEING HER SHOW UP TODAY WAS A MAJOR SHOCK, Y'KNOW. I'M STILL REELING.
SORRY ABOUT THAT.
YOU SEE, WHAT I WANT...
IS FOR AMI TO BE ABLE TO RELATE WITH OTHER PEOPLE AS HER TRUE SELF.
I KNEW IT WOULDN'T BE EASY. BRINGING HER TO SCHOOL, SHE'S BOUND TO STICK WITH HER FALSE FACE.
SO THAT'S WHY I SET THINGS UP SO AISAKA WOULD SEE THE REAL HER.
DON'T YOU THINK AMI'LL GET SERIOUSLY MAD AT YOU FOR DELIBER-ATELY BLOWING HER COVER?
WIPE
IT'S NOT LIKE I'M GOING TO START A RUMOR ABOUT HER.
THIS METHOD IS BETTER THAN EXPLAINING HOW I WANT THINGS TO TURN OUT.
WIPE
HUH?!

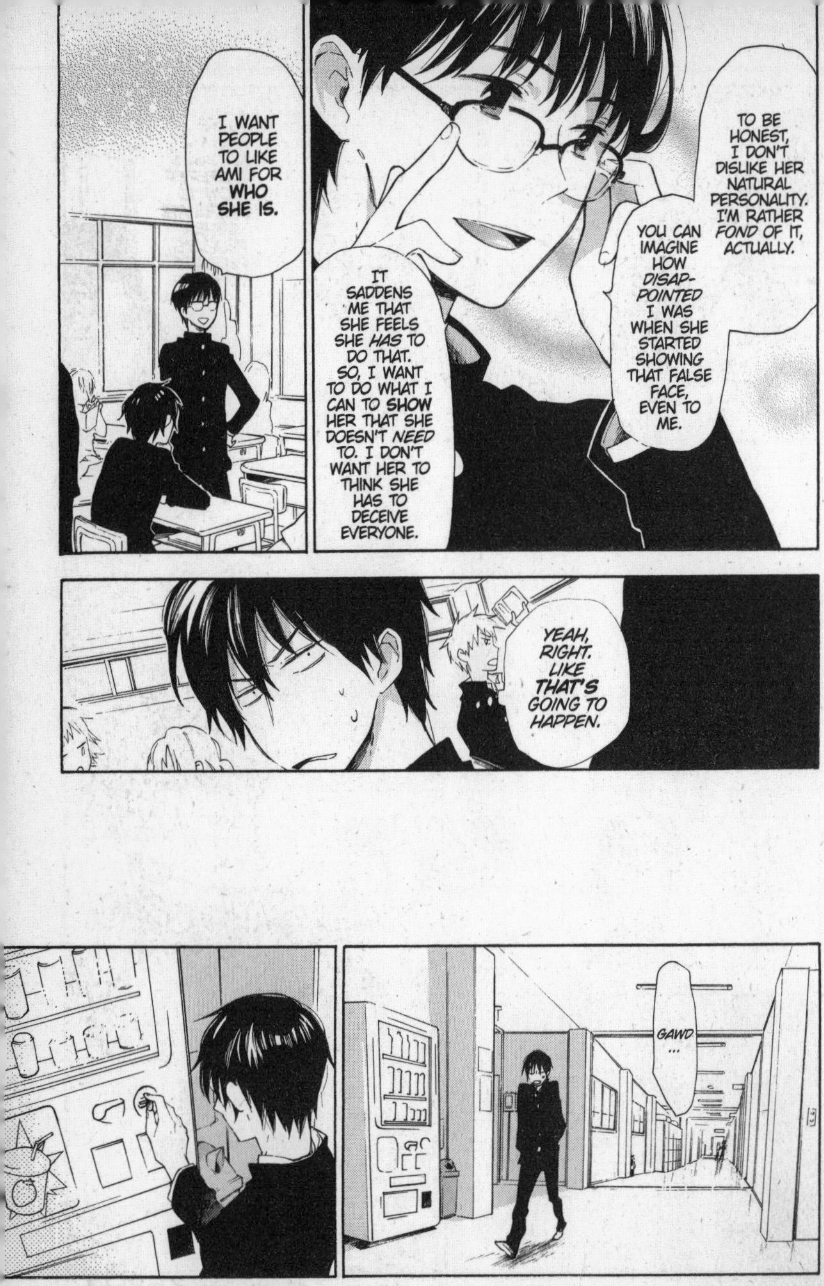
TO BE HONEST, I DON'T DISLIKE HER NATURAL PERSONALITY. I'M RATHER FOND OF IT, ACTUALLY.
YOU CAN IMAGINE HOW DISAPPOINTED I WAS WHEN SHE STARTED SHOWING THAT FALSE FACE, EVEN TO ME.
IT SADDENS ME THAT SHE FEELS SHE HAS TO DO THAT. SO, I WANT TO DO WHAT I CAN TO SHOW HER THAT SHE DOESN'T NEED TO. I DON'T WANT HER TO THINK SHE HAS TO DECEIVE EVERYONE.
I WANT PEOPLE TO LIKE AMI FOR WHO SHE IS.
YEAH, RIGHT. LIKE THAT'S GOING TO HAPPEN.
GAWD...

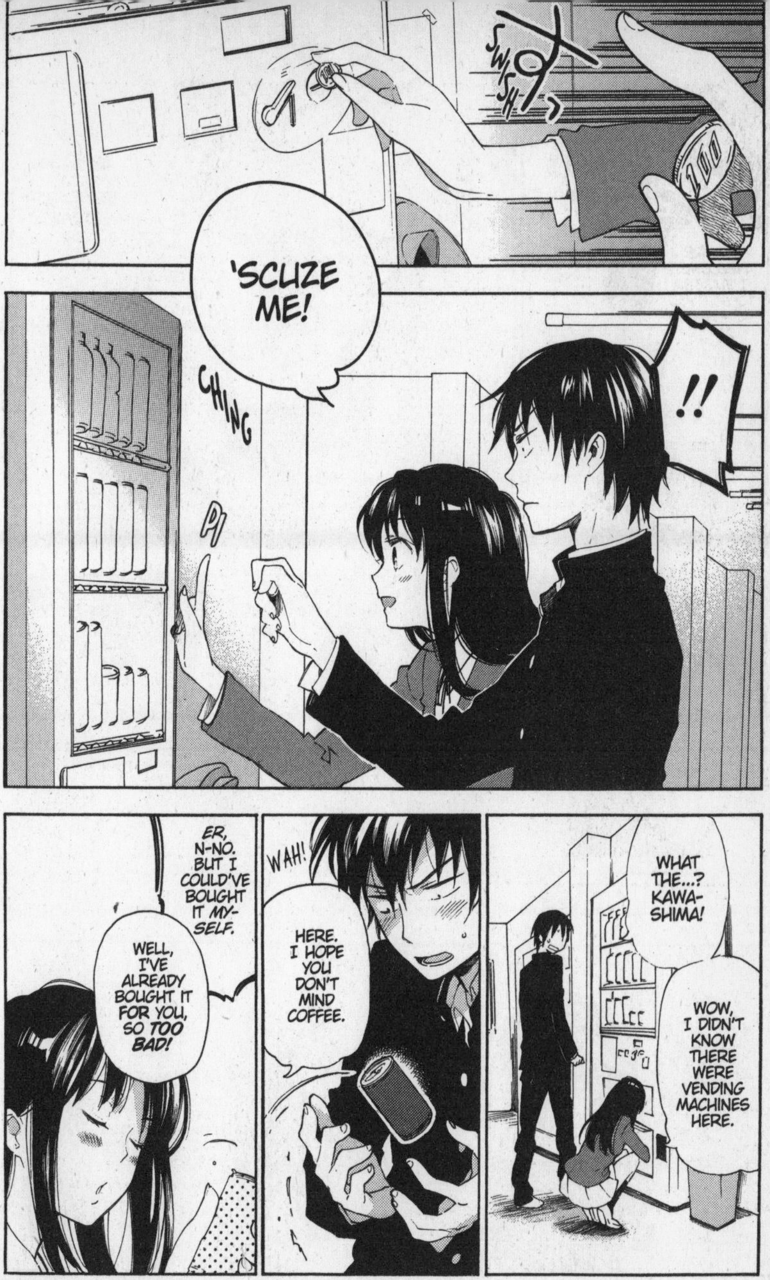
SWISH
'SCUZE ME!
!!
CHING
PI
WHAT THE...? KAWASHIMA!
WOW, I DIDN'T KNOW THERE WERE VENDING MACHINES HERE.
WAH!
HERE. I HOPE YOU DON'T MIND COFFEE.
ER, N-NO. BUT I COULD'VE BOUGHT IT *MYSELF*.
WELL, I'VE ALREADY BOUGHT IT FOR YOU, SO *TOO BAD!*

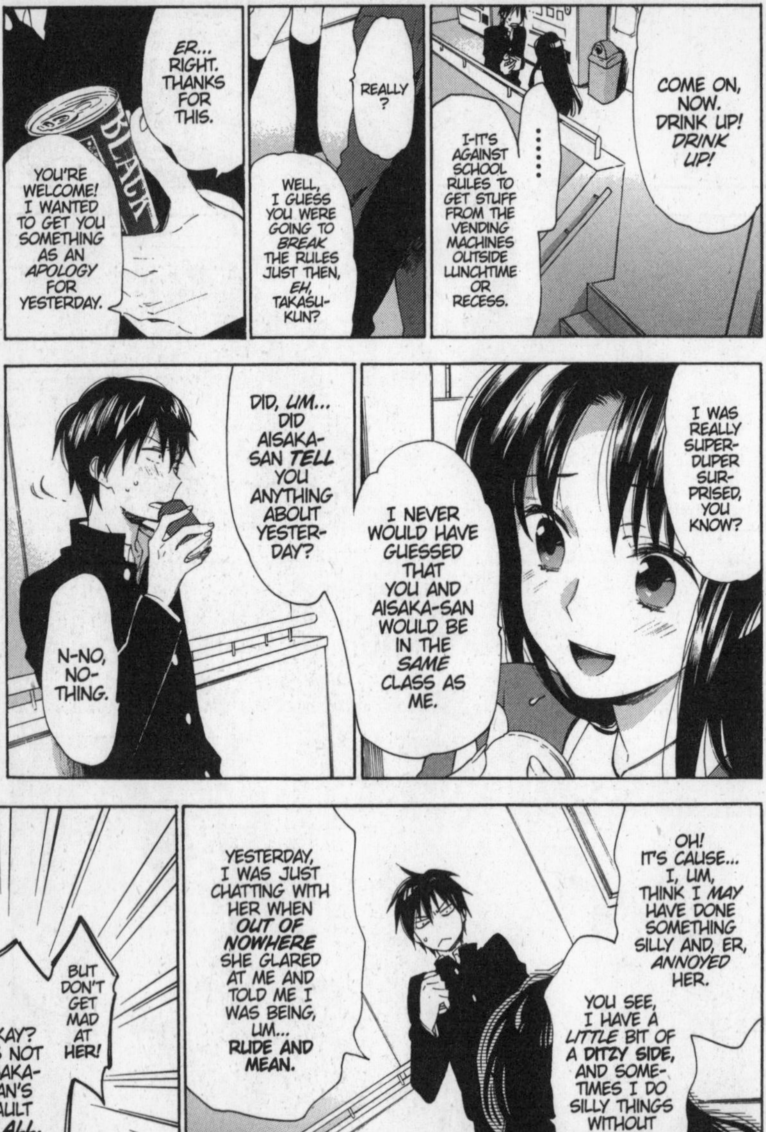
COME ON, NOW. DRINK UP! *DRINK UP!*
......
I-IT'S AGAINST SCHOOL RULES TO GET STUFF FROM THE VENDING MACHINES OUTSIDE LUNCHTIME OR RECESS.
REALLY?
WELL, I GUESS YOU WERE GOING TO *BREAK* THE RULES JUST THEN, *EH,* TAKASU-KUN?
ER... RIGHT. THANKS FOR THIS.
BLACK
YOU'RE WELCOME! I WANTED TO GET YOU SOMETHING AS AN *APOLOGY* FOR YESTERDAY.
I WAS REALLY SUPER-DUPER SURPRISED, YOU KNOW?
I NEVER WOULD HAVE GUESSED THAT YOU AND AISAKA-SAN WOULD BE IN THE *SAME* CLASS AS ME.
DID, *UM...* DID AISAKA-SAN ***TELL*** YOU ANYTHING ABOUT YESTERDAY?
N-NO, NOTHING.
OH! IT'S CAUSE... I, UM, THINK I *MAY* HAVE DONE SOMETHING SILLY AND, ER, *ANNOYED* HER.
YOU SEE, I HAVE A *LITTLE* BIT OF A **DITZY SIDE,** AND SOMETIMES I DO SILLY THINGS WITHOUT THINKING.
YESTERDAY, I WAS JUST CHATTING WITH HER WHEN ***OUT OF NOWHERE*** SHE GLARED AT ME AND TOLD ME I WAS BEING, UM... **RUDE AND MEAN.**
BUT DON'T GET MAD AT HER!
OKAY? IT'S NOT AISAKA-SAN'S FAULT ***AT ALL.***

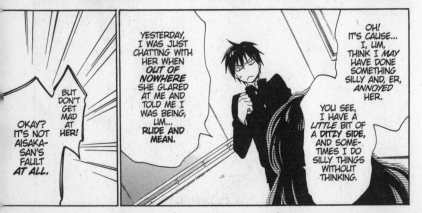

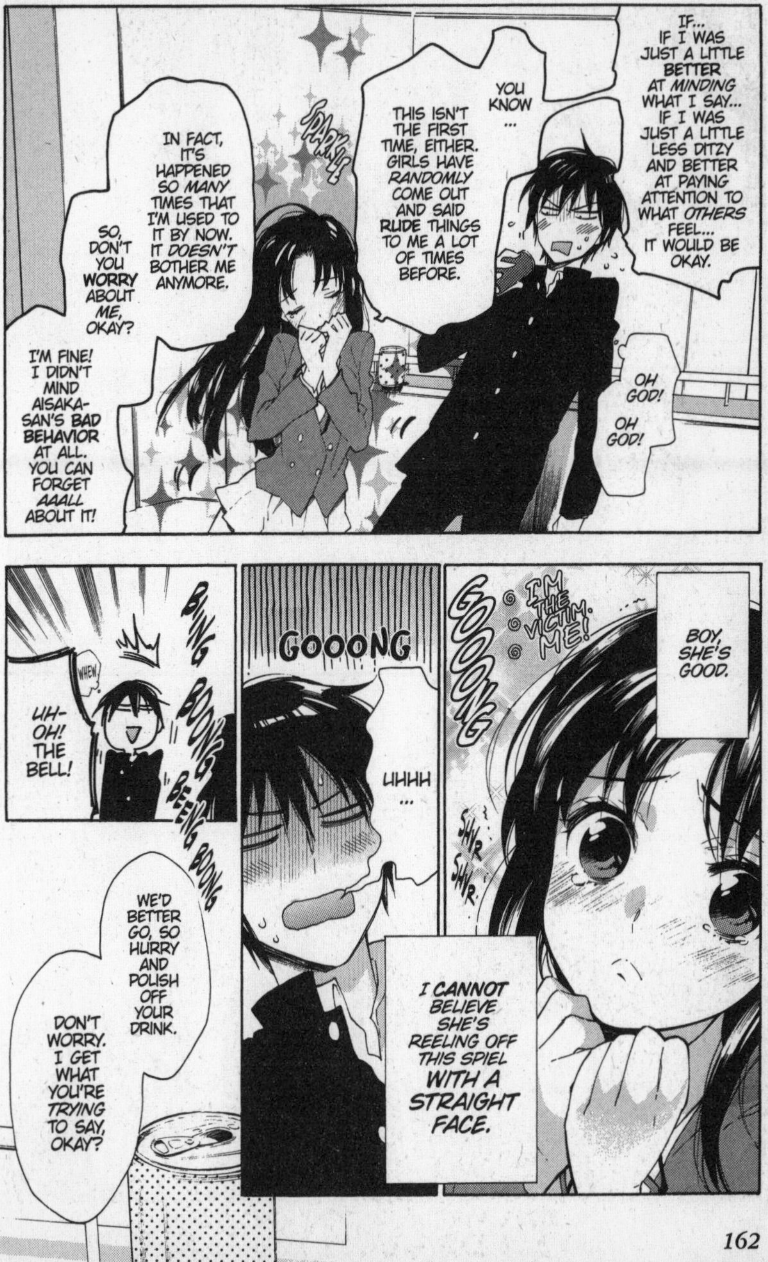
IF... IF I WAS JUST A LITTLE BETTER AT MINDING WHAT I SAY... IF I WAS JUST A LITTLE LESS DITZY AND BETTER AT PAYING ATTENTION TO WHAT OTHERS FEEL... IT WOULD BE OKAY.
YOU KNOW ...
THIS ISN'T THE FIRST TIME, EITHER. GIRLS HAVE RANDOMLY COME OUT AND SAID RUDE THINGS TO ME A LOT OF TIMES BEFORE.
SPARKLE
IN FACT, IT'S HAPPENED SO MANY TIMES THAT I'M USED TO IT BY NOW. IT DOESN'T BOTHER ME ANYMORE.
SO, DON'T YOU WORRY ABOUT ME, OKAY?
OH GOD! OH GOD!
I'M FINE! I DIDN'T MIND AISAKA-SAN'S BAD BEHAVIOR AT ALL. YOU CAN FORGET AAALL ABOUT IT!
BOY, SHE'S GOOD.
GOOOONG
I'M THE VICTIM. ME!
SHVR SHVR
I CANNOT BELIEVE SHE'S REELING OFF THIS SPIEL WITH A STRAIGHT FACE.
GOOONG
UHHH ...
BING BOONG BEENG BOONG
WHEW.
UH-OH! THE BELL!
WE'D BETTER GO, SO HURRY AND POLISH OFF YOUR DRINK.
DON'T WORRY. I GET WHAT YOU'RE TRYING TO SAY, OKAY?

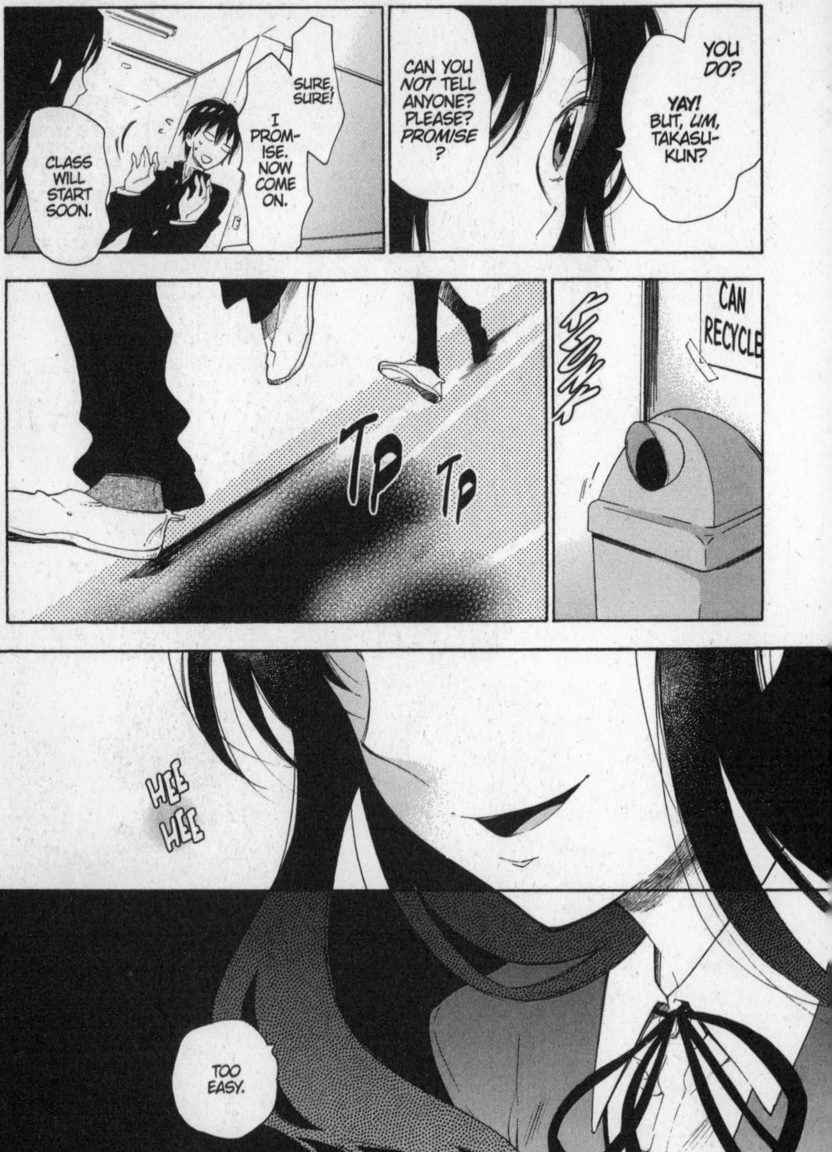
YOU DO?
YAY! BUT, UM, TAKASU-KUN?
CAN YOU NOT TELL ANYONE? PLEASE? PROMISE?
SURE, SURE!
I PROMISE. NOW COME ON.
CLASS WILL START SOON.
CAN RECYCLE
KLONK
TP TP
HEE HEE
TOO EASY.

TO BE CONTINUED!!

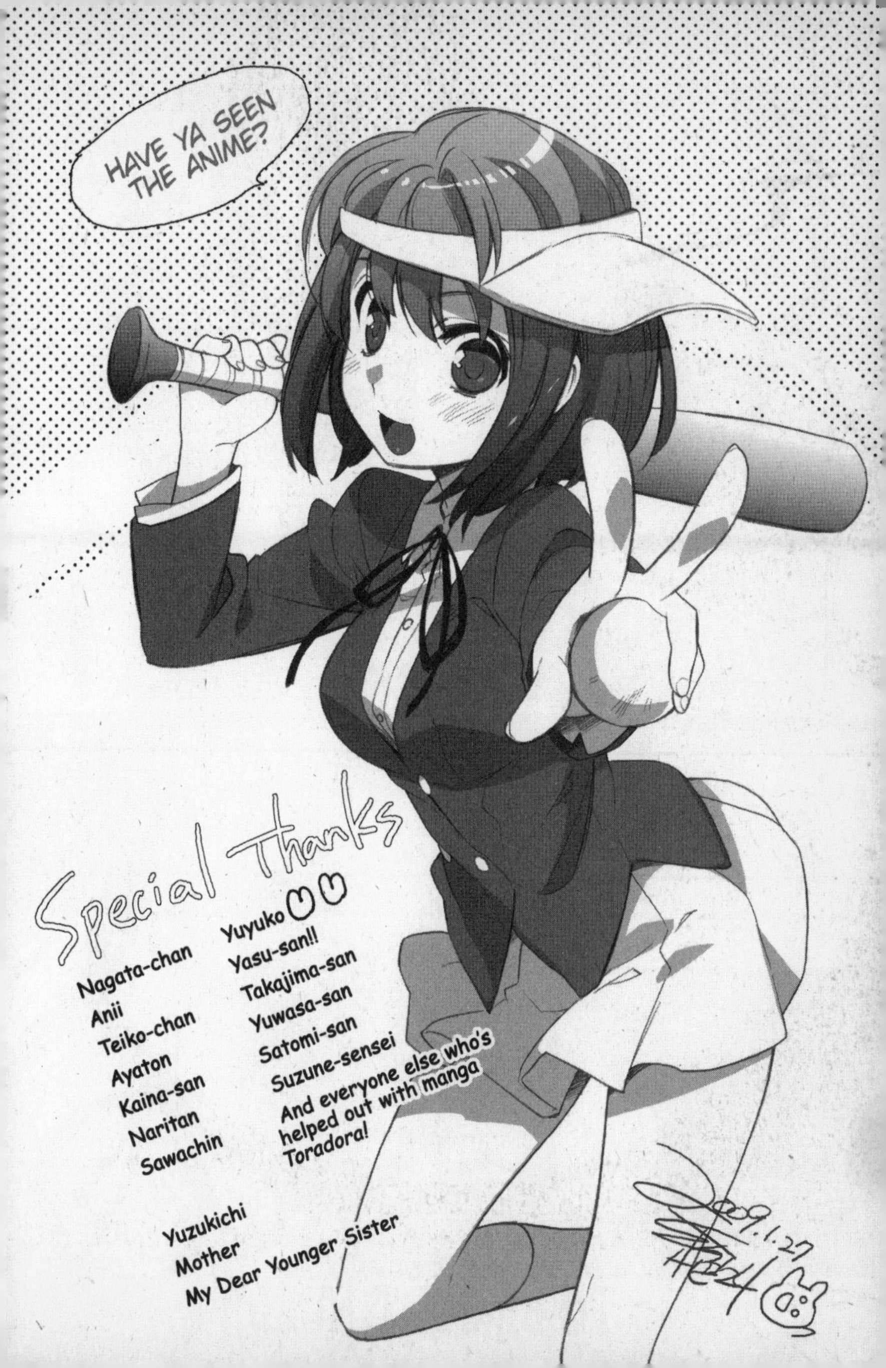
HAVE YA SEEN THE ANIME?
Special Thanks
Yuyuko
Yasu-san!!
Takajima-san
Yuwasa-san
Satomi-san
Suzune-sensei
And everyone else who's helped out with manga Toradora!
Nagata-chan
Anii
Teiko-chan
Ayaton
Kaina-san
Naritan
Sawachin
Yuzukichi
Mother
My Dear Younger Sister
2009.1.27

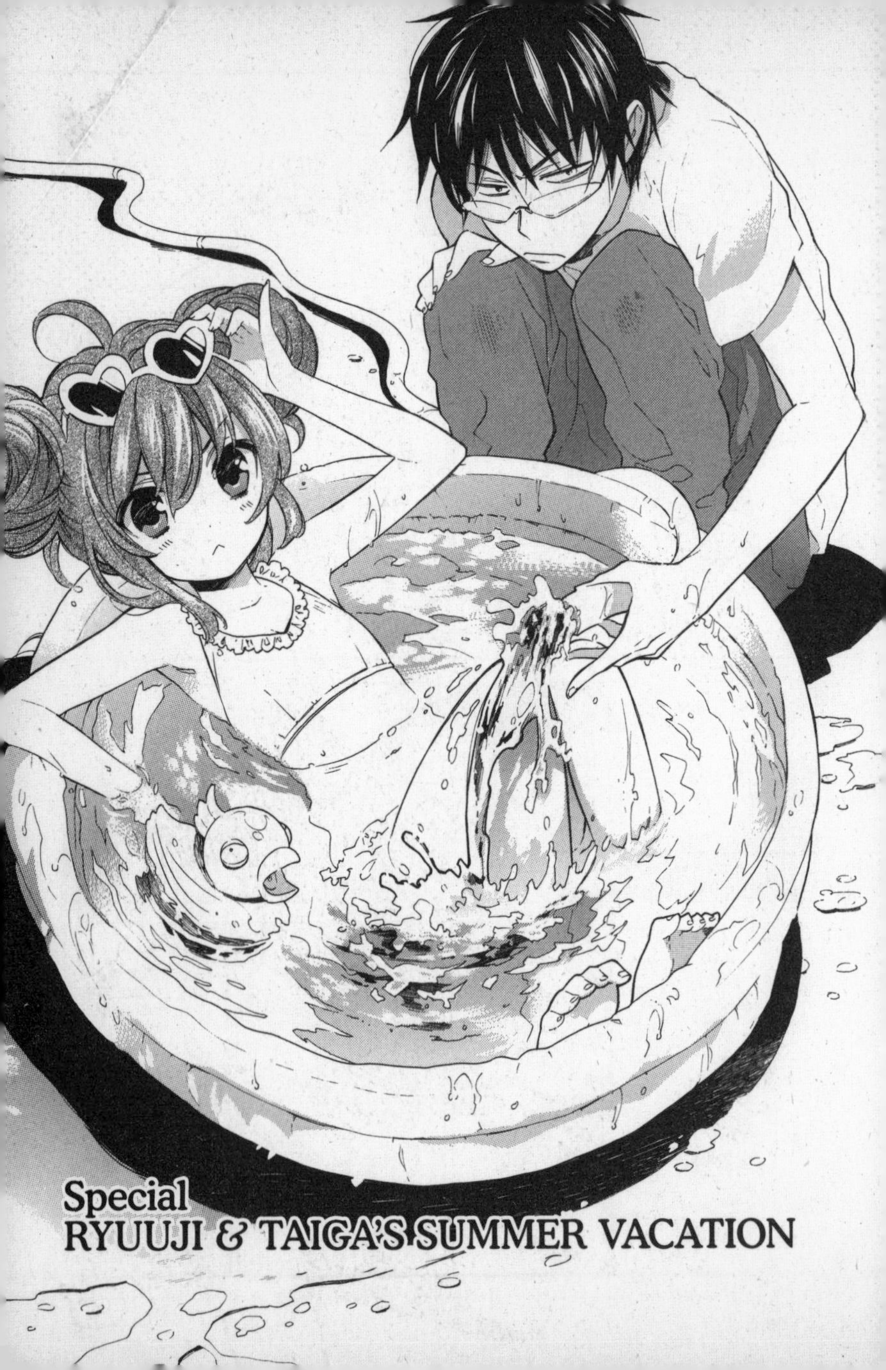

Special
RYUUJI & TAIGA'S SUMMER VACATION

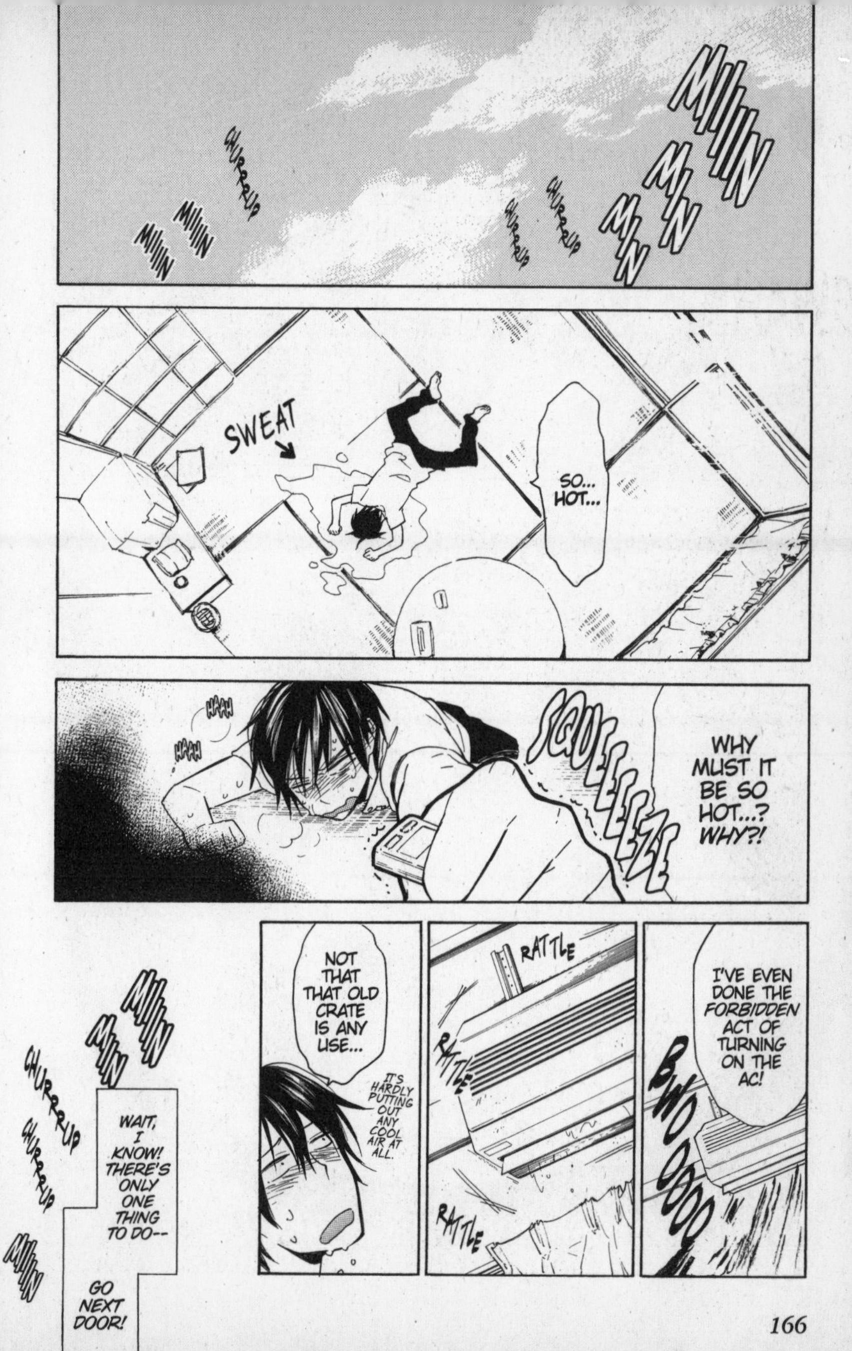
MIIIN MIN MIN
CHURRRUP
CHURRRUP
CHURRRUP
MIIIN
MIIIN
SO... HOT...
SWEAT
WHY MUST IT BE SO HOT...? WHY?!
SQUEEEEZE
HAAH
HAAH
I'VE EVEN DONE THE FORBIDDEN ACT OF TURNING ON THE AC!
BWOOOOOH
RATTLE
RATTLE
RATTLE
NOT THAT THAT OLD CRATE IS ANY USE...
IT'S HARDLY PUTTING OUT ANY COOL AIR AT ALL.
WAIT, I KNOW! THERE'S ONLY ONE THING TO DO--
GO NEXT DOOR!
MIIIN MIN
CHURRRUP
CHURRRUP
MIIIN

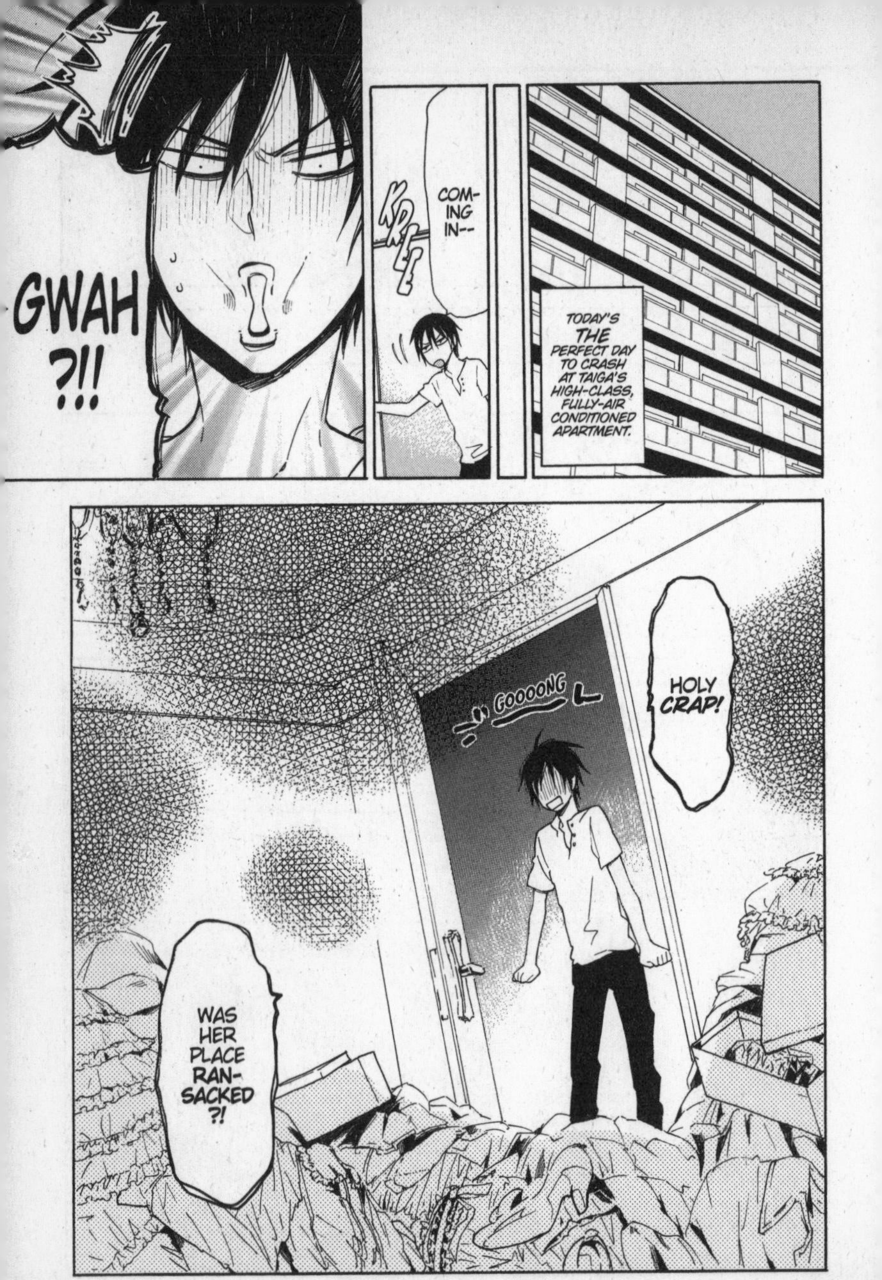
TODAY'S THE PERFECT DAY TO CRASH AT TAIGA'S HIGH-CLASS, FULLY-AIR CONDITIONED APARTMENT.
COMING IN--
KREE
GWAH ?!!
HOLY CRAP!
GOOOONG
WAS HER PLACE RAN-SACKED ?!

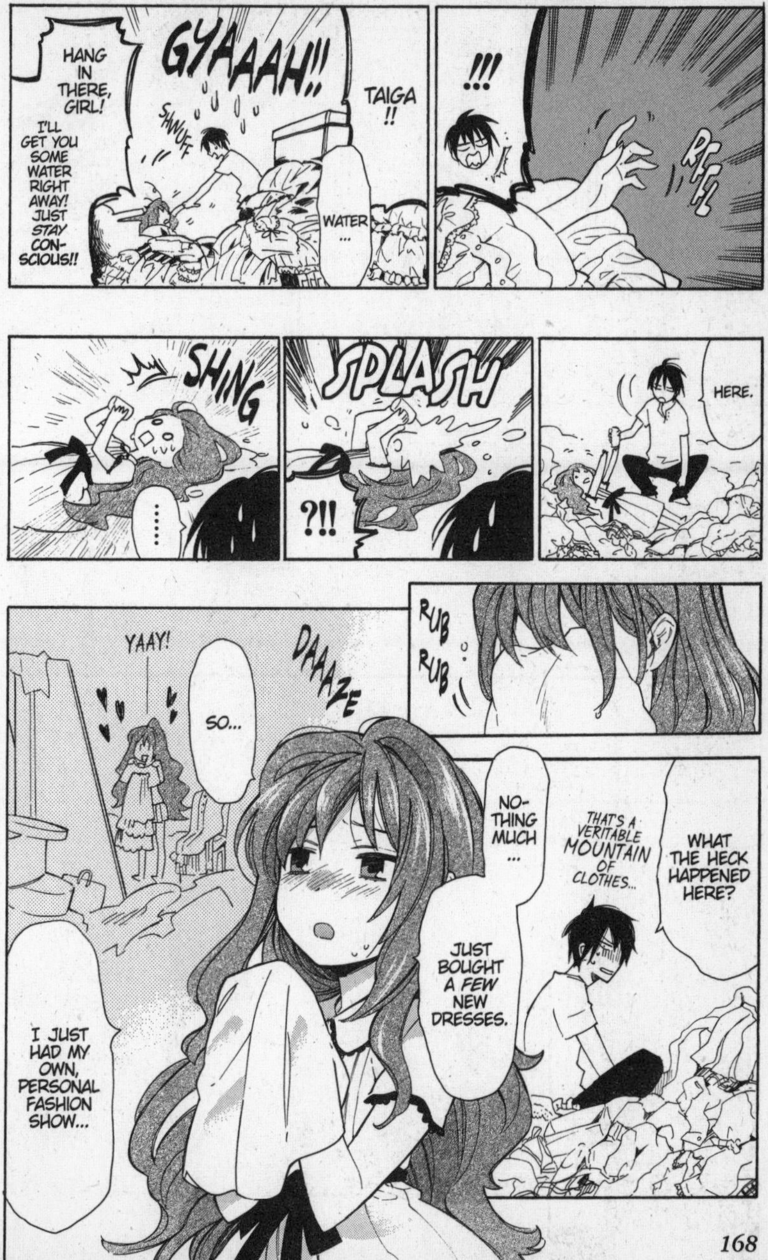
!!!
REEL
TAIGA !!
WATER ...
GYAAAH!!
SHNUFF
HANG IN THERE, GIRL! I'LL GET YOU SOME WATER RIGHT AWAY! JUST STAY CONSCIOUS!!
HERE.
SPLASH
?!!
SHING
......
RUB RUB
WHAT THE HECK HAPPENED HERE?
THAT'S A VERITABLE MOUNTAIN OF CLOTHES...
NO-THING MUCH ...
JUST BOUGHT A FEW NEW DRESSES.
DAAAAZE
SO...
YAAY!
I JUST HAD MY OWN, PERSONAL FASHION SHOW...

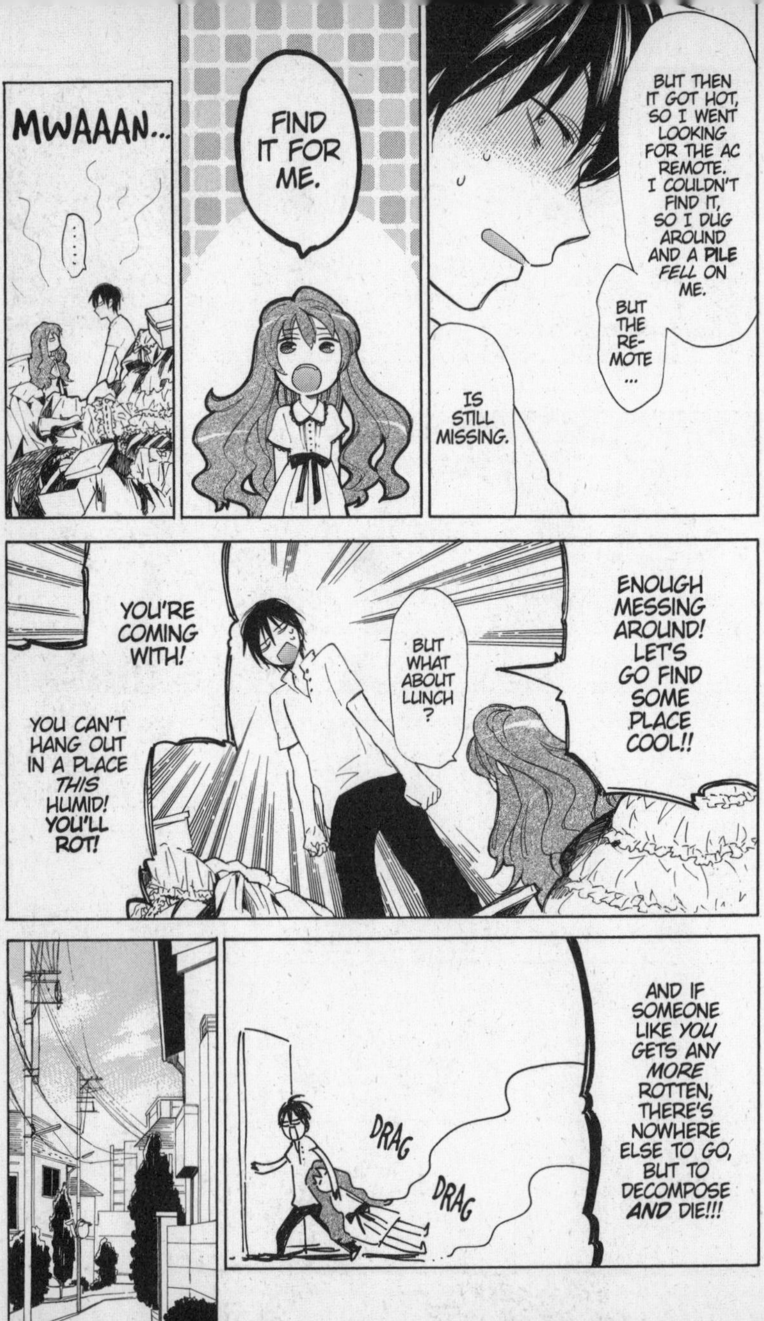
BUT THEN IT GOT HOT, SO I WENT LOOKING FOR THE AC REMOTE. I COULDN'T FIND IT, SO I DUG AROUND AND A PILE FELL ON ME.
BUT THE RE-MOTE ...
IS STILL MISSING.
FIND IT FOR ME.
MWAAAN...
......
ENOUGH MESSING AROUND! LET'S GO FIND SOME PLACE COOL!!
BUT WHAT ABOUT LUNCH?
YOU'RE COMING WITH!
YOU CAN'T HANG OUT IN A PLACE THIS HUMID! YOU'LL ROT!
AND IF SOMEONE LIKE YOU GETS ANY MORE ROTTEN, THERE'S NOWHERE ELSE TO GO, BUT TO DECOMPOSE AND DIE!!!
DRAG
DRAG

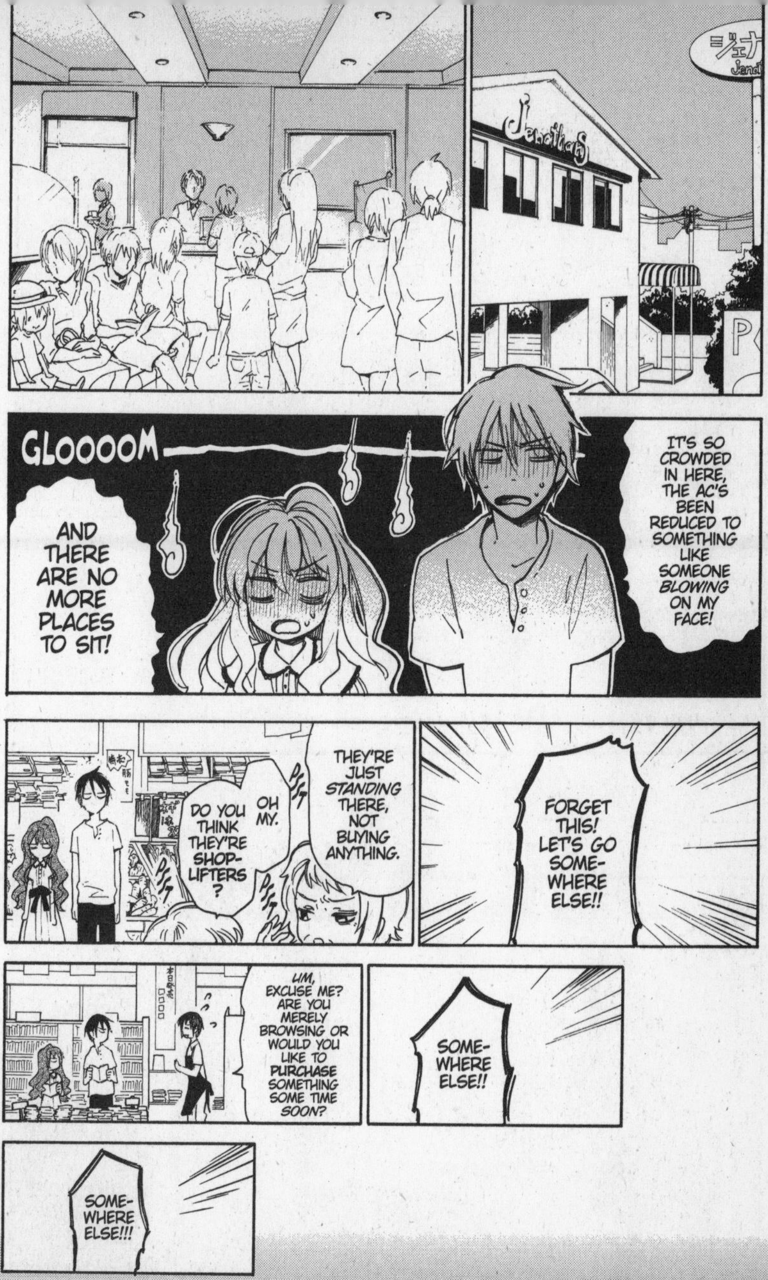
Jenathans
IT'S SO CROWDED IN HERE, THE AC'S BEEN REDUCED TO SOMETHING LIKE SOMEONE *BLOWING* ON MY FACE!
GLOOOM
AND THERE ARE NO MORE PLACES TO SIT!
FORGET THIS! LET'S GO SOME-WHERE ELSE!!
THEY'RE JUST *STANDING* THERE, NOT BUYING ANYTHING.
OH MY.
DO YOU THINK THEY'RE SHOP-LIFTERS?
SOME-WHERE ELSE!!
UM, EXCUSE ME? ARE YOU MERELY BROWSING OR WOULD YOU LIKE TO PURCHASE SOMETHING SOME TIME *SOON*?
SOME-WHERE ELSE!!!

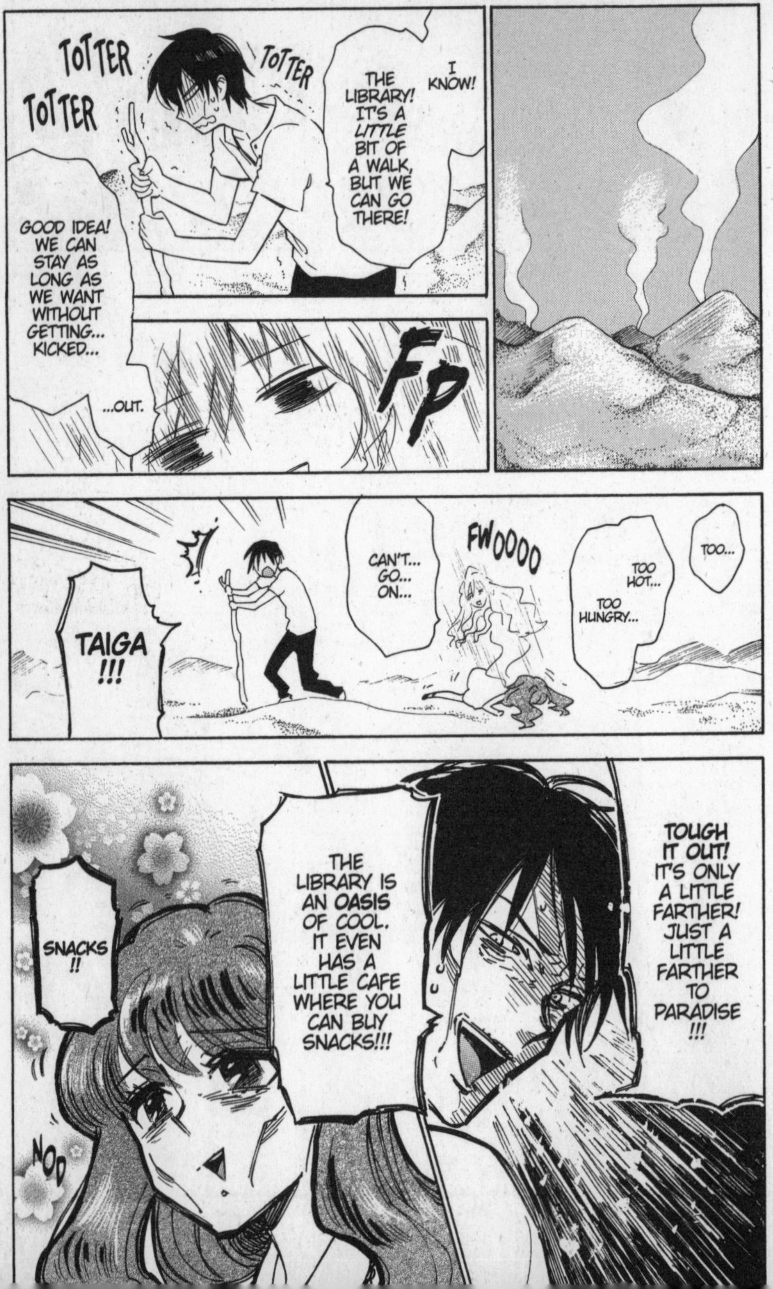
I KNOW!
THE LIBRARY! IT'S A LITTLE BIT OF A WALK, BUT WE CAN GO THERE!
TOTTER
TOTTER
TOTTER
GOOD IDEA! WE CAN STAY AS LONG AS WE WANT WITHOUT GETTING... KICKED...
FP
...OUT.
TOO...
TOO HOT...
TOO HUNGRY...
FWOOOO
CAN'T... GO... ON...
TAIGA !!!
TOUGH IT OUT! IT'S ONLY A LITTLE FARTHER! JUST A LITTLE FARTHER TO PARADISE !!!
THE LIBRARY IS AN OASIS OF COOL. IT EVEN HAS A LITTLE CAFE WHERE YOU CAN BUY SNACKS!!!
SNACKS !!
NOD

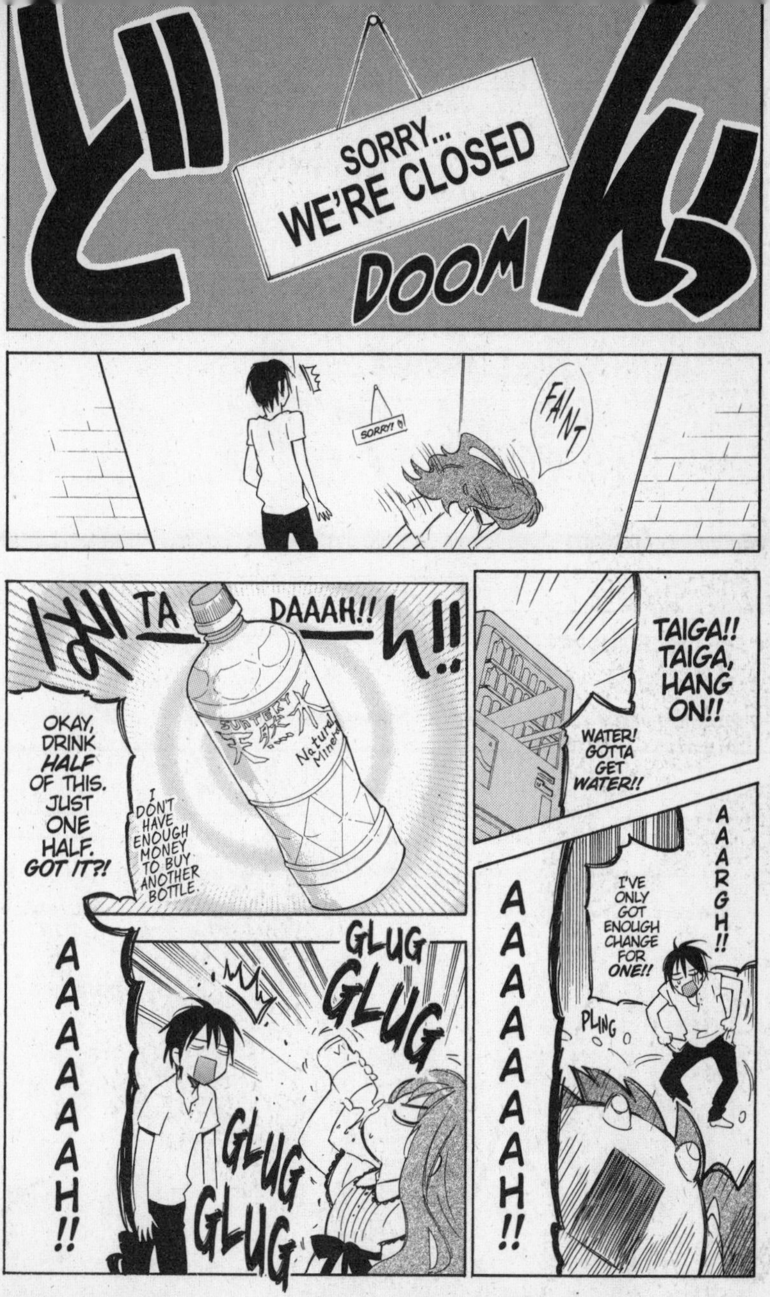
SORRY... WE'RE CLOSED
DOOM
SORRY!
FAINT
TAIGA!! TAIGA, HANG ON!!
WATER! GOTTA GET WATER!!
TA DAAAH!!
OKAY, DRINK HALF OF THIS. JUST ONE HALF. GOT IT?!
I DON'T HAVE ENOUGH MONEY TO BUY ANOTHER BOTTLE.
AAAARGH!!
I'VE ONLY GOT ENOUGH CHANGE FOR ONE!!
PLING
AAAAAAAAAH!!
GLUG GLUG
GLUG GLUG
AAAAAAAAH!!

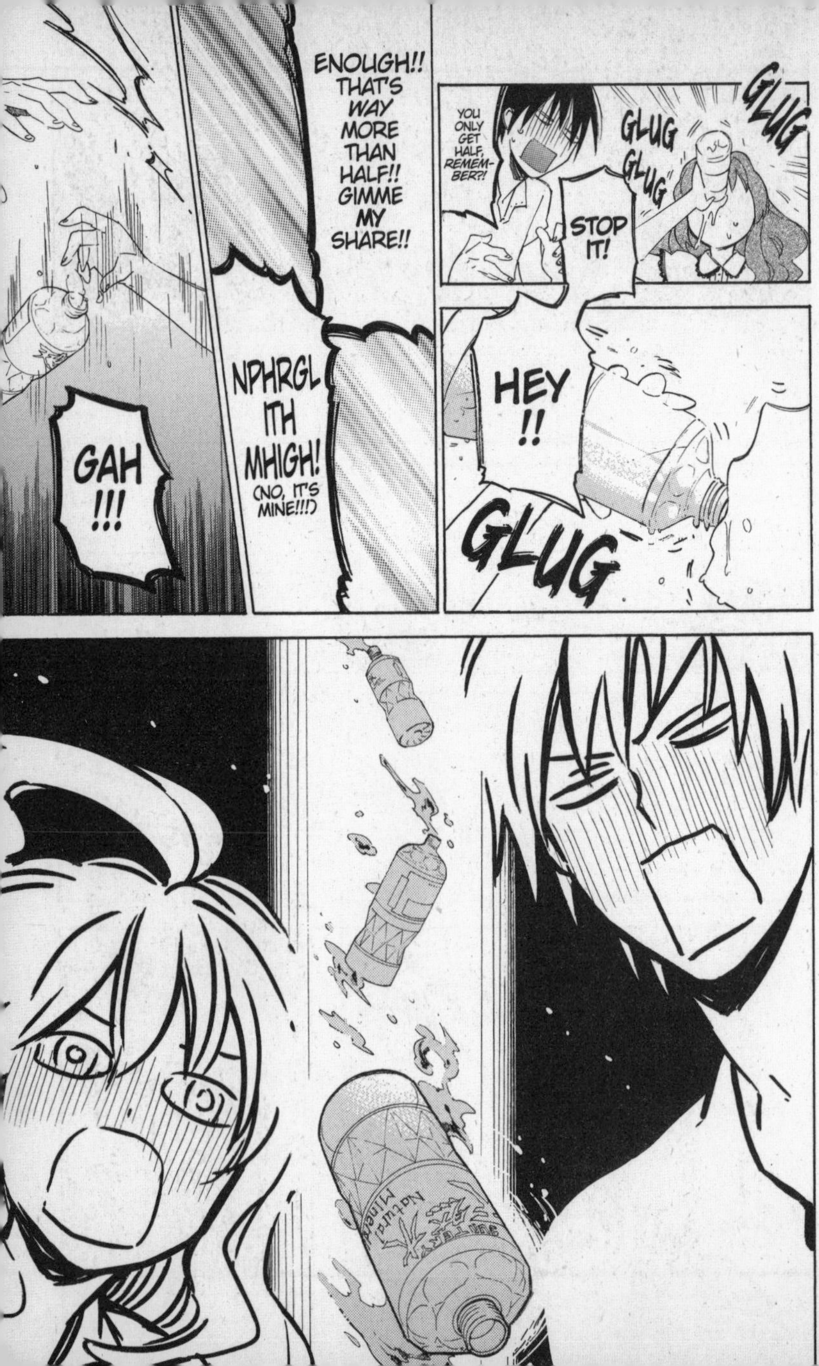
GLUG
GLUG
GLUG
YOU ONLY GET HALF, REMEMBER?!
STOP IT!
HEY !!
GLUG
ENOUGH!! THAT'S WAY MORE THAN HALF!! GIMME MY SHARE!!
NPHRGL ITH MHIGH!
(NO, IT'S MINE!!!)
GAH !!!

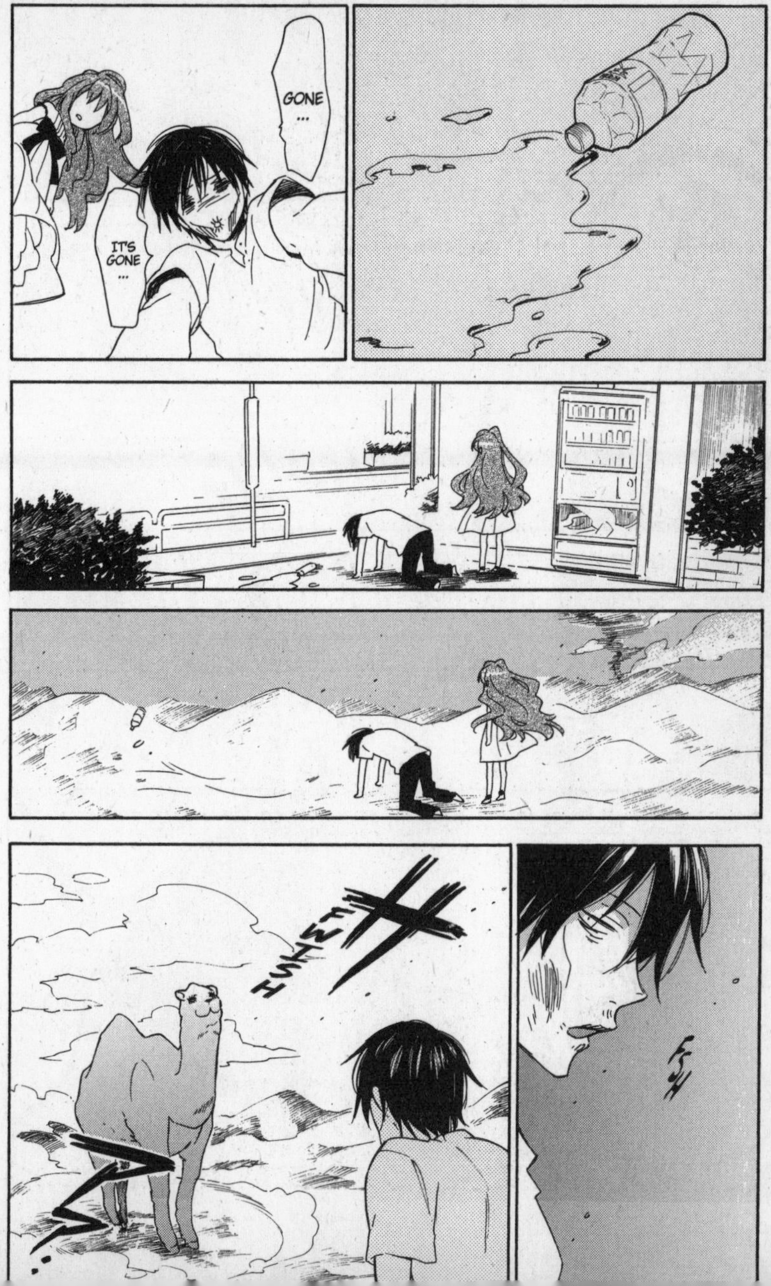
GONE ...
IT'S GONE ...

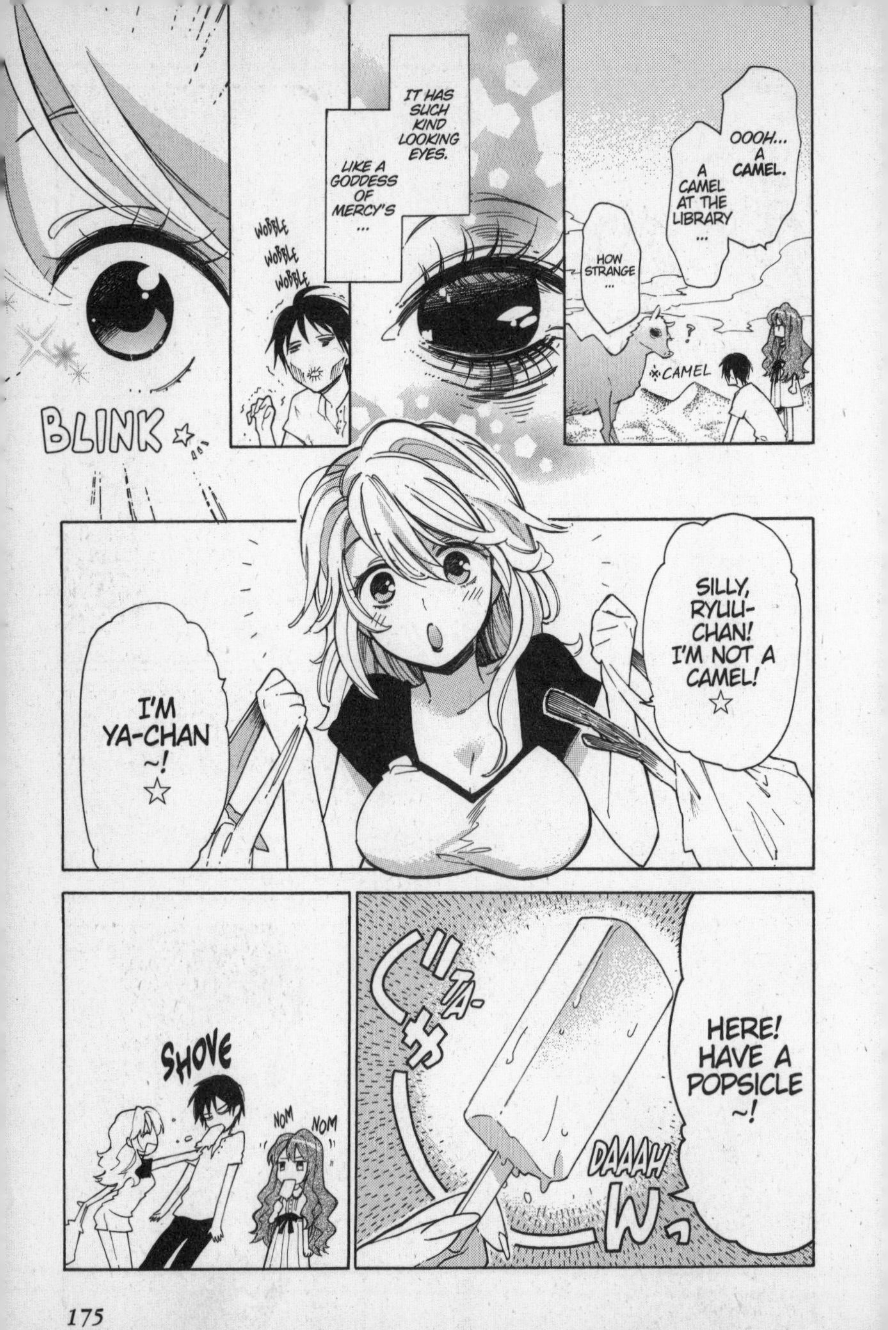
OOOH... A CAMEL.
A CAMEL AT THE LIBRARY ...
HOW STRANGE ...
※CAMEL
IT HAS SUCH KIND LOOKING EYES.
LIKE A GODDESS OF MERCY'S ...
WOBBLE WOBBLE WOBBLE
BLINK ☆
SILLY, RYUU-CHAN! I'M NOT A CAMEL! ☆
I'M YA-CHAN ~! ☆
HERE! HAVE A POPSICLE ~!
DAAAH
W
ITA-
SHOVE
NOM NOM

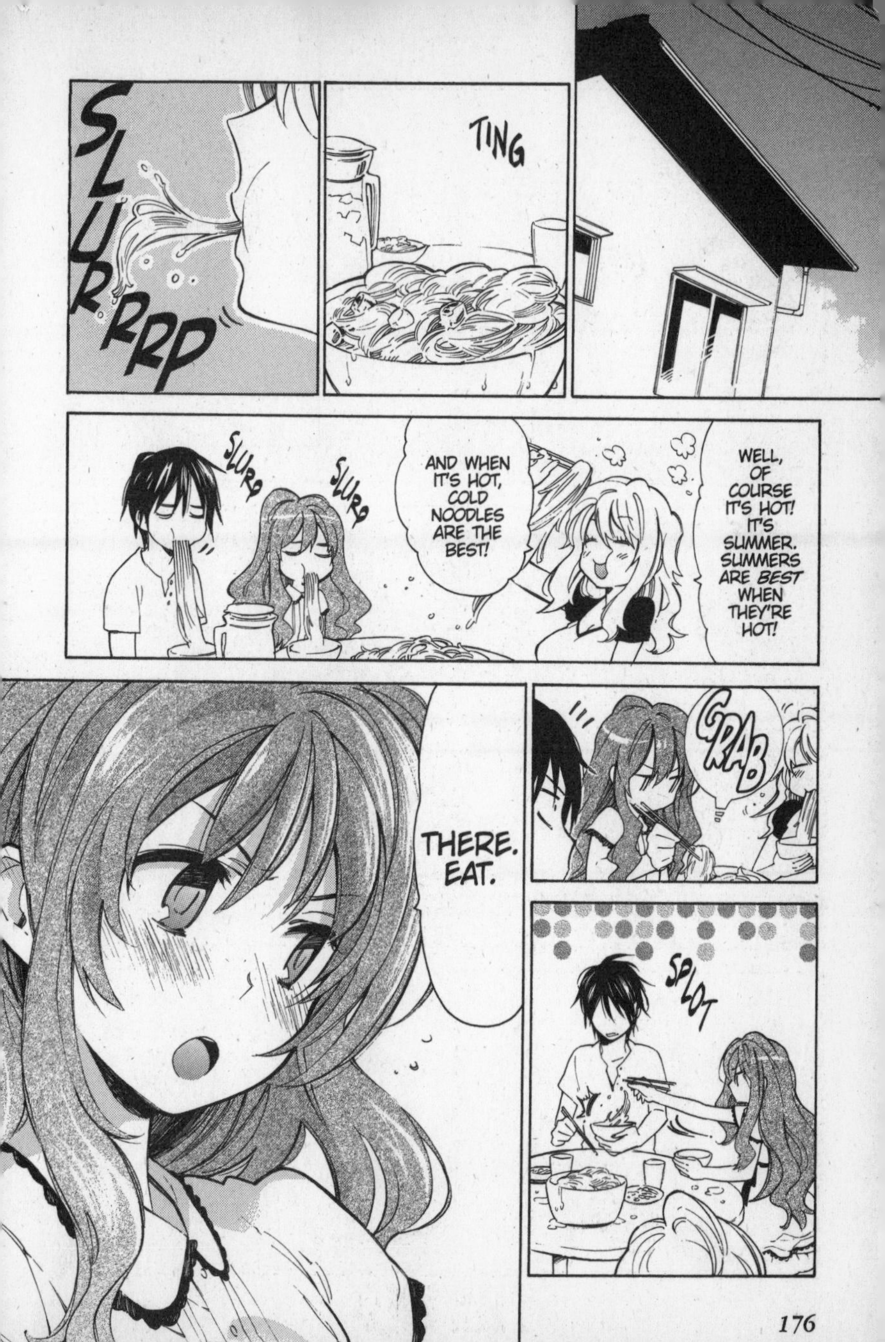
TING
SLURRRP
WELL, OF COURSE IT'S HOT! IT'S SUMMER. SUMMERS ARE *BEST* WHEN THEY'RE HOT!
AND WHEN IT'S HOT, COLD NOODLES ARE THE BEST!
SLURP
SLURP
GRAB
SPLOT
THERE. EAT.

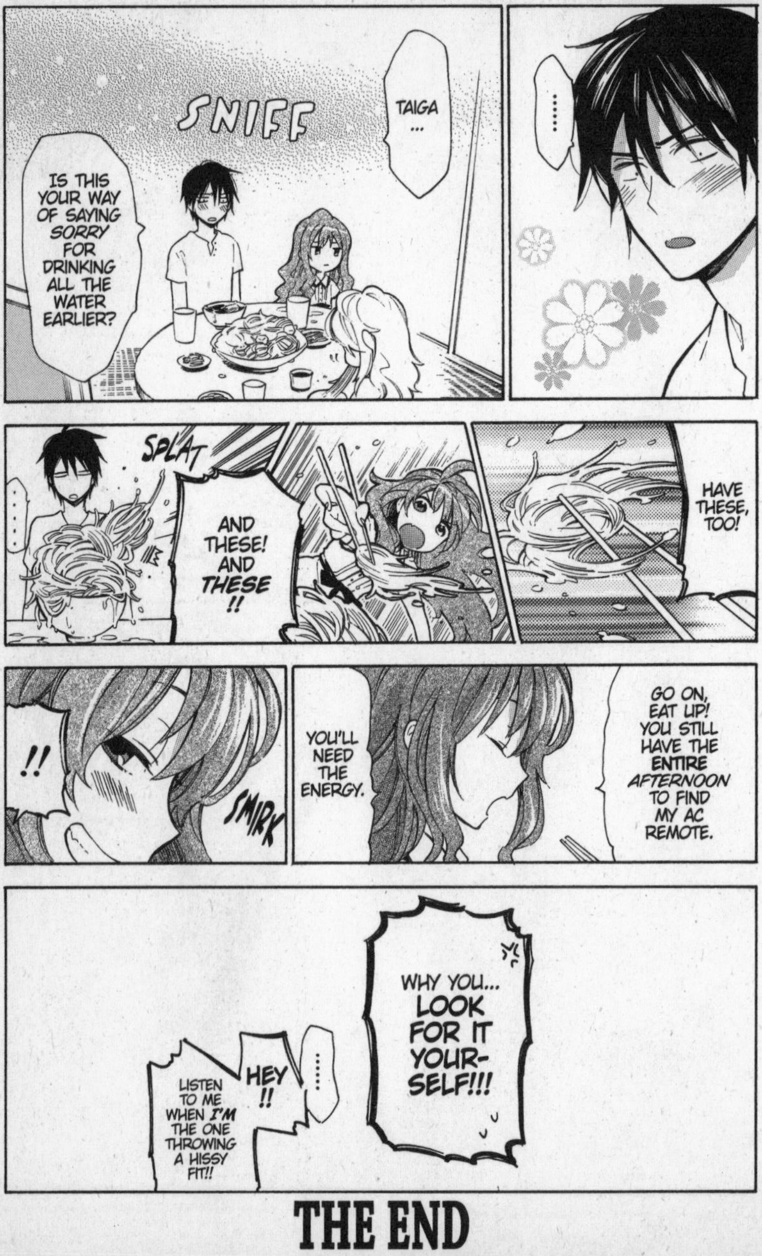
......
TAIGA ...
SNIFF
IS THIS YOUR WAY OF SAYING SORRY FOR DRINKING ALL THE WATER EARLIER?
HAVE THESE, TOO!
AND THESE! AND THESE!!
SPLAT
...
GO ON, EAT UP! YOU STILL HAVE THE ENTIRE AFTERNOON TO FIND MY AC REMOTE.
YOU'LL NEED THE ENERGY.
SMIRK
!!
WHY YOU... LOOK FOR IT YOURSELF!!!
......
HEY!!
LISTEN TO ME WHEN I'M THE ONE THROWING A HISSY FIT!!

THE END

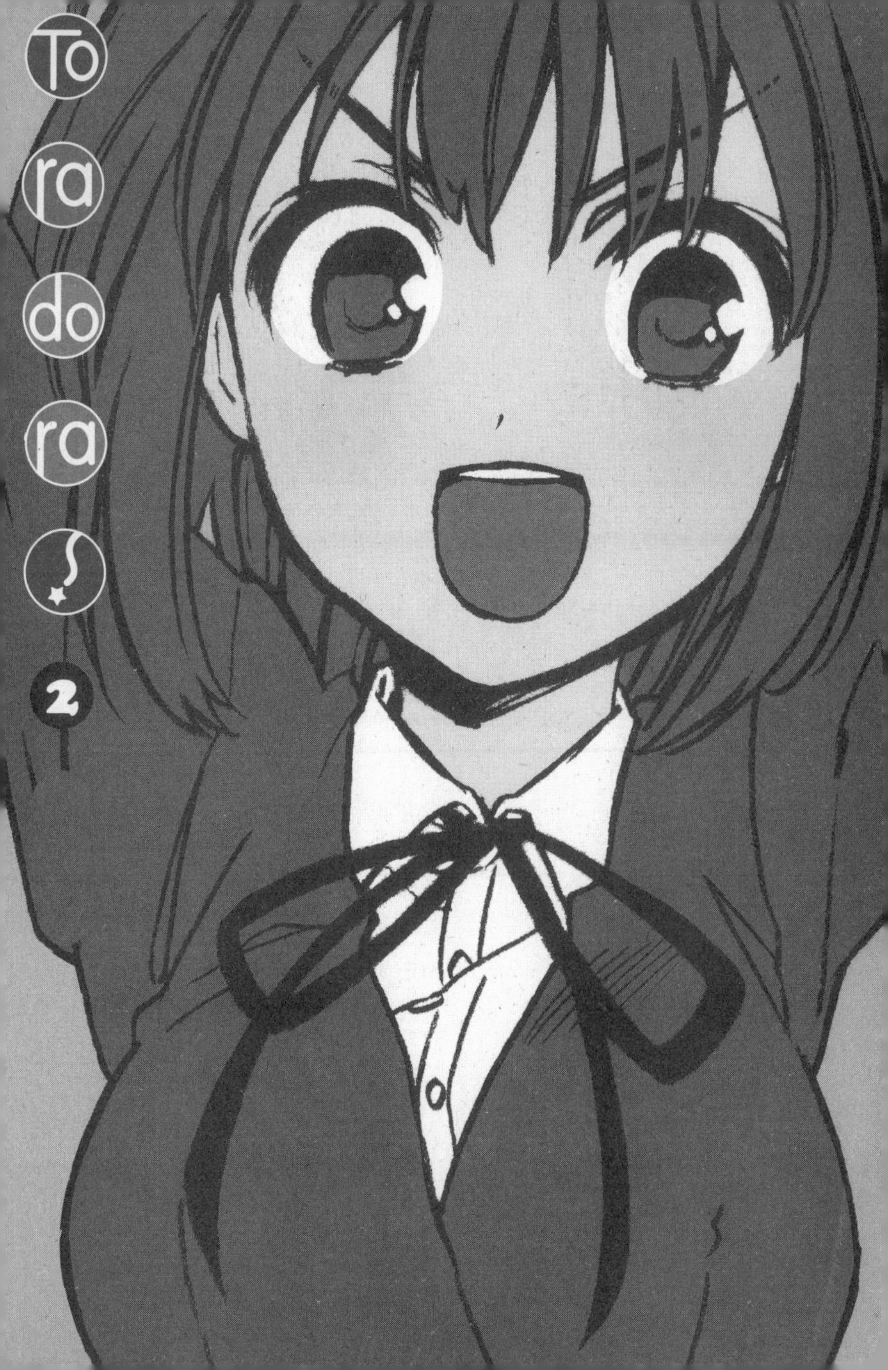
Toradora!
2

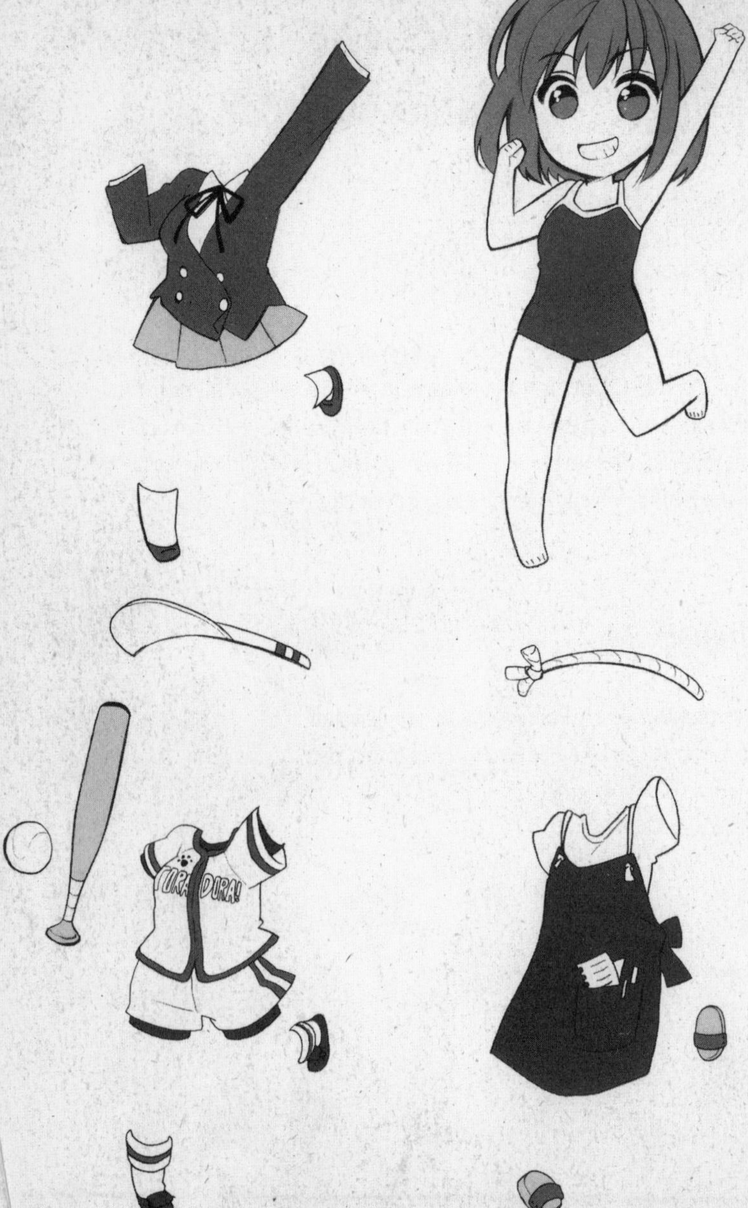
TORA DORA!

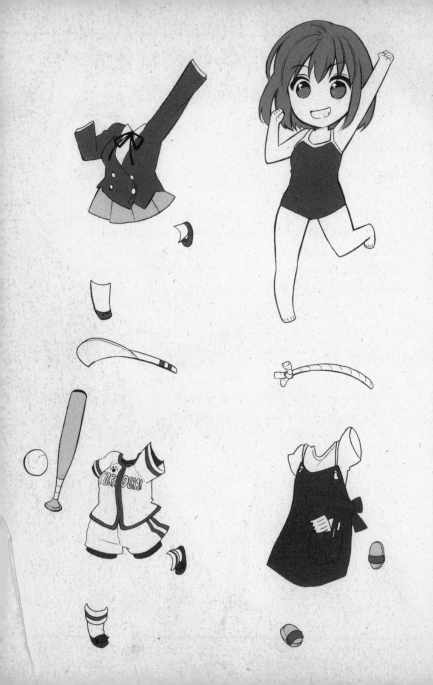

TRANSLATION NOTES

Chapter 13

The "Great Pine Corridor" refers to one of the more famous hallways in the old Edo Castle. It was in this hallway that Asano Takumi drew his blade—an act forbidden within the castle walls—and assaulted Kira Kozuke after an insult. That was the incident that kick started the story of the revenge of the Forty-seven Ronin.

Chapter 14

Ojisama/Obasama – Polite ways of saying Aunt and Uncle. These terms can also be used to refer to the parents of a close friend.

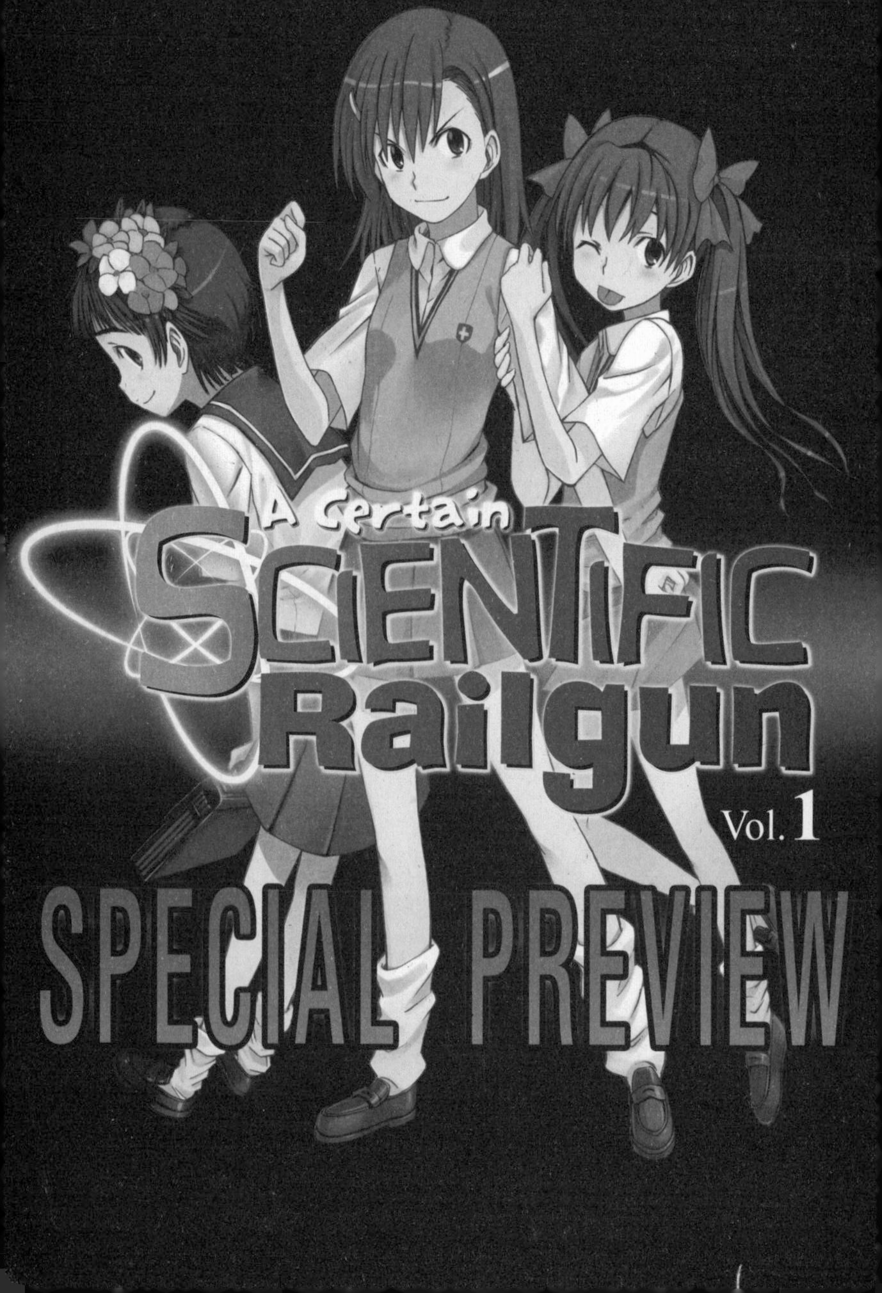
A Certain
SCIENTIFIC
Railgun
Vol. 1
SPECIAL PREVIEW

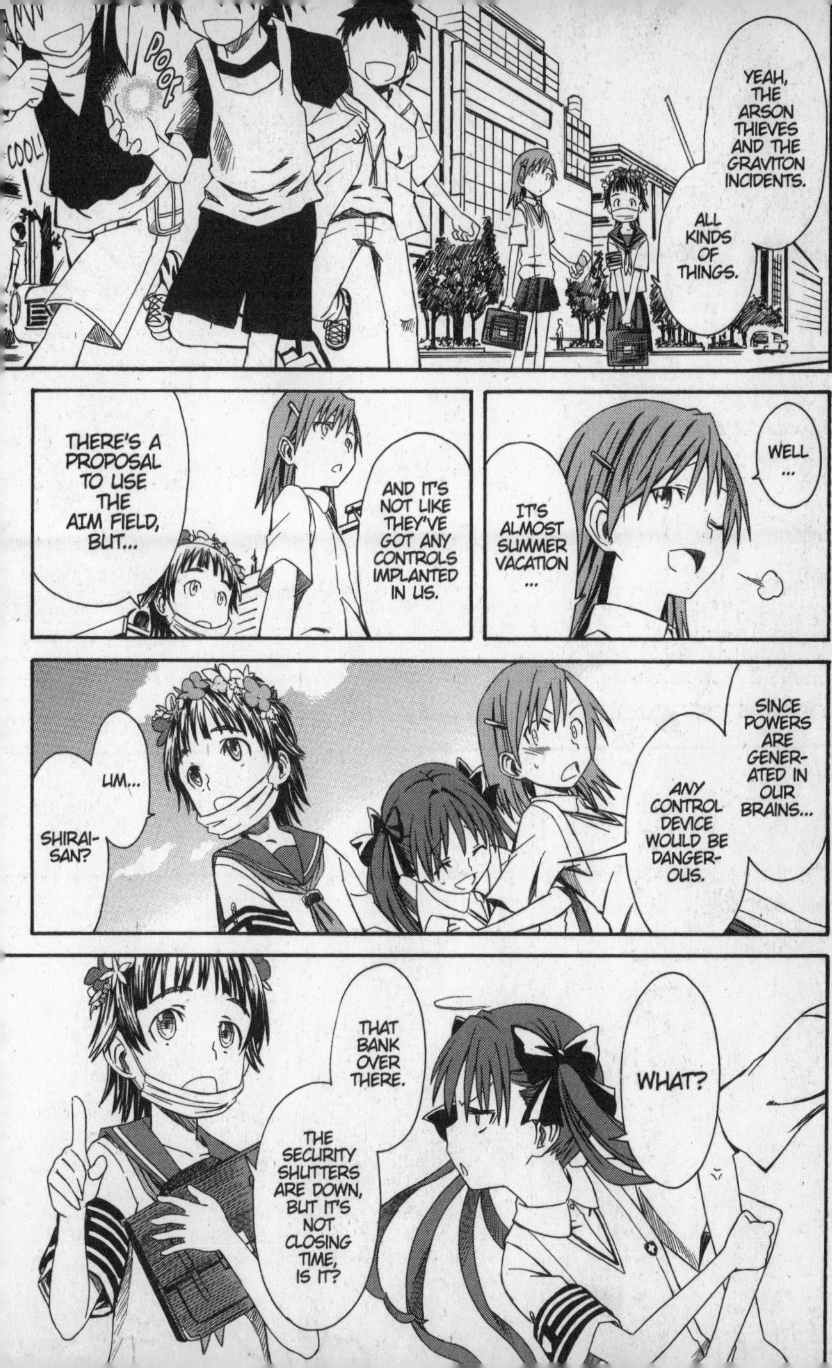
YEAH, THE ARSON THIEVES AND THE GRAVITON INCIDENTS.
ALL KINDS OF THINGS.
POOF
COOL!
WELL ...
IT'S ALMOST SUMMER VACATION ...
AND IT'S NOT LIKE THEY'VE GOT ANY CONTROLS IMPLANTED IN US.
THERE'S A PROPOSAL TO USE THE AIM FIELD, BUT...
SINCE POWERS ARE GENER-ATED IN OUR BRAINS...
ANY CONTROL DEVICE WOULD BE DANGER-OUS.
UM...
SHIRAI-SAN?
WHAT?
THAT BANK OVER THERE.
THE SECURITY SHUTTERS ARE DOWN, BUT IT'S NOT CLOSING TIME, IS IT?

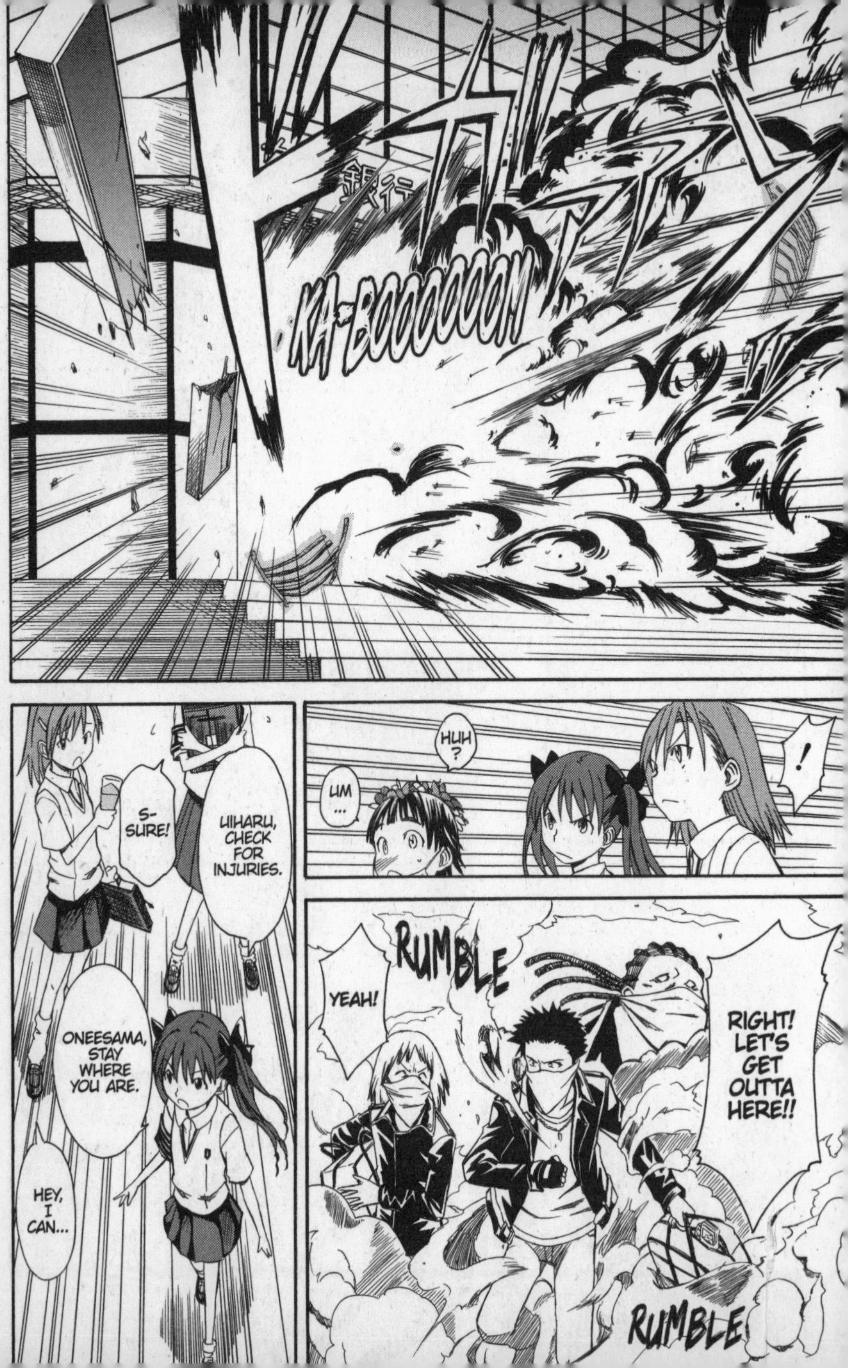
KA-BOOOOOOM!
!
HUH?
UM...
RIGHT! LET'S GET OUTTA HERE!!
RUMBLE
YEAH!
RUMBLE
UIHARU, CHECK FOR INJURIES.
S-SURE!
ONEESAMA, STAY WHERE YOU ARE.
HEY, I CAN...

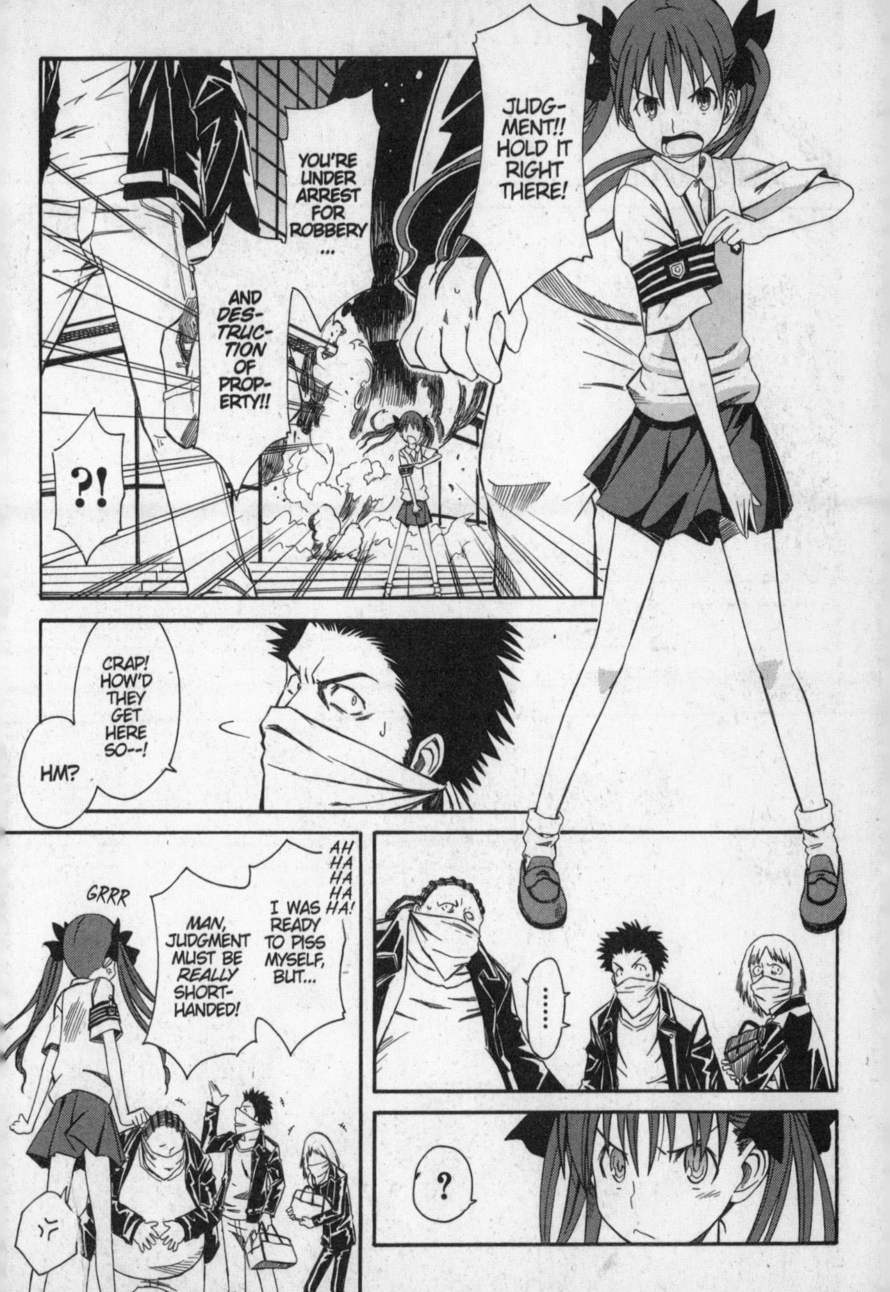

JUDG-MENT!! HOLD IT RIGHT THERE!
YOU'RE UNDER ARREST FOR ROBBERY...
AND DES-TRUC-TION OF PROP-ERTY!!
?!
CRAP! HOW'D THEY GET HERE SO--!
HM?
......
?
AH HA HA HA HA!
I WAS READY TO PISS MYSELF, BUT...
MAN, JUDGMENT MUST BE *REALLY* SHORT-HANDED!
GRRR

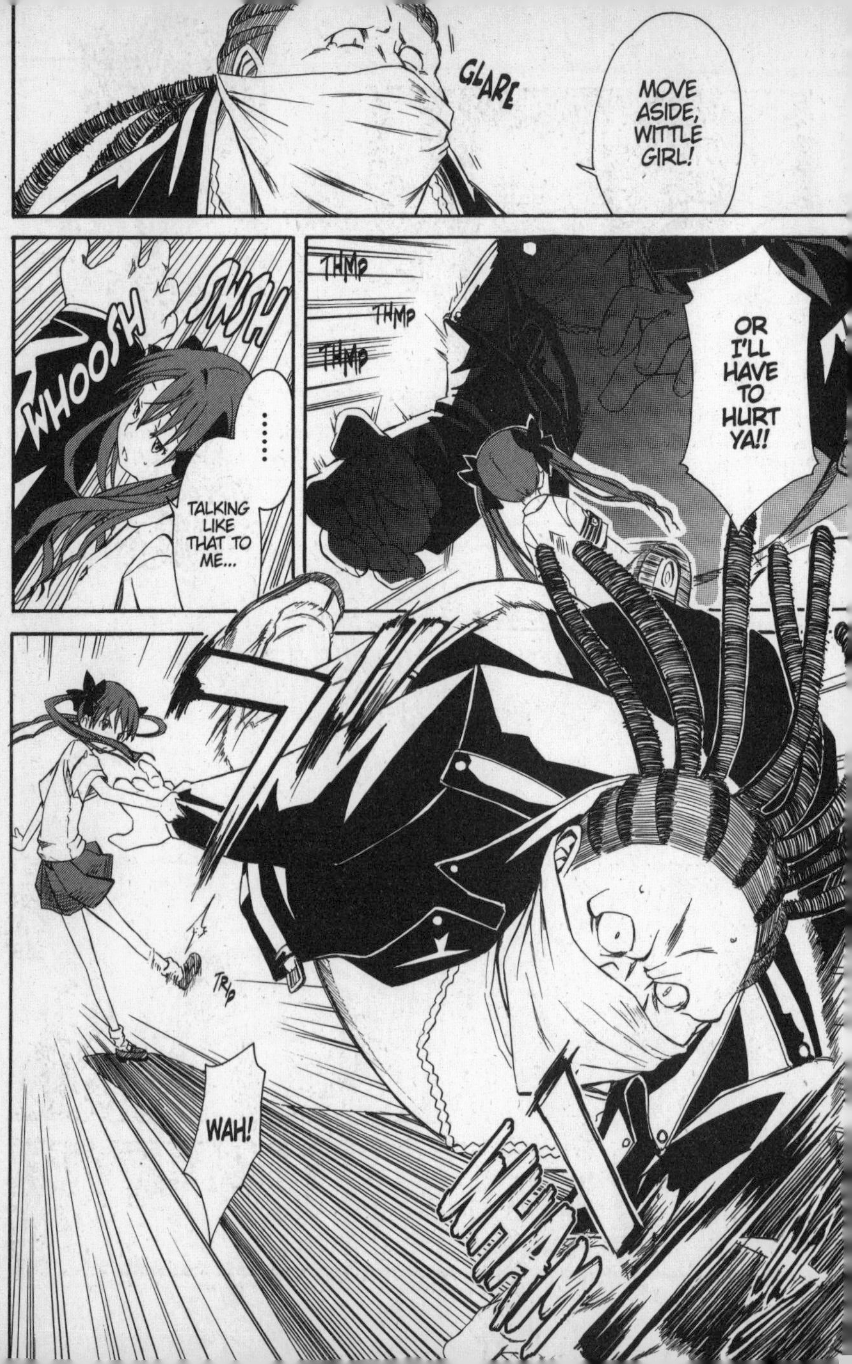
GLARE
MOVE ASIDE, WITTLE GIRL!
THMP
THMP
THMP
OR I'LL HAVE TO HURT YA!!
WHOOSH
SWSH
......
TALKING LIKE THAT TO ME...
TRIP
WAH!

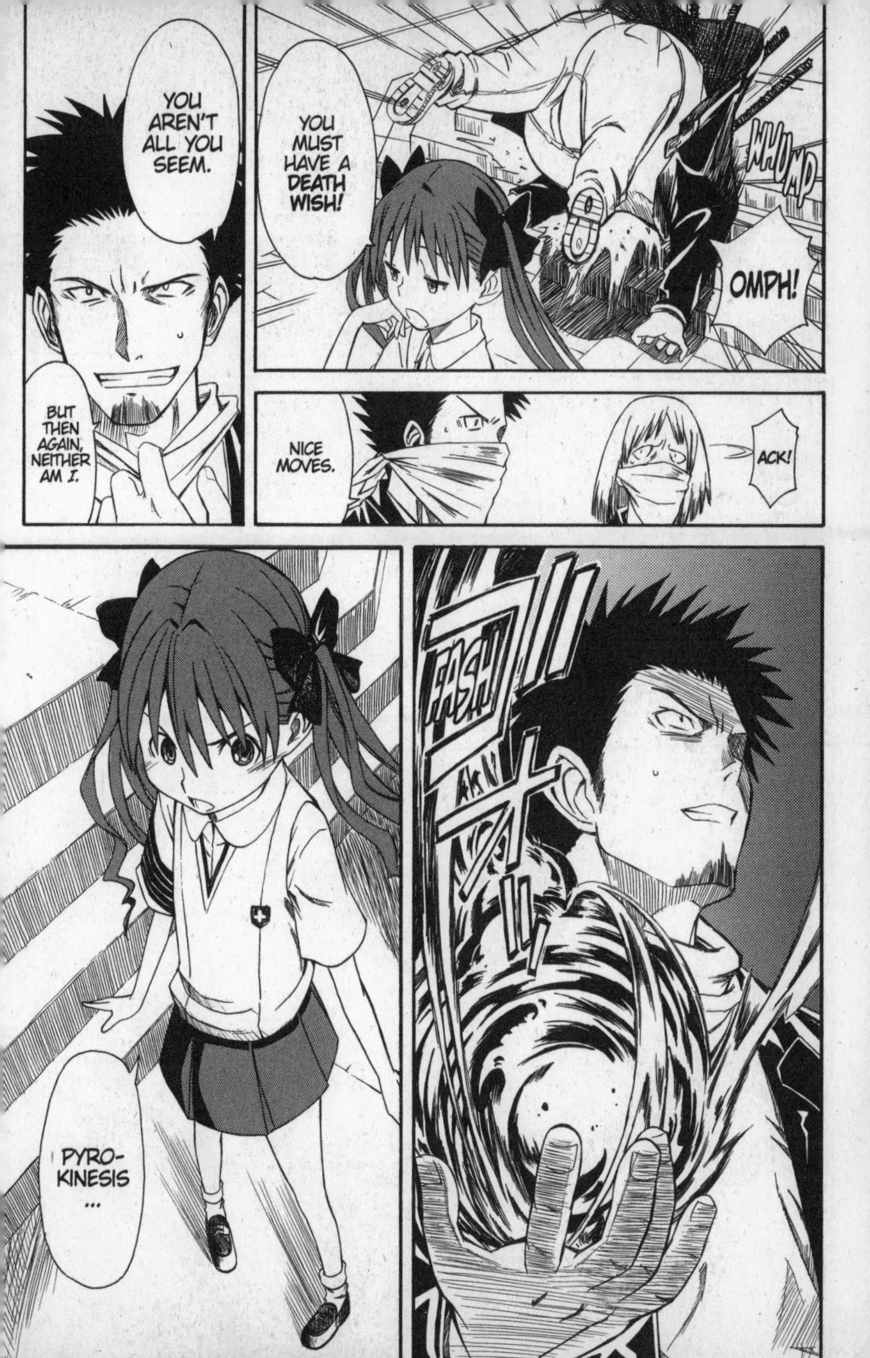
WHUMP
YOU MUST HAVE A DEATH WISH!
OMPH!
ACK!
NICE MOVES.
YOU AREN'T ALL YOU SEEM.
BUT THEN AGAIN, NEITHER AM I.
PYRO-KINESIS ...

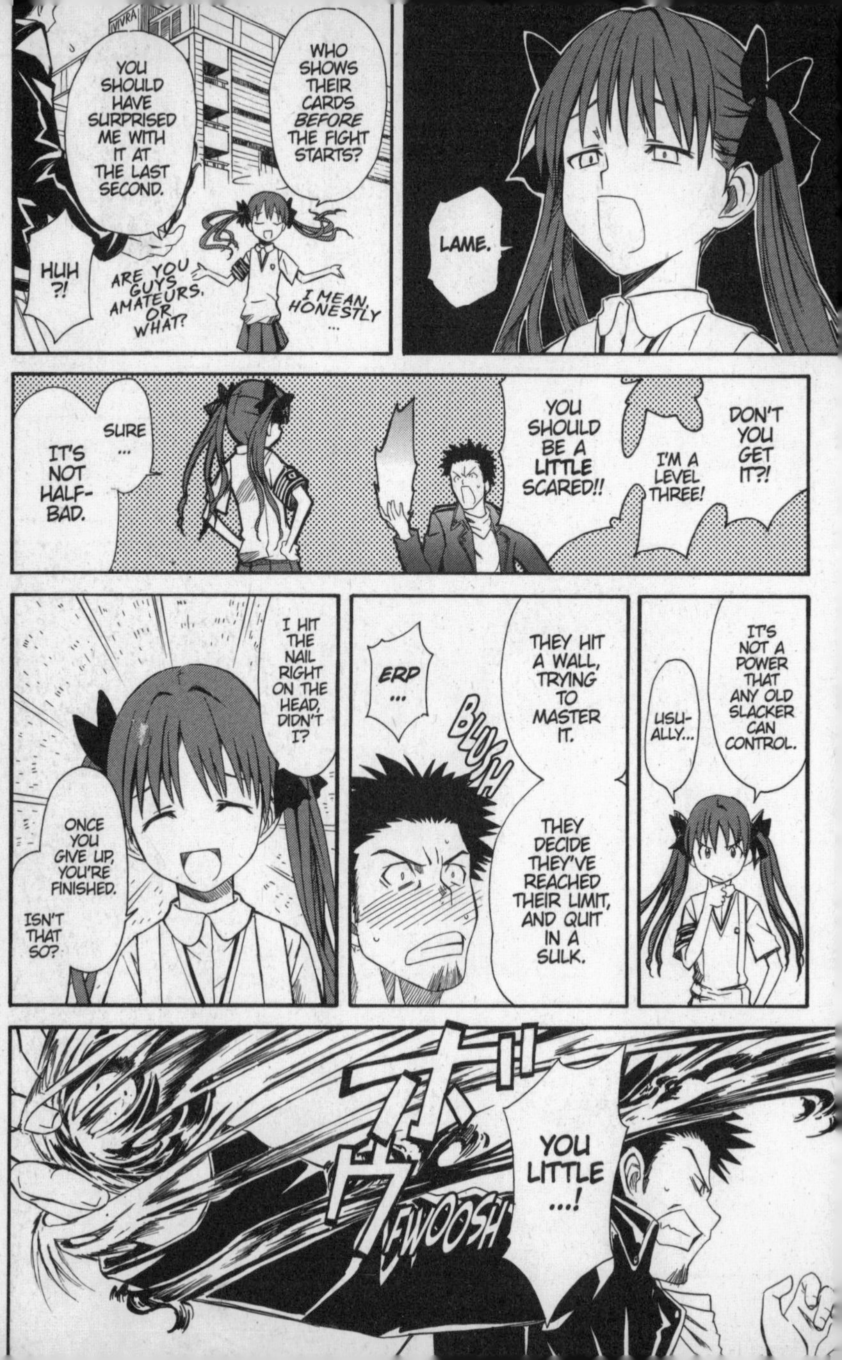
LAME.
WHO SHOWS THEIR CARDS *BEFORE* THE FIGHT STARTS?
YOU SHOULD HAVE SURPRISED ME WITH IT AT THE LAST SECOND.
I MEAN, HONESTLY ...
ARE YOU GUYS AMATEURS, OR WHAT?
HUH ?!
DON'T YOU GET IT?!
I'M A LEVEL THREE!
YOU SHOULD BE A LITTLE SCARED!!
SURE ...
IT'S NOT HALF-BAD.
IT'S NOT A POWER THAT ANY OLD SLACKER CAN CONTROL.
USU-ALLY...
THEY HIT A WALL, TRYING TO MASTER IT.
THEY DECIDE THEY'VE REACHED THEIR LIMIT, AND QUIT IN A SULK.
BLUSH
ERP ...
I HIT THE NAIL RIGHT ON THE HEAD, DIDN'T I?
ONCE YOU GIVE UP, YOU'RE FINISHED.
ISN'T THAT SO?
YOU LITTLE ...!
FWOOSH

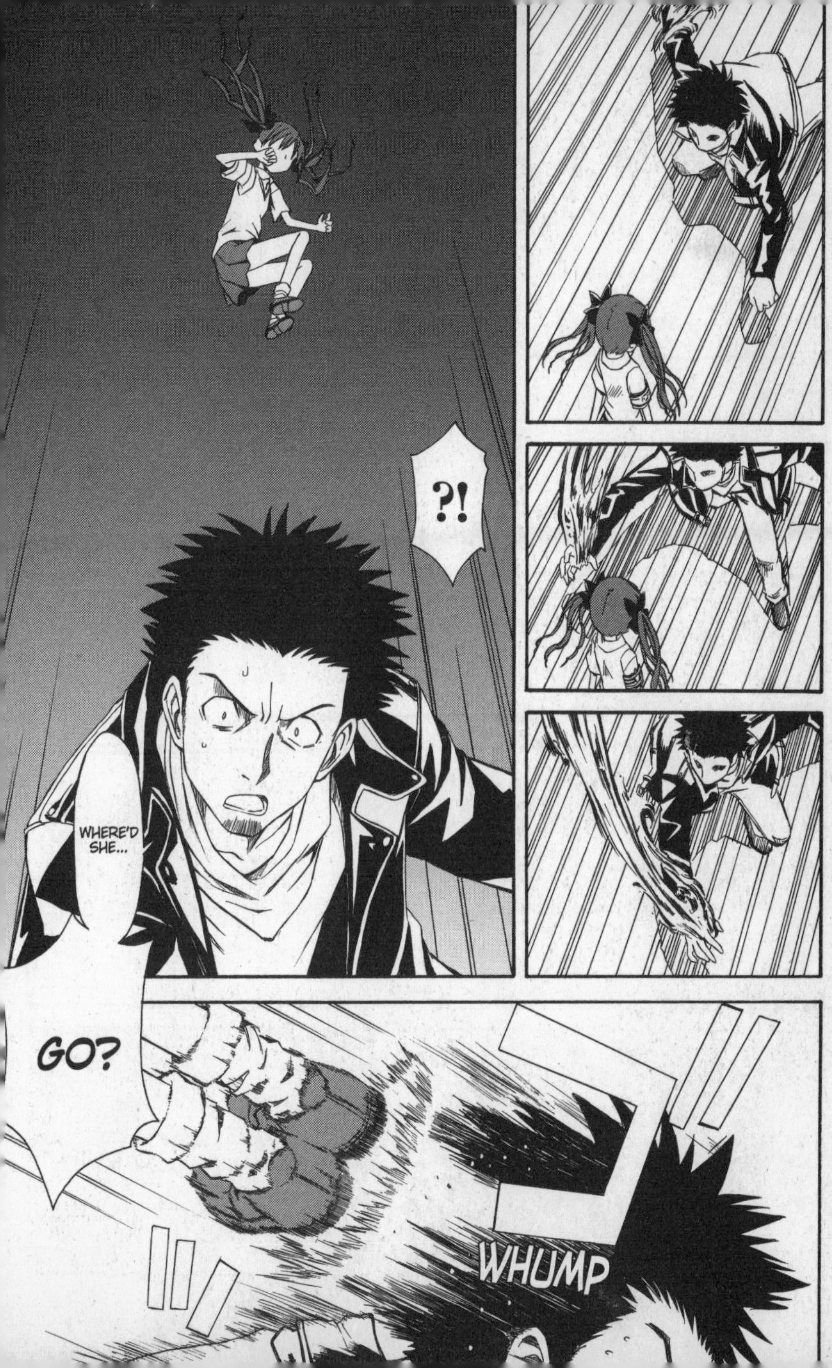
?!
WHERE'D SHE...
GO?
WHUMP